ENCYCLOPAEDIA OF
CYBER LAWS AND CRIME

ENCYCLOPAEDIA OF CYBER LAWS AND CRIME

Vol. 4

Laws on Intellectual Property

Edited by

S.R. Sharma

ANMOL PUBLICATIONS PVT. LTD.
NEW DELHI - 110 002 (INDIA)

ANMOL PUBLICATIONS PVT. LTD.
4374/4B, Ansari Road, Daryaganj
New Delhi - 110 002
Ph.: 23261597, 23278000
Visit us at: www.anmolpublications.com

Encyclopaedia of Cyber Laws and Crime

First Edition, 2003

ISBN 81-261-1432-0 (Set)

PRINTED IN INDIA

Published by J.L. Kumar for Anmol Publications Pvt. Ltd., New Delhi - 110 002 and Printed at Mehra Offset Press, Delhi.

CONTENTS

PREFACE

In the last years of the twentieth century a phenomenon has been witnessed which is likely to change the shape of human civilization. This is the explosion which has taken place in electronics and as a result of which there has been infinite expansion of knowledge that is commonly described as information explosion. The most astounding development in this area has been the geometric expansion of trade commerce entertainment and information jointly known as the internet or the web. The web accepts no restrictions of the country, race religion or country and has been totally responsible as a decisive factor in taking the world into what is now known as globalisation.

It is generally believed that a website is created every minute and along with its positive aspect it also brings about a new sense of responsibility. The free trade and commerce available through website in what is known as cyber space has also given birth to a mobile population where intent may be basically criminal. Thus we have hachers, virus carriers, sleepers and moles, who may constitute a real threat to the creativity of the web. There is, therefore, the eternal question of intellectual copyright and the policing of vast cyber space to protect and maintain what manhood can truly achieve.

Consequently the TRAI Act 1997 has been enacted by the Indian parliament in the 48th year of Republic of India on 28th March 1997 to provide for the establishment of the Telecom Regulatory Authority of India (TRAI) to regulate the telecommunication services and for matters connected therewith are incidental thereto.

As per Section 11 (2) of the TRAI Act TRAI is empowered to fix/revise tariff for various telecom services provided in India and service providers including the Department service provisions have to implement the tariffs, notified by the TRAI as per provisions of law.

The TRAI has been mandated to fix/revise tariff for various telecom services by virtue of section 11 (2) of TRAI Act.

The Encyclopaedia tries to cover as many laws as possible, promulgated by various countries and unions of countries like the European Union in this area to give a comprehensive and comparative view of CYBER Law.

The editor has no claims to originality and has simply compiled and edited the material collected from various sources. In view of the English language being the medium most of the material has been collected from American, British and Indian sources.

The editor is grateful to the Librarians of the library of the Supreme Court, the Indian Law Institute and the Ministry of Law, Justice and Company Affairs, for their kind assistance in locating the material from various sources.

The editor is specifically grateful to Shri Jawahar Lal Kumar, Managing Director, Anmol Publications Pvt. Ltd., New Delhi for venturing to publish the Encyclopaedia on Cyber Laws.

—Dr. S.R. Sharma

1 THE POLITICAL ECONOMY OF INTELLECTUAL PROPERTY

The political-economic theory of communications has already made a significant contribution to our understanding of mass communications and society. Denis McQuail identified three prominent trends in media business and technology, that have greatly increased its pertinence in the current age: the concentration of media systems into the hands of a few transnational corporations; the expansion of the "information economy" and the convergence of technologies; and the decline of public control over communications systems.[1] With its focus on institutional structures and practices, the political economy of communications is poised to help explain the forces driving these processes and to offer up predictions about their implications.

The political economy of communications properly belongs to the larger set of critical approaches to the study of culture and communications that began to challenge the "dominant paradigm" or "orthodox consensus"[2] during the 1960s. In North America, researchers such as Dallas Smythe, Herbert Schiller, and Thomas Guback sought to fill the gaps in our understanding of communications processes and systems caused by the lack of attention to institutional structures and practices by mainstream communications researchers. The focus of the dominant approaches on media content, audience uses and gratifications, and effects largely left the issues of media ownership and control unexplored.

However, social movements of the 1960s prompted academics to bring questions of ideology, power, and domination to the fore. For political economists, this involved an analysis of the ownership and control of communications industries, interconnections between the communications sector and big business, and links between the communications sector and government, including the military. A substantial body of political-economic research has demonstrated how the logic of capital has resulted in the concentration of ownership and control of the communications system in the hands of the richest members of the capitalist class. The dominant class thus earns profits from ownership of communications firms, further enhancing its wealth. Political economists underscore the point that ownership and control of the means of communication also significantly augment the ideological power of this class. Furthermore, the dominant class, with its superior resources and communications networks, is generally able to organise its hegemony within the political system. Consequently, government policies regarding communications have generally tended to favor property rights over access to channels of communication.

Thematic Overview

The purpose of this book is to extend the main lines of inquiry running through the political economy of communications into the relatively unexplored area of intellectual property, particularly copyright. The traditional concern of political economy with ownership and control of the means of communication is taken one step further to examine ownership and control of content, through the mechanism of copyright. In that chapter I demonstrate how copyright serves as an instrument of wealth that can be utilised in the cycle of capital accumulation to generate more wealth. Copyright can also serve as the basis for expanding market power. The cases of media capitalists Ted Turner and Rupert Murdoch show how they used ownership of rights to filmed entertainment to expand their operations into new lines of business. In these cases, the tendency of copyright to be monopolistic is exacerbated by the oligopolistic structure of the media marketplace. Ultimately, the effects of concentrated ownership of the means of communication and of the messages themselves are the same: high barriers to entry in the "marketplace of ideas" and a narrow and limited range of informational and cultural works.

Political economists highlight the logic of capital as the primary determining factor in shaping the form and structure of the communications system. Economists of information, in contrast, have sought to explain how the structure of the information marketplace is determined by the peculiar nature of informational and cultural commodities. These commodities have the characteristics of what economists call a "public good," meaning that the product cannot be used up by any one consumer. This feature also makes it difficult to exclude consumers from using the good without paying for it. It is also characteristic of informational and cultural commodities to have relatively low reproduction costs in comparison to tangible commodities. Both of these characteristics make markets dealing in informational and cultural commodities prone to failure. For example, the videocassette recorder (VCR) opened a new market for the filmed entertainment industry, but it was a market prone to failure from the beginning. Although it was possible to sell prerecorded videocassettes to consumers, video recording technology made it easier and cheaper for a person to make multiple copies from an original cassette at a fraction of the cost.

Providers of informational and cultural goods and services utilise a variety of mechanisms to deal with the peculiar characteristics of the commodities they sell, including copyright, patents, trademarks, advertising, compulsory licensing packaging, encryption, price discrimination, and so on. Oscar Gandy concluded that informational and cultural markets would inevitably be far from perfect and generally require state intervention to prevent market failure.[3] The logic of the commodity thus has a determining influence on market structure. However, political economists insist that the logic of the commodity must be situated within the larger context of the logic of capital. Markets within which informational and cultural goods are exchanged may take a variety of forms given the logic of the commodity, but their general purpose always remains the valorisation of capital. Accordingly, these markets follow the same tendencies toward concentration found in other economic sectors.

Although political economy provides the overarching framework for this inquiry into intellectual property, the richness of the topic facilitates an extension of the main lines of political economic analysis using related theoretical approaches within the critical paradigm. The history of copyright is explored and interpreted through the historical materialist lens of political economy in combination with the systems approach to the history of communications pioneered by Harold Innis. The central problematic taken up in this chapter concerns the notion of determination. Traditionally, the method of historical materialism involved delineating the determining influence of the mode of production on particular forms and functions of various components of the superstructure, that is, politics, law, culture, ideology, and so on. Similarly, historians of communications systems have sought to identify how particular modes of communications determine the structure of social organisations as well as human cognition.

The analytical framework utilised to study the history of copyright adopts a refined notion of determination to trace the origins of literary property rights. Copyright appears on the historical stage when conditions for it are ripe: the dawn of capitalism and the birth of the printing press. This history also demonstrates the crucial role of the state in recognising, conferring, and protecting intellectual property rights. Political economy again proves useful with its specific attention to the *political* forces influencing the form and structure of communications systems.

Intellectual property rights are both economic and statutory in nature. Claims to ownership of intellectual and artistic works must be recognised by law to be effective. We look at the history of cable copyright in the United States, with particular attention to the policymaking apparatus. In that chapter, radical and neo-Marxist theories of the capitalist state are drawn upon to explain the outcomes of state intervention into intellectual property matters. The effects of new communications technologies on the filmed entertainment copyright system, in both cases, new communications technologies—cable television and VCRs—were introduced into the marketplace before a set of copyright laws had been implemented to govern their uses). How the filmed entertainment industry, broadcasters, and cable operators clashed within the state apparatus over the structure and form of a copyright mechanism for cable retransmission of television broadcasts are also explored. Thus, the state became the site in which this particular incident of market failure was resolved. The outcome of this intraclass struggle once again reveals the workings of the logic of capital. Although cable television technology carried the potential to disrupt filmed entertainment markets and to undermine the market power of the major filmed entertainment producers based in Hollywood, it has become thoroughly integrated into the prevailing market structure. This pattern was repeated with the VCR.)

I draw upon critical legal studies (CLS) to help inform a case study of how the filmed entertainment industry sought to assert control over its copyrights in the face of the infringing uses afforded by video recording technology. The major producers of filmed entertainment for television perceived the VCR as a threat to their established distribution system. The VCR offered home tapers the ability to decide when they wanted to watch particular programs, taking some scheduling control out of the hands of broadcasters. Television program producers also feared losing income from advertisers as home tapers deleted or fast-forwarded through commercials. The apparent threat of this new technology caused the filmed entertainment industry to seek to protect its markets through judicial and legislative action. However, when the dust settled, the VCR, like television and cable television before it, had become yet another ancillary market for the major filmed entertainment companies.)

The expansionary logic of capital drives the expansion of the realm of intellectual property at the global level as well. However, copyright owners find the tendencies toward market failure in international markets identical to those that operate on the national level. For example, the ability of filmed entertainment copyright owners to exploit cable television and VCR technology in foreign markets is based upon the copyright mechanisms governing them. The combined efforts of the U.S. filmed entertainment industry and U.S. government to extend the law of intellectual property into new technological and geographical domains. Cable television and the VCR are used in two case studies to explore the relationship between technology, communications markets, and the state.

The first case examines efforts by U.S. copyright owners and U.S. government officials to compel the Canadian government to change its copyright law to require cable operators to pay for the use of programs contained in the broadcast signals retransmitted by cable. The U.S. filmed entertainment industry effected the requisite changes in Canadian copyright law through the U.S.-Canada Free Trade Agreement. Free trade agreements have become a vehicle for U.S. foreign policy makers to advance the interests of intellectual property owners. Indeed, the North American Free Trade Agreement (NAFTA) contains provisions that provide the strictest intellectual property protection of any international agreement.

Access to the large and wealthy U.S. market drove both Canada and Mexico to ward free trade agreements. Access to the U.S. market also proves pivotal in the second case study. Which addresses the efforts of U.S. copyright owners to eradicate piracy of video and musical recordings, software, trademarks, and other forms of intellectual property. This case study spotlights Hollywood's international antivideocassette piracy campaign. As the major filmed entertainment companies sought to extend their home-video market abroad, they found rampant market failure in the form of videocassette piracy. Videocassette pirates take advantage of the low reproduction costs of filmed entertainment. Because they do not have to pay original production costs or royalties, they are able to undercut the market for "legitimate" sales and rentals. Accordingly, Hollywood put pressure on the U.S. government, which in turn put pressure on foreign governments, to "update" their copyright laws and practices and to halt infringements on U.S. property rights. Trade leveraging, a practice by which access to the U.S. market for foreign imports is conditioned in part upon the protection of U.S. intellectual property rights by the trading partner, is the means by which this, has been largely accomplished. Trading privileges have been similarly linked to protection of human rights, treatment of labor, and efforts to eliminate drug trafficking.

The evidence reveals a pattern wherein the eradication of video-cassette piracy in a foreign market is followed by entry of U.S. home-video distributors that eventually take over the market. The ranks of the top ten rentals or sales in market after market are dominated by feature films distributed by major U.S. companies. Often, these are the same films that ranked at the top in box-office revenues. In sum, Hollywood has successfully supplemented its control of the world's theater screens with control of the world's television screens.

The global proliferation of communications technologies and the expansion of the realm of intellectual property is a process that clearly benefits the advanced economies of the United States, Europe, and Japan. The incorporation of intellectual property protection into the General Agreement on Tariffs and Trade (GATT) signaled the consolidation of control over intellectual and artistic creativity in the hands of transnational corporations based in the rich countries. The consequences of expanded intellectual property rights are always the same: the continuing enclosure of the intellectual and artistic commons. More and more, knowledge and culture are being privately appropriated and submitted to the logic of the marketplace. Political economists continue to document the negative effects of this profess on democracy.

The enclosure of the intellectual and artistic commons is not inevitable or necessary, even though the emphasis on the logic of capital makes it seem as if it is. I explore some of the ways that individuals and groups have confronted or resisted the expansionary logic of intellectual property. More specifically, I isolate the struggles of human subjects in making their own history. The point of a political economic analysis is to reveal how existing structures and practices have become reified, making them appear to be inevitable and necessary and beyond the realm of human intervention. These structures and practices are critiqued to support claims that "what exists" falls far short of "what ought to be" in terms of a society that maximises the attainment of full human potential.

A Note on Theory and Method

The relationship between structural determination and human agency is a central concern of political economy. Indeed, the conceptualisation of this relationship is at the core of the theory and method of this approach. As noted, political-economic communications theory, along with other critical approaches to the study of communications and culture, gained its foothold in the challenge to the dominant paradigm. Therefore, political economists are critical of the "abstracted empiricism" of much mainstream work. However, they do seek to support their claims empirically. At the same time, they are critical of purely interpretive approaches that lapse into idealism.

Political economists adopt a formal framework through which the empirical world is examined. Research is conducted and empirical data are organised and tested according to an interpretive framework grounded in political-economic theory. This is not very different from the procedures taken by empirical researchers. However, as Graham Murdock argued, it is "the way available research materials are contextualised theoretically and the way that explanations are constructed" that distinguishes this approach.[4] The political economist moves from the realm of theory and the abstract to the realm of the specific and empirical and back again. Evidence gathered at the empirical level is seen as a surface manifestation of the structural forces that lie below.

Linking structures to practices involves interpretation, a procedure readily acknowledged and not disguised behind a claim that "the data speak for themselves." For example, much of the data from this study comes from the pages of the business press and trade journals. These sources provide much of what we know about what occurs in the realm of business practice. However, the topics and events described by business journalists still require interpretations as to their structural causes. The political-economic framework offers a map with history and context. Thus, the announcement of a merger between two media companies is not treated as an isolated event, but as evidence of the larger tendencies within capitalism toward concentration. The political economist is not concerned with how the deal will affect stock prices, but with its impact on employment, market structure, and democracy. The analysis is linked to underlying structural forces that are at work determining the general developments at the level of business practice.

This brings us back to the relationship between structures and human agency. Political economists have rejected the strict notion of determination associated with structuralism. Human subjects are not simply actors performing their scripted roles on the stage of world history. Therefore, no social theory can make guaranteed predictions as to the future of the human condition. However, it is one thing to recognise that history is contingent and quite another to reject the concept of determination entirely.

Anthony Giddens's revised conception of the relationship between structures and human agency has proven useful in analysing topics in mass communications research.[5] Giddens reiterated that economic and social structures are created by active human subjects and that they operate both to constrain and enable human activity.[6] Furthermore, these structures are not self-perpetuating but must be re-created through everyday practice.[7]

Giddens developed his *structuration theory* to "explain how it comes about that structures are constituted through action, and reciprocally how action is constituted structurally."[8] Accordingly, the task of political economists is to conceptualise economic and social structures and then to tease out the ways in which they affect everyday practice.[9] The routines of everyday life may result in the reproduction, modification, or alteration of these larger social formations. Obviously, this process is affected by the dynamics of class, gender, race, and ethnic struggles. The terms of these struggles are shaped by the overall distribution of wealth, political authority, and knowledge. The unequal distribution of these resources, particularly the control of capital, results in the general tendency toward the reproduction of structures of domination despite the efforts of conscious and active human subjects to modify and challenge them.

Political economists have never forgotten that human beings are the makers of their own history. Even classical writers understood that their purpose was not just to describe the existing political-economic system but also to see how it measures up to various normative principles. For Marx, the capitalist political-economic system failed miserably in providing enabling structures for the full development of human potential. A society that fulfilled human potential could only come about through, a revolutionary transformation of the existing mode of production. Similarly, it is possible to evaluate how the actually existing intellectual property system compares to the normative principles upon which it is premised. The central assumption upon which the copyright system is based is that creators of intellectual works need an incentive to be creative. The pecuniary reward implied in the exclusive right to exploit a copyrighted work is meant to supply the motivation for intellectual and artistic activity and, more practically, to serve as the source of income from which artists, authors, and other creators of intellectual works could make a living. If the copyright system works this way, it is functional in terms of the social good since it stimulates intellectual creativity.

The evidence presented in this book suggests that the copyright system does not operate according to the ideal. First, the basic premises of copyright were worked out at a time when the production of intellectual creativity, mainly books, was a far simpler process, mainly involving a single author bargaining with a publisher over the terms of exploiting a literary work. Currently, most artistic and intellectual creativity involves the participation of many actual creators in the production of "works for hire." Ownership of copyrights increasingly rests with the capitalists who have the machinery and capital to manufacture and distribute them.

Second, there has always been a tension between the monopolistic character of intellectual property and its normative goal of enhancing the flow of information and ideas. Copyright seeks to restrict the use of a work to those willing and able to pay for it. This exclusivity can have the opposite result than that intended by the founders of the system and may exacerbate the gaps between the information-rich and the information-poor. The oligopolistic structure of the communications system contributes further to the widening of these gaps. The incorporation of new communications technologies into this oligopolistic structure have undermined their potential to bring about an increase in the range and forms of intellectual and artistic creativity. In sum, their potential to significantly enhance participation in the communications system has been thwarted. These problems are rooted in the political-economic structure of communications, as the following chapters demonstrate.

NOTES

1. Denis McQuail, Mass *Communication Theory: An Introduction* (3rd ed.), London: Sage, 1994, p. 83.
2. Anthony Giddens, "The Orthodox Consensus and the Emerging Synthesis," in B. Dervin et al. (eds.), *Rethinking Communication, Volume 1: Paradigm Issues,* Newbury Park, CA: Sage, 1989, pp. 53-65.
3. Oscar Gandy, "The Political Economy Approach: A Critical Challenge," *Journal of Media Economics,* 5:2, 1992, pp. 23-42.
4. Graham Murdock, "Critical Inquiry and Audience Activity," in B. Dervin et al. (eds.), *Rethinking Communication, Volume 2: Paradigm Exemplars,* Newbury Park, CA: Sage, 1989, pp. 226-249, p. 227.
5. Compare Murdock with Patrick Parsons, "Defining Cable Television: Structuration and Public Policy," *Journal of Communication,* 39:2, 1989, pp. 10-26.
6. Anthony Giddens, *The Constitution of Society: Outline of the Theory of Structuration,* Cambridge: Polity Press, 1984, pp. 25-28.
7. Anthony Giddens, *Central Problems in Social Theory,* Berkeley: University of California Press, 1979; Anthony Giddens, "Action, Subjectivity, and the Constitution of Meaning," *Social Research,* 53:3, 1986, pp. 529-545.
8. Anthony Giddens, *New Rules of Sociological Method,* London: Hutchinson, 1976, p. 161.
9. Murdock, "Critical Inquiry," p. 228.

2 HISTORY AND PHILOSOPHY OF COPYRIGHT

Critical research on intellectual property, including the relatively unexplored history of copyright, is still pioneering work. Traditional histories of copyright provide adequate descriptions of the origins and evolution of copyright but lack any real explanation for its emergence and functions.[1] These histories are also teleological; they treat the "evolution" of the concept of literary property as a reflection of the natural progressiveness of human beings. The history of copyright developed in this chapter is based on an analytical framework that stresses the modes and relations of production and communications as the key explanatory variables in accounting for the origin and development of a concept of literary property. Accordingly, this history of copyright suggests that there is an essential connection between the rise of capitalism, the extension of commodity relations into literary and artistic domains, and the emergence of the printing press.

The first section of this chapter looks for evidence of intellectual property rights in ancient and medieval times. In a second section, an analysis of the dawn of capitalism and the development of the printing press is linked to the emergence of copyright, a crucial connection that is generally neglected in traditional histories. The evolution of copyright in England and the United States forms the central focus of the third section, which includes a significant revision and expansion of previous copyright histories that explore the connection between John Locke and the articulation of literary property rights. Lyman Patterson argued that a historical analysis of copyright "removes obstacles —long-continued acceptance of certain ideas, self-interest, and the pressing need to resolve immediate problems—which may be present when analysis occurs in a wholly contemporary context."[2] It also provides the occasion to compare the earliest ideas concerning copyright to current copyright practices, as well as patterns of ownership and control of intellectual and artistic creativity.

Theoretical Approaches

Historical analysis is inherent to the political-economic approach to communications. Marx grounded his dialectical analysis in historical materialism, situating the analysis of economics, politics, law, society, and culture within the larger context of the modes and relations of production. Traditionally, such an analysis identifies various stages in human history—Asiatic, ancient, feudal, and capitalist—that are defined by how people go about making a living. Focusing on how people go about communicating, cultural historians of communications, following Innis,[3] substitute the modes and relations of communication for modes and relations of production in an attempt to identify how communications shapes social organisation and structures human cognition.

One criticism of historical materialism is aimed at its periodisation scheme. For example, Jack Goody argued that shifting our attention to communications technologies and systems makes an "overdetermined stage theory" of history problematic.[4] To illustrate, he showed how "trading and banking of a capitalistic kind" can be traced back to the early civilisations of the Middle East, where humans developed writing as a technology for managing the economic affairs of the palace and temple.[5] He suggested that certain nascent features of capitalism, made possible by writing, appear well before the emergence of what is generally recognised as the capitalist mode of production. Goody incorrectly charged historical materialism with treating each mode of production as a totality in which there can be no coexistence with other modes of production. Actually, Marx's theory of history, as presented in the preface to *A Contribution to the Critique of Political Economy* and *The German Ideology*,[6] requires such coexistence, for it is out of the contradictions inherent to the dominant mode of production that the new economic system emerges. Innis held a parallel view of the evolution of modes of communication: Monopolies of knowledge generate contradictions that prompt humans to develop new decentralising modes of communication. Thus, change is a result of conflicts inherent to any given system—economic or communicative. Of course, the poststructuralist vantage point leads us now to stress that actual human beings must serve as historical agents for such change to occur.

This brings us to another criticism of historical materialism: its teleological nature, or the assumption that history unfolds according to some underlying plan. To dispute this approach critics regularly pointed to "actually existing" socialist societies that seemingly had skipped capitalism. A reformulated Marxist view of history does not see evolution of the modes of production as an absolutely linear or inevitable process. Although still evolutionary, historical development is now seen as a process with many dead ends, backward steps, uneven development in different areas, diffusion from one area to another, and skipping of some stages in other areas.[7] In sum, contemporary Marxists retain economic stages as organising principles for historical analysis, but they no longer make claims of holding the key to the future.

A third criticism of the orthodox Marxist view of history is also implicit in Goody's example above. Marxist political economists are regularly charged with economic reductionism, in particular their "monocausal economic explanations" for everything.[8] Similarly, Innis, Marshall McLuhan, Walter Ong, and others are branded as "technological determinists" for making communications the central focus of change. Orthodox Marxism and the early work of historical-cultural studies certainly can be faulted for disregarding the dialectical interaction between base and superstructure or technology and society. Again, reformulations have been made as a result of such criticisms to take into account interactions between economic structure (relations and forces of production) and social structure (ideas and institutions) or between technology and society.[9]

However, these approaches do not entirely dispense with notions of determination as organising principles for research but do disinherit the claim that determination operates only in one direction or in every instance. They resurrect dialectical analysis while recognising the efficacy of ideology and culture. Additionally, the concept of determination has been revised along the lines suggested by Raymond Williams, from a strict one-to-one causal relationship to a process involving "the setting of limits" and the "exertion of pressures."[10] Nevertheless, within communications history and political economy, special attention is given to discover those instances or domains in which technology or economics are determining. In this historical account of the origins of intellectual property, capitalism and the printing press are stressed as determining forces.

The Prehistory of Intellectual Property Rights

As Edward Ploman and L. Clark Hamilton pointed out, nascent aspects of the modem conception of copyright existed in ancient Greece, in the Talmudic principles of ancient Jewish law, and in the Roman publishing system.[11] The oral poetry of ancient Greece, including the Homeric poems, was developed and recited who today remain anonymous.[12] The reasons are rooted in both the nature of oral cultures and the organisation of artistic and literary production. At of communications practice, oral cultures are less conducive to the preservation of exact versions of texts and records due to the limits of human memory;[13] therefore the, recording of claims to authorship is similarly constrained. Furthermore, claims to personal creativity may not have been made in the first place, for the poets of Greek orality saw their work as a "collective achievement, the common and indivisible possession of a school, guild or group" rather than as an individual effort that could be personally owned.[14] Arnold Hauser claimed that intellectual property appears and takes root in Athens during the sixth century B.C., when a new sense of the individual self emerges in all fields of cultural life. This is indicated by the first recorded personal claims to literary and artistic creativity and is attributed by Hauser to the development of commerce and urban society. To this equation cultural historians of communications would add literacy and the highly evolved Greek alphabet, which permitted authors to discover and explore intersubjectivity. Nevertheless, books remained rare, and no evidence of anything resembling a copyright exists for the Greek classical period, only this new notion of the individual creative self.

The oral reporters of the Hebrew Talmud were required to identify the contributors of new principles to that body of civil and religious law. Victor Hazen suggested that this mandate to report a thing "in the name of him who said it" links ancient Jewish law to a modern "universal copyright."[15] Although such a practice might imply a "natural" recognition of an author's right to attribution, our understanding of oral cultures suggests this practice may just as well have been an attempt to preserve a historical record of scholarship. Perhaps more important than preservation, citation in scholarship involves a claim to the authority of the spoken word or text. In sum, the practice of attribution seems rooted in concerns about the accuracy and authority of the oral record rather than, as Hazen suggests, a notion of property rights. At most, ancient Jewish law provides something akin to an author's moral right to attribution, whether it was conceived of as such or not.

There is no recognition of a copyright in written Roman law, though there is evidence that some authors signed "publishing" contracts with booksellers.[16] Ploman and Hamilton argued that a viable trade in literary works existed in Rome, making the conditions right for a copyright.[17] L. D. Reynolds and N. G. Wilson stated that by the middle of the third century A.D. "the world of books had become very much a part of the world of the educated Roman" and writing was accepted as a "serious occupation of the leisured class."[18] However, this does not mean that authors and poets made a living by selling their works and earning royalties, as some currently do, since the dominant form of literary compensation at this time was the patronage system.[19] Also, much of the manuscript production of the time was geared toward the copying, emendation, and correction of existing works. In this regard, "most readers depended on borrowing books from friends and having their own copies made for them"[20] by either their own slaves or those owned by and working for booksellers. Moreover, unless an author or poet was wealthy enough to publish his own book, he would have to give or sell it to a bookseller, who as owner of the parchment and slaves came to own the copies of the work. Finally, it is not at all clear whether the publishing agreements cited above were based on some notion of author's right, since Roman law makes no mention of it or of property interests in immaterial things in general.[21]

Societies without copyright include ancient India, whose early history is one of peoples rather than individuals and where the great literary and philosophical masterpieces are all anonymous. In this oral culture, "who said what" was not as important as "what was said."[22] Similarly, in the more recent oral culture of Bali, artistic property, in the sense of personal possession, did not exist. The Balinese viewed the production of culture as an anonymous, community-oriented, participatory process, and they intended art to be "the expression of collective thought."[23] Thus, artistic knowledge could not be centralised in the hands of a particular intellectual class.[24] Until 1991, the People's Republic of China did not have a copyright system reflecting the fact that the concept of intellectual property also did not exist in the societies of Southeast Asia.

Ploman and Hamilton maintained that different cultural attitudes, social organisation, and legal conceptions may explain why copyright emerged in Europe and not in Asia.[25] To this equation we might add the mode of communication. Although the Chinese developed writing during the third millennium B.C. and introduced paper to the world, writing in China was first used in service to the empire instead of for literary or religious purposes.[26] Additionally, the logographic system of writing limited the rates of attainment of fluent literacy[27] and certainly limited the audience for written works and the possibilities of a market for manuscripts.

Turning to the European medieval period, we again find a conception of literary property lacking due to several factors: the general relations of production, the specific organisation of literary production, the dominant mode of communication, and the role of culture in society. Beginning with the specific organisation of literary creativity, we know that the Roman Catholic Church centralised the production, preservation, and dissemination of artistic and intellectual knowledge within a monastic system. The Church held a monopoly on knowledge, especially during the Early Middle Ages, through its control of manuscripts and their reproduction and through control of education and, consequently, literacy. As the Benedictine monasteries developed methods for loaning and exchanging manuscripts, they soon discovered the value of their libraries. Access to manuscripts could command land, cattle, money, or other privileges. George Putnam called the practice of requiring payment for the right to copy a manuscript the first European copyright, though one that had "nothing whatever to do with the rights of an original producer in the literary production."[28]

Medieval Europe was also primarily an oral culture; consequently the dominant mode of communication was not conducive to a conception of literary property. Accordingly, "the medieval listener had a greater respect for form than for authorship."[29] Additionally, it was difficult for the *troubadours* and *jongleurs* to protect their work from copiers and imitators. The real historical events upon which the poems and songs of the Middle Ages were based belonged to a literary commons from which anyone could draw.[30] Nor was the oral performance itself something that could be kept or owned in any way. For an oral poet, the moment of composition takes place at the time of performance, and each actualisation of the songs and stories is different.[31] Thus, there is no "original," only a combination of formula, spontaneity, and forgetfulness, a "creative artist making the tradition."[32] Variation is inherent to oral performance, due to the personality and creativity of the performer, the context of reception, and the limits of human memory. Elizabeth Eisenstein proposed that scribal culture of medieval Europe "worked against the concept of intellectual property rights" because this mode of communication lacked the power necessary for preserving individual contributions to art, literature, and inventions.[33]

Hauser, in contrast, held that concepts of "the artist as genius" and intellectual property could not emerge until "Christian culture" disintegrated.[34] In his view, the "cultural unity of the Middle Ages" deprived art of any structural autonomy within the larger social system. Artistic creativity, in the medieval worldview, entailed the embodiment of the Divine as spoken through the artist, the medium through which the "eternal, supernatural order of things [was] made visible."[35] Lacking structural autonomy, different forms of intellectual expression derived all meaning and purpose from above while the value of any creative work was based on its fidelity to the "Truth."[36] It follows that monastic chronicles and church music were not formally encumbered with property rights in the modern sense, because monks, who functioned equally as copyists, scholars, and authors, freely used and reproduced literary works, often without concern for attribution. Instead, authorship was attributed to the monastery as a moral entity whose duty it was to record and preserve the Word of God.

When we turn directly to the relations of production that dominated medieval Europe, we again find factors working against a conception of literary property. The corporate structure of medieval society meant that people saw themselves primarily as members of a group rather than as individuals.[37] Since every person was assigned to a station in life by God, few believed that they could earn their way out through fame or fortune (though oral fairy tales did allow them to imagine this).[38] On these grounds, E. K. Hunt argued that the feudal ideology, based on a Christian paternalist ethic, was decidedly anticapitalist.[39] Hence, "greed, selfishness, covetousness, and the desire to better oneself materially or socially" are qualities that "were uniformly denounced and reviled in the Middle Ages."[40] This is illustrated by the doctrine of the just price and the prohibition against usury.[41] Clearly, the result of such practices was to prevent social mobility and to preserve the class relationships that characterised the European feudal system. Hunt concluded that the Christian paternalist ethic had to be abandoned for capitalism to take root.

In sum, Eisenstein stressed the mode of communication and Hauser emphasised the structural position of artistic creativity as the keys to understanding the absence of a conception of literary property up through medieval times. Both, however, glossed over consideration of the relations of production based on collective forms of creativity and consumption. Combining the analysis of modes and relations of production and communication provides a materialist grounding that links the origin of intellectual property to the emergence of the printing press and the rise of capitalism.

The Origins of Copyright

Sophia Menache argued that the needs and interests of Europe's *culture savante,* including the clergy and the nobility, led it to begin developing a European communications system at the advent of the Central Middle Ages (1000-1400 A.D.). Correspondence and books constituted two important means of communication within this emerging system. A secular trade in manuscripts emerged during the twelfth century, first in Paris and then in other university towns, signaling the impending demise of the Church's monopoly of knowledge. The book trade of the "Secular Age" was organised around the universities found in growing urban centers and was mainly based on the reproduction of the works of religious authorities and classical authors.[42] Copies of texts were still made by hand, but this system was "rationalised" by the "stationer" who, for a fee, organised the reproduction of texts on behalf of buyers looking for particular titles. The first stationers worked under the strict regulation of the universities, whose authorities checked essential works for textual correctness, controlled prices, and required that books be loaned to anyone wishing to make copies or have copies made for them.[43] Thus, it was not possible for anyone owning or producing a text to demand remuneration for making his work available since the system forbade exclusivity.[44]

With the appearance of an embryonic bourgeoisie and the increasing autonomy of the nobility from the Church, a growing reading public allowed some stationers to break free from university and guild control. The response to the literary needs of these emerging class forces prompted the production of books on practical concerns such as law, politics, and science and also of "works of literature, edifying moral treatises, romances and translations."[45] At first, stationers turned out adaptations of outdated works and Latin translations of medieval classics; later they began seeking out original works to keep their operations going. Thus, the structural autonomy of literature, which Hauser linked to the disintegration of Christian culture, developed as the rising bourgeoisie and secular nobility demanded their own cultural fare and as enterprising stationers sought to exploit new markets.

As this suggests, the midwives of the birth of printing were the stationers, who as merchant capitalists laid the foundation for the transformation of the book trade by using their accumulated capital for investment in print technology and manuscripts and by organising the book trade along capitalistic lines. This required the printing press, for as Eisenstein argued, the manuscript-based production system could never have generated the surplus of books necessary for a capitalist book trade.[46] Indeed, the printing press is among the first inventions to be exploited by capitalists. Johann Gutenberg developed the printing press only with the assistance of a merchant capitalist named Johann Fust, who ended up with the equipment when Gutenberg could not repay the loans. This appropriation of Gutenberg's intellectual creativity symbolises the nature of the dawning capitalist system.

Copyright in Venice

When seeking the origins of capitalism, Marxist historians and political economists usually begin with the Italian republics of the thirteenth and fourteenth centuries. Venice, in particular, was a core state of a smaller Mediterranean regional economy during the High Middle Ages.[47] At that time, Venice was a center of commerce, banking, finance, and textile production. By 1500, trade with Venice "affected directly all of the Mediterranean and the whole of Western Europe."[48] Both the internal factors and external factors necessary for the emergence of capitalism came together in this Italian republic. Internally, there was capital accumulation through application of new technologies and exploitation of wage labor, which in turn generated the surplus production required for external trade. Furthermore, the wealthy merchant classes of this thriving metropolis effectively controlled the state.[49] Venice is also cited as the first city in Italy, and practically the first in Europe, in which the business of printing and publishing becomes important.[50]

When John of Speyer brought the printing press to Venice in 1469, the Venetian Collegio granted him an exclusive printing privilege for a five-year term. By extending grants and privileges of this sort, the city government sought to encourage the importation of new industrial techniques and stimulate the growth of local industry and commerce. Similar laws regulating the printing and publishing trade became common in many European countries by the beginning of the sixteenth century. Such grants of exclusivity by the state, first appearing in fifteenth-century Venice, "were the precursor and the foundation of the later system of copyright."[51]

Early government regulation of industry in general took the form of patent monopolies, an exclusive right to operate in a particular industry sector or to produce a certain type of commodity. Governments granted patents in the book trade, such as the one granted to John of Speyer, that secured for printers exclusive control over the right to copy certain titles or classes of literary work in order to encourage them to invest in an "expensive and speculative undertaking."[52] Such privileges were also granted as favors or rewards to selected entrepreneurs in exchange for political loyalty and as a way of supporting infant industries. Conveniently, they served to control who printed and what was printed. Eisenstein concluded that the granting of these privileges to printers forced governments to begin to define what belonged in the public domain and what areas of literary creativity could be appropriated for private use and profit.[53] This brings us to the essential connection between intellectual property rights and capitalism.

Patent and copyright laws supported the expansion of the realm of creative human activities that could be commodified. Copyright, in particular, reflected the existence of newly developed print technology that allowed the "fixing" of literary works in a tangible medium—books—

that could be mass produced on an unprecedented scale and then sold in the marketplace. As governments decided what printing privileges to grant to whom, the "literary 'Common' became subject to 'enclosure movements.'"[54] Intellectual property laws facilitated the private appropriation of intellectual creativity, which is always based upon socially constructed knowledge and culture, in the same way that property laws in general served as the basis for the commodification of tangible property, the common land in particular. At the same time, copyright and patent laws, most often enacted and enforced by the state, legitimised the concentration of ownership of inventions, art, and literature in the hands of the expanding capitalist class. In the literary domain, copyright first appears primarily as an economic privilege for publishers in the form of monopolies over individual titles or classes of works.

At first glance, the state's role in establishing and enforcing intellectual property rights seems essential for a capitalist-based publishing industry, but this is not always the case. Special privileges for the encouragement of a book publishing industry, both imperial and municipal, appear in sixteenth-century Germany.[55] They dealt mainly with the property interests of publishers and printers in classical and medieval texts. Even though Germany's early publishing industry had these official privileges available to it, the leading publishers found it more convenient, given the fragmented nature of state authority in Germany at that time, to protect their economic investments against piracy and competition through noninterference agreements. These were exercised through a guild and through the Frankfurt and Leipzig book fairs. We find a similar evolution of the regulation of literary property in the Netherlands, where the chief protection enjoyed by publishers seems to have been an informal understanding or system of agreements among themselves.[56] As the national publishing industries became increasingly international, these agreements broke down to be supplanted by national and international copyright regimes. The evolution of copyright law in Great Britain, which is cited as the source of inspiration for the U.S. copyright system, involved both private cooperation and state intervention from the outset.

History of Copyright in Britain

Print technology reached England in 1476 when a successful merchant capitalist named William Caxton set up a printing press in the precincts of Westminster Abbey.[57] Early government regulation included efforts to entice printers and booksellers to England and to encourage the development of a book trade. Further regulation of the book trade involved licensing of printing presses, printing patents for titles and classes of books, and censorship. In 1557, Philip and Mary granted a charter for the incorporation of the Stationers Company, giving it a firm monopoly over printing and publishing in England for the next 150 years. Only members of the company could secure government licenses to operate a printing press, and the total number of printers, bookbinders, and book sellers was limited (for example, a Star Chamber decree of 1586 limited the number of master printers to twenty-five). The licenses were granted in exchange for the company's policing of its own members (for instance, in the publication of seditious and heretical material) as well as of pirate operations. Additionally, printing patents gave members of the company exclusivity over titles or classes of books in exchange for loyalty to the crown. Copyright laws emerged simultaneously with censorship out of the trade practices of this monopoly.

The Stationers Company kept a registry in which member printers and publishers listed the titles of their publications and thereby procured exclusive rights to copy them. Stationers were allowed to transfer copyrights as secured by registration to other members. Only members of the company could register titles and secure copyrights, and they registered only those titles that were deemed by members (or at times, government officials) to be religiously and/or politically safe.

Although British law protected the economic rights of company members, nothing in it referred to the protection of authors' rights in their own creative works. Furthermore, since only licensed printers and booksellers could legally make copies, authors were in a weak position to bargain when seeking publication of their works. Consequently, the economic rewards generated by the commodification of literature flowed to printers, publishers, and booksellers, not to authors.[58] The importance of authorship did begin to increase as printers and publishers neared completing the enclosure of public domain works from classic and medieval times and began seeking new and "original" works to keep the presses running and to meet the demands of the expanding reading public.

Patronage remained the major form of support for authors from the dawn of printing until roughly the mid-eighteenth century. However, by the second half of the seventeenth century, publishers also began paying authors for the right to copy and publish their works. We see this with the publication of Milton's *Paradise Lost* in 1667. For this work, Milton left us the first recorded agreement in which a publisher paid "copy money" for an original work, though it earned him a mere ten pounds total before his death in 1674. His widow, who inherited the copyright, sold all further rights to the "copy" for eight pounds. Ploman and Hamilton concluded that such payments were not based so much upon legal or moral grounds as economic grounds.[59] Publishers willingly paid for the best "originals" that authors could produce, as these commanded higher value in the marketplace. Eisenstein also attributed many improvements of the printed book, such as title pages, table of contents, and indices,, to the commercial motives of printers and booksellers.

There seemed to be little question that authors should be paid for their manuscripts, though the prevailing attitude during this period was one of contempt for authors who wrote especially for publication. Up through the seventeenth century, writing was viewed as a leisure pursuit of the educated and financially independent man, but after two centuries of printing, the compensation system for authors was completely transformed. Goldsmith makes the familiar qualitative judgment of the printing age as "that fatal revolution whereby writing is converted to a mechanical trade."[60] By the end of the seventeenth century, authorship was clearly becoming a way of making a living for some writers. Daniel Defoe, a respected English writer, could note in 1725 that "writing ... is become a very considerable Branch of the English Commerce. The Booksellers are the Master Manufacturers or Employers. The several Writers, Authors, Copyers, Sub-writers and all other operators with Pen and Ink are the workmen employed by the said Master-Manufacturers."[61] Defoe observed that writing was increasingly an individual pursuit conducted for personal recognition and pecuniary rewards and that competition in the marketplace increasingly determined who could make a living producing art and literature. Here lies the crucial link between libertarian theory and copyright: As literary and artistic works were progressively commodified, "possessive individualism began to characterise the attitude of writers to their work."[62]

The Role of John Locke

Both authors and publishers latched onto popular

notions of natural rights as they sought to define the concept and practice of copyright. Two important contemporary texts on intellectual property attribute the development of authors' rights in literary creativity to John Locke as laid out in his *Two Treatises of Civil Government*, published in 1690.[63] Accordingly, Ploman and Hamilton claim that John Locke "postulated a theory of an intellectual property right in the author."[64] Later they conclude: "John Locke's attempt to shift the rights of intellectual property from a statutory right to a naturally given right meant in practical terms a shift of the right from the publisher to the author."[65] The congressional Office of Technology Assessment report on intellectual property repeats the claim that "in 1690, John Locke argued in his *Two Treatises of Civil Government* that the author has a natural right in his work since he had expended his own labor in creating it."[66] However, such an argument is nowhere to be found in Locke's Two *Treatises*. Indeed, it is debatable whether Locke extended his labor theory of property, as applied to the production of tangible goods, to intellectual and artistic labor.

According to C.B. Macpherson,[67] Locke built upon the theory of possessive individualism offered by Thomas Hobbes[68] but retained certain aspects of traditional moral law that made Locke more acceptable to the rising capitalist class than Hobbes. Seventeenth-century individualism conceived of the male individual as essentially the proprietor of his own person and capacities, for which he owed nothing to society. Locke began with the assumption that "the earth and all inferior creatures [are] common to all men" in the state of nature but then developed his labor theory of property to justify the private appropriation of the common wealth of nature.[69] Since every male individual is the proprietor of his own person, "the labour of his body and the work of his hands, we may say, are properly his.

Whatsoever then he removes out of the state that nature hath provided and left it in, he hath mixed his labor with, and joined to it something that is his own, and thereby makes it his property."[70]

Inherent to the notion of private property is the right to exclude others from using it. It is clear that the forms of property to which Locke referred were "the fruits of the earth and the beasts that subsist on it [and] the earth itself."[71] But Locke did not explicitly extend private appropriation to the realm of inventive, artistic, or literary creativity. In fact, in one relevant passage Locke notes that "invention and arts," when applied to the process of appropriation from land and nature, allow one to increase one's private property holdings, but nothing is mentioned here or elsewhere about the private ownership of these same "invention and arts."[72]

It is therefore doubtful that Locke had intellectual creativity in mind when articulating his labor theory of property; it is not specifically addressed in the central text in which this theory is presented. When we turn to Locke's biography, we find that he earned his livelihood as a political writer for the third earl of Shaftesbury and that he also received income from property holdings, government commissions, and the lease or sale of publishing rights to his works. It is clear that Locke did not earn a living from the publication of his books, so he probably did not see the need to make a case for authors' rights. Additionally, *Two Treatises* was published anonymously, suggesting that Locke did not prioritise claims to ownership over political expediency. Richard Ashcraft found that Locke published the work anonymously to avoid alienating personal friends and allies.[73]

Aside from Locke's own publishing practices, we can look at his political record to seek evidence of conscious and explicit articulation of a natural right of authorship. Locke was directly involved in legislation concerning the licensing of printing. When the Act for the Regulation of Printing of 1662 came up for renewal in Parliament in 1692, "Locke took a lively interest in the discussions it provoked."[74] Opponents to renewal, especially independent booksellers and printers, attacked the law for the monopoly privileges it conferred. John Feather contended that a small inner circle of copyright owners within the Stationers Company, holding dozens of valuable copies that they had been inheriting and purchasing since the 1590s, had gained control of the British publishing industry in the mid-seventeenth century.[75] This inner circle operated in classic monopoly fashion, buying up all of the rights to copy books, colluding among themselves to limit competition, and charging monopoly prices for books (prices higher than those that would exist in competitive markets). Locke's primary problem with the monopoly was the poor quality of the books its members produced and the high prices they were nevertheless able to charge.

The attack on the Stationers Company came with the general assault on monopoly privileges associated with aristocratic authority. As Ashcraft showed, Locke assailed monopolistic bankers and sections of the landed aristocracy for hoarding money and property to the detriment of the kingdom. In a letter to Edward Clark written in 1692, following the renewal of the licensing Act of 1662, Locke added the monopoly held by "the company of ignorant and lazy stationers" to his list of unproductive capital holders.[76] In the letter he listed the "inconveniencys of that [A]ct," referring mainly to the restrictions on book imports and the exclusivity that publishers were able to claim on "Ancient Latin Authors" by registering titles in the Stationers Company's book. In seeking to define a public domain for literature, Locke argued that anyone should have the right to publish or import "any Latin booke whose author lived above a thousand year since."[77] This way publishers would have to compete to put out the best editions of ancient Latin texts and thereby lift "a great oppression upon Schollars."[78] Nothing in this complaint against the licensing system pertained to censorship or freedom of the press.

When the Licensing Act again came up for renewal in 1694, Locke sent a memorandum to Clark, a member of the House of Commons and a member of the committee overseeing preparation of new legislation regarding printing, in which he added freedom of the press to his rhetorical attack on the publishing monopoly.[79] In the eighteen-point memorandum, only one point questioned the principle of censorship, whereas thirteen of the points constituted an attack on the Act as the basis for the monopolistic book trade. The remainder targeted the Act for its general ineffectiveness in suppressing seditious publications. Within the memorandum, Locke moved toward greater precision in defining the public versus private literary domains, proposing that books of contemporary authors be publishable by anyone after fifty or seventy years in print. He seemed to take as given the idea that authors merit protection for a certain period of time, but his reasoning was expressed in terms of limits on the author's rights in order to *preserve literature* rather than in terms of an author's natural right. His concern was that "many good books come quite to be lost" as a result of the perpetual licenses held by the monopolistic book industry.[80] He again called for bringing the works of a "Tully, Caesar, or Livy" into the public domain, as was the practice in Holland, where books were "cheaper" and "better" because "the printers all strive to outdo one another."[81]

When the House of Commons voted to repeal the Act and the House of Lords voted for renewal, the Commons submitted to the Lords a paper citing Locke's eighteen reasons against renewal.[82] Frederick Siebert claimed that in adopting Locke's position paper the Commons followed his reasoning and thus emphasised the commercial constraints produced by the Act.[83] Maurice Cranston noted an irony here: that "freedom of the Press came to England all but incidentally to the elimination of a commercial monopoly." He contrasted Locke's call for "liberty in the name of trade" to Milton's call for "liberty in the name of liberty" and again found it ironic that the former "achieved his end" while the latter failed.[84]

Locke, it seems, never explicitly articulated a theory of an author's natural right to his work, for that argument surely would have been made in the above context. Either he was taking this right for granted or he failed to see the connections between his labor theory of property and intellectual and artistic creativity. Milton, in contrast, writing some fifty years earlier, found it necessary to explicitly identify a natural proprietary right in the "copy" of a work, but this probably referred to printers and booksellers, not authors.[85] In "Areopagitica," just before he launched his attack on the licensing ordinance of 1643 entitled "An Act for Redressing Disorders in Printing," Milton made the disclaimer that he would not be addressing that part of the law "which preserves justly every man's copy," although he advised that this too could be abused.[86]

The traditional copyright histories of Bruce Bugbee, Patterson, and Putnam argued that by the late seventeenth century, the basic principles of English copyright included an author's perpetual right to his copy under common law. Even if such a right existed, and the evidence is not all that clear that it did, the realities of publishing at this time were still such that only a licensed printer could legally make copies, and "dealing from this superior bargaining position, he paid for the author's manuscript as he saw fit."[87] Accordingly, Bugbee maintained that this property right in the manuscript therefore was not a "true copyright," by which he means the "exclusive control over multiplication of copies" of a manuscript.[88]

The First Modern Copyright Law

Upon expiration of the Licensing Act in 1694, the argument of the author's or inventor's natural property right in his artistic and intellectual labor proved expedient to the copyright-based monopoly now seeking ways to preserve its exclusive control over valuable literary properties. The most useful aspect of this theory for capitalists is this: Although the male individual is proprietor of his own person, which he cannot alienate, he is free to alienate his capacity to labor, for "property in the bourgeois sense is not only a right to enjoy or use; it is a right to dispose of, to exchange, to alienate."[89] With the lapse of the Licensing Act, the publishing monopoly began to argue that since authors had a natural copyright in their works as a result of their creative labor, the transfer of the right to copy a work gave the publisher a license in perpetuity.

The monopoly developed two practical strategies to cope with the lapse of its government-sanctioned privileges. One marketing response was to set up an exclusive wholesale distribution system, tying wholesalers to the dominant publishers and copyright owners. The other was a legal strategy; the monopoly continued to defend its copyrights, now claimed in perpetuity, through civil action. The distribution system offered only partial protection, and "the courts were slow, expensive and unsympathetic to the few members of the trade who went to Chancery to take civil proceedings against those who infringed their rights."[90] Consequently, members of the industry continued their efforts to gain renewal of some form of statutory protection through repeated petitioning of the House of Commons for new legislation.

The petitioners—including copyright-owning publishers, a few printers who still owned valuable copyrights, the wholesalers tied to the monopoly, but no authors or translators—sought legal protection for their copies and finally secured it in April 1710 with passage of the Copyright Act or Statute of Queen Anne (known as "An Act for the Encouragement of Learning and for Securing the Property of Copies of Books to the Rightful Owners Thereof"). Copyright historians generally cite the Statute of Queen Anne as the first modern copyright law. It granted copyright protection to existing titles in the Stationers Register, for twenty-one years; entries made after the Act took effect were protected for fourteen years with the possibility of a fourteen-year extension beyond that. It was not immediately clear whether the work would go into the public domain when the statutory periods were over or whether perpetual rights were retained at common law. Ploman and Hamilton summed up the provisions of the Act this way: "The Statute concerned the right to copy and no more. The protection afforded was against the piracy of printed works. There was nothing in this Statute that touched upon the creative or moral rights of the author. The right protected was a property right."[91] According to Patterson, the Act "was basically a trade-regulation statute" aimed at ordering the book industry and preventing monopoly. [92] To a certain extent, the strategy of the monopolists backfired, for by granting authors the right to register their own copyrights the exclusive privileges enjoyed by members of the Stationers Company were undermined. In an indirect way then, the Act confirmed the authors' natural right of copyright ownership at common law; yet its very existence had the effect of bringing the period of common law copyright in England to an end.[93]

Following passage of the Statute of Queen Anne, two important legal proceedings helped to sort out the conflicting claims made for copyright, whether based on statutory or natural right. The first case, brought by the major copyright holders still seeking to perpetuate their monopoly, was *Millar v. Taylor* (1769). There, the House of Lords recognised the common law right of authors and concluded that the Statute of Queen Anne simply provided extra protection upon publication of a work.[94] This decision had the effect of firmly fixing the idea of copyright as an author's right but also supported the publishers' claim to perpetual copyrights; thus it preserved their monopoly. In a second case, *Donaldson v. Beckett* (1774), the House of Lords again recognised the author's natural copyright at common law but decided that the Statute of Queen Anne supplanted this right with a statutory right.[95] Consequently, in the Anglo-American tradition, copyrights are governed by statute, and once a work is published it becomes subject to the limits established by the law. Feather believed that the underlying intent of the *Donaldson* decision was again to break up the system of long-term monopoly control of copyrights still held by the inner circle of the former Stationers Company.[96] The decision had this effect but at the same time contributed to the emergence of the publisher alone as the dominant figure in the book industry.

Origins and Development of U.S. Copyright Law

U.S. copyright law descends directly from the legal theory and practice established in Britain. This is evident from the wording used to codify the U.S. laws, the mechanisms by which copyright was procured, and the legal decisions upon which U.S. courts drew to define copyright.

The General Court of the Massachusetts Bay Colony granted the first recorded copyright in the colonies in 1672 in response to a petition by John Usher, a wealthy merchant-bookseller.[97] Usher sought to publish a revised edition of *The General Laws and Liberties of the Massachusetts Colony*, and to protect his investment he secured legislation that forbade printers from printing copies or selling the work without his permission. This "private" copyright is the only one recorded during the first hundred years of the colonial era.

Patterson showed that "copyright was the subject of widespread legislation almost as soon as the new nation was founded."[98] He found this remarkable given the "absence of an author class" that might have lobbied for such legislation, and he attributed this legislative activity to "the intellectual quality of the leaders of the day" and "the intellectual ferment that characterised the young United States."[99] Patterson is widely off the mark with this interpretation. Instead, the early history of U.S. copyright lawmaking is a classic demonstration of the instrumental role of the state in advancing the interests of capital and aligned elites. [100] Bugbee described how, beginning in the 1780s, a handful of "literary gentlemen" launched a campaign to secure the protection of literary property.

Thomas Paine set the rhetorical tone of the copyright crusade in a letter to the abbe Raynal in 1782, in which he stressed the link between protectionism and the national development of literature: "It may, with propriety, be remarked, that in all countries where literature is protected, (and it never can flourish where it is not), the works of an author are his legal property; and to treat letters in any other light than this, is to banish them from the country, or strangle them at birth."[101] Paine's *Common Sense*, of course, was one of the first "best-sellers" produced in the United States, making him someone who stood to benefit from copyright. Calling attention to "the state of literature in

America," he predicted that the legislature would one day have to consider the subject; that up to that time, writing was "a disinterested service of the Revolution" for which "no man thought of profits." But, he continued, "when peace shall give time and opportunity for study, the country will deprive itself of the honour and service of letters, and the improvement of science, unless sufficient laws are made to prevent depredation on literary property."[102]

This charge was picked up by Noah Webster, another important literary figure of the era. Seeking copyright protection for his English textbook, Webster launched the lobbying campaign for literary property rights with a petition to the Connecticut and New York legislatures. Though pursuing specific protection for their own works, Webster and other members of the embryonic U.S. literati cast their arguments in terms of the national interest and the development of a national literature. The Connecticut legislature responded to this appeal with the first state copyright statute (January 1783). Shifting its attention to the Continental Congress, this "small but significant group of men interested in letters"[103] prompted the passage of a resolution in March 1783 recommending that the individual states secure to "authors and publishers of new books the copyright of such books."[104]

Twelve of the thirteen original states, all but Delaware, passed copyright laws between 1783 and 1786. These were generally based in language and in form on the Statute of Queen Anne. According to Ploman and Hamilton, the goals of these statutes, in order of importance, were: first, to secure the author's right; second, to promote learning; third, to provide order in the book trade; and fourth, to prevent monopoly.[105] The preambles to the state copyright acts reflect these goals. They also assume an "inherent" connection between creativity, profit, and social welfare.

For example, Connecticut's 1783 "Act for the Encouragement of Literature and Genius" mandated "that every author should be secured in receiving the profits that may arise from the sale of his works, and such security may encourage men of learning and genius to publish their writings; which may do honor to their country, and service to mankind."[106] Similarly, the Massachusetts copyright act passed in 1783 determined that in order to encourage "learned and ingenious persons in the various arts and sciences ... to make great and beneficial exertions of this nature," there "must exist legal security of the fruits of their study and industry to themselves."[107] The underlying assumption here is that human beings require economic reward to be intellectually or artistically creative. The philosophy of intellectual property reifies economic rationalism as a natural human trait. Yet from our historical analysis we see that throughout most of human history there existed no concept of intellectual property rights. Nevertheless, humans still produced technological and cultural artifacts.

Early state lawmakers did ground their copyright statutes in Locke's natural rights theory. The copyright protection conferred by Massachusetts law proclaimed such legal security as "one of the natural rights of all men" that is most self-evident. For when it came to literary activity there is "no property more peculiarly a man's own than that which is produced by the labour of his mind."[108] Not all of the state copyright laws appealed to natural law. The Pennsylvania version passed in 1784 aimed instead at halting the practice whereby printers or booksellers printed, reprinted, and published books without the consent of the "authors or proprietors" of copyrights "to their very great detriment" and "damage" to their families.[109] South Carolina and Virginia extended copyright protection to booksellers and printers who "have purchased or acquired the copy or copies of any book or books" in order to reprint them.[110]

Two types of "limits" on copyrights are found in these statutes. The first is the limit on the duration of the term of protection, varying from an initial period of fourteen to twenty-one years for different states, with some states allowing renewal for an additional fourteen years by authors or their heirs or assigns. In addition, five states—Massachusetts, South and North Carolina, Georgia, and New York—had limits on the copyright monopoly in the form of a "just price." These clauses stipulated that if the copyright owner, author, or publisher set an unreasonable price on any book, that is, above the costs figured for labor, expenses, and risk, the court could in fact set a reasonable price. Similarly, if a copyright owner attempted to limit the supply of a work, the court could grant a license to publish it to another party (for example, to a petitioner bringing forth charges). This "limit" on the copyright monopoly recognised that exclusive rights can backfire and-actually hinder access to published works.

All of these statutes required registration of copyrights with local courts as the basis of protection and possible litigation. Pirates were punished by forfeiture or destruction of all infringing copies ana by fines levied on a per-page basis. Despite the underlying principles and explicit rhetoric of natural rights/these statutes served to protect the author's or publisher's copyright from piracy for a statutorily determined length of time. Usually, publishers provided the capital to bring a book to the marketplace, with publication being necessary to secure copyright protection. Consequently, copyright continued in its early U.S. form to function much like the Stationers Company copyright, that is, as a publisher's economic right. The author's right to authorise the display, public reading, translation, alteration, or derivation after publication was not recognised.

Federalism and U.S. Copyright Law

The separate state copyright statutes could not be enforced very successfully, as each had its own registry of copyrighted works by local authors and publishers. It was clear that a national system of copyright was necessary for the purposes of enforcement and support of a national book trade. With a growing interstate economy, the new nation required standardised laws for the regulation of commerce, including intellectual property. In this regard, James Madison wrote in *The Federalist* that the "states cannot separately make effectual provision" of copyright and patent protection and that congressional action was therefore required.[11] Madison's efforts, traced back by Bugbee[112] to the personal influence of Noah Webster led to the adoption of the copyright and patent clause of the U.S. Constitution (Article 1, section 8, clause 8), which reads: "The Congress shall have the power ... to promote the progress of science and useful arts, by securing for limited time to authors and inventors the exclusive right to their respective writings and discoveries."

The clause emerged out of a set of nation-building proposals—one by James Madison and one by Charles Pinckney—that would authorise Congress to: "grant charters of incorporation in cases where the public good may require them"; "establish a university"; "grant patents for useful inventions"; "secure to literary authors their copy rights for a limited time"; and "establish public institutions, rewards, and immunities for the promotion of agriculture, commerce, trade and manufacture."[113] These proposals reflect the role of the federal government would play in supporting the rise of a national U.S. economy within the context of competitive capitalism. The rewards and monopolies had much the same function as the patents granted earlier by governments in Europe out of which copyright emerged, that is, to support the development of infant industries. Although Bugbee underscores the role of a small but influential class of manufacturers and "war-born capitalists" seeking stable investment opportunities in securing these measures,[114] we can again recognise the underlying structural logic of capital at work. Copyright and patent protection also reflects the larger political agenda of this class in favor of stronger and more centralised defense of private property as a check on popular sovereignty.

Madison, for one, was sensitive to the power of exclusive privileges with his knowledge of the European history of patent monopolies. In a letter to Thomas Jefferson dated October 17,1788, he expressed his hope that the new nation could avoid the stifling effects of mercantilist-based monopolies, which he classed "among the greatest nuisances in Government" but deemed "too valuable to be wholly renounced" as "encouragements to literary works and ingenious discoveries."[115] Discovering the fundamental contradiction inherent in intellectual property law, he argued that the public and individual interests were commensurate in the U.S. system of intellectual property as long as copyrights were broadly held by authors and for a limited time. In this passage, Madison sounded much like Jefferson, who advocated the broad distribution of landed property, or Paine, who argued for a republic made up of artisans and craftspersons.[116] Both saw their particular constituency as the essential basis for an interested and democratic body politic.

Madison believed that "where power is in the few, it is natural for them to sacrifice the many to their own partialities and corruptions," which is what he saw when he looked back on Britain's monopoly-dominated mercantile system and the state-conferred privileges upon which it was based.[117] Yet when Madison and his fellow framers of the Constitution looked forward, they saw a potentially more troubling future: a tyranny of the propertyless majority to which "the few will be unnecessarily sacrificed" (that is, deprived of their property).[118] Therefore, with regard to the copyright or patent, Madison expressed willingness to "reserve in all cases a right to the public to abolish the privilege" but "at a price to be specified in the grant of it."[119] Implicitly, Madison recognised that the concentration of intellectual property could thwart the very creativity it was supposed to encourage, but he also recognised it as an essential foundation for a private property-based economic system.

Congress followed up on the constitutional mandate adopted in 1789 and passed the first federal copyright law in the Act of May 31, 1790. Following the English precedent, this law provided protection only for the created statutory term, granting the U.S. author or his or her heirs or assigns "the sole right and liberty of printing, reprinting, publishing and vending" of such works. It stated explicitly that it did not intend to prohibit publication and sale of works in the United States that were first written, printed, or published abroad. Ploman and Hamilton argued that this piracy provision can be seen "as the action of a developing country to protect its burgeoning culture while exploiting the cultural products of more developed nations."[120]

However, it was again not immediately clear after passage of the Act whether the author's common law copyright had been supplanted. The notion of natural rights in inventive and intellectual creativity was losing its resonance by the early nineteenth century. The U.S. Supreme Court addressed this tension in *Wheaton v. Peters* (1834), which set the terms for U.S. copyright protection for the next 150 years. The *Wheaton* decision drew heavily from *Donaldson v. Beckett*, concluding that copyright was a statutory right created by Congress and was "secured" by following the formalities of registration, notice, and deposit.[121] The Court thereby rejected the notion that an inventor or author had a perpetual right in the patent or copyright as well as the idea that certain legal rights of authors are retained even after publication. In reaching its decision, the Court framed copyright litigation as a matter of protecting the copyright owner's exclusive rights to exploit and profit from effort and risk put into the work versus protecting public access to literary creativity.

By concluding that copyright was a statutory right of limited duration, the Court struck against the notion of unlimited monopoly that a natural, perpetual right implied. Thus, once the statutory period of protection expired, the published, copyrighted works passed into the public domain. An author did retain a common law copyright, but only as long as the work remained unpublished. This fact again highlights the central role of capital in bringing a work to the public, a process through which the publisher takes control of and benefits the most from the author's copyright privileges. This pattern is subsequently replicated as copyright law is extended each time a new form or medium of artistic and literary creativity and expression is developed and deployed, from etched and engraved prints in 1802 to computer software programs in 1980. The result has been the concentration of ownership of the copyrights to cultural and literary artifacts with the highest exchange value in the hands of the capitalist class, which will be demonstrated in the next chapter.

NOTES

1. Bruce Bugbee, *The Genesis of American Patent and Copyright Law*, Washington, DC: Public Affairs Press, 1967; Lyman Patterson, *Copyright in Historical Perspective*, Nashville, TN: Vanderbilt University Press, 1968; George Putnam, "Literary Property: An Historical Sketch," in G. Putnam (ed.), *The Question of Copyright*,

New York: Knickerbocker, 1896, pp. 351-411; Royce F. Whale, *Copyright*, London: Longman, 1971.

2. Patterson, p. 223.
3. Harold Innis, *Empire and Communication*, New York: Oxford University Press, 1950; Harold Innis, *The Bias of Communication*, Toronto: University of Toronto Press, 1951.
4. Jack Goody, The Logic of Writing and the Organisation of Society, Cambridge: Cambridge University Press, 1986, p. 179.
5. Goody, p. 179.
6. Karl Marx, *Preface to a Contribution to the Critique of Political Economy*, London: Lawrence and Wishart, 1971; Karl Marx and Frederick Engels, *The German Ideology*, New York: International Publishers, 1970.
7. Howard Sherman, *Foundations of Radical Political Economy*, Armonk, NY: M. E. Sharpe, 1987, p. 69.
8. Bob Jessop, "Mode of Production," in J. Eatwell, M. Milgate, and P. Newman (eds.), *The New Palgrave: Marxian Economics*, London: Macmillan, 1990, pp. 289-296, p. 295.
9. Brian Winston, *Misunderstanding Media*, Cambridge: Harvard University Press, 1986.
10. Raymond Williams, *Marxism and Literature*, Oxford: Oxford University Press, 1977, p. 87.
11. Edward Ploman and L. Clark Hamilton, *Copyright: Intellectual Property in the Information Age*, London: Routledge and Kegan Paul, 1980.
12. Rosalind Thomas, *Oral Tradition and Written Records in Classical Athens*, Cambridge: Cambridge University Press, 1989.
13. Walter Ong, *Interfaces of the Word*, Ithaca: Cornell University Press, 1977.
14. Arnold Hauser, *The Social History of Art*, New York: Alfred A. Knopf, 1952, p. 87.
15. Victor Hazen, "The Origins of Copyright in Ancient Jewish Law," *Bulletin of the Copyright Society of the U.S.A.*, 18:1, 1970, pp. 23-28, p. 25.
16. Ploman and Hamilton, p. 7; Putnam, pp. 355-356.
17. Ploman and Hamilton, p. 7.
18. L.D. Reynolds and N. G. Wilson, *Scribes and Scholars*, Oxford: Clarendon, p. 19.

19. Reynolds and Wilson, p. 24; Oswald Dilke, *Roman Books and Their Impact*, Leeds: Elmete, p. 14.
20. Reynolds and Wilson, p. 23.
21. P. Wittenberg, *The Law of Literary Property*, Cleveland: World Publishing, 1957, p.15
22. Robert Oliver, *Communication and Culture in Ancient India and China*, Syracuse, NY: Syracuse University Press, 1971, p. 21.
23. M. Covarrubias, *Island of Bali*, New York: Alfred A. Knopf, 1937, p. 164.
24. Covarrubias, pp. 160-166.
25. Ploman and Hamilton, pp. 141-142.
26. Goody, p. 91.
27. Goody, p. 96.
28. George Putnam, *Books and Their Makers During the Middle Ages*, New York: Hillary House, 1962, p. 484.
29. M. Kline, *Rabelais and the Age of Printing*, Geneva: Librairie Droz, 1963, p. 5.
30. James Burke, *The Day the Universe Changed*, Boston: Little, Brown, 1985, p. 97.
31. A. Lord, *The Singer of Tales*, Cambridge: Harvard University Press, 1960, p. 5.
32. Lord, p. 13.
33. Elizabeth Eisenstein, *The Printing Press as an Agent of Change*, Cambridge: Cambridge University Press, 1979, p. 229.
34. Hauser, p. 327.
35. Hauser, p. 327.
36. Hauser, p. 328.
37. Sophia Menache, *The Vox Dei*, Cambridge: Oxford University Press, 1990, p. 9.
38. Robert Darnton, *The Great Cat Massacre and Other Episodes in French Cultural History*, New York: Basic Books, 1984.
39. E.K. Hunt, *Property and Prophets* (6th ed.), New York: Harper and Row, 1990, pp. 8-10.
40. Hunt, p. 9.
41. Hunt, p. 10.

42. Michel Thomas, "Introduction," in L. Febvre and H. Martin, *The Coming of the Book*, London: Verso, 1984, pp. 15-27.
43. M. Thomas, p. 21.
44. Lucien Febvre and Henri-Jean Martin, *The Coming of the Book*, London: Verso, 1984, pp. 159-160.
45. M. Thomas, p. 22.
46. Eisenstein, p. 49.
47. Immanuel Wallerstein, *The Capitalist World-Economy*, Cambridge: Cambridge University Press, 1979, p. 42.
48. Michel Beaud, *A History of Capitalism, 1500-1980*, New York: Monthly Review Press, 1983, p. 23.
49. Wallerstein, p. 42.
50. Putnam, 1962, pp. 404-405.
51. Putnam, 1962, p. 486.
52. Putnam, 1962, p. 487.
53. Eisenstein, p. 120.
54. Eisenstein, pp. 120-121.
55. Putnam, 1962, p. 412.
56. Bugbee, p. 49.
57. For histories of British printing, see John Feather, *A History of British Printing*, London: Croom Helm, 1988; Frank Mumby, *Publishing and Bookselling* (5th ed.), London: Jonathan Cape, 1974; Marjorie Plant, *The English Book Trade* (3rd ed.), London: George Allen and Unwin, 1974.
58. Feather, p. 25.
59. Ploman and Hamilton, pp. 11-12.
60. Cited in Raymond Williams, *The Long Revolution*, New York: Columbia University Press, 1961, p. 162.
61. Williams, 1961, pp. 161-162.
62. Eisenstein, p. 121.
63. Ploman and Hamilton, 1980; U.S. Congress, Office of Technology Assessment, *Intellectual Property Rights in an Age of Electronics and Information*, Washington, DC: U.S. Government Printing Office, 1986 (hereinafter OTA Report).
64. Ploman and Hamilton, p. 13.

65. Ploman and Hamilton, p. 17.
66. OTA Report, p. 36.
67. C. B. Macpherson, *The Political Theory of Possessive Individualism: Hobbes to Locke*, Oxford: Oxford University Press, 1962.
68. Thomas Hobbes, *Leviathan, or the Matter, Forme, and Power of a Commonwealth Ecclesiastical and Civil*, New York: Collier Books, 1962.
69. John Locke, *Two Treatises of Civil Government*, New York: Hafner, 1947, p. 134.
70. Locke, p. 134.
71. Locke, p. 136.
72. Locke, p. 143.
73. Richard Ashcraft, *Revolutionary Politics und Locke's Two Treatises of Civil Government*, Princeton: Princeton University Press, 1986, p. 600.
74. Maurice Cranston, *John Locke: A Biography*, London: Longman 1957, p. 368.
75. Feather, p. 41.
76. John Locke, *The Correspondence of John Locke*, E. S. DeBeer (ed.), Oxford: Oxford University Press, 1979, p. 615.
77. Locke, 1979, p. 615.
78. Locke, 1979, p. 615.
79. Cranston, pp. 386-387.
80. Peter King, *The Life and Letters of John Locke*, London: Bell and Daldy, 1864, p. 205.
81. P. King, p. 205.
82. Cranston, p. 387.
83. Frederick Siebert, *Freedom of the Press in England*, Urbana: University of Illinois Press, 1952, p. 261.
84. Cranston, p. 387.
85. H. Ranson, *The First Copyright Statute: Art Essay on an Act for the Encouragement of Learning, 1710*, Austin: University of Texas Press, 1956.
86. John Milton, *Areopagitica and of Education*, New York: Appleton-Century-Crofts, 1951, p. 5.
87. Bugbee, p. 51.

88. Bugbee, p. 51.
89. Macpherson, p. 215.
90. Feather, p. 73.
91. Ploman and Hamilton, p. 13.
92. Patterson, p. 14.
93. Putnam, 1962, p. 472.
94. *Millar v. Taylor*, 4 Burr. 2303, Eng. Rep. 201 (1769).
95. *Donaldson v. Beckett*, 4 Burr. 2408, 98 Eng. Rep. 257 (1774).
96. Feather, p. 83.
97. U.S. Library of Congress, Copyright Office, *Copyright Enactments*, Washington, DC: U.S. Government Printing Office, 1963, p. 140; Bugbee, p. 65.
98. Patterson, p. 180.
99. Patterson, p. 180.
100. See G. W. Domhoff, *Who Rules America Now?* Englewood Cliffs, NJ: Prentice Hall, 1983; Ralph Miliband, *The State in Capitalist Society*, New York: Basic Books, 1969.
101. Cited in Bugbee, p. 104.
102. Cited in Bugbee, p. 105.
103. Bugbee, p. 112.
104. U.S. Library of Congress, 1963, p. 1.
105. Ploman and Hamilton, p. 15.
106. U.S. Library of Congress, 1963, p. 1.
107. U.S. Library of Congress, 1963, p. 4.
108. U.S. Library of Congress, 1963, p. 4.
109. U.S. Library of Congress, 1963, p. 10.
110. U.S. Library of Congress, 1963, pp. 12, 14.
111. Alexander Hamilton, John Jay, and James Madison, *The Federalist*, New York: New American Library, 1961, pp. 271-272.
112. Bugbee, p. 125.
113. Cited in Bugbee, p. 126.
114. Bugbee, p. 128.
115. James Madison, *Letters and Other Writings of James Madison*, New York: R. Worthington, 1884, p. 427.

116. Eric Foner, *Tom Paine and Revolutionary America*, London: Oxford University Press, 1976.
117. Madison, p. 427.
118. Madison, p. 427.
119. Madison, p. 427.
120. Ploman and Hamilton, p.16.
121. *Wheaton V. Peters*, 8 Pet, 591 (1834).

3 CONTROL OF CULTURE AND INFORMATION

This chapter begins to lay out the theoretical framework that guides this inquiry into the relationships among filmed entertainment, new communications technology, and intellectual property rights. The framework combines radical political economy with information economics, Marxist and radical theories of the capitalist state, and critical legal studies. Radical political-economic communications theory and research can be organised into three fundamental categories: (1) the economic structure of communications industries; (2) the effects of the logic of capital on the production, distribution, and consumption of culture and information; and (3) the contradictions and forms of resistance within capitalist communications systems.[1] This chapter contributes primarily to research in the first category, the analysis of the structure of the communications industry. More precisely, the focus here is on the structure of the filmed entertainment industry and on who owns and controls the communications industry and its core asset, intellectual property.

Attempts arfe made to examine how the logic of capital and the peculiar nature of the product of this industry sector affect the structure and performance of the communications system. This interdisciplinary combination of critical theory produces a holistic framework for the analysis of the filmed entertainment industry's structure and performance, the role of the state vis-a-vis this industry, and the specific relationship between communications technology and the filmed entertainment copyright system. The normative purpose of this study is to contribute further to our understanding of the relationships between capitalism, the state, and communications media.

The Radical Political Economy of Communications

The roots of the radical political-economic approach to communications can be traced to the historical dialectics of Hegel and Marx, the radical political economy of Marx, Rudolf Hilferding, Rosa Luxemburg, Paul Baran, and Paul Sweezy, and the analysis of imperialism by Lenin and Nikolai Bukharin.[2] These critics of capitalism have provided us with a basic understanding of the logic of capital accumulation and of the contradictions inherent to this form of organising economic life. Robert Heilbroner defines the logic of capitalism as "the driving need — to extract wealth from the productive activities of society *in the form of capital*"[3] What distinguishes capitalism from earlier modes of production, in which wealth was sought for purposes of luxury consumption, is that wealth as capital is generated primarily to be reinvested for the accumulation of more wealth. This makes the underlying inherent tendency within capitalism an expansionary one. Capital never rests; it "inhabits material things only transiently."[4] Therefore, this tendency, which manifests itself in the world of capitalist praxis, leads to a never-ending search for new territories and markets to conquer and exploit. Foreshadowing the contemporary phase of capitalism, Luxemburg concluded long ago that capitalism "reaches into every corner of the earth so as to find productive employment for the surplus it has realised."[5]

This expansionary logic of capital infiltrates the vast

ranges of human labor and activity including intellectual and artistic creativity. Thus, when it comes to the domains of information and culture, the logic of capital drives an unending appropriation of whatever tangible forms of intellectual and artistic creativity people may come up with, as long as this creativity can be embodied in a tangible form, claimed as intellectual property, and brought to the marketplace. In David Harvey's summation: "Precisely because capitalism is expansionary and imperialistic, cultural life in more and more areas gets brought within the grasp of the cash nexus and the logic of capital circulation."[6]

The members of the Frankfurt School made the industrialisation of culture an important theme in their work.[7] These theorists and other Marxists have also focused on the ideological nature of capitalist media systems.[8] The exploration of both of these themes begins with research that seeks to empirically identify and outline patterns of capitalist ownership and control of communications media. Political economists insist that this analysis is a necessary starting point for understanding the output of the communications media.[9] They are particularly interested in the effects of capitalist structures of ownership and control of information and culture upon the ideological nature of media output and upon the accessibility to and diversity in the media marketplace.

Ownership and Control of the Culture Industries

Sut Jhally, borrowing from Hans Enzensberger, calls political-economic communications research that examines patterns of ownership and control in relation to ruling-class ideology the "consciousness industry " approach.[10] The theoretical inspiration for such an analysis comes from the famous passage in Marx and Engels's *German Ideology*, which states that "the ideas of the ruling class are in every epoch the ruling ideas" since this class "has the means of material production at its disposal" as well as the "means of mental production."[11] Marx and Engels recognised that every ruling class possesses "consciousness." Accordingly, the individuals who compose the dominant class "rule also as thinkers, as producers of ideas" and "regulate the production and distribution of the ideas of their age."[12]

Marx and Engels took it for granted that within capitalism the ruling capitalist class owns and controls the means of communication and is therefore able to manage the production and distribution of information and culture. They recognised that with this control the dominant class is privileged in the struggles over the making of meaning in the cultural and ideological realms; they stressed in particular how this class is able to represent its specific interests as the general interests of society as a whole. Contemporary analysts extend this idea by highlighting the important role of the media in the economic and ideological production and reproduction of capitalist social relations.

The focus of this book is not so much on the ideological function of the consciousness industry, but rather on the appropriation and commodification of information and culture. This approach is taken at the suggestion of Nicolas Garnham, who has argued that political economists ought to "shift attention away from the conception of the mass media as ideological apparatuses of the State" and toward seeing them "first as economic entities with both a direct role as creators of surplus value through commodity production and exchange and an indirect role, through advertising, in the creation of surplus value within other sectors of commodity production."[13] Whereas Marx and Engels took the ruling class/ruling ideology relationship for granted, this is no longer possible after nearly a century of empirical academic work seeking to disprove that the capitalist class exists, that it controls the economy, and that it has class consciousness. Consequently, political economists of communications are compelled to demonstrate the theoretical utility of class analysis.

A class analysis of communications reveals that there is a capitalist class that has come to largely own and control the means of communication as well as the rights to the forms of artistic and literary activity embodied in books, screenplays, songs, films, recordings, symbols, images, paintings, photographs, and so on that flow through them—what Bernard Edelman has called *intellectual primary material.*[14] Precisely because the capitalist class owns the means of communication, it is able to extract the artistic and intellectual labor of actual creators of media messages. For to get "published," in the broad sense, actual creators must transfer their rights to ownership in their work to those who have the means of disseminating it. With ownership of the means of communication and the exclusive control over the media product conferred by copyright, capitalists decide when and where to distribute artistic or literary works to achieve the highest possible return on their investments.[5] Thus, cultural artifacts and informational goods are transformed into investment instruments for the expansion of capital much like real estate, bonds, stock, licenses, franchises, precious metals, and so on. Furthermore, capital generated by tangible productive property or investment instruments frequently is expanded through investments in intellectual property and the means of disseminating it.

The control of intellectual primary material, in particular copyrights in television programs and motion pictures, facilitated Hollywood's capture of new cable and video technology. Rather than undermining the oligopolistic structure of filmed entertainment distribution, these new technologies have become means for perpetuating concentrated ownership and control of communications and information industries and for heightening barriers to access into these sectors. Consequently, because we are talking about the ownership and control of knowledge, we inevitably come to the consideration of the ideological effects suggested by Marx and Engels.

Concentrated media ownership and control results in, to use Edward Herman's terminology, "marginal" or "meaningless" diversity.[16] Moreover, the commodity process itself conditions the output of the communications system. For example, Guback argued that within capitalism motion pictures are manufactured and sold as commodities "with regard neither for the medium's instructive capacity, its ability to be used for social transformation, nor its potential for contributing to solutions of society's problems."[17] It is in this sense that political economists conceive the determining effects of economics upon the communications sphere.

Concentration in Media Ownership

The U.S. economy is controlled by a few dominant corporations—the top 1,200 or so largest firms in the country - that form the core of a dual economic structure. In 1980, the core firms accounted for half of all corporate sales, 65 per cent of all nonfinancial assets, and 70 per cent of total corporate profit. [18] This wealth and power distinguishes the core from the periphery, which is made up of millions of small and midsised firms that are diverse in operations and have little market power. The dual economy emerged during the late nineteenth and early twentieth centuries because competition effected an incessant tendency toward economic concentration.

At first, the expansionary logic of capital and the concentration and centralisation of capital may appear to be contradictory tendencies, but upon closer examination they turn out to be complementary processes. On the one hand, capitalists are continually penetrating new territories, markets, and realms of human activity in their constant search for profits. On the other hand, capitalists seek ways to eliminate competition in order to reduce the costs and risks that competition engenders. Therefore, even though competition constitutes a major and continuing force of change in a capitalist economy, the overriding tendency within capitalism is toward concentration.

Daniel Fusfeld argued that to eliminate competition reduce the risk that characterise laissez-faire capitalism, capitalists seek to increase their control over production, distribution, and sales within their market sector and to increase their economic and political power generally.[19] This may mean buying out competition through horizontal mergers, the pattern of economic integration that characterised the first merger wave in the U.S. economy at the turn of the century. Or it could mean buying up suppliers of production inputs, distributors, and retail outlets in a vertical pattern of integration to guarantee cheap and ready supplies as well as assured markets for finished goods or services—the dominant merger trend in the U.S. between the mid-1920s and early 1930s. It is precisely this period during which the "studio system" emerged in Hollywood—a system that involved the control of motion picture production, distribution, and exhibition by five major and three minor firms. This also is roughly the time when other media sectors became increasingly concentrated, including the radio broadcasting,[20] music recording and publishing,[21] and newspaper, magazine, and book publishing industries.[22]

Capitalists turned to conglomeration after World War II and pursued this strategy until about 1970 in order to diversify their holdings and stabilise income and revenue flows in spite of business cycles. With this trend, dominant firms branched out from their core activities to a wide range of related and unrelated sectors. Additional advantages of conglomeration include increased access to investment capital, enhanced market power within each line of business stemming from cross-subsidisation possibilities, and the augmented political power that comes with bigness. Gulf + Western Inc. represented the ultimate in this form of conglomeration, when in the mid-1960s it expanded from its original line of business, auto parts, to a bizarre assortment of more than a hundred companies including manufacturers of cigars, jet engine and missile parts, traffic lights, nuclear power plants, steel and zinc products, as well as lingerie, providers of insurance and financial services, owners of race horses and sports teams, producers of film and television program production (Paramount Pictures and Desilu Productions), and books (Simon & Schuster).

The current wave of mergers and acquisitions, which began around 1970, is a process of reorganisation around core and related lines of business along with an effort to establish alliances across national boundaries with market-dominant firms in other countries. Again, we can identify communications companies that typify this trend. For example, Gulf + Western sold business lines not related to communications through the 1980s and became Paramount Communications Inc., a fully diversified media and entertainment conglomerate. Its lines of business included film and television production and distribution (Paramount Pictures and Paramount Television), movie theaters in twelve countries, television broadcasting (83 per cent of TVX Broadcast Group), part ownership of the USA Network (with MCA Inc.), the MSG cable network, music publishing (Famous Music), book publishing (Simon & Schuster/ Prentice Hall), the Madison Square Garden sports arena, the New York Rangers hockey team, the New York Knicks basketball team, and Kings Entertainment theme park. In 1994, Viacom Inc. bought Paramount to create an even more extensive, vertically integrated media conglomerate; peripheral lines of business, such as the sports group, were shed to reduce debt. Other major media conglomerates involved in the filmed entertainment industry that are similarly diversified include Time Warner Inc., News Corp. Ltd., and the Walt Disney Company. In 1989, Sony Corp. bought Columbia Pictures Entertainment, and in 1991 Matsushita Electric Industrial Company bought MCA, parent of Universal Pictures, in both cases in effort to support their hardware lines and improve their chances of winning technology format wars.

Communications scholars, analysts, and executives agree that a handful—six to ten vertically integrated communications companies—will soon produce, own, and distribute the bulk of the culture and information circulating in the global marketplace.[23] In the United States, the concentration of the communications industry as a whole is already quite high. This concentration accelerated during the 1980s, according to Ben Bagdikian, a foremost scholar of "media monopoly." In the early 1980s, by various means of calculation for each sector, he found that about fifty firms controlled more than half of the output of the newspaper, magazine, book publishing, television, and motion picture industries.[24] His most recent calculation found that by the early 1990s, the bulk of media output in the United States was in the hands of only twenty major media corporations.[25] In early 1989, before its merger with Warner Communications, Inc., J. Richard Munro, then chairman and chief executive of Time, Inc., predicted that by the mid-1990s "the media and entertainment industry will be composed of a limited number of global giants" and that Time intended to be one of those companies. These firms needed to be vertically integrated, large enough to produce, market, and distribute worldwide, and able to amortise the costs of doing global business through as broad a distribution network as possible.[26]

Economic Structure of the Filmed Entertainment Industry

The filmed entertainment industry has long been oligopolistic, reflecting the dual economic structure of the U.S. economy as a whole. From the monopolistic Motion Picture Patents Company (1908-1915) to the early 1990s, a handful of core production, distribution, and exhibition firms have accounted for the bulk of the industry's revenues and market shares while countless others have struggled at the periphery. Guback estimated that there were probably over 10,000 corporations involved in the filmed entertainment business in the mid-1980s but that a small number dominated the industry by virtue of their volume of revenue and profit, their share of total industry assets, and the number of people they employed.[27]

The real power in the industry lies with the distribution sector, and typically just six or seven firms have accounted for 80 to 90 per cent of the revenues generated from the business of distributing films to theaters.[28] In 1991, the top six distribution firms (Sony Pictures, Warner Bros., Disney, Paramount, Twentieth Century Fox, and MCA/Universal) accounted lor 82.2 per cent of the distributor's share of the total domestic box-office gross. Orion Pictures Corp. took another 8.5 per cent, leaving just 9.3 per cent of the box-office gross to other peripheral distributors.[29] In 1992, the top three distributors, Time Warner, Disney, and Sony, accounted for about 60 per cent of the theatrical box-office gross. Adding the next three, Fox (14 per cent), MCA (12 per cent), and Paramount (10 per cent), gives the top six distributors 96 per cent of the 1992 box-office gross.[30] And though the theatrical market represents a decreasing share (25-30 per cent) of the total filmed entertainment market, it nevertheless remains the showcase for establishing the commercial value of any particular movie in the ancillary markets (videocassette, pay-cable, and broadcast).[31]

The exhibition sector is also partitioned into a core-periphery structure. Guback estimated that the five largest domestic circuits—United Artists Communication, AMC Entertainment, General Cinema, Cineplex Odeon Corp., and Carmike Cinemas—owned roughly 28 per cent of all indoor screens during the mid-1980s.[32] He showed further that the revenues taken in by these top five firms constituted a greater share than the number of screens they owned, since low-grossing theaters in small towns typically are not part of the major chains. Standard & Poor's figured that about 45 per cent of U.S. movie screens were operated by the ten largest theater companies in 1992.[33] The reintegration of the filmed entertainment industry along vertical lines is a notable trend with regard to the exhibition sector. MCA/Universal (Cineplex Odeon), Paramount (Mann Theaters), and Sony (Loews Theaters) have become major players in the U.S. theatrical exhibition market, which gave the major distributors about 9 per cent of the nation's 2,200 screens in 1993.[34] Time Warner has formed partnerships in Japan, Spain, Portugal, Italy, Australia, Germany, Denmark, and Russia to open multiscreen complexes in those countries. MCA and Paramount also have interests in theater chains in Europe and Canada.

A basic premise of this book is that holding a dominant market share in one sector of the filmed entertainment business permits entry and success in another sector. The control of filmed entertainment copyrights—the rights to movies and TV programs—provides a significant advantage to the core companies in the contest over the formats and uses of new technologies. As VCRs and cable penetrated US. households in the mid-1980s, the value of MGM/UA's 4,459 films stood at $733 million, MCA/Universal's 2,000 films at $367 million, Columbia's 1,800 films at $330 million, Warner Bros.'s 1,800 films at $330 million, Twentieth Century Fox's 1,000 films at $183 million, Paramount's 720 films at $132 million, Orion's 600 films at $110 million, and Disney's 169 films at $500 million.[35] These core firms use their libraries as collateral to secure lines of credit from banks, or they split up the rights to these libraries to raise revenues for new productions and expansion of operations. They have the software to drive the mass deployment of film and video hardware. It is not surprising then that it is largely these same firms that dominate the cable and home-video marketplace.

In the pay-cable market, Time Warner (Home Box Office and Cinemax, with 17.4 million and 6.2 million subscribers in 1992, respectively) was the clear leader among providers of movie networks. Its total subscriber base across these two pay-TV channels was twice that of its nearest competitor, Viacom (Showtime and The Movie Channel, with 7.6 million and 2.7 million subscribers in 1992, respectively). The pay-TV triopoly was rounded out by the Disney Channel, with 7.1 million subscribers in 1992.[36]

The videocassette market, accounting for about 35 to 45 per cent of the worldwide revenues earned by the filmed entertainment industry in the early 1990s,[37] has been captured by the same Hollywood-based majors that dominated the theatrical market. In 1992, Disney's Buena Vista videocassette distribution division accounted for 21.3

per cent of the revenues earned from videocassette sales in North America (the United States and Canada).[38] Disney was followed by Warner Home Video (18.1 per cent), FoxVideo (14.1 per cent), Columbia Tri-Star Home Video (9.7 per cent), Paramount (7.3 per cent), and MCA/Universal Home Video (6.6 per cent), giving the six active major filmed entertainment companies 77 per cent of the total revenues earned from videocassette sales in the North American market.[39]

Another important sector of the filmed entertainment industry is television program production. Once seen as a threat to the major producers and distributors of feature films, the television broadcast market is now an integral part of the filmed entertainment industry, providing the movies, television series, and other programming to television networks and stations. The filmed entertainment industry earns between 10 and 20 per cent of its worldwide revenues just from the sale of feature-length motion pictures to broadcast television.[40] The number of hours of prime-time series programming provided by the major producers to the television networks accounted for approximately 75 per cent of the total hours carried by the networks in the early 1990s, up from 39 per cent in 1970.[41] This increase is due to the "Financial Interest and Syndication Rules" passed in 1970 by the Federal Communications Commission (FCC), which limited the number of hours of prime-time entertainment programming that the networks could produce "in-house."[42] It reflects the transfer of sectoral control from one oligopoly— the networks—to another—the major filmed entertainment companies. Syndication of this programming is also controlled by the seven major studios, which account for about two-thirds of the $4.3 billion earned in the U.S. syndication market and about 80 per cent of the international syndication market.[43]

Intellectual Property as Strategic Corporate Asset

The core filmed entertainment companies are actually media conglomerates. Murdock noted that this gives them significant stakes in a range of major media markets and ultimately "an unprecedented degree of potential control over the range and direction of cultural production."[44] Control over intellectual property rights permits them to extend this control. With increasing globalisation, privatisation, and commercialisation of the communications media, the value of these rights promises to soar. A president of a stock management firm suggests that the most lucrative returns on investments in communications industries will come not from the firms that lay the systems but from those that provide the software, such as Disney, with its "extensive library of nearly timeless entertainment, and characters that can be restructured and reconfigured using new media," or Time Warner, which derives 60 per cent of its income from copyrighted media.[45] For this reason too, a *Wall Street Journal* investment columnist put the "buy" recommendation on Paramount in the early 1990s as "one of the best ways to play the growing demand for 'software' in the media and communications businesses," seeing the company as "fat with trophy assets waiting to be better managed."[46]

Indeed, the filmed entertainment in the vaults of the core firms, especially classic films, are now being mined for video and cable, for they are the closest the industry can get to a "sure thing" in terms of investment returns. Marketing costs are low and the costs of restoration are a mere fraction of producing new films and programs. For example, 1989's fiftieth-anniversary edition of *Gone with the Wind* was restored and marketed at a total cost of about $350,000 and earned $2.5 million at the box office plus another $4.5 million from the sale of 220,000 copies on videocassette.[47]

Eileen Meehan's study of Batman demonstrates how a single copyrighted character can be used synergistically by a communications conglomerate to exploit several media outlets and audiences.[48] Warner Communications acquired the copyright to the character when it bought DC Comics. In addition to new editions of Batman comic books, Time Warner produced a series of motion pictures as well as music soundtracks, music videos, and novelisations of the films and licensed a wide variety of Batman products—from cereals to bedding—to enhance the hype of the films and squeeze more revenue out of the character.

Software-hardware synergies motivated the Sony Corporation to purchase Columbia Pictures from the Coca-Cola Company for about $5 billion in 1989; the same reason led to its acquisition of CBS Records in January 1988 for $2 billion. Sony's purpose in buying CBS Records and Columbia Pictures, according to Anthony Smith, was twofold: vertical integration and diversification.[49] Like the Matsushita-MCA deal that it prompted, Sony's vertical integration involves linking up its hardware lines of consumer electronic goods to the entertainment divisions' software products—records, movies, and television programs. Sony's move into software follows the hard lesson it learned from the failure of the Betamax VCR format, namely, that to win consumer electronic-format wars it must control software.[50] Sony is now in the position to capitalise on its control of software to promote its new hardware lines, which include eight-millimeter video cameras and VCRs; the Mini Disc, a compact audio disc player/recorder; compact video disc players; and high-definition television cameras and sets (HDTV). The next move involves the melding of the hardware and software divisions and a move into computer-related software businesses. For this move, control of copyrights and the use of copyrighted material will be essential.

Sony's takeover of Columbia Pictures and CBS Records underscores how intellectual property serves as the raw material that is fed into the communications system. Through these mergers, Sony gained the rights to the television industry's largest library of some 2,600 television shows, including game shows (with over 10,000 episodes of "Wheel of Fortune," "Jeopardy," "The Dating Game," and "The Gong Show") and television series (over 26,000 episodes), a library of roughly 3,000 feature films, the copyrights to over 35,000 songs, and one of the largest catalogs of musical recordings.[51] Although the sale of communications hardware is prone to market saturation, cultural software can be repackaged and sold continuously; given the peculiar nature of intellectual property, it is never used up. The ownership of intellectual property thus permits the extension of oligopolistic control by the core firms while simultaneously perpetuating the existence of the capitalist class, for it is the members of this class who own and control the means of communication and the messages that flow through them.

(Re)Discovering the Capitalist Class

Among the ideas that have been intensely promoted by what Marx and Engels called "the thinkers" of the ruling class are that U.S. society is basically classless and pluralist in structure; that ownership of the means of production is widely diffused; and that through a managerial revolution corporate business has come under the control of a stratum of managers rather than the capitalist class. Marx was among the first to identify the changing structure of the ownership and control of capital that began with the rise of corporations and stock markets. He described this process in terms of a transformation of private, individual capital into collective, social capital.[52] The increasing capital costs required for the startup and operation of large-scale industrial firms necessitated this pooling of individual private capital. However, instead of the wider diffusion of capital ownership, he correctly predicted the concentration of capital into the hands of a few very large, dominant corporations and their owners.

German Social Democrat Eduard Bernstein, writing in 1899, downplayed the significance of economic concentration and focused instead on the public stock corporation, which he came to see as a means for increasing democratic control over economic life in his country. Although he provided no empirical data on stock ownership, he claimed there were "armies of shareholders" exerting "a most influential power over the economic life of society."[53] Indeed, the shareholder had supplanted the "captains of industry" that commanded the German economy before the concentration of business. With shareholder diversity, consumer cooperatives, democratic conditions in the political domain, and a colonial empire, Bernstein believed that a peaceful and gradual transformation of the German nation from capitalism to socialism was possible.

Writing ten years later, Hilferding showed that continued development of public stock corporations in the advanced capitalist economies had, indeed, led to a separation of ownership and control of capital for most shareholders. Although it appeared that property ownership was becoming more diffused, control of the corporation had come to rest in the hands of a very few shareholders holding as little as one-quarter to one-third of a company's stock. Consequently, the few large shareholders had gained control over the capital of the many small shareholders. They also had effective command of the corporation through control of the board of directors and appointment of chief executive officers (CEOs). Furthermore, these large shareholders were largely industrialists and investment bankers fused into a hegemonic bloc that Hilferding called "finance capital." Finance capitalists, seeking to protect their broad range of capital investments, encouraged corporate concentration through mergers and acquisitions in order to reduce business risks, increase guaranteed market shares, and stabilise investment returns.

Adolf Berle and Gardiner Means published a study in 1932 showing that the U.S. economy was dominated by some 200 major firms and that economic power was increasingly concentrated in the hands of the few executives that ran them.[54] Management had come to reign in the corporate world because ownership of corporate stock had become so widely diffused that no single individual or block of shareholders could exercise control over the modern corporation. Consequently, chief executives and upper-level managers, constituting a "managerial class," commanded the largest U.S. corporations on behalf of the vast army of shareholders, none of whom could exercise owner influence. Berle and Means expressed concern about this situation, fearing that managers would pursue their own interests in divergence from those of actual stock owners. Thus, they argued that this leadership stratum of the modern corporation had to be transformed into a "purely neutral technocracy" that served neither themselves nor their stock owners alone, but rather all of society.[55] By the late 1950s, Berle concluded that these fears had been unfounded, as it turned out that the power of core corporate managers was subject to a number of systemic limitations, including political pluralism and oligopolistic competition, the need for profits, "public consensus" and the "corporate conscience," and political intervention.[56]

In *The End of Ideology*, Daniel Bell repeated many of the same arguments in rejecting the relevance of class analysis for the study of the U.S. political economy, particularly due to the shift from "family capitalism," a system in which ownership and control of a firm was synonymous, to "modern American capitalism," in which "new managers" served as the controllers of capital.[57] The larger claim invoked by these perspectives was that capitalism had become more democratic and business more socially responsible now that professional managers were in charge of business, rather than the capitalist captains of industry.

There is a notable parallel between the managerial control hypothesis and the "social responsibility theory of the press" developed at approximately the same time. Both took the concentration of economic power as a given. Thus, social responsibility theorists hoped that just as the captains of industry were giving way to managers of industry, media moguls and press barons would ultimately give way to professionally trained managers and mass communicators who would conduct the press in a more socially responsible manner. The social responsibility theory asserted that for the media to achieve the normative goals set for them in a democratic society, publishers would have to adopt "codes of ethical behavior" and make the "concern for the public good" a priority.[58] As Roya Akavan-Majid and Gary Wolf pointed out, social responsibility theorists took the concentrated, privately owned media structure as a given, consequently making social responsibility on the part of mass communicators a virtue out of necessity.[59] It was all but an admission of the failure of libertarian media theory, which assumed that competitive capitalism would sustain a "free" marketplace of ideas. Herbert Altschull argued even more strongly that "press responsibility' represents a layer of intellectual cosmetics used to coat over the raw power needs of those in a position to control their environment."[60]

Consequently, by the midpoint of the twentieth century, the capitalist, corporate, oligopolistic basis of the U.S. mass media system was already off-limits as a legitimate subject for political discussion. Robert McChesney argued that once Congress passed the Communications Act of 1934, it essentially terminated the debate over a public versus private radio broadcasting structure.[61] Also off-limits is any discussion of the implications of the private appropriation of intellectual and artistic creativity and its increasing concentration in the hands of the oligopolistic firms controlling not only the communications industry but, as David Noble showed, research and development as well.[62]

Radical political economy has sought to reopen the discussion of media ownership and control and make it a legitimate topic of political debate. Murdock launched one of the first salvos into the ownership and control debate with an exploration of the ideological effects of capitalist ownership and control of the mass media.[63] In this chapter I will shift the focus to the ownership of rights to informational and cultural artifacts in order to find out who profits most from the extension and protection of intellectual property rights. In so doing I question the validity of the two basic philosophical justifications for granting private intellectual property rights: first, that these rights encourage the production and dissemination of artistic and intellectual creativity through pecuniary rewards to actual creators; and second, that they stimulate the dissemination of this work to the benefit of society as a whole. The counterclaim developed here is that the intellectual property system results in the unequal distribution of the rewards for human intellectual and artistic creativity, especially to the detriment of actual creators, and that it primarily benefits the capitalist class rather than society as a whole.

TABLE 3.1

Concentration of Wealth in the United States in 1983

Per cent Rank U.S. Households	*Per cent Net Wealth Held*	*Per cent Real Estate Held*	*Per cent Corp. Stock Held*	*Per cent Bonds Held*
Top .5 per cent (Super Rich)	35	15	46.5	43
Next .5 per cent (Very Rich)	7	4	13.5	8
Next 9 per cent (Rich)	30	30	29	39
Total Top 10 per cent	*72*	*49*	*89*	*90*
Bottom 90 per cent (Everyone Else)	28	51	11	10

Source: U.S. Congress, Joint Economic Committee, *The Concentration of Wealth in the United States: Trends in the Distribution of Wealth Among American Families*, July 1986.

Control of Wealth and Income

Putting the discussion of the ownership and control of the means of communication and its messages back on the political agenda requires a response to the myth of classlessness and the managerial control hypothesis. To address the myth of classlessness it is possible to make an empirically grounded case that there is a U.S. capitalist class that owns and controls the bulk of the nation's accumulated wealth. This wealth takes the form of such tangible property as land, buildings, the means of production and communication, raw materials, goods in process and for sale, works of art, precious metals and jewelry, and agricultural products and animals, as well as intangible property such as money, financial instruments, franchises, patent rights, copyrights, trademarks, and goodwill.

Some of the best recent evidence came from a study commissioned by the Democratic Staff of the Joint Economic Committee of Congress that looked at who holds wealth in the United States. It provided powerful evidence that U.S. household wealth is concentrated in the hands of a relatively few families.[64] The Staff report, based on 1983 survey data, found that U.S. households held a total aggregate net worth of about $10.6 trillion, primarily in the form of real estate, corporate stock, and business assets. It found that the wealthiest 10 per cent of U.S. households owned 72 per cent of total net wealth and the richest .5 per cent of U.S. households (400,000 households) held 35 per cent. When broken down by categories of wealth, the wealthiest 10 per cent of U.S. households owned nearly half the value of real estate, 89 per cent of corporate stocks, and 90 per cent of all bonds. The richest .5 per cent of U.S. households owned 15 per cent of all real estate and 46.5 per cent of all corporate stock and assets (see Table 3.1). Once the researchers excluded equity in personal residences, which represents the primary form of wealth held by most people, the "super rich" (the top .5 per cent of U.S. households) were found to hold 45 per cent of all net wealth while the top 10 per cent of U.S. households held a total of 83 per cent (see Table 3.2). Additional evidence from a U.S. Federal Reserve study indicated that the share of wealth held by the richest 1 per cent of U.S. households increased under Reagan-Bush monetarist economic policies, from 31 per cent in 1983 to 37 per cent in 1989.[65] The super rich increased their share of the wealth between 1983 and 1989, from 24 per cent to 29 per cent. Rather than a trickling down of wealth, this figure represents a gushing upward. The survey sample indicated that the top 1 per cent of U.S. households held 49 per cent of all publicly held stock, 62 per cent of business assets, and 45 per cent of nonresidential real estate. For Maurice Zeitlin, these data indicated that the capitalist class has not vanished from the U.S. social stratification scene. Indeed, he found remarkable stability in the makeup of the capitalist class, pointing out that the richest 1 per cent of *individuals* in the U.S. owned 24 per cent of all wealth in 1860 and 24.9 per cent about a century later in 1969.[66]

TABLE 3.2

Concentration of Wealth in the United Stales (Minus Home Equity)

Per cent Rank U.S. Households	*Net Wealth*
Super Rich	45
Very Rich	8
Rich	30
Everyone Else	17

Sources: U.S. Congress, Joint Economic Committee, *The Concentration of Wealth in the United States: Trends in the Distribution of Wealth Among American Families*, July 1986.

Unequal distribution of wealth is inextricably linked with unequal distribution of income. The families with the highest incomes derive most of their annual earnings from dividends, capital gains, rents, royalties, and interest (for example, 1980 U.S. tax returns showed that in 1979, 77 per cent of the income of families earning $1 million or more was property income).[67] The Congressional Budget Office also reported that annual income share of the top 1 per cent of U.S. families was 12 per cent in 1989, up from 7 per cent in 1977. Again, "Reaganomics" largely benefited the wealthiest 1 per cent of U.S. households; the 600,000 families earning over $310,000 per year took 60 per cent of the growth in average after-tax family income between 1977 and 1989, and 75 per cent of the increase in pretax income during this same span.[68] At the same time, the tax burden became less progressive after 1977 as the effective tax rates rose for families in the lowest income decile and fell for families in the highest income decile.[69]

Income inequalities also extend along race and gender lines, with large income gaps between whites on one hand and blacks and Hispanics on the other and between men and women. The Federal Reserve reported that between 1983 and 1989 single parents, nonwhites, and Hispanics suffered sharp declines in net worth.[70] D. Stanley Eitzen and Maxine Zinn argued that structural transformations within U.S. capitalism have served to exacerbate certain patterns of class, gender, and racial inequalities.[71] Samuel Bowles and Richard Edwards concluded that these gaps between wealth and income illustrate the unfairness of U.S. capitalism when measured by the normative criterion of who suffers the burdens and who reaps the benefits of this economic system.[72]

Based on evidence indicating that a tiny minority controls most of society's productive wealth, radicals and Marxists agree that a ruling class does indeed exist in the United States, that it is primarily based in the upper social class, and that it is primarily a capitalist or business class. The precise boundaries of this class, and what terminology to use in describing it, are the subjects of intense debate between and among Marxists and radicals. Radical political economists Bowles and Edwards defined the capitalist ruling class as the top 2 per cent of the richest families in the United States; "those who own capital goods used in production and exercise control over the labor of others; they receive their income in the form of profits or other payments (like interest and rent) for the use of their capital goods."[73]

Howard Sherman and E. K. Hunt, also radical political economists, designated the richest 2 per cent of the population, at most, as the capitalist class and identified the top 1 per cent as the elite, powerful capitalists.[74] They included the corporate executives of the largest firms in the economy within this category. Similarly, Sweezy spoke in terms of a national ruling class at the core of which are big capitalists.[75] On the numerous fringes of the ruling class are smaller property owners, high-level government officials and business executives (insofar as they are not big capitalists themselves), professionals, and the like. For Zeitlin, the top 1 per cent constituted the real owners and controllers of U.S. corporations.[76] He noted that their existence and their activities remain largely hidden from view, helping to perpetuate the myth of classlessness and to legitimate the managerial revolution hypothesis.

Social Cohesion and Ideological Unity

For radical sociologist G. William Domhoff, the top .5 per cent of U.S. families, with nearly half of all wealth in the United States, constitutes a social upper class, which is also the ruling class.[77] Besides its commonality in terms of enormous wealth and annual income, this upper class is "socially cohesive and clearly demarcated" and shares a "distinctive style of life."[78] It is an interacting and intermarrying upper social stratum (or social elite) that maintains its social cohesion through constant meetings in countless face-to-face small groups. The sites for cultivating this social cohesion include private schools, social clubs, corporate board meetings, exclusive resorts, the pages of elite media, and annual retreats. These contacts make conscious policy coordination by the upper class possible.

Drawing on the findings of social psychology, Domhoff argued that members of the upper class are "eager to reach an agreement on issues of common concern to them."[79] The opposite is argued by culturalists and poststructuralists who emphasise the fragmentation and incohesiveness of class identities in general and the divisiveness within the ruling class in particular. For instance, Stuart Hall criticised the political economy approach for its "continuing crudity and reductionism" and demanded that its adherents give up their view of "the conspiratorial and class-originated source of ideology" and instead incorporate a "theory of articulations" that considers the "struggle for meaning."[80] Furthermore, he suggested that it is not possible to "ascribe positions of power . . . permanently to anybody" and that establishing hegemony "requires people to do specific concrete work."[81] Contemporary political economists avoid this reductionism by specifically revealing the mechanisms by which the dominant classes are able to forge their unity and define and direct political debates so that their specific interests become defined as the general interests of society as a whole.

This is not to say that the ruling ideology or "worldview" of the dominant class or classes is "always already in place," but rather that they have an extraordinary ability to "structure their own unity" and produce "their own meanings." The members of the ruling class are better able to overcome any divisiveness than those of other classes due to their substantial resources, their numerous sites of contact, and their common interest in maintaining existing social relations. Accordingly, Domhoff *did* differentiate the upper social class from the capitalist economic class. Even though business and finance are by far the primary preoccupations of the social upper class, thus meaning it is "capitalist based," not all members of this upper class are capitalists; they are also corporate lawyers, investment bankers, policy experts, university professors, and politicians,[82] who together with the business leaders of the upper class constitute a "power elite." In the course of protecting the vast wealth and social power of the upper class to which they belong, the members of the power elite ultimately serve as the leadership group of the capitalist class, which Domhoff agreed is a class segmented along industry-sector and regional lines. The power elite therefore helps unify the interests of the capitalist class. A central purpose of this book is to precisely describe and analyze how this power elite is involved in the extension of the law of intellectual property into new technological and geographical domains.

Domhoff argued further that by virtue of controlling the majority of public stock, the business leaders of the upper class are overrepresented in the upper ranks of corporate management and on the boards of directors of the nation's largest firms. Top executives, shareholders, and shareholder representatives (such as investment advisers, lawyers, or bank officials) occupy the majority of board seats that interlock with one another. The business leaders of the upper class therefore also make up the majority of the inner group of the corporate community.[83] These interlocks extend into the state system. Because upper-level executives are often involved in the making of intellectual property policy and law, they become the surrogates for capital in defending and expanding the property rights of the owners of intellectual primary material.

Although we should not overemphasise the divisiveness within the capitalist class, segmentation along industrial and sectoral lines does lead to intraclass conflict.[84] For example, Nicos Poulantzas described the capitalist class as segmented into landed, commercial, industrial, and financial segments.[85] But what interested Poulantzas was how the capitalist class was able to overcome its fragmentation. He argued that at certain times under specific conditions of capitalist accumulation any one or combination of these factions is able to establish a "hegemonic bloc" by working through the stale to unify its interests and ideologically legitimate its hegemony. In the structuralist theory of Poulantzas, the degree and form of capitalist development ultimately determine which of the segments of the capitalist class becomes the dominant class faction. Of course, actual human subjects must actively forge this hegemonic bloc.

Since the early 1970s, an ascending fraction of the capitalist class, centered in the knowledge, culture, and high-technology sectors, has begun to organise the transition to a new phase of capitalism—post-Fordism or "technocapitalism"[86]— in which the ownership of intellectual property rights to information, knowledge, and cultural goods is central. Working in and through the power elite, capitalists have begun to forge and solidify a new hegemonic bloc comprising those segments of the capitalist class involved in the production, distribution, and sale of intellectual property. But rather than undermining or fragmenting capital as a whole, these efforts, because intellectual property rights are broadly held within the core of the capitalist class, serve to unify the interests of this class as a whole. This shift is rooted in the underlying logic of capital that prompts the necessity of structural transformation as a response to declining profit rates and the deterioration of U.S. global economic hegemony.

Ownership and Control of Media and Copyrights

Political economists of communications demonstrate that the major media companies—and thus their essential assets, copyrights—are owned and controlled by the capitalist class. For example, Herman and Noam Chomsky examined control of the twenty-four largest firms that constitute the media industry's top tier in terms of prestige, resources, and outreach and found that in 1986 two-thirds of these companies were either closely held or still controlled by members of the founding families who continue to own large blocks of stock.[87] For Herman and Chomsky, this evidence provided powerful refutation of the managerial control hypothesis. They concluded that by virtue of their great wealth and strategic position atop one of the major institutions in society, these families and individuals have a "special stake in the status quo"[88] and exercise their power by determining the general policy aims of their companies and selecting its top management.

Taking a consciousness-industry approach, Herman and Chomsky primarily explored the ownership of media companies involved in the production and distribution of news in order to identify how this "filter" works to shape news media coverage of U.S. foreign policy. More relevant to the purposes of this project, Guback examined ownership and control of the largest publicly held U.S. filmed entertainment companies in 1984 and 1985.[89] His study represents the most systematic test of the validity of the managerial revolution hypothesis for this media sector. Although he found stock ownership widely diffused, with the average holding of shares in any one company at less than 1 per cent, a closer look revealed that controlling interests of feature film production, distribution, exhibition, and pay television companies rested in the hands of either executive officers, board members, financial institutions, or other firms. Banks and other financial institutions that provided term loans and revolving lines of credit to the filmed entertainment industry were found to temper the control exercised by dominant stockholders by imposing various stipulations on how the debt capital could be used. However, Guback argued that rather than being in conflict equity owners and capital lenders tend to form a "community of interest in which the expertise of the bankers assists, if not guides, corporate management to achieve sound financial results."[90] Guback concluded that a few individuals and small groups own and control the film industry. They "share a class interest that shapes their posture toward social resources: how they are used, by whom, for what purpose and in whose interest."[91]

Media Ownership Among the Super Rich

Both the means and messages of communications in the United States are largely owned and controlled by the super rich. A review of *Forbes* magazine's annual listing of the 400 richest individuals and families in the United States demonstrates that owners or former owners of media and information corporations constitute approximately 25 per cent of the people listed.[92] Thirty-eight of the sixty-four North Americans on *Fortune* magazine's 1992 list of the world's billionaires owed all or part of their wealth to media ownership.[93] Within the Forbes 400 we find that several of the richest capitalists hold (or have held) major stakes in the filmed entertainment business. The following survey puts the spotlight on some of these media owners to illuminate the role of copyrights in capital accumulation.

One of the richest individuals in the world is John Kluge (estimated worth in 1992, $5.5 billion according to *Forbes*, $8.1 billion according to *Fortune)*, who liquidated his Metromedia Co. assets (radio and television stations) in 1984 for $4.65 billion. Kluge used a small portion of the money to buy 70 per cent of Orion Pictures, at one time a thriving independent film production company *(Silence of the Lambs, Dances with Wolves, Robocop)* until it filed for bankruptcy in 1991. In late 1992, Kluge assumed the position of chairman of Orion as part of a federal bankruptcy reorganisation plan. In the plan, the cash flow from Orion's principal asset, its 750-film library, was to be used to pay off its creditors, $270 million owed to banks and $70 million owed to Sony Corp.'s Columbia Pictures. Orion immediately generated $45 million proceedings by selling Japanese broadcast rights to 200 films and making a deal with McDonald's to sell three Orion videos, including *Dances With Wolves*, through the fast-food outlet.[94] It is precisely because of its valuable library that Orion even had a chance of returning to its "glory days" as a "minimajor" producer-distributor. Without such assets, most independent filmed entertainment companies are never able to recover twin bankruptcy. At the same time, however the core companies that make up the filmed entertainment oligopoly are able to maintain their core status, or return to it after off years, because of the significant intellectual property assets they hold.

Another exemplary figure, Sumner M. Redstone, regularly in the top ten on the Forbes 400 list with $3.25 billion, took over his father's drive-in theater business in 1954 and built it into National Amusements Inc., with over 750 movie screens in the United States and Great Britain. He significantly expanded his wealth in the 1980s through investments in Twentieth Century Fox, Columbia Pictures, and MGM/UA Home Video. In 1987, he initiated a hostile takeover of Viacom and immediately took it public while holding on to a controlling share of 76 per cent of its common stock. Viacom was a media conglomerate that included Showtime, The Movie Channel, MTV, Nickelodeon, cable systems, and radio and television stations. Television program, feature film, and video rights figured prominently in Viacom's activities, from exclusives with music recording companies for new music video releases on MTV and VH-1 and feature film exclusives with filmed entertainment companies for its pay-movie networks, Showtime and The Movie Channel, to the rights to old television series it uses to program its Nickelodeon network.

Viacom was spun off from CBS in 1972 as a result of the U.S. federal government's intervention into the prime-time television program marketplace. The FCC prohibited the networks from syndicating these programs, in an effort to break up vertical integration in the television program production/distribution/exhibition marketplace. Viacom stepped in to take up this line of business and used the income to successfully expand into a bona fide media conglomerate. Redstone further enlarged his media empire by acquiring 50.1 per cent of Paramount's stock in 1994, a deal valued at $10 billion.

Another media entrepreneur, Walter H. Annenberg, worth an estimated $1.6 billion, cashed in on his media investments when he sold *TV Guide,* a publication of his Triangle Publications, to Rupert Murdoch in 1988 for $3.2 billion. The significant portion of Annenberg's wealth earned by *TV Guide* was not made *in* the filmed entertainment business but rather *on* it.

Rupert Murdoch used control of particular media sectors to spawn other lines of business and to expand the range of his media investments. Murdoch, a contemporary media mogul who jumped dramatically from forty-fifth on the 1991 Forbes 400 with an estimated personal worth of $1.1 billion to tenth in 1992 with an estimated $2.6 billion, gives us a successful example of the propagation of media business through mergers and acquisitions. Murdoch's estimated $2.6 billion fortune came from his 35 per cent stake in News Corp. Ltd., a multinational media and entertainment empire that includes newspapers in the United States, Europe, and the Far East, magazines (including *TV Guide,* the largest weekly publication in the United States), an international book-publishing house (HarperCollins), filmed entertainment production and distribution (Twentieth Century Fox), television stations and the fourth largest U.S. television network (Fox Broadcasting Company), and a 48 per cent interest in the European six-channel satellite television service, British Sky Broadcasting, Ltd.[95]

The U.S.-based Fox television network gained its foothold in 1986 through News Corp.'s ownership of six of the strongest independent television stations that directly reached nearly one-fourth of U.S. households.[96] Moreover, many of the network's prime-time series are produced by or in association with Fox's television production arm, and its news division has access to overseas news coverage produced by Sky News, the twenty-four-hour news channel offered as part of the British Sky satellite television service. To capitalise on the trend toward digitised multimedia formats, News Corp. announced in early 1992 the creation of a new division, News Electronic Data, that would make its publications, including the *London Times* and *TV Guide*, available for use with handheld personal computers.[97]

With over one-third of News Corp.'s stock, Murdoch remains in control of the media conglomerate and again provides a visible counterexample to the managerial revolution hypothesis, as well as to the claims of social responsibility theorists, who insist that media managers and media professionals are relatively autonomous from media owners. Accordingly, in this case of ownership and control, the claims of the consciousness-industry variant of political economy can be supported. Indeed, when Barry Diller, the chairman and chief executive of Fox, Inc., from 1984 to 1992, resigned his position (reportedly out of the desire to experience the autonomy that comes with media ownership),[98] Murdoch stepped in to directly supervise the movie and television subsidiaries of News Corp. To justify the move, Murdoch stressed his experience in the industry by claiming to have "been a party to every decision made" since News Corp. acquired Fox seven years earlier, a situation clearly at odds with the managerial revolution hypothesis.[99]

For many of these rich individuals or families, media firms and intellectual property investments are simply one more means of expanding their capital. Among those whose wealth originated in other sectors, but which has been significantly augmented through such investments, is Robert Bass, who used his oil money to diversify into stock, holding stakes at one time or another in Disney, Taft Broadcasting, Times Publishing, Bell & Howell, and cable television systems. Robert's brothers, Sid and Lee, hold about 18.5 per cent of Disney's stock (worth well over $2 billion), giving them effective control of this media and entertainment conglomerate.[100] Walt's nephew, Roy, is also on the Forbes 400 and is another large shareholder, with nearly 2 per cent of the company's stock. He has served as vice chairman of the board of directors at Disney since 1984 and heads the animation department. Other Disney heirs also have substantial holdings, including Sharon Disney Lund, daughter of Walt, who holds 1.6 per cent of the company's shares and sits on its board.

Disney figures prominently in the case studies that follow, since it has been one of the most assiduous defenders of its copyrighted works. It signed on as coplaintiff with Universal Pictures in the suit against Sony over the alleged infringing uses of the Betamax VCR. Since then, of all filmed entertainment companies, Disney has learned to make the most profitable use of the new technology through the sales and rental of prerecorded videocassettes. Accordingly, it has been a major player in the war on videocassette piracy. Disney regularly sues or threatens to sue unauthorised users of its copyrighted works and trademarked images for infringement, oftentimes using its property rights to censor freedom of expression. With Disney, property rights take precedence over communicative rights.

Holding similar sentiments is Samuel J. LeFrak, who used his wealth from real estate interests to move into oil and gas, entertainment, music publishing, and copyrights. The attitude that the super rich take toward culture as just one more site of investment, rather than as something valuable in its own right, is reflected in LeFrak's remark that "the music business is like real estate, except you don't have to paint it every two years."[101] Marvin Davis (estimated worth $1.4 billion in 1992) used some of his oil and real estate money to buy Twentieth Century Fox in 1981, together with Marc Rich, a commodities trader worth $800-$900 million. Davis later bought out Rich and sold the film production/distribution company to Murdoch in 1985. Investor Kirk Kerkorian, who made his billion dollars in airlines and hotel casinos, dabbled in the film industry with a hostile takeover of MGM in 1969, a buyout of United Artists in 1981, and a merger of the two companies to form MGM/UA in 1986. He then sold MGM/UA to Ted Turner's Turner Broadcasting System Inc. in 1986 for $1.5 billion and immediately bought back the bulk of the company's assets, leaving Turner with certain broadcast and videocassette rights to the MGM library of old films.

In 1990, Kerkorian sold his 76 per cent stake in MGM/UA to Giancarlo Parretti's Pathe Communications Corporation for $1.3 billion. The deal nicely demonstrates the divisibility of intellectual property as well as its use as a means of raising capital. In this transaction, the Turner Broadcasting System came to own the U.S. television broadcasting rights to 1,000 United Artists films, along with all MGM/UA movies released between 1986 and 1988, and some 1989 releases, plus the rights to some 300 films for its "TNT South" Latin American satellite network. United Communication S.A. of France acquired the French-language television rights to most of MGM/UA's film library, and Time Warner Inc. put up $125 million for home-video rights. By splitting up and selling off rights, plus borrowing some $560 million from Credit Lyonnais, Parretti managed to raise the money to complete the $1.3 billion deal.

The deal engendered conflicts over who actually owns what rights, demonstrating the unique problems that result from the intangibility of intellectual property. The Turner company claimed that Parretti sold its home-video rights to Time Warner, and MGM's library of James Bond films was excluded from the deal due to contested ownership by Switzerland-based Danjaq Inc., which owns the exclusive rights to produce feature films and television series based on the James Bond character. The fact that Time Warner owned 17 per cent of the Turner Broadcasting System while Turner was already broadcasting films for television licensed from MGM-Pathe when the deal was being negotiated in 1991 reveals further just how intertwined media ownership and control has become.[102]

With Parretti unable to make loan payments, control of MGM-Pathe passed into the hands of its largest creditor, the state-owned French bank Credit Lyonnais, following a foreclosure sale in May 1992. Despite its financial problems, MGM's significant assets based in its film library still permitted it to make a bid for Orion Pictures in 1992. MGM-Pathe unsuccessfully offered a restructuring plan to bring that company out of bankruptcy and make it a viable producer-distributor once more. MGM-Pathe also was part of a joint venture effort with an affiliate of Italy's Rizzoli Corriere della Sera Group; Le Studio Canel Plus, a unit of France's Canal Plus S.A.; and a unit of Pioneer Electronic Corp. of Japan to rescue Carolco Pictures Inc., producers of *Rambo, Terminator*, and *Terminator 2: Judgment Day*, from bankruptcy.[103] In early 1993, Credit Lyonnais hired Michael Ovitz, chair of Creative Artists Agency (CAA), Hollywood's most powerful talent agency, to manage its entertainment portfolio. Competing studios and talent agencies complained that vertical integration between CAA, the supplier of talent, and MGM, the producer of the film, gave the alliance an unfair competitive advantage.

Those who have used wealth generated primarily in nonmedia sectors to invest in media and entertainment firms are listed in Table 3.3. The evidence presented here suggests that far from being deeply divided as a result of being positioned atop different industry sectors, these capitalists have widely diversified interests that would tend to unite them around the general defense of private property rights, given that they serve as the essential basis of capitalism. These capitalists have both the purposes and the means for organising themselves against challenges to the rule of capital.

Several additional members of the super rich whose *core* assets are media- and communications-based are notable for the purposes of this study. Climbing rapidly up the list of the most wealthy is Ted Turner, worth an estimated $ 1.9 billion in 1992, already mentioned in the account of the MGM/UA deal with Kerkorian. Besides the broadcast rights to the 3,000-film MGM library used primarily to program his cable television network, Turner Network Television (TNT), Turner's media and entertainment empire included the Cable News Network (CNN), the Headline News network, and two sports franchises, the Atlanta Braves baseball team and Atlanta Hawks basketball team. In 1991, he bought Hanna-Barbera Productions Inc., a unit of Great American Communications Co., bringing him the rights to some 3,000 half-hours of its library of cartoons in order to program the new cable Cartoon Network. In 1992, the Turner Broadcasting System entered the emerging multimedia sector with a new division designed to create interactive news documentaries for CD-ROM systems drawing on CNN footage as well as interactive games based on characters from the Hanna-Barbera film library. Turner played a significant role in shaping the structure of the cable television market when, in 1976, he began national distribution of the broadcast signal of his UHF-TV station, WTBS, via satellite.

TABLE 3.3

The Super Rich: Initial Wealth Outside Media

*Est'd Worth 1991**	*Name*	*Initial Source of Wealth*	*Meida Investments*
4.8	Warren E. Buffett	Stock equities	Cap Cities/ABC, *Washington Post*
4.5	Jay A. and Robert A. Pritzker	Finance, manufacturing	Savoy Pictures Entertainment
3.1	Ronald O. Perelman	Investments	Marvel Comics, New World Entertainment
2.0	Sid and Lee Bass	Oil	18.5 per cent Disney Stock
1.5	Samuel J. Heyman	Chemicals, building materials	Broadcasting
1.5	Leonard N. Stern	Pet supplies, real estate	Publishing
1.4	Samuel J. LeFrak	Real estate	Music publishing
1.3	Marvin Davis	Oil, real estate	Twentieth Century Fox
1.0	Jack Kent Cook	Real estate, investments, sports	*LA. Daily News*, cable TV
1.0	Kirk Kerkorian	Hotels, casinos	MGM/United Artists
.93	Orville W. Rollins	Auto dealerships, bottled water, radio	Rollins Communications
1.7	Donald J. Hall and sisters	Hallmark Cards	Media groups
1.1	Carl H. Lindner Jr. and family	Insurance, banking	Taft Broadcasting
1.15	Ted Field and Marshall Field V	Department store, inheritance	Newspapers, cable TV, encyclopedias, Muzak, film production

*Est'd Worth 1991**	*Name*	*Initial Source of Wealth*	*Meida Investments*
.56	George L. Lindemann	Cosmetics, pharmaceuticals	Cable TV
.55	Erskin B. Ingram	Oil, barges	Book, video, software distr.
.55	Richard Mellon Scaife	Inheritance	Scaife Newspapers
.545	John J. Louis	Inheritance	Combined Communications
.45	Robert A. Lurie	Real estate, inheritance	Broadway and film production
.355	David T. Chase	Real estate	TV, radio stations
.35	Susan Thompson Buffett	Marriage	Cap Cities/ABC, *Washington Post*
.29	H. Wayne Huizenga	Waste disposal	Blockbuster Entertainment

*in $billions

Source: "Forbes Four Hundred," *Forbes*, October 21,1991, pp. 150-171; "The Billionaires 1991," *Fortune*, September 9, 1991, pp. 59-113.

A centimillionaire who comes up in connection with the cable copyright case study is August C. Meyer, a regular on the Forbes 400 list until he died in 1992, leaving an estate worth some $300 million. Meyer, as owner of Midwest Television, Inc., initiated the legal deliberations over the status of distant-signal importation of television broadcasts by cable system operators. In this action, he sought to stop San Diego cable operators from importing broadcast signals from Los Angeles, as this brought competition into the San Diego market for his television station there.[104]

Lew Wasserman, who was chairman of MCA/Universal until his retirement in 1995 and is still among the wealthiest people in the United States, figures prominently in the home-video recording case study (see Chapter 6). It was Wasserman, along with Disney executives, who sought to control the introduction and use of the VCR with their suit against Sony. Not realising the revenue potential of the new technology, the filmed entertainment companies sought to halt the sale of VCRs, fearing that the use of the device to tape television broadcasts would undermine the value of their copyrighted television programs. Eventually, the U.S. Supreme Court determined home taping of television broadcasts was a fair use of copyrighted works in what came to be known as the Betamax case.[105] Now the purchase and rental of videocassettes used on VCRs produce a significant portion of the Hollywood-based filmed entertainment industry's revenues.

Wasserman built his wealth through ownership and control of MCA, originally a talent agency. Guback found Universal Pictures to be under the control of Wasserman, who in the mid-1980s held 7.3 per cent of MCA shares outright and probably controlled another 12.6 per cent as trustee for several trusts that owned shares.[106] In 1990, he sold his controlling interest in MCA/Universal for $327 million in preferred shares of Matsushita stock while continuing as its board chair and CEO. Again showing the strong link between ownership and management, MCA president Sidney Sheinberg traded in his 1.3 million shares of MCA stock for $150 million in Matsushita shares. David Geffen, chair of MCA subsidiary Geffen Records, received $710 million in cash for his 10 million MCA shares. Thomas Pollack, chairman of Universal Pictures, sold his MCA stock for $30 million and stayed on as head of the film company. In total, Matsushita, the world's second largest electronics company in 1990,[107] took over MCA by obtaining about 97 per cent of its outstanding shares in a $6.1 billion deal. It acquired the record, book publishing, and filmed entertainment properties to provide the software for its growing line of consumer electronics.

Although Wasserman and his handpicked president of nineteen years, Sidney Sheinberg, remained as top officers of MCA/Universal, control passed into the hands of the parent corporation. This became evident when Matsushita refused to allow the subsidiary to enter the bidding for British-based Virgin Records in order to expand its global music recording operations.[108] Just a few months after taking over MCA, Matsushita named three of its officials to MCA's executive commttee, the highest managerial decision making body of the company. Additionally, it expanded MCA's board from its existing eleven members by naming twelve additional Matsushita representatives.[109] In October 1994, Wasserman and Sheinberg publicly admitted their lack of autonomy and sought tc regain control of MCA by asking to reacquire 51 per cent of the company's stock.[110] Matsushita's chairman, Masdaharu Matsushita, the adopted son of founder Konosuki Matsushita, refused the offer. The continuing clash of corporate culture between Japanese and U.S. management, coupled with the failure of the hardware-software merger to produce significant synergies, prompted Matsushita to sell 80 per cent of MCA's stock to the Seagram Corp. in 1995. As a result of the deal, ownership and control of MCA passed into the hands of the Bronfman family. Edgar Bronfman Sr. was worth an estimated $2.3 billion in 1991, according to *Forbes*. Edgar Jr., president of Seagram, immediately asserted managerial control over MCA.

The ranks of the super rich are replete with several individuals whose core interests are in media and entertainment (see Table 3.4). *Forbes* magazine has a separate category within its 400 list that identifies the wealthiest *families* that share the fortunes left by predecessors. Several significant media fortunes appear on this list, including some at the billion-dollar level, as shown in Table 3.5. Although actual ownership of the stock of these media assets may be dispersed among various family members, usually as a result of inheritance but also for the purpose of reducing tax burdens, control of the shares and shareholder voting rights may often be exercised by trusts operating on behalf of the family as a whole.[111] Domhoff identified continuing patterns of family ownership through family offices, holding companies, and voting on significant holdings of stock and concluded that a notable number of large corporations continue to be controlled by founding owners. [112] The introduction to the 1987 Forbes 400 notes that 40 per cent of those listed accrued their fortunes primarily or completely from inheritance.[113] As this analysis of the richest individuals and families in the United States indicates, the super rich hold significant stakes on media companies and copyrights,. In fact, the introduction to *Fortune* magazine's 1992 billionaire survey identified media ownership as " as one of the surest roads to big riches" worldwide.[114]

TABLE 3.4

The Super Rich: Initial Wealth from Media

*Est'd Worth 1991**	*Name*	*Company*	*Media Holdings*
7.0	Newhouse brothers	Advance Publications	Conde Naste, Random House, news paper chain, cable TV
5.5	John W. Kluge	Metromedia	Orion Picts., Lin Broadcasting
4.4	Hearst family	Hearst Corp.	Newspapers, consumer and trade magazines, TV and radio, books
4.2	Cox sisters	Cox Enterprises	Newspapers, cable, broadcasting

*Est'd Worth 1991**	*Name*	*Company*	*Media Holdings*
3.25	Sumner Redstone	National Amusements, Viacom	Theater chain, TV stations, cable systems, cable networks
1.5	McCaw family	McCaw Cellular	Cellular telephone
1.4	Ted Turner	Turner Broadcasting	Cable networks, film libraries
1.25	William B.Ziff	Ziff Comus.	PC Magazine, PC Week, PC /Computing
1.15	Lawrence and Preston Tisch	Loews Corp.	25% CBS, Inc., stock
1.1	Rupert Murdoch	News Corp.	Film/TV prdn., newspapers, magazines, broadcasting
1.1	Edward L. Gaylord	Oklahoma Publishing company	Newspapers, TV and radio, cable
.95	Donald W. Reynolds	Donrey Media Group	Daily and weekly newspapers TV, cable, billboards
.88	David Geffen	Geffen Records, brought by MCA	Performing rights
.655	Andrew J. Perenchio	Cofounder Embassy Pcts. (sold in 1985)	TV and film rights
.64	Helen K. Copley	Copley Press	Daily and weekly newspapers, cable TV
.6	Frank Batten Sr.	Landmark communications	Daily and weekly newspapers, TV and radio, Weather Channel
.515	Roy H. Park	Park Communications	Channel TV and radio stations, newspapers
.5	Patrick J. McGovern	International Data Group	Publishing and information services
.5	Amos B. Hosteller, Jr.	Continental Cablevision	Cable systems
.5	Robert S. Howard	Howard Publications	Newspapers
.48	Jane B. Cook	Dow Jones & Co.	Newspapers, wire services, radio and TV programming

cont...

Est'd Worth 1991*	Name	Company	Media Holdings
.47	Roy E. Disney	Walt Disney Company	Theme parks, copyrights, Disney Channel
.46	Richard A. Smith	General Cinema	Movie theaters
.45	Bob J. Magness	TCI, Inc., United Artists Entertainment	Cable TV, movie theaters
.45	Overta Culp Hobby and family	Cowles Boradcasting	TV and radio stations
.44	Charles F. Dolan	Cablevision Systems Corp., Sky Cable	Cable TV, DBS
.4	Harry H. and Mary Jane Hoiles Hardie	Freedom Newspapers	Newspapers, TV stations
.4	Mark Goodson		TV programming, newspapers
.4	Joe L. Allbritton		TV stations, newspaper
.36	Dean S. Lesher		Newspapers
.35	William S. Morris III	Morris Communications	Newspapers, billboards
.35	Lew Wasserman	MCA, Inc.	Films, music recording, book publishing
.32	Rober A. Naify	TCI, Inc., United Artists Entertainment	Cable TV, theaters
. 31	Robert Guccione	Penthouse Intl.	Magazines
.3	Malcom A. Borg	Macromedia Inc.	Newspapers, TV stations
.3	Stanley S. Hubbard		TV and radio stations, cable programming, DBS
.3	Gene Autry		Radio stations
.3	Robert E. Petersen	Petersen Publishing	Magazsines
.3	Michael R. Forman		Movie theaters
.295	Aaron Spelling		TV programming
.29	Russell Solomon	Tower Records	Music recording, retail

* in $ billions

Source: "Forbes Four Hunderd," *Forbes*, October 21, 1991, pp. 150-271; "The Billionaires 1991," *Fortune*, September 9, 1991, pp. 59-113.

TABLE 3.5

Family-Shared Media Fortunes

*Est'd Worth 1991**	*Family Name*	*Media Interests*
1.5	Bancroft	Dow Jones & Co. (Ottaway Newspapers, *Wall Street Journal, Barrens,* Dow Jones ticker)
.35	Bingham	Newspapers
.4	Bullitt	Radio and TV stations, cable TV
1.3	Chandler	Times Mirror, Inc. (newspapers, magazines, broadcasting, cable TV)
.525	Cowles (Gardner)	Cowles Media, New York Times Co. stock
.75	de Young	Chronicle Publishing (newspapers, TV broadcasting, cable)
1.0	Donnelly	Dun & Bradstreet, largest U.S. commercial printer
.36	Graham	Washington Post Co. (newspapers, *Newsweek,* TV broadcasting, cellular telephone)
.645	Jordan	Affiliated Publications, McCaw Cellular
.5	King	King World Productions (syndication rights to "Wheel of Fortune," "Jeopardy!" "Oprah")
.5	McClatchy	Newspapers
.47	McGraw	McGraw-Hill (magazines and book publishing)
.57	Pulitzer	Pulitzer Publishing (newspapers, TV and radio broadcasting, satellite network)
.5	Sammons	Cable TV
1.4	Scripps (E. W.)	Scripps Howard (United Media syndicate, newspapers, TV and radio broadcasting, cable)

cont...

*Est'd Worth 1991**	*Family Name*	*Media Interests*
.9	Scripps (J. E.)	Evening News Association (sold 1976), Booth Newspapers (sold to Gannett in 1985)
.5	Sulzberger	New York Times Co. (newspapers, magazines, broadcasting)
.455	Taylor	McCaw Cellular (sold), Affiliated Publications stock
.5	Wolfe	*Columbus Dispatch, Ohio Magazine,* TV and radio broadcasting

*in $billions

Source: "Forbes Four Hundred: Great Family Fortunes," *Forbes,* October 21, 1991, pp. 274-296.

Who Controls Capital? Countering the Managerial Revolution

Answering the question of who owns productive capital still leaves unanswered the question of who controls it. Despite the long history of research seeking to prove or disprove the managerial revolution hypothesis, the question of control should not preoccupy us so. Energies spent refuting it only demonstrate how academic agendas reflect hegemonic interests. Whether a corporation is run by family owners, by the largest shareholder(s), or by nonowning executives, the logic of capitals compels all capitalists to pursue the same basic goals, thai is, to defend property rights, to seek new markets, to reduce risks by eliminating competition, and to maximise profits. In light of this fact, Beth Mintz simply concluded that "the behavioral implications of the separation of ownership and control are overstated.[115]

However, since the academy itself is a site of struggle, it is necessary to challenge hegemonic theories and perspectives, for they ultimately have very real effects when they are tested and applied. Moreover, not only is theory based on normative assumptions, it is also laden with political intentions. Thus, proponents of the managerial revolution theory suggest that the broad holding of stock equities democratises capitalism, constituting a "people's capitalism" in Berle's terminology, and that the separation of ownership and control brings about a socially responsible business behavior, making alternatives to the system unnecessary. If the opposite can be shown to be true, it becomes necessary to change the system to achieve economic democracy and socially responsible production and consumption.

Corporate managers who control intellectual property would also have to exhibit social responsibility toward the use of and access to it (if the managerial revolution hypothesis may be extended in such a manner). This responsibility would manifest itself in a number of ways. For example, managers of intellectual property might exercise less stringent control of intellectual property rights, recognise more the historical and social nature of human creativity, feel freer to share this property with competitors, or give stronger support to the moral rights of actual creators. In the realm of copyrighted culture, socially responsible management of this property would include encouraging and facilitating the increasing intertextual uses of cultural creativity, such as sampling in music and video making, by permitting freer access to copyrighted work. Managers of copyrighted scientific and technical works might find ways to permit cheaper and freer access through reprographic technologies and compulsory licensing systems, especially in poorer regions and nations. In the realm of patented knowledge, social responsibility might mean wider and cheaper dissemination of patented seeds and medicines to the poorer nations and peoples of the world. However, questions about the validity of the managerial control hypothesis lead one to be skeptical about such behavioral implications.

Extensive evidence does indeed exist to demonstrate that (1) a significant proportion of the executives and directors of the largest firms in the U.S. economy come from the families of the upper class; (2) top executives tend to have a stake in the corporations they manage as a result of stock ownership and bonus plans; and (3) those executives not born into the upper class have been assimilated into it.[116] This subjective stake in the capitalist system reinforces their structural positioning as managers of capitalist firms that must produce profits to survive. To begin with stock ownership, we find that although the percentage of shares held by upper-level managers may not constitute controlling interests in their firms, these stakes tend to comprise significant portions of their personal financial portfolios.[117] In 1992, the typical large corporation reserved 6.5 per cent of common shares for executive incentives, up from about 4.5 per cent in the early 1980s, the result of greater use of stock option programs and "megagrants" to recruit and retain upper-level executives.[118] A 1991 Conference Board survey of executive compensation found that a majority of companies paid CEOs with stock options.[119] Stock ownership in one's employing company can only increase the tendency of upper-level managers to focus on profitability. Recognising this, the Eastman Kodak Co. developed a policy requiring top managers to invest up to four times the amount of their annual salaries in the company's stock.[120]

The annual incomes of the nation's top corporate officers also propel them into the ranks of the super rich. *Business Week* and the *Wall Street Journal* provided 1992 estimates of annual salaries plus short-term bonus payouts of the 1,000 chief executives of the most valuable publicly held

TABLE 3.6

Twenty Highest Executive Salaries in 1992

Executive	*Company*	*1992 Salary Plus Short-Term Bonus ($millions)**
Bernard L. Schwartz	Loral	5.8
Charles P. Lazarus	Toys 'R' Us	5.5
Michael Eisner	Disney	5.4
Richard B. Fisher	Morgan Stanley Group	5.3
Patrick H. Thomas	First Financial Management	3.8
Donald B. Marron	PaineWebber Group	3.6
James Wood	Great Atlantic & Pacific Tea	3.6
David A. Brandon	Valassis Communications	3.6
P. Roy Vagelos	Merck	3.3
John F. Welch	General Electric	3.2
Louis V. Gerstner	RJR Nabisco Holdings	3.2
Roberto C. Goizueta	Coca-Cola	3.1
Linda J. Wachner	Warnaco Group	3.1
Sanford I. Weill	Primerica	3.1
Charles R. Schwab	Schwab	3.0
Dwayne O. Andreas	Archer Daniels Midland	2.8
Rand V. Araskog	ITT	2.8
Gerald M. Levin	Time Warner	2.8
Charles B. Wang	Computer Associates Intl.	2.8
Martin Davis	Paramount Communications	2.8

*** 'rounded to the nearest $100.000**

Source: "The Coporate Elite," *Business Week*, October 12, 1992, pp. 119-146; The Boss's Pay," *Wall Journal*, April 22, 1992, pp. R9-R11.

companies.[121] The top twenty income earners are listed in Table 3.6. Such incomes, if wisely invested in diversified portfolios, only increase, only the stakes these executives have in the exploitation of private property rights within the capitalist system When long-term bonus and stock option plans are added to annual compensation figures, the status of CEOs as members of the capitalist class becomes even clearer. Surveys of income packages, including long-term compensation, paid to CEOs of the nation's largest public companies add substantially to what the highest paid among them took home in 1991 (see Table 3.7).

Kevin Philips argued that the significant increase in the size of CEO compensation packages that occurred during the 1980s allowed many of these individuals to leap to decamillionaire capitalist status and blurred the economic divisions between top managers of major corporations and entrepreneur-capitalist founders or owners.[122] What is significant for the purposes of this study is the sprinkling of communications executives in these lists. In Table 3.6, seven of the twenty highest-paid CEOs run companies with a direct stake in the ownership or dissemination of information and communications. Also notable are the CEOs of some of the nations largest pharmaceutical firms (Eli Lilly & Co., Bristol-Squibb Meyer, Bausch & Lomb, Merck, American Home Products, Glaxo) and agricultural firms (Archer Daniels Midland, ConAgra), as the wealth and power of these firms are primarily based on patented knowledge. Several CEOs of media companies, not in the top ranks, made at least $1 million in salary and short-term and long-term compensation in 1991, as shown in Table 3.8. Two studies indicated that executives of entertainment and information companies were the highest-paid group among all industry sectors in 1991.[123]

A close look at the pattern of ownership and control of the Disney empire underscores Phillips's point about the blurring of the boundaries between capitalists and upper-level managers that occurred during the 1980s. Since being recruited by the Bass brothers in 1984 to run Disney as

TABLE 3.7

Top Twenty-Five Executive Compensation Packages in 1991

Executive	*Company*	*Salari Plus Long-Term Bonus ($millions)**
Anthony O' Reily	H.J. Heinz	74.8
Leon C. Hirsch	U.S. Surgical	22.5
Richard K. Earner	National Medical	16.9
Sanford I. Weill	Primerica	16.7
Hamish Maxwell	Philip Morris	15.8
William P. Stiritz	Ralston Purina	13.8
Richard L. Gelb	Briston-Meyers Squibb	12.2
William A. Schreyer	Merrill Lynch	11.4
W.E LaMothe	Kellogg	9.8
Lawrence G. Rawl	Exxon	9.2
Richard B. Fisher	Morgan Stanley	7.6
Charles M. Harper	ConAgra	7.2
August A. Busch III	Anheuser-Busch	6.7
David A. Jones	Humana	6.4
Robert Cizik	Cooper Industries	6.3
Richard D. Wood	Lilly (Eli)	6.1
James B. Williams	SunTrust	6.0
Orin B. Smith	Englehard	5.8
John R. Stafford	American Home Products	5.6
Daniel E. Gill	Bausch & Lomb	5.5
Michael Eisner	Disney	5.4
Alan C. Greenberg	Bear Stearns	5.3
George D. Kennedy	Imcera	5.2
John F. Welch	General Electric	5.1
Martin Davis	Paramount	5.0

*rounded to the nearest $ 100,000

Source: *Wall Street Journal,* " Boss's Pay, ", April 22, 1992, pp. R9-R11.

CEO and chairman of the board, Michael Eisner has consistently ranked at the top of executive salary and compensation charts. In 1988, Eisner topped *Business Week's*, survey of executive pay with a salary of $7.5 million and stock options that earned another $32.6 million, giving him a total compensation package of $40.1 million that year.[124] His salary and cash bonus in 1989 totaled $9,589,360,[125] and in 1990 it was $11,233,000.[126] Eisner also held 1.65 per cent (353,467 shares) of Disney's stock in 1991 with options on another 1.8 million shares.

Frank G. Wells, deceased president and chief operation officer of Disney and former member of the board of directors, also consistently ranked high in executive compensation charts. He placed second to Eisner on *Business Week's* 1988 executive pay scoreboard with salary, cash bonus, and stock options totaling over $32 million.[127] The 1990 *Business Week* list had him as the highest-paid non-CEO in the United States in 1989, with a salary of $4.8 million plus $46 million earned in stock options for a total that year of nearly $51 million.[128] Also in 1989, Gary L. Wilson, Disney's executive vice president and chief financial officer at the time, garnered $47.5 million from stock options plus an additional $500,000 in salary and $1.5 million in cash bonuses.[129]

The exercise of Eisner's and Wells's stock options at the end of 1992 underscored the beneficial tax policies of the Reagan-Bush era for the rich and their concern about the Clinton administration's promise to raise taxes on the wealthy. Eisner and Wells went ahead and exercised their options to buy Disney stock at the 1984 market price, which after two 4-for-l splits worked out to $3.60 a share. They then immediately sold off a large percentage at the actual market price of $40 a share. For selling off 3.45 million of his 5.425 million shares Eisner made $197.5

million while Wells, selling off 1.64 million shares of the 1984 option package, earned about $60 million.[130] Both men retained substantial holdings of Disney stock, Eisner with 3 million shares and options on another 8 million from his 1989 contract; Wells held options on 3 million shares.

TABLE 3.8

CEOs of Public Media Companies Earning More than $1 Million in 1991

Executive	*Company*	*Salary Plus Bonus ($millions)*
John C. Malone	Tele-Communications	19.0
Michael Eisner	Disney	5.4
Martin Davis	Paramount	5.0
George V. Grune	Reader's Digest	4.3
Daniel B. Burke	Capital Cities/ABC	3.7
Steven J. Ross	Time Warner	3.4
Michael King	King World	2.8
Charles W. Moritz	Dun & Bradstreet	2.2
John J. Gurley	Gannett	2.1
Charles T. Brumback	Tribune	2.0
Frank J. Biondi Jr.	Viacom	1.7
Robert J. Tarr	General Cinema	1.6
Robert F. Erburu	Times Mirror	1.5
Laurence A. Tisch	CBS	1.4
Joseph L. Dionne	McGraw-Hill	1.3
James K. Batten	Knight-Ridder	1.2
Arthur Ochs Sulzberger	New York Times	1.1

Source: "Boss's Pay," *Wall Street Journal*, April 22, 1992, pp. R9-R11; "The Corporate Elite," *Business Week*, October 12, 1992, pp. 119-146; "What 800 Companies Paid Their Bosses," *Forbes*, May 25, 1992.

Other top managers of the major media conglomerates involved in filmed entertainment have scored high on the executive compensation charts as well. Steven J. Ross, the co-CEO and chair of Time Warner until his death in 1992, earned approximately $34 million in 1989 and $78 million in 1990 in salary and equity participation.[131] Ross, the key force behind the Time and Warner Communications merger in 1989, received $196 million for selling out his founding stake in Warner. Graef Crystal, an executive compensation analyst, rated Ross and his co-CEO, Nicholas J. Nicholas, as the most overpaid executives in 1990 in terms of a comparative analysis of their salaries with the firm's profit performance.[132] Between 1989 and 1991, Martin Davis, the chair of Paramount Communications, (formerly Gulf + Western), earned nearly $23 million in combined salary and bonuses during a period in which he earned stockholders a mere .6 per cent return on their investments.[133] In 1989, the president of MCA/Universal, Sidney Sheinberg, and its executive president, Thomas Pollack, ranked in the top ten of the highest-paid non-CEOs (approximately $8 million and $6 million, respectively).[134]

The spectacular growth in the incomes of CEOs during the past few decades was not paralleled by similar gains for "everyone else." Holly Sklar stressed that the average income of a U.S. CEO in 1988 was seventy-two times that of a school teacher and ninety-three times that of a factory worker.[135] The gap has increased significantly since 1960, when CEOs made roughly fifty times what a school teacher or factory worker made in annual income.[136] The income gaps between top management and workers again indicate a basic unfairness in the U.S. economy. Such gaps are greater in the United States than in Europe and Japan. Crystal estimated that CEOs in the United States yearly earn 160 times what the average employee earns in a year, whereas in Japan CEOs earn only 16 times that of the average employee.[137] A United Nations survey of the top twenty-one industrialised countries found that only Australia had a higher rate of income inequality than the United States.[138]

Furthermore, top-level corporate management is composed primarily of white males. A *Fortune* survey of 799 companies on its combined lists of the 1,000 largest U.S. industrial and service companies found that in 1990 only .5 per cent of the highest-paid officers and directors were women.[139] Only 5 per cent of upper-level managers at 255 major corporations surveyed by *Fortune* were women. Another survey commissioned by *Fortune* in 1991 surveyed the annual reports of 201 of the nation's largest companies and confirmed that only 4.8 per cent of senior officers were women, up from only 2.9 per cent in 1986.[140] The Feminist Majority Foundation surveyed the composition of upper-level management, from vice president on up, at the nation's largest corporations and found that only 3.5 per cent were women.[141] *Business Week's* 1,000 "Corporate Elite" list added its first African American, Erroll Davis Jr. of WPL Holdings, in 1990, a list that also included only two women.[142] These data again illustrate how capitalism unfairly distributes the burdens and benefits of the economy and intensifies .the exploitation of people on the basis of gender and race.

There is also evidence pointing to the fact that top officers of the largest U.S. corporations are actively recruited for membership in the social upper class if they fit the profile: rich, white, male. Domhoff argued that they are assimilated socially into the upper class, so that they "come to share its values, thereby cementing the relationship between the upper class and the corporate community."[143] This cultivation of corporate values begins in the education system at elite universities and business schools. Accordingly, *Business Week's* composite profile of the typical member of the corporate elite described him as having attended Yale, Princeton, or Harvard, where he played varsity football and where "he met a lot of fellows very much like him who also turned out to be CEOs."[144] Domhoff concluded that "in terms of their wealth, their social contacts, and their values, successful managers become part of the upper class as they rise in the corporate hierarchy."[145] Ralph Miliband argued further that conflicts between managers and owners, like those between segments of the capitalist class, "are safely contained within a particular ideological spectrum, and do not preclude a basic political consensus in regard to the crucial issues of economic and political life."[146] Surely the sanctity of intellectual property falls well within this ideological spectrum.

Zeitlin reiterated that corporate executives inevitably must peform in a way that maximises corporate profitability, not only to reap the lucrative rewards that come with their high status but also to keep their jobs.[147] Pressures to produce high profits appear to be on the increase with growing involvement of institutional investors (trust funds, mutual funds, and government and corporate pension funds) and outside directors in corporate boardrooms.[148] This is reflected in the ouster of several board chairmen and CEOs of major U.S. firms in the early 1990s, including Robert C. Stempel of General Motors Corp., James D. Robinson III of American Express Company, and John F. Akers of IBM Corp., among others.[149] Institutional investors have become particularly interested in linking executive compensation to corporate performance. They have also begun to demand that more independent, outside directors be named to the board and to its major committees.[150] Their main clout remains based on the threat of massive stock sell-offs that exacerbate, management's preoccupation with short-term profitability, as does the fact that the average institutional investor holds stock for only about two years.[151] Accordingly, CEOs must increasingly produce immedia l e profits. This is confirmed in data showing that new chief executives who fail to deliver high profits in their first year face quicker termination than just five years ago (eight out of every 100 in 1992, as opposed to one out every 100 in 1987).[152] These developments have led both executives and some business scholars to begin to question the relevance of the managerial revolution hypothesis.[153]

The findings on ownership of wealth, in particular the concentrated ownership of productive capital, the overrepresentation of upper-class people in the corporate community, and the socialisation of executives into the upper class, led Domhoff to conclude that "the upper social stratum is a business class based in the ownership and control of large corporations."[154] He took these findings as evidence that the upper class has been reorganised into a "corporate rich" that includes both top-level executives and major owners. These owners, upper-level executives, and major stockholders constitute a small inner group of directors who sit on the boards to produce interlocks among about 90 per cent of the largest U.S. corporations and banks.[155] These interlocks are a primary site for forging the unification of the interests of the capitalist class. They provide its corporate-based leadership with a "dense and flexible communication network,"[156] with commercial bank boards serving as the central "switch." Thus, nominally competitive and independent firms are formally linked into a "network of relationships that makes cousins of entire broods of economic giants."[157]

Surveys of media industry board members show that they too are plugged into this network through interlocks with banks and other financial institutions, media firms, and core corporations.[158] An examination of the interlocks of boards of directors of filmed entertainment companies reflects the pattern at the level of industry sector. In 1993, Paramount's board members had interlocks with NYNEX Corporation, Pennzoil, Lazard Freres & Co., Swiss Bank Corporation, Philip Morris Companies, and the Federal National Mortgage Association.[159] While in the hands of

Coca-Cola, Columbia Pictures was tied to the Cox media empire through Anne Cox Chambers and to Security Pacific National Bank, Dow Chemical Company, American Express, Sun Trust Banks, Inc., Trust Company of Georgia, and other investment firms.[160] Before linking with Time, Warner Communication's interlocking directorates included Chris-Craft Industries, Inc., Salomon Brothers, Inc., and several law and investment firms.[161] In 1992, Disney's board was linked to the Federal Reserve Bank of San Francisco, Bank America Corp., Pacific Mutual Life Insurance Co., Bank of California, Northwest Airlines, and L.A. Gear Inc. Additional ties linked it to oil and gas exploration, law, and real estate development firms.[162] These networks serve to extend and broaden the shared stake held by the corporate core of the capitalist class in the existing economic system. At the same time, these common interests are highly concentrated in the hands of a tightly knit big-business community, making U.S. capitalism much more coordinated than competitive.

Conclusion

As this brief survey demonstrates, the ownership and control of informational and cultural industries, intellectual property, and the means of embodying and disseminating it constitute a valuable portion of the productive capital owned and controlled by the capitalist class. However, the task of defending and extending intellectual property rights is necessarily complex given the peculiar nature of intellectual property. This peculiarity of informational and cultural products distinguishes them from tangible forms of property and requires special mechanisms to facilitate the appropriation and exploitation of intellectual property. It also necessarily implicates the state in the process of conferring, extending, and protecting intellectual property rights. These themes are explored in the next two chapters.

NOTES

1. This breakdown of the political economy of communications is used by Jeffrey Halley, "Culture in Late Capitalism," in S. McNall (ed.), *Political Economy: A Critique of American Society*, Glenview, IL: Scott, Foresman, 1981, pp. 137-155. A slightly more elaborate categorisation scheme for "critical communications research" is developed by Vincent Mosco, *The Pay-Per Society: Computers and Communication in the Information Age*, Norwood, NJ: Ablex, 1989, pp. 41-66.
2. Georg Hegel, *The Philosophy of History*, New York: Dover, 1956; Rudolf Hilferding, *Finance Capital*, London: Routledge, 1981; Rosa Luxemburg, *The Accumulation of Capital*, New York: Monthly Review Press, 1964; Paul Sweezy, *The Theory of Capitalist Development*, New York: Oxford University Press, 1942; Paul Baran and Paul Sweezy, *Monopoly Capital*, New York: Monthly Review Press, 1966; V. I. Lenin, *Imperialism*, New York: International Publishers, 1939; Nikolai Bukharin, *Imperialism and the World Economy*, New York: International Publishers, 1929.
3. Robert Heilbroner, *The Nature and logic of Capitalism*, New York: W. W. Norton, 1985, p. 33.
4. Heilbroner, p. 35
5. Luxemburg, p. 358.
6. David Harvey, *The Condition of Postmodernity* Oxford: Basil Blackwell, 1989, p. 344.
7. Sec Douglas Kellner, *Critical Theory: Marxism and Modernity, Baltimore*: Johns Hopkins University Press, 1989.
8. See, for example, Hans Magnus Enzensberger, The *Consciousness Industry*, New York: Seabury Press, 1974, or Peter Golding and Graham Murdock, "Ideology and the Mass Media: The Question of Determination," in M. Barrett et al. (eds.), London: Croon Helm, 1979, pp. 198-225.
9. Murdock argued for a shift from economics as a determinant in the last instance, as first proposed by Marx and stressed by Louis Althusser ("Contradiction and Overdetermination: Notes for an Investigation," *For Marx*, London: Verso Editions/NLB, 1986, pp. 87-128), to the determining role of economics in the first instance as the starting point of communications research (see Graham Murdock, "Critical Inquiry and Audience Activity," in B. Dervin et al. [eds.], *Rethinking Communication, Volume 2:*

*Paradigm Exemplars;*Newbury Park, CA: Sage, 1989, pp. 226-249).

10. Sut Jhally, "The Political Economy of Culture," in I. Angus and S. Jhally (eds.), *Cultural Politics in Contemporary America*, New York: Routledge, 1989, pp. 65-81.
11. Karl Marx and Frederick Engels, *The German Ideology*, New York: International Publishers, 1970, p. 64.
12. Marx and Engels, p. 64.
13. Nicolas Garnham, "Contribution to a Political Economy of Mass Communication," in *Capitalism and Communication*, Newbury Park, CA: Sage, 1990, p. 30.
14. Bernard Edelman, *Ownership of the Image: Elements for a Marxist Theory of Law*, Boston: Routledge and Kegan Paul, 1979.
15. Stephan Morawski, "Introduction," in L. Baxendall (ed.), *Marx and Engels on Literature and Art*, St. Louis, MO: Telos, 1973, pp. 3-47.
16. Edward Herman, "Diversity of News: 'Marginalising' the Opposition," *Journal of Communication*, 35:3, 1985, pp. 135-146.
17. Thomas Guback, "Theatrical Film," in Benjamin M. Compaine et al. (eds.), *Who Owns the Media? Concentration of Ownership in the Mass Communications Industry*, White Plains, NJ: Knowledge Industries, 1979, pp. 179-249, p. 190.
18. Samuel Bowles and Richard Edwards, *Understanding Capitalism: Competition, Command, and Change in the U.S. Economy*, New York: Harper and Row, 1985, p. 201.
19. Daniel Fusfeld, *Economics: Principles of Political Economy* (3rd ed.), Glenview, IL: Scott, Foresman, 1988.
20. Erik Barnouw, *A History of Broadcasting in the United States, Volume 1: To 1933: A Tower in Babel*, New York: Oxford University Press, 1966; Robert McChesney, "The Battle for the U.S. Airwaves, 1928-1935," *Journal of Communication*, 40:3,1990, pp. 29-57; Robert McChesney, "An Almost Incredible Absurdity for a Democracy," *Journal of Communication Inquiry*, 15:1, 1991, pp. 89-114.
21. Simon Frith, "The Industrialisation of Popular Music," in J. Lull (ed.), *Popular Music and Society* (2nd ed.), Newbury Park, CA: Sage, 1992, pp. 49-74.
22. B Bagdikian, *The Media Monopoly* (4th ed.), Boston: Beacon, 1992; Benjamin Compaine, "Newspapers" and "Magazines," and J. Kendrick Noble Jr., "Books," in Compaine et al., *Who*

Owns the Media? pp. 11-53, 127-178, and 251-291; Janice Radway, *Reading the Romance: Women, Patriarchy, and Popular Literature*, Chapel Hill: University of North Carolina Press, 1984.

23. Bagdikian, 1992; Herbert Schiller, Culture *Inc.: The Corporate Takeover of Public Expression*, New York: Oxford University Press, 1990; Anthony Smith, The Age of *Behemoths: The Globalisation of Mass Media Firms*, New York: Priority Press, 1991; Jeremy Tunstall and Michael *Palmer, Media Moguls*, London: Routledge, 1991.
24. Ben Bagdikian, *The Media Monopoly*, Boston: Beacon, 1983.
25. Bagdikian, 1992, p. ix.
26. Edwin McDowell, "Time Inc.'s Grand Plan Leaves Room for Books," New *York Times*, January 30, 1989, p. D 10.
27. Thomas Guback, "Ownership and Control of the Motion Picture Industry," *Journal of Film and Video*, 38:1, 1986, pp. 7-20.
28. David Waterman, "Rerecorded Home Video and the Distribution of Theatrical Feature Films," in Eli Noam (ed.), *Video Media Competition*, New York: Columbia University, 1985, pp. 221-243, p. 229.
29. Data cited from *Variety* in Laura Landro, "Sony's Holiday Films Surprise Skeptics," *Wall Street Journal*, January 15, 1992, pp. BI, B6.
30. Data cited from *Daily Variety* (January 1993) in Thomas R. King, "Three Hollywood Studios Wage Close Fight for Box-Office Crown," *Wall Street Journal*, January 4, 1993, pp. B1, B8.
31. A. D. Murphy, "'Majors' Global Rentals Totaled $3.27 Bil in '91," *Variety*, June 15, 1992, pp. 1, 5.
32. Thomas Guback, "The Evolution of the Motion Picture Theater Business in the 1980s," *Journal of Communication*, 37:2, 1987, pp. 60-77, p. 74.
33. Tom Graves, "Leisure-Time: Current Analysis," *Standard & Poor's Industry Surveys*, November 11, 1993, pp. L1-L68, p. L24.
34. Graves, p. L24.
35. Suzanne M. Donahue, *American Film Distribution*, Ann Arbor: UMI Research Press, 1987, p. 192.
36. Mark Robichaux, "Premium Cable Channels Gain Viewers with Original Programs, Package Deals," *Wall Street Journal*, March 24, 1993, pp. BI, BIO. The closest pay-TV channel on the periphery is the Encore Channel, with 3.8 million subscribers in 1992, which is partly owned by the Liberty Media Corp.

37. Graves, p. L21.
38. Marc Berman, "Rentals Reap Bulk of 1991 Vid Harvest," *Variety,* January 6, 1992, pp. 22, 104.
39. Berman, pp. 22, 104.
40. Graves, p. L21
41. "The Stale Rules That Stifle TV," *New York Times,* November 30, 1990, p. A32; Elizabeth Jensen, "Networks Gain in Syndication Dispute, but Many See Rerun of Battles Ahead," *Wall Street Journal,* November 9, 1992, pp. BI, B6.
42. Federal Communications Commission, *Competition and Responsibility in Network Television Broadcasting: Report and Order,* 1970, 23 FCC 2d 384.
43. Jensen, p. B6.
44. Graham Murdock, "Large Corporations and the Control of the Communications Industries," in M. Gurevitch, T. Bennett, J. Curran, and J. Woolacott (eds.), *Culture, Society, and the Media,* New York: Methuen, 1982, pp. 118-150, p. 120.
45. Mark Robichaux and Craig Torres, "Heard on the Street: Playing Cable-TV Stocks May Be Trickier Than It Looks," *Wall Street Journal,* February 4, 1993, pp. Cl, C2.
46. Johnnie L. Roberts, "Paramount 31/2-Point Stock lump Spotlights Brighter Outlook, Investors and Analysts Say," *Wall Street Journal,* January 22, 1993, p. C2.
47. Larry Rohter, "New Profits (and Prestige) from Old Films," *New York Times,* April 25,1991, pp. C15, C16.
48. Eileen Meehan, "*Holy Commodity Fetish, Batman!* The Political Economy of Commercial Intertext," in R. Pearson and W Uricchio (eds.), *The Many Lives of the Batman: Critical Approaches to a Superhero and His Media,* New York: Routledge, 1991, pp. 47-65.
49. Smith, p. 36.
50. The success of VHS was the result of JVC's decision to license the format to other manufacturers of VCRs. Once the majority of the VCRs in people's homes were VHS, the filmed entertainment industry came out with more products in that format. Additionally, as owners of video rental establishments sought to maximise diversity of tides and cut back on duplicate inventory, they increasingly went with the dominant format. This further exacerbated the decline of Betamax, even though some would argue that it was the superior format.

51. Geraldine Fabrikant, "Deal Is Expected for Sony to Buy Columbia Pictures," *New York Times*, September 26, 1989, pp. Al, D8; Laura Landro, "Sony Unit Set to Enter Cable Programming," *Wall Street Journal*, May 4, 1992, pp. BI, B8. Thomas Schatz, "Boss Men: Executive Decisions," *Film Comment*, January 1990, pp. 28-31; Bagdikian, 1992, p. 4.
52. See chapter 27 of Karl Marx, *Capital III*, New York: International Publishers, 1967.
53. Eduard Bernstein, *Evolutionary Socialism*, New York: Shocken Books, 1961, p. 54.
54. Adolf Berle Jr. and Gardiner Means, *The Modern Corporation and Private Property*, New York: Macmillan, 1932.
55. Berle and Means, p. 356.
56. Adolf Berle, *Power Without Property*, New York: Harcourt Brace, 1959, pp. 87-93.
57. Daniel Bell, *The End of Ideology* (rev. ed.), New York: Free Press, 1962.
58. Frederick S. Siebert, Theodore Peterson, and Wilbur Schramm, *Four Theories of the Press*, Urbana: University of Illinois Press, 1956.
59. Roya Akavan-Majid and Gary Wolf, "American Mass Media and the Myth of Libertarianism: Toward an 'Elite Power Group' Theory," *Critical Studies in Mass Communication*, 8:2,1991, pp. 139-151. While taking a capitalist media system as a given, social responsibility theorists did argue that public or government intervention was necessary when the market failed to deliver vital communications services.
60. Herbert Altschull, *Agents of Power: The Role of the News Media in Human Affairs*, New York: Longman, 1984, p. 5.
61. Robert W. McChesney, "Off Limits: An Inquiry into the Lack of Debate over the Ownership, Structure, and Control of the Mass Media in U.S. Political Life," *Communication*, 13:1 1992, pp. 1-19.
62. David Noble, *America by Design: Science, Technology, and the Rise of Corporate Capitalism*, New York: Knopf Publishing, 1977. See particularly chapter 6, "The Corporation as Inventor," pp. 84-109.
63. Murdock, 1982.
64. U.S. Congress, Democratic Staff of the Joint Economic Committee, *The Concentration of Wealth in the United States: Trends in the*

Distribution of Wealth Among American Families, Washington, DC: Joint Economic Committee, July 1986, pp. 23,29.

65. U.S. Federal Reserve, *Survey of Consumer Finances,* April 1992. Data cited in Sylvia Nasar,"Fed Gives Evidence of 80s Gains by Richest," *New York Times, April 21,*1992, pp. Al, A17, 72

66. Maurice Zeitlin, *The Large Corporation and Contemporary Classes,* Oxford: Polity Press, 1989, p. 146.

67. Zeitlin, 1989, p. 147.

68. U.S. Congress, Congressional Budget Office, *Measuring the Distribution of Income Gains,* CBO Staff Memorandum, Washington, DC: Congressional Budget Office, March 1992, p. 3. Data also cited in Sylvia Nasar, "However You Slice the Data the Richest Did Get Richer," *New York Times,* May 11, 1992, pp. Dl, D5.

69. U.S. Congress, Congressional Budget Office, *The Changing Distribution of Federal Taxes: 1975-1990,* Washington, DC: U.S. Congress, 1987.

70. U.S. Federal Reserve, "Changes in Family Finances from 1983 to 1989: Evidence from the Survey of Consumer Finances," *Federal Reserve Bulletin,* January 1992, pp. 1-18.

71. D. Stanley Eitzen and Maxine Baca Zinn, "Structural Transformation and Systems of Inequality," in D. Stanley Eitzen and Maxine Baca Zinn (eds.), *The Reshaping of America: Social Consequences of the Changing Economy,* Englewood Cliffs, NJ: Prentice Hall, 1989, pp. 131-143.

72. Bowles and Edwards, p. 22.

73. Bowles and Edwards, p. 80.

74. E.K. Hunt and Howard J. Sherman, *Economics: An Introduction to Traditional and Radical Views* (4th ed.), New York: Harper and Row, 1981, p. 249.

75. Paul M. Sweezy, *The Present as History: Essays and Reviews on Capitalism and Socialism,* New York: Monthly Review Press, 1953, pp. 128-129.

76. Zeitlin, 1989.

77. G. William Domhoff, "State and Ruling Class in Corporate America," *Insurgent Sociologist,* 4:3, 1974, pp. 3-14; *The Powers That Be,* New York: Vintage Books, 1979; *Who Rules America Now?* Englewood Cliffs, NJ: Prentice Hall, 1983.

78. Domhoff, 1983, p. 13.

79. Domhoff, 1983, p. 50.

80. Stuart Hall, "Ideology and Communication Theory," *Rethinking Communication, Volume 1: Paradigm Issues*, B. Dervin et al. (eds.), Newbury Park, CA: Sage, 1989, pp. 40-52.
81. Hall, 1989, pp. 51-52.
82. G. William Domhoff, *The Power Elite and the State: How Policy Is Made in America*, New York: Aldine de Gruyter, 1990, p. 39.
83. Domhoff, 1983, pp. 67-76.
84. Maurice Zeitlin, "On Classes, Class Conflict, and the State: An Introductory Note," in M. Zeitlin (ed.), *Classes, Class Conflict, and the State*, Cambridge, MA: Winthrop, 1980, pp. 1-37.
85. Nicos Poulantzas, *Political Power and Social Classes*, London: New Left Books, 1975, p. 296.
86. Kellner, pp. 176-203.
87. Edward Herman and Noam Chomsky, *Manufacturing Consent: The Political Economy of the Mass Media*, New York: Pantheon, 1988, pp. 7-10.
88. Herman and Chomsky, p. 8.
89. Thomas Guback, "Ownership and Control in the Motion Picture Industry," *Journal of Film and Video*, 38:1, 1986, pp. 7-20.
90. Guback, 1986, p. 17.
91. Guback, 1986, p. 17.
92. "The Forbes Four Hundred: The Richest People in America." Forbes October 21, 1991, pp. 145-272; "The Forbes Four Hundred: Great Family Fortunes," *Forbes*, October 21, 1991, pp. 274-296; "The Forbes Four Hundred: The Richest People in America, *Forbes*, October 19, 1992, pp. 90-208; "The Forbes Four Hundred: Great Family Fortunes," *Forbes*, October 19, 1992, pp. 218-243.
93. Stephanie Losee, "The Billionaires," *Fortune*, September 7, 1992, pp. 86-88.
94. Johnnie L. Roberts, "Orion Struggles to Return to Its Hollywood Glory Days," *Wall Street Journal*, January 26, 1993, p. B4.
95. In order to retain control of the company, Murdoch expanded his media holdings by borrowing money rather than issuing stock and diluting his stock holdings. Consequently, News Corp. has a huge debt load that ran as high as $8.7 billion in 1990 and still stood at $7.2 billion in 1992. The high debt load forced Murdoch to sell off some of News Corp.'s noncore assets as well as some very core properties, namely eight magazines (*New York, Premiere, New Woman, Seventeen, European Travel and Life,*

Soap Opera Weekly, Soap Opera Digest, and *Automobile)* and the racetrack newspaper, the *Daily Racing Form.*

96. News Corporation Limited, *Annual Report,* 1986, p. 16.

97. Patrick M. Reilly, "Murdoch to Digitise His Publications for Hand-Held PCs," *Wall Street Journal,* March 12, 1992, p. B7.

98. Laura Landro and Thomas R. King, "Diller Steps Down at Fox and Murdoch Takes the Reins," *Wall Street Journal,* February 25, 1992, pp. BI, B7. As a result of Diller's resignation, management's stake in TCF has been dissipated. At that time Diller held News Corp. stock that he acquired in the sale of TCF to Murdoch by Marvin Davis. At this time Diller also acquired a 5 per cent interest in the profits of Fox, Inc., of which he served as chairman and CEO. Before resigning in 1992, Diller had earned at least $70 million in compensation through stock, salary, and profit participation ("In Hollywood, a Nouveau Royalty Made by Mergers," *New York Times,* March 1,1992, p. F5). His total worth was estimated at $100 million in 1992; he has begun to reinvest that wealth in the media, first of all in the Home Shopping Channel, which he planned to develop into a leader in the emerging interactive television business.

99. Laura Landro and Johnnie L. Roberts, "Murdoch Plays Role of Hollywood Mogul," *Wall Street Journal,* February 26, 1992, pp. BI, B3. Upon taking over Diller's role as chief executive, Murdoch announced he had no plans to be involved in "creative decisions." Joe Roth, president of TCP, maintained that Murdoch did not delve into "the editorial side" of filmmaking but was reading film scripts and approving budgets (see Bernard Weinraub, "Rupert Murdoch, in Hollywood, Learns the Value of 'No,'" *New York Times,* July 21,1992, pp. C11, C15). The distinction Roth draws is problematic since financial decisions are actually the initial creative moment when it comes to making movies within a capitalist system. Murdoch also supposedly sent cautionary messages concerning the levels of explicit sex and violence in TCF films (Richard Turner, "Roth Will Leave Twentieth Century Fox to Produce Movies at Walt Disney," *Wall Street Journal,* November 3,1992, p. B6). Murdoch's vision for Fox Broadcasting's news programming is also being felt, where he advocates reporting that is quick-paced, visually oriented, and packaged into memorable thirty-second stories. Murdoch has been active in planning and programming the Fox network since it began (Bill Carter, "Rivals Say the Heat Is Off; Top Fox Executives Bristle," *New York Times,* March 2, 1992, p. D8).

100. Walt Disney Company, *Notice of Annual Meeting of Stockholders and Proxy Statement, Statement*, 1992, Burbank, CA.
101. "Forbes 400," 1991, p. 164.
102. Ted Turner, the chair of Turner Broadcasting System, also has given up some control over his company as a result of the need to lower debt. Besides the stake held by Time Warner, now about 22 per cent, another major shareholder is Tele-Communications Inc. (TCI), the largest multisystem cable operator in the United States. Time Warner and TCI stopped Turner from pursuing purchase of one of the major U.S. television networks (CBS, ABC, NBC) and from bidding on Orion Pictures ("Turner Rejects Rumor on Deal," *New York Times*, March 4, 1992, p. D6.).
103. Richard Turner, "Carolco Submits Restructuring Plan Involving MGM," *Wall Street Journal*, December 28, 1992, p. B4.
104. Midwest Television continues to be family controlled, with son Chris running the three television and four radio stations.
105. *Universal City Studios, Inc. v. Sony Corporation of America, Inc.*, 480 F. Supp 429 (C.D. Cal. 1979); *Sony Corporation of America, Inc. v. Universal City Studios, Inc.*, 659 F.2d 963 (9th Cir. 1981); *Sony Corporation of America, Inc. v. Universal City Studios, Inc.* 464 U.S. 417(1984).
106. Guback, 1986, p. 12.
107. Christopher Murray, "Here's the Electronic Business International 100," *Electronic Business*, December, 1992, pp. 83-85.
108. Geraldine Fabrikant, "The Osaka Decision," *New York Times*, May 3, 1992, pp. FI, F6. During negotiations for Matsushita's takeover of MCA, officials of the former iterated that they had no intention of trying to influence the subjects or content of the latter's creative output. Although there was some suggestion that changes in the script for "Mr. Baseball," a film about a U.S. baseball player playing in Japan, were the result of self-censorship on the part of Universal Pictures producers, the claim is hard to prove and easy to deny (see Steven R. Weisman, "Film Changes After Japanese Buy Studio," *New York Times*, November 20, 1991, pp. Al, C21).
109. Yumiko Ono and Richard Turner, "Matsushita Names Officials to MCA's Highest Committee," *Wall Street Journal*, January 21, 1991, p. B2.
110. Andrew Pollack, "At MCA's Japanese Parent, No Signs Yet of Letting Go," *New York Times*, October 14, 1994, pp. Dl, D16;

Geraldine Fabrikant, "Matsushita's Chief May Meet on MCA," *New York Times*, November 17, 1994, p. D5.

111. See, for example, the case of the cable-system merger between the Times Mirror Company and Cox Cable. The Chandler family trust, holder of preferred shares of Times Mirror stock, controls shareholder votes despite a minority ownership of overall stock. This would have allowed the trust to make out better in the merger deal than common stock holders, who protested the terms of the deal (Floyd Norris, "At Times Mirror, 2 Roads Diverge," *New York Times*, June 7, 1994, pp. Dl, D8).

112. Domhoff, 1983, pp. 60-65.

113. Eric Schuckler, Ralph King Jr., and Dolores A. Lataniotis, "The 400 Richest People in America," *Forbes*, October 26, 1987, pp. 106-110, p. 110.

114. Losee, p. 88.

115. Beth Mintz, "United States of America," in T. Bottomore and R. Brym (eds.), *The Capitalist Class: An International Study*, New York: New York University Press, 1989.

116. C. Wright Mills, *The Power Elite* New York Oxford University Press, 1956; Don Villarejo "Stock Ownership and the Control of the Corporation," *New University* Thought 2, 1961, pp. 33-77; G. William Domhoff, Who Rules America? Eaglewood Cliffs, NJ: Prentice Hall, 1967, and *The Higher Circles*, New York: Random House, 1970; Edward Herman, *Corporate Control, Corporate Power*, New York: Cambridge University Press, 1981; Domhoff, 1983.

117. Michael Useem, *The Inner Circle*, New York: Oxford University Press, 1984, p. 30.

118. Figures cited from William M. Mercer Inc., a New York business consulting firm, in "Executive Stockpile," *Wall Street Journal*, August 13, 1992, p. Al.

119. Elizabeth Arreglado, "Compensation Survey," New York: Conference Board, December 1992.

120. Joan E. Rigdon, "Kodak to Require Stock Ownership by Top Managers," *Wall Street Journal*, January 14, 1993, p. A6.

121. "The Corporate Elite," *Business Week*, October 12, 1992, pp. 119-146; "The Boss's Pay," *Wall Street Journal*, April 22, 1992, pp. R9-R11.

122. Kevin Phillips, *The Politics of Rich and Poor: Wealth and the American Electorate in the Reagan Aftermath*, New York: Random House, 1990, p. 178.

123. Steve Kichen and Eric Hardy, "Corporate America's Most Powerful People," *Forbes,* May 25, 1992, p. 174; Arreglado.
124. John A. Byrne, Ronald Grover, and Todd Vogel, "Is the Boss Getting Paid Too Much?" *Business Week,* May 1, 1989, pp. 46-52.
125. Walt Disney Company, *Notice of Annual Meeting of Stockholders and Proxy Statement,* 1990, p. 9.
126. Walt Disney Company, *Notice of Annual Meeting of Stockholders and Proxy Statement,* 1991, p. 9.
127. Byrne, Grover, and Vogel, p. 47.
128. John Byrne, Ronald Grover, and Robert D. Hof, "Pay Stubs of the Rich and Corporate," *Business Week,* May 7, 1990, pp. 56-64.
129. Walt Disney Company, *Notice of Annual Meeting of Stockholders and Proxy Statement,* 1990, pp. 9, 11.
130. Steve Lohr, "Avoiding the Clinton Taxman," *New York Times,* December 2, 1992, pp. Dl, D5; James Bates and Jube Shiver Jr., "Disney's Chief Makes Out Big from Stock *Options"Philadelphia Inquirer,* December 3, 1992, pp. D9-D10; David J. Jefferson,"Disney Officials Get $185 Million from Stock Sale," *Wall Street Journal,* December 2, 1992, p. A3.
131. Byrne, Grover, and Hof; Steve Kichen and Eric Hardy, "Turnover at the Top," *Forbes,* May 27, 1991, pp. 214-218.
132. Alison Leigh Cowan, "The Gadfly C.E.O.'s Want to Swat," *New York Times,* February 2, 1992, pp. F1, F6.
133. John Byrne, "What, Me Overpaid? CEOs Fight Back," *Business Week,* May 4, 1992, pp. 142-148.
134. Byrne, Grover, and Hof.
135. Holly Sklar, "Who's Who: The Truly Greedy," *Z Magazine,* July/August 1990, pp. 56-57.
136. Byrne, Grover, and Vogel.
137. Graef Crystal, *In Search of Excess: The Over-Compensation of American Executives,* New York: Norton, 1993.
138. United Nations Development Programme, Human Development Oxford University Press, 1992.
139. Jaclyn Fierman, "Why Women Still Don't Hit the Top," *Fortune,* July 30, 1990, pp. 40-62.
140. Anne B. Fisher, "When Will Women Get to the Top?" *Fortune,* September 21, 1992, pp. 44-56.
141. Feminist Majority Foundation, *Empowering Women in Business,* Arlington, VA: Feminist Majority Foundation, 1991, p. 1.

142. "The Corporate Elite," *Business Week*, October 19, 1990, pp. 55-274.

143. Domhoff, 1983, p. 73.

144. Robert Mims and Ephraim Lewis, "A Portrait of the Boss," *Business Week*, October 19, 1990, pp. 8-14.

145. Domhoff, 1983, p. 76.

146. Ralph Miliband, *The State in Capitalist Society*, New York: Basic Books, 1969, p. 46.

147. Zeitlin, 1989, p. 160.

148. Kevin Salwen, "Institutions Are Poised to Increase Clout in Boardroom," *Wall Street Journal*, September 21, 1992, pp. BI, B7.

149. Steve Lohr, "Pulling Down the Corporate Clubhouse," *New York Times*, April 12, 1992, pp. FI, F5; Allen R. Myerson, "A Corporate Storm Blows in at American Express," *New York Times*, December 7, 1992, pp. Al, D3.

150. Mutual fund brokers controlled 9.1 per cent of all stock in investors' hands in 1991, and government and corporate pension funds held another 25 per cent (Randall Smith, "Mutual Funds Have Become Dominant Buyers of Stock," *Wall Street Journal*, May 22, 1992, pp. Cl, C2). In total, by 1992 all institutional investors combined controlled 53 per cent of all U.S. stock outstanding (Alison Leigh Cowan, "The High-Energy Boardroom," *New York Times*, October 28, 1992, pp. D1-D2; Kevin Salwen and Joann Lublin, "Activist Holders: Giant Investors Flex Their Muscles More at U.S. Corporations," *Wall Street Journal*, April 27, 1992, pp. Al, A5).

151. Salwen and Lublin, p. A5.

152. Joann S. Lublin, "More Chief Executives Learn Entrance to Office Is a Rapidly Revolving Door," *Wall Street Journal*, October 7, 1992, pp. BI, B3.

153. Lohr, April 12, 1992, pp. FI, F5.

154. Domhoff, 1983, p. 77.

155. Domhoff, 1983, p. 71.

156. Domhoff, 1983, p. 77.

157. Fusfeld, p. 416.

158. Peter Dreier and Steven Weinberg, "The Ties That Blind: Interlocking Directorates," *Columbia Journalism Review*, November 1979, pp. 51-68; Peter Dreier, "The Position of the Press in the U.S. Power Structure," *Social Problems*, 29:3, February 1982, pp.

298-310; Doug Henwood, "Corporate Profile: The New York Times," *Extra!* Mar/Apr 1989, pp. 8-9; "NBC: The GE Broadcasting Co.," *Extra!* May/June 1989, pp. 8-9; "CBS: Tiffany Goes to K-Mart," *Extra!* Oct/Nov 1989, pp. 8-10; "The *Washington Post:* The Establishment's Paper," *Extra!* Jan/Feb 1990, pp. 9-11; "Cap Cities/ABC: No. 2, and Trying Harder," *Extra!* Mar/Apr 1990; U.S. Senate, Committee on Governmental Affairs, Subcommittee on Reports, Accounting, and Management, *Interlocking Directorates Among Major U.S. Corporations, Parts 1 and 2*, Staff Study, 95th Cong., 2nd Sess., Washington, DC: U.S.Government Printing Office, 1978, U.S. Senate Committee on Governmental Affairs. *Structure of Corporate Concentration*, Staff Study, 96th Cong., 2nd Sess.. Washington, DC: U.S. Government Printing Office, 1981.

159. Kathryn Harris, "Paramount Board Setting Up Bidding Format," Los *Angeles Times,* December 14, 1993, p. Dl.

160. Coca-Cola Company, *Annual Report*, I987, p. 53.

161. Warner Communications, Inc., *Annual Report*, 1987, p. 56.

162. Walt Disney Company, *Annual Meeting of Stockholders and Proxy Statement*, 1992.

4 INTELLECTUAL PROPERTY ON THE INTERNATIONAL STAGE

Introduction

1. One of the most significant and distinctive features of intellectual property is its ability to transcend national boundaries in a way which is simply not open to real property. A book, film or song enjoyed in one country may well take root within the culture of another with very little effort; the pharmaceutical compound which treats a skin ailment in Germany will be equally efficacious in Austria; the customer at McDonald's Hamburger Restaurant in Geneva will bring with him the expectations drawn from his experiences of similar establishments in London, New York or Tokyo, and so on. It is not therefore surprising that there has been much activity in the international field with regard to both the protection of intellectual property and the dissemination of the information protected by it. This chapter will give a brief overview of this international activity, in the hope that the reader will be able to derive a general impression of it. The subject is of very much more legal, political and economic importance than this brief treatment suggests.

The Players

2. The international stage is occupied by the following players :

(i) *Sovereign states* Techniques for counting sovereign states vary as to one's preparedness to recognise particular countries for particular purposes, but a rough and non-political estimate is that there are some 160 of them, de facto or de jure. These countries may be categorised accordingly:

(a) Developed capitalist economies (United States, Japan, United Kingdom, France, Germany, Italy, The Netherlands, Canada, Australia and a few others), which both produce and consume great quantities of intellectual property. These countries generally perceive their interest as being served by the greatest degree of protection and enforcement of intellectual property rights, of which they create most of the world's current stock. They are known as the 'Group B countries' in international trade terms[1].

(b) The formerly socialist economies (USSR, Poland, Hungary, Czechoslovakia, Bulgaria and a few others), which may be industrially advanced or not, and which are torn between their desire to create products and stimulate production on the one hand, and their recently discarded but still influential practice of supporting state enterprise and public trusteeship of the means of production on the other. These countries are neither conspicuous producers nor consumers of intellectual property, at least in comparison with the developed capitalist economies. They are often known as the 'Group D' countries[2].

(c) Developing countries (most of the world's

nations), which currently consume far more intellectual property than they can produce or pay for, and which they can obtain largely through foreign aid and co-operation, charity or theft[3]. This is the 'Group of 77'[4]. Within this group is a large body of countries known as LDCs ('Least Developed Countries'), the poorest in terms 01 money, physical resources and manpower, and usually the least able to assist themselves.

(d) The Islamic world (largely the Middle Eastern states), which, with some honourable exceptions, has little interest in the phenomenon of intellectual property; in some cases this is because a strong national or cultural homogeneity makes the countries of this group culturally self-sufficient, and in some cases because the wealth-creating possibilities of intellectual property have failed to shine beneath the brilliant light of the petro-dollar.

These various sovereign states sometimes form themselves into groupings which have great significance for intellectual property, for example the European Community and the Andean Pact, and indeed show a greater tendency to work in groups and through regional consensus than to enter into bilateral agreements with each other (the predominant practice until the late nineteenth century).

(ii) *International bodies* Sovereign states have, during the last half-century, shown a marked tendency to establish international bodies which, while deriving their status and authority only from the consensus of sovereign states, often appear to wield more power and influence than such states. The United Nations Organisation is the best known example of such a body, but the three which most greatly occupy the international stage of intellectual property law are WIPO (the World Intellectual Property Organisation). UNESCO (the United Nations Educational, Scientific and Cultural Organisation) and UNCTAD (the United Nations Committee on Trade and Development). In short their roles are as follows : WIPO seeks to establish intellectual property laws which maintain at least a minimum standard of protection in all countries, without regard to the economic or cultural necessity to do so, UNESCO seeks to encourage the widest exploitation of educational and scientific materials on reasonable terms, without worrying too much about the proprietary implications of so doing[5], while UNCTAD is at work in establishing intellectual property licensing norms which will give equal weight to the claims of both owners and users of intellectual property to be allowed to determine the terms under which it may be exploited[6]. UNCTAD's stewardship of GATT (the General Agreement on Tariffs and Trade), in its Third (Uruguay) Round, has also focused on the issue of whether developed countries are justified in applying punitive trade sanctions against developing countries which fail to provide adequate domestic remedies against counterfeiting.

(iii) *International pressure groups* Intellectual property rights owners, and those who make it their business to service them, have organised themselves into cogent and articulate exponents of the case for promoting intellectual property rights. Of these the best-known are ALAI (L'Association Litteraire et Artislique Internationale), which speaks for authors and creators in numerous countries, AIPPI (L'Association Internationale pour la Protection de la Propriete Industrielle), which speaks for those who deal in industrial property rights, IFPI (the International Federation of Producers of Phonograms and Videograms) and CISAC (La Confederation Internationale des Societes des Auteurs et des Compositeurs), which represents the interests of the world's most important copyright collecting societies. A small number of national groupings are so powerful that their influence is felt internationally, for example, the USTA (United States Trademark Association).

Types of international activities

3. Now that some account has been given of the various parties to international agreements and activities, it falls to describe some of the types of activity in question.

Reciprocity of Protection

4. In the early nineteenth century any British author would have found, to his annoyance, that anyone in France who wished to publish there an issue of his work could do so without the fear of any legal reprisals; it would be of little comfort to him, especially in the light of British 'Francophobia' and ignorance of the French language, to know that he could, with impunity, publish in the UK the work of any of France's leading authors. The solution to this problem was for the British and French governments to get together and to do a deal with each other : French authors would thus be protected by British copyright law if the French protected British authors in return[7]. By the

mid- to late-nineteenth century there were numerous such reciprocal treaties, despite the potential problems of balancing out inequalities of protection (eg if country A, but not country B protects a particular right, should an author from country B be able to enjoy that right in country A, or vice versa?).

5. Bilateral treaties of this nature did much to ease the immediate needs of the then most developed countries, but the preparation and negotiation of a multiplicity of bilateral agreements require an inefficient duplication of skilled labour and do not result in any establishment of general norms of protection. That is why it was felt necessary to replace bilateral treaties, where possible, with international treaties made between as many as possible of the economically significant nations. Two such international treaties, the Paris Convention for the Protection of Industrial Property in 1883[8] and the Berne Convention for the Protection of Literary and Artistic Works of 1886[9], contributed greatly to the establishment of principles of reciprocity by requiring that signatory nations adhere to the obligation to treat nationals of other member states as they would their own. The importance of the principle of reciprocity may be drawn from the number of countries signatory to one or other of the various texts of the Paris and Berne Conventions (100 and 841 respectively, on 1 January 1990); most of these countries have little or nothing to gain from joining them apart from the resulting protection of their nationals overseas.

Economies of Labour or Scale

6. Some international agreements are not designed to establish principles of reciprocity or to establish new norms of protection (discussed below); they are primarily intended to give their member states (or their nationals) the benefits of economies of labour or of scale. For example, in the

absence of the Patent Co-operation Treaty (PCT) of 1970[10], a person who wants worldwide patent protection for his invention would have to pay fees for the filing, examination and novelty search conducted in each of over one hundred countries which have patent systems. This is useless, repetitive labour for which the application would have had to pay a hundredfold. The PCT, however, provides that a single application, a single partial search and examination, will cover all the countries which adhere to it. Even though, by 1 January 1990, only 43 countries (including the UK) belonged to the PCT, the saving in terms of liberated bureaucratic time and application funding is immense. Along the same lines as the PCT but of a rather more advanced nature is the European Patent Convention (EPC) by which an applicant to the European Patent Office (EPO) in Munich can designate his patent application to cover one or more of its twelve member states. The EPO processes each applications at a fraction of the cost of making separate applications in all the signatory states (both under the PCT and EPC the cost of a treaty application is cheaper than the cost of three separate national applications). Similarly, savings can be made in trade mark applications under the terms of the Madrid Agreement on the International Registration of Trade Marks of 1891 to which some 29 countries (but not the UK) adhere. Under this Agreement a person who has successfully registered a trade mark in his own country can deposit that mark with WIPO; the mark will then be registered in any member state designated by the trade mark's proprietor and which does not within twelve months object to its registrability under the provisions of its national law. A revised and more versatile version of the Madrid Agreement, known as the Madrid Protocol, was signed on 29 June 1989. It is expected to prove more popular than the Madrid Agreement, which it is eventually expected to replace, because it contains fewer idiosyncrasies and allows English as a working language besides French.

7. Economies of scale, as distinct from labour, are achieved by two African treaties of relatively recent provenance which established AIPO[11] and ARIPO[12]. AIPO is a group of thirteen French-speaking African states, and ARIPO contains twelve of its English-speaking counterparts. In each group of countries a single patent application and grant procedure will result in the applicant obtaining a single patent to cover each set of territories (AIPO), or as many member states as the applicant designates (ARIPO). This makes great sense from an economic point of view. If lots of small and relatively disadvantaged African states each maintain their separate patent systems, they must establish and pay for the infrastructure of patent systems which will be substantially under-utilised, given that in a small jurisdiction one can often secure a powerful de facto monopoly by being first on the market without ever needing patent protection. AIPO and ARIPO both offer attractively large and thus more viable markets for would-be patentees, and free their member states from the financial burdens of running a whole Patent Office.

Establishment of Norms of Protection

8. While the Paris and Berne Conventions both encouraged the adoption in many countries of higher levels of legal protection than had been enjoyed within them previously, that improvement in general standards might be viewed as a fortunate, if important, by-product of the reciprocity-seeking process. In modern conventions, however, the setting of new standards of protection and the identification of new subject matter for protection have supplanted reciprocity as their most important object. Much of the groundwork in the examination of norms and the identification of subject matter has been done by WIPO,

which administers, or is at least associated with, almost all the major modern world intellectual property conventions. Examples of such agreements are the Rome Convention of 1961 for the Protection of Performers, Producers of Phonograms and Broadcasting Organisations, which attempted to set new standards for the protection of 'neighbouring rights', the Geneva Convention of 1971 for the Protection of Producers of Phonograms Against Unauthorised Duplication of their Phonograms, and the Union for the Protection of Plant Varieties Convention (the 'UPOV Convention') of 1961.

9. Not all of the conventions set up to establish norms are successful. The number of states party to the Rome and Geneva Conventions mentioned in the previous paragraph (35 and 43 respectively, as of 1 January 1990 with 28 overlaps), indicates that the piracy, rather than the protection, of Part II works should be regarded as the generally agreed international level of behaviour; another convention, the Brussels Convention of 1974 on the Protection of Satellite Transmissions, has only attracted eleven members to 1 January 1986, which is perhaps a reflection on the small number of countries whose 'point-to-point' satellite broadcasts are in danger of being intercepted by pirates, and a third, the Vienna Agreement for the Protection of Typefaces and their International Deposit (1973), has attracted little international support because its subject matter so rarely arises as a national issue.

Harmonisation and Integration

10. Since the European Community has as one of its aims the integration of separate markets into one large market within which there are no artificial barriers, it is not surprising that the Cyber Laws European Commission has promoted the causes of harmonisation of domestic

trade mark laws[13], the Community Patent[14] and the Community Trade Mark.[15] When the respective proposals are implemented, there will be only one application, registration office and registration procedure in respect of the totality of the EC. On a less grand scale, international co-operation can determine even standards of an arbitrary or bureaucratic nature which are subservient to the law. Of such a nature are the Nice Agreement of 1957 on the Classification of Goods and Services, which fixed internationally recognised categories of registration for trade marks, and the International Patent Classification which provides formulaic descriptions of fields of science in order to render the prior art accessible to researchers in any language[16].

The Facilitation of the Greater Dissemination of Intellectual Property

11. Until the mid-1960s the voice of the developing world was scarcely heard in the auditorium of intellectual property debate. Most of today's poorest and least privileged regimes were still subject to colonial rule or protection, and those which had achieved independence had yet to find their voice. The only thing they sought was independence, and it was assumed that, with independence, they could harness their indigenous potential and develop themselves. Whatever the merits of this assumption, the factual basis for it was swept aside by the sudden surge in technological applications experienced by the developed nations in the mid-1960s. From that time onwards it has become increasingly apparent that technological information in the form of both pure and applied science is a necessary ingredient, it not a sufficient one, of sustained industrial and agricultural growth.

12. The demand made by developing countries for greater access to intellectual property on reasonable terms

has been reflected by international developments in at least two major aspects. First, the Berne Convention[17], and its 'shadow', the Universal Copyright Convention[18], relaxed their standards of protection, in their Paris revision in 1971, so as to allow developing countries to institute in their own laws a regime of non-exclusive, non-transferable licences to translate, broadcast and reproduce works for educational purposes, on payment of reasonable royalties-Second, the UNCTAD Transfer of Technology Code, now in its sixth draft[19], aims at establishing model terms under which developing countries can enjoy the technological benefits of cooperation with sophisticated corporations based in developed countries.

REFERENCES

1. This designation stems from the division of the UNCTAD Trade and Development Board into four groups of countries from which that Board is composed. See W Fikentscher, The Draft International Code of Concoct on the Transfer of Technology (1980), p. 4.
2. *Ibid.*, Yugoslavia is a 'Group A' country, and Mongolia a 'Group of 77' country (seen 4 below).
3. For a sympathetic account of the position of developing countries see Aruda 'Third World View of Technology Transfer'(1984) Les Nouvelles 12.
4. Fikentscher, n 1 above, p. 4. The 'Group of 77' comprising both Groups A (Afro-Asian) and C (Latin America).
5. On the current attitudes of UNESCO towards the New International Economic Order see its General Conference Resolution 9.1.1978, much of which may seem incompatible with its stewardship of the Universal Copyright Convention of 1952.
6. On which see Fikentscher, n 1.
7. Such treaties were brought into domestic law by orders made under the International Copyright Acts 1844, 1852 and 1875.
8. Revised to the Stockholm text of 14 July 1967.
9. The most recent revision is the Paris text of 24 July 1971.

10. Washington 1970; amended and modified to 3 February 1984. For a usefully simplified view of PCT procedure see B Reid A Practical Guide to Patent Law'(1985): p 369.
11. The African Intellectual Property Organisation (established in March 1977).
12. Formerly ESARIPO, Industrial Property Organisation for English-speaking Africa (established in December 1982).
13. See the Approximation Directive 89/104/EEC of 21 December 1988.
14. Convention for the European Patent for the Common Market, 15 December 1975.
15. See the Amended Proposal for Council Regulation on the Community Trade Mark, 9 August 1984.
16. The International Patent Classification Agreement of 24 March 1971.
17. Appendix to the Paris text of 24 July 1971.
18. Para 14.2, n 5 above, articles *Vbis* to *Vquater*.
19. Draft International Code of Çonduct on the Transfer of Technology, on which see M Blakeney Legal Aspects of the Transfer of Technology to Developing Countries (1989), pp. 131-161.

5 THE ECONOMICS OF INTELLECTUAL PROPERTY

As a marketable commodity, intellectual property has come under the scrutiny of economists specialising in the "economics of information." This chapter reviews some of the key concepts from the field of "information economics," particularly those germane to intellectual property issues, among them:

- the nature of information as a public good
- the problem of excluding nonpaying consumers of information
- the relationship between the first-copy costs of producing information and the costs of reproducing and distributing it
- price discrimination in information markets
- the nondepletability of information and entertainment goods, and
- the economies of scale and scope in the production and distribution of informational and cultural goods.

The chapter concludes with a discussion of the debate between neoclassical economists and radical political economists over differing conceptions of "efficiency."

The Economics of Intellectual Property

Thomas Jefferson recognised early the difference between the nature of ideas and information and that of material goods. He said of "an idea": "Its peculiar character, too, is that no one possesses the less, because every other possesses the whole of it. He who receives an idea from me, receives instruction himself without lessening mine; as he who lights his taper at mine, receives light without darkening me."[1] Jefferson was describing what contemporary economists call "public goods," which allow joint, or nonrival, consumption by all potential consumers. Like Jefferson's taper, the use of a radio broadcast or lighthouse signal by one person does not prevent its actual or potential consumption by another. A related distinguishing feature of public goods is their nonexclusive nature, that is, once a public good is provided, it is impossible or very costly to exclude nonpayers from access to it. Economists expect that rational consumers will take a "free ride" when they can have access to a public good without paying for it.

Stanley Besen made the important distinction between the intangible expressions of intellectual or artistic creativity, such as songs, computer programs, novels, or scientific articles, and their materialised forms—audio tapes, phonograph records, computer diskettes, books, or journals.[2] Only the former are public goods, because their consumption is nonrivalous and because of the impossibility of excluding individuals from using them once they are produced and made available to consumers. The embodied, material forms of the artistic or intellectual expression, such as the videocassette or the book, are private goods and can be exclusive in terms of ownership and use. In the case of broadcasting, exclusion remains problematic because of the intangibility of this form of information delivery.

Due to the peculiar nature of informational and cultural commodities, markets for information-based goods and services are inefficient and prone to failure. From the economist's perspective, this is "a situation where the operation of markets will not result in pareto-optimality or the *fair* distribution of wealth."[3] Therefore, in intellectual property markets the problem is, in W. Curtiss Priest's term, one of "in-appropriability," where property owners have difficulty "receiving the full market compensation for the creation of information due to the problem of exclusion."[4] Besen argued that if owners of intellectual property are unable to exclude non-payers, their revenues will decline and their willingness and ability to produce new types of intellectual property will diminish; being rational capitalists they will invest elsewhere.[5] The bottom line in this argument is that fewer books, movies, information systems, and so on are produced than is socially "efficient."[6]

Therefore, other mechanisms must be found to deal with the problem of exclusion, because direct sale of intellectual property goods to consumers is often problematic. Garnham listed five main strategies intellectual property owners use to deal with the peculiar characteristics of informational and cultural commodities: copyright; control of access to consumption at the direct point of sale (e.g., the box office); built-in obsolescence through the manipulation of time; bundling (e.g., the creation, packaging, and sale of audiences to advertisers rather than direct sale of cultural and informational goods to consumers); and state patronage.[7] The next section of this chapter focuses on those exclusion mechanisms utilised in the distribution of motion pictures and other filmed entertainment programming.

The evolution of these mechanisms represents the filmed entertainment industry's *private* efforts to incorporate various communications technologies (i.e., television, cable television, videocassettes, and satellites) into its marketing structure. However, in each case government-defined and -mandated copyrights and related "neighboring" rights serve as the guarantee upon which private mechanisms are built. Copyright laws therefore serve to regulate the flow of communications and information through various industry sectors and communications hardware, Copy, distribution, and performance rights permit the transfer of ownership claims and thereby facilitate the realisation of exchange value from informational and cultural commodities. The critical moment in this process, which this book explores, is when new technologies for embodying and distributing intellectual and artistic creativity are introduced and, in turn, generate struggles over who should be able reap the benefits from their use — actual creators, copyright owners, or consumers.

The Exclusivity Inherent in Theatrical Exhibition

Traditionally, the problem of exclusion of nonpayers from viewing motion pictures was a simple matter. In the days of the kinetoscope ("peep show" viewing machines widely used between 1893 and 1896), watching "movies" was originally limited to one customer per exhibition device.[8] Guback has noted the inefficiency of this means of exhibition in terms of revenue produced per exhibition and of the rate of amortising production costs.[9] Large-screen projectors introduced to the market in 1896 provided a more efficient system in this regard, projecting movies onto a silver screen so they could be viewed by a large audience, thereby increasing the revenue produced per exhibition. Such audiences were already gathered in vaudeville theaters. Hence, producers of vaudeville shows incorporated movies as a novelty and labor-saving technology. Eventually, filmed entertainment replaced live entertainment as the dominant mode of cultural production and consumption.

Vaudeville served as the primary exhibition outlet for motion pictures up to 1906. It also provided the film industry with a marketing model: vertical and horizontal integration; a national distribution system that handled bookings and exchanges with regional circuits of theaters; and the strategy of targeting the middle-class audience.[10] By 1905, with the rise of nickelodeons and film exchanges, the theatrical motion picture became a mass-produced and mass-distributed cultural product. Film producers found the narrative form most conducive to "regularising and stabilising production," a prime example of how the logic of industrialised culture influences the form of cultural commodities.[11]

As in the early history of book publishing, the new medium drew on accumulated intellectual creativity as it appropriated classics, novels, plays, and other popular literature. No compensation was paid to authors of original works because copyright did not contemplate these rights.[12] This was just one incident in the evolution of the industry's copyright system where technological and structural changes outpaced legislative and legal developments. Congress amended the 1909 Copyright Act in 1912 to specifically include "motion-picture photoplays" and "motion pictures other than photoplays" and, by extension, the right to authorise their exhibition.[13] In short, copyright law was broadened to conform to the industry's structure and mode of operation.

Consumer access to theatrical motion pictures was originally attained only through direct payment at the theater box office. At this retail level, going to the motion picture theater is much like buying a book; access to the motion picture theater is a system of direct payment lor the privilege of consuming the product. Unlike the consumer of the book, however, the consumer of the motion picture at the theater can only secure access for a single use per payment. Unlike a book itself, the movie consumed in the theater cannot be "kept" in any tangible way by the consumer nor shared with others beyond oral or written accounts. Thus, motion picture exhibition in theaters remains an effective way of dealing with the public-good character of film by excluding nonpayers at the turnstile. At this level, exclusion is more a function of the communications technology (film, projector, screen) and tangible property (land, the building, furnishings), than of copyright law.

Still, copyright is fundamental to addressing the problem of appropriability because it serves as the basis for contracts between the different sectors of the motion picture industry—production, distribution, and exhibition. It prevents unauthorised copying of prints and unlicensed exhibition through the threat or pursuit of civil litigation and criminal complaints. In this regard, the industry has a functional need for a copyright system. It enforces the right of exclusion by permitting legal action against those not authorised to use the copyrighted work. It also facilitates the transfer of rights concerning the use of particular properties between industry sectors while punishing those who attempt to make unauthorised use of the property. As long as the filmed entertainment industry could monitor the use of film prints and collect compensation for their use, the copyright system functioned rather effectively. This became more difficult as new communications technologies broadened the stream through which filmed entertainment flowed.

Broadcasting: The Problem of Exclusion

When television first appeared as a mass medium during the 1950s, there was some reluctance by the major motion picture producers to sell their products to broadcasters, mainly out of fear of losing their audiences.

By keeping theatrical feature films from television, the filmed entertainment industry owners sought to compel consumers to keep coming to the theater to view them. Obviously, theaters provided a better response to the problem of excluding nonpayers than the system of broadcasting.

Direct sales of programming to consumers via broadcasting is inherently problematic. Consequently, in the early days of radio broadcasting, the medium's public-good character generated some uncertainty about how programming would be paid for and nonpayers excluded. Broadcasters developed various mechanisms to receive remuneration for the delivery of information and entertainment to consumers. At first, radio manufacturers and department stores provided programming to consumers without charge as a means of promoting the sale of radio receivers. However, as radio receiver sales reached market saturation, it was clear that the one-time sale of radio sets could not cover the high costs of programming, which at that time consisted mainly of copyrighted musical recordings and live musical and dramatic performances. For this reason, Canada and Great Britain controlled access and payment for programming at the point of the receiver set under a licensing system. In such systems, radio-set owners pay an annual tax on their receiving device with the proceeds earmarked tor the support of public broadcast program production.[14]

The U.S. system of advertiser-supported broadcasting, which commodified audiences and concentrated on excluding advertisers, addressed the problem of charging consumers for radio programming and excluding nonpayers. In this system, the audience's time and attention is the private property of broadcasters. Broadcasters are able to commodify the audience as a result of their ownership of the means of transmission and their exclusive license to transmit on government-allocated frequencies. In turn, they purchase the right to use copyrighted works and transmit them in hopes of generating an audience to sell to advertisers.

The same companies that pioneered and came to dominate network radio broadcasting in the United States (CBS, NBC, and NBC spinoff ABC) played a central role in establishing television broadcasting. For radio station owners, advertisers, and recording companies that owned music copyrights, the national-network, advertiser-supported broadcast model had proven its efficiency and profitability. The "logic" of industrialised culture determined that television would be an important outlet for copyrighted filmed entertainment programming, even if film industry owners resisted this at first. By the mid-1950s, minor producers began licensing films from their libraries for broadcast, and the major Hollywood studios followed soon after.

In 1961, NBC bought rights to exhibit a package of theatrical motion pictures from copyright owner Twentieth Century Fox for a regular, weekly broadcast of movies during prime time (NBC's "Saturday Night at the Movies"). Both advertisers and networks were delighted to discover by the mid-1960s that feature films could often attract larger audiences than regular series and other programming. Eventually, the revenues generated from the sale of television exhibition rights became an integral part of the system for financing the production of motion pictures. Motion picture theaters and broadcast television provided the primary outlets for filmed entertainment up to the mid-1970s.

"Efficient" Filmed Entertainment Delivery Systems

Still, when dealing with the problem of exclusion,

broadcasting cannot be considered as efficient, in terms of per-consumer net revenue, as direct payment at the box office. Producers and distributors of film and television entertainment have recognised that higher returns are possible from direct payment for home viewing of film and video entertainment. Accordingly, in the belief that consumers are willing or can be convinced to pay more, they have set about the task of shifting more of their production from advertiser- to consumer-supported viewing.[15] "Basic" cable, pay-cable, pay-per-view, microwave, and satellite television are various forms of subscription television that can significantly improve the revenues generated per consumer for film and video entertainment. The better the technology for excluding nonpayers, the higher the revenue potential per viewer. For example, a single pay-per-view exhibition of a movie generates S3-$4 per household compared to only $10 per month per household for as many as sixteen to twenty movies typically offered in a pay-movie channel package.

"Event" programs, such as major boxing matches, the Olympics, or rock concerts, can generate even more income per household. In 1989, 270,000 pay-per-viewers paid $22.50 to see a televised Rolling Stones concert. The Evander Holyfield-George Foreman heavyweight title fight, in April 1991, drew 1.4 million homes paying $35.95 each. NBC, in partnership with Cablevision Systems Corp., spent about $200 million to sccurc rights, produce, and promote various pay-per-view packages of the 1992 Olympic games held in Barcelona. Although NBC probably lost money on this deal, Thomas Rogers, president of NBC Cable, said it served the larger purpose of easing the way for pay-per-view projects and transforming the way sports will be broadcast and sold in the future.[16] In terms relevant to this discussion, Rogers described pay-per-view as "a theater with infinite seats."[17] However, the pay-per-view industry is concerned that too many people are sitting in the same seat. It seems that pay-per-view often is used when entertaining guests, a practice that reduces potential revenues per viewer. For this reason, Tom Neville, Showtime Event Television's vice president of research, admitted that the long-term growth strategy for the business involved encouraging people to view events in smaller groups, that is, to promote the privatised consumption of film and video programming.[18]

Although pay-TV channels, such as Home Box Office and the Disney Channel, improve the efficiency of per-use revenues over broadcasting, they still represent a form of bundling, another common marketing mechanism for dealing with the problem of exclusion.[19] In pay-cable television and other subscription systems, movies are bundled and sold in a per-channel package. Access is essentially controlled by limiting the availability of the transmitted signals to those who have paid for their use. Scrambling and descrambling systems are utilised to prevent unauthorised uses. Copyright law provides the grounds for stopping those who attempt to make unauthorised use with the threat of fines and/or prison terms. Under the 1984 Cable Act, a person who willfully makes unauthorised use of cable communications can be fined up to $1,000 and/or imprisoned for up to six months.[20] Anyone who pirates cable services for commercial gain can be fined up to $50,000 and/or imprisoned for up to two years.[21]

In contrast to pay-TV channels such as Home Box Office and Showtime, pay-per-view cable and over-the-air pay-per-view TV represent direct, unbundled, and unsponsored delivery of motion pictures and other entertainment programming. David Waterman argued that pay-per-view permits the same kind of self-selection of high-value customers for individual movies as does the theater turnstile.[22] These marketing systems make exclusion possible on a per-program, per-customer basis. In this case, a payment is required for access to each program that is carried on the delivery system. Foreseeing a shift to marketing mechanisms based on pay-per-view, Besen predicted that advertiser support is likely to become proportionately less important for the support of television.[23]

The filmed entertainment industry's interest in pay-per-view can be traced back to the early 1980s. In 1983, Universal conducted the first pay-per-view day-and-date theatrical release with the feature film *The Pirates of Penzance.* Columbia Pictures, then a subsidiary of the Coca-Cola Company had a mid-1980s "growth strategy" that sought "to maximise the efficient use of distribution systems."[24] To encourage the growth of pay-per-view, Columbia released the film *Ghostbusters* to pay-per-view in 1985, breaking all previous records for earnings by this outlet.

The shift to pay-per-view suggests that new communications technologies are not being developed in response to consumer demand for new delivery mechanisms but rather in response to the desire of copyright owners to exploit their intellectual property more efficiently. Accordingly, Vincent Mosco described "the essence of our time" as the *"Pay-per Society"* in which the "driving force *is* commodification"; a society in which we increasingly "pay-per call, pay-per view, pay-per bit or screenful of information, etc."[25]

There is a long history of concern about the effects of this shift from advertiser-supported television to pay-per-view upon the availability of information and entertainment programming to those who lack economic means or technological access.[26] Given the logic of informational and cultural commodities, the attrition of programming from broadcast to pay and videocassette formats is occurring to a significant degree. As noted above, sports programmers increasingly are shifting major sporting events to pay-TV, pay-per-view, or cable-delivered "superstations." For example, portions of the Wimbledon or U.S. Open tennis championships are only available on Home Box Office; early rounds of the National Basketball Association playoffs are exclusively on the Turner Broadcasting System's cable networks, TNT and WTBS; other major-league sports are available only on regional cable sports networks; and ESPN's 1989 deal with Major League Baseball greatly increased the number of games available per season on cable but resulted in a net reduction of the number of games available on network television.[27] The chair of Showtime (Viacom Inc.'s pay-TV channel) predicted that the Super Bowl "will eventually be on pay-per-view."[28] Several sports teams already run pay-per-view operations, among them the San Diego Padres, Minnesota Twins, Cincinnati Reds, the Louisiana State University's football program, and the Portland Trailblazers.

Furthermore, much film and video entertainment will not make it to broadcast television (network or local), for example, those cable network or superstation "broadcast" premieres and special "made-for-cable movies" that do not get picked up by the broadcast networks or are not affordable or interesting to the small and midsised independent or network-affiliated broadcasters. Networks, their affiliates, and independents know that ratings for motion picture broadcasts are lower if the film has been available on cable and videocassette for some time. Some interesting made-for-cable motion pictures, specials, or scries programming also may never appear on broadcast television because of language, nudity, or the alternative lifestyles they depict, primarily due to broadcasters' fears of alienating portions of the audience that they must sell to advertisers.

Cost and access to new communications technology are factors creating further gaps between the information-rich and the information-poor. Cable television passed about 95 per cent of U.S. homes by 1993, but only 62 per cent of those households subscribed.[29] In mid-1993, the average monthly basic-cable bill was $21, and cost was cited as the primary reason by nonsubscribers for not taking the service.[30] The U.S. Commerce Department predicted that household cable penetration would level out at 70 per cent by the turn of the century.[31] Pay-per-view capacity, in terms of addressable cable households, was available to only about 20 million cable subscribers in 1993.[32] Converter boxes for interactive television systems range from $600 to $1,000. To receive Hughes Communications Inc.'s 150-channel, direct-broadcast satellite service requires a $700 satellite dish.

The attrition of information and entertainment from broadcast to pay programming and the threat this poses to the quality of "free" TV[33] has regularly been invoked in policy discussions surrounding the development and deployment of new communications technologies, as it was in the cases of both the cable retransmission copyright and home-video recording rights. In the former case, broadcasters convinced the FCC in the mid-1960s that their industry suffered an unfair disadvantage when they had to pay royalties for the use of copyrighted programming while cable operators did not. Later broadcasters argued that pay-TV and cable would eventually siphon "quality" programming and major sporting events from broadcast television, a successful argument that led to a set of rules promulgated by the FCC to prevent this.

Similarly, in response to home taping of broadcasts on VCRs, copyright owners argued that the value of broadcast markets would decline as advertisers began accounting for commercials "zapped" by home tapers or "zipped" through upon replay, thereby reducing the number of audience members who view the commercial messages contained in the broadcast. Filmed entertainment industry officials predicted that the "quality" of broadcast television would decline because of the resulting decrease in advertising revenues. Implicit in this prediction is the threat of an investment strike. Capitalist media owners are suggesting that if they are unable to appropriate what they see as adequate compensation for the use of their property they will make their investments elsewhere.

These cases make apparent the contradiction between the search for greater efficiency through new technologies and the loss of control over intellectual property that these technologies engender. For example, the VCR facilitates direct, unbundled sale of filmed entertainment and other video programs to consumers and overcomes the problem ol exclusion by rebuilding them with a private good (i.e., the recorded videocassette). Compared to bundled delivery systems, such as broadcasting or pay-TV channels, the videocassette is more efficient in terms of net-revenue earnings per viewer. At the same time, the VCR has reduced the control that filmed entertainment copyright owners have traditionally held over their property. Consumers can now record movies and other programs from broadcast and cable television, they can buy or make copies of them, and they can use them when they choose. The VCR has also prompted piracy of filmed entertainment on an unprecedented scale around the world. Finally, the rental of prerecorded videocassettes represents a whole new industry over which the filmed entertainment producer-distributors have only indirect control. Because of the first sale doctrine embodied in the federal copyright provisions,[34] filmed entertainment copyright owners receive remuneration only from the first sale of the prerecorded videocassette to the video rental operator but not from each subsequent rental.

Hollywood studios earned an estimated $2 billion from selling videocassettes to rental operations in 1991 and about the same in 1992.[35] Their take from the videocassette outlet could be much larger if they could benefit from each rental of the video. It is logical, therefore, for filmed entertainment production-distribution companies to pursue alternatives to the video rental system. One highly successful strategy is to sell videocassettes directly to consumers, which earned video distributors about $2.5 billion in 1992.[36] The Walt Disney Company has led the shift from video rentals to video sales with its strategy of "selling through" classic and current theatrical feature films. In 1992, Disney captured 40 per cent of the total U.S. video sell-through business.[37] *Beauty and the Beast* carried a suggested retail price of $24.99 and wholesaled for about $13.50. Each videocassette costs about $2 to manufacture and $2 to market. Disney expected to sell 20 million copies of this film, earning it an estimated $270 million from just this one video.[38] This comes on top of the $145 million the film earned at the U.S. box office and the additional $200 million taken in at box offices around the world.[39] It is estimated that Disney earned more than three-quarters of its 1992 fiscal year operating profit of $508.2 million from home video.[40] Disney's success in the video sell-through market demonstrates the viability of this market, which now surpasses the revenues earned by the Hollywood majors from sales to rental operators. It also points to the importance of copyright protection of prerecorded videocassettes to Disney, since video piracy could have an enormous effect on the company's profits.

The filmed entertainment industry's other strategy to gain greater efficiency in delivery of its products is to continue to develop pay-per-view. The movie studios were already earning an average of about $250,000 for each film shown on pay-per-view in 1988, for a total take that year of $36 million.[41] Showtime Event Television estimated that total gross pay-per-view revenue earned by feature films in 1992 would be $140 million out of a total take of $329 million, the remainder to come largely from boxing ($86 million) and wrestling ($68 million).[42] Paul Kagan Associates Inc. estimated that total gross pay-per-view revenues for 1992 came to $337.7 million; out of this, $108.2 million (28.6 per cent) was earned by mainstream movies and $76 million (20.1 per cent) by "exploitation/adult" programming, giving filmed entertainment about half of all pay-per-view revenues.[43]

Adult programming has become the most stable category in terms of pay-per-view revenue, taking up to 40 per cent of all movie revenue on some cable systems.[44] Film and video pornography also drove the worldwide penetration of the VCR by offering the opportunity to watch this type of programming in the privacy of one's home rather than at the theater. Pay-per-view offers even greater anonymity since the videocassette still must be purchased, either through the mail or at adult bookstores, or purchased or rented from video retailers, a factor especially important in small towns and morally conservative regions.

The filmed entertainment industry is seeking to capture the pay-per-view market as it did the cable and videocassette markets. Twentieth Century Fox was the first studio to make a direct move into pay-per-view in 1992 when it, along with Tele-Communications Inc. (TCI), bought into Request Television, which delivers pay-per-view channels via satellite to cable system operators. Request Television planned to offer 30-50 pay-per-view channels by 1994.

Request Television and Viewer's Choice, a similar service, are strategically positioned to dominate the pay-per-view market, having linked up with the major multisystem cable operators. Both companies also have contracts with the major filmed entertainment companies, though the form of these agreements remains in flux. Warner Bros. Pay Television has sought contracts with Request Television and Viewer's Choice that tie pay-per-view network shelf space to box-office revenues, meaning that if Warner Bros, generated 20 per cent of all box-office revenues in any one year, then the pay-per-view networks would have to devote 20 per cent of their schedules to the studio's films.[45] Under this system, pay-per-view movie services will simply become one more outlet for filmed entertainment controlled by the same core firms, as have cable delivery systems and VCRs.

The next step toward more efficient delivery systems is called "video on demand." Existing pay-per-view systems that deliver movies are still bundled. The prototype was Time Warner's 150-channel cable-TV system in Queens, New York, which included fifty-five channels delivering a choice of seventeen pay-per-view movies around the clock. With movies starting every half-hour and costing $3.95 each, the cable operator determined the choice of movies to run on each channel as well as the times they played. In such a system, the viewer cannot control the flow of the film as one can a videocassette playing on a VCR. Actual video-on-de-mand systems would allow consumers to call up movies of their choice from a central database in which they are digitally stored. A control box at the viewer's television set would permit storage and playback of the film by the viewer. The choice of product that consumers make, of course, depends upon what films have been stored and what they know about what is available.

Major information and media firms began earnest testing

of several variations of video-on-demand systems during the early 1990s. For information and communications companies, video-on-demand, interactive television, and multimedia systems are the future. Killen & Associates, Inc., a provider of multimedia information products, issued a report in early 1993 predicting that by the year 2000 the interactive television market would be worth $200 billion to consumer electronics and computer suppliers alone.[46] TCI, the largest multiple system operator (MSO) in the United States, took the first major step toward an actual video-on-demand system, announcing in December 1992 that it would introduce digital compression technology allowing the transmission of digitised data from a central operations post, via satellite, to its cable systems. The compressed data would permit the systems to deliver as many as 500 channels to TCI's 11 million or so customers, though they will require set-top converters to navigate their way through the myriad of channels. This is still only a virtual video-on-demand system, since TCI will be programming the 500 or so channels.

An even more significant step in the direction of video on demand was taken in 1993 when the US West telephone company bought a $2.5 billion, 25 per cent stake in Time Warner Entertainment, a limited partnership controlled by Time Warner that operated the company's cable systems, Warner Bros., and HBO/Cinemax. Two Japanese companies, C. Itochu Corp., a trading company, and Toshiba Corp., the electronics firm, owned 11.5 per cent of the partnership. Time Warner brought the software and the cable infrastructure to the deal while US West provided the expertise in storage, delivery, and switching technologies required to handle the large amount of data contained in filmed entertainment. Thus, the alliance linked the data, the storage systems, and the retrieval technology required for video on demand.

Another phone company, Southwestern Bell, has taken similar steps toward providing video on demand. Early in 1993, Southwestern became the first phone company to buy into the cable-TV business, purchasing two cable systems from Hauser Communications Inc. located in Montgomery County, Maryland, and Arlington County, Virginia (together serving a total of 500,000 homes). Soon thereafter, the company announced it was selling a 25 per cent stake in its British cable systems to Cox Cable Communications. Cox's emphasis has been on upgrading its coaxial cable systems to fiber optics, giving it the potential to do such things as send specialised advertising to different neighborhoods as well as to provide video on demand. The company has also moved into the software side of the business, taking stakes in cable networks, Discovery Channel, and the E! entertainment network; producing shows such as *Star Search and Lifestyles of the Rich and Famous;* buying a syndication company, Rysher Entertainment, that has several new series in production; and taking a 35 per cent stake in U.K. Gold, a British television network that mines the archives of the British Broadcasting Corp. and Thames Television.[47] In mid-1994, Cox announced the purchase of the cable systems owned by Times Mirror, significantly expanding its multisystem operations.

Signaling a willingness to cross the lines in the battle between newspaper companies and phone companies over who should control electronic information systems, Cox began discussions with another phone company in June 1993, BellSouth Corp., to jointly provide classified advertising and yellow pages data through household and business phones and computers.[48] Another regional phone company, Bell Atlantic, announced plans in late 1992 to deliver fully interactive cable-TV programming over its phone lines in Morris County, New Jersey, to some 8,000 customers.

Another notable alliance, announced in mid-1993, involved AT&T and Viacom and signals the further blurring of boundaries between the information and entertainment industries. The companies began testing interactive programming services on Viacom's advanced, two-way cable system already operating in Castro Valley, California. AT&T brought its all-digital network video server technology to the deal, which permits the simultaneous delivery of video games, video on demand, home shopping, and interactive advertising to customers by compressing data and delivering information or movies at different speeds depending upon user demand for the product. Viacom would draw upon its software lines to provide the programming for the system. With this system, viewers could select a video from MTV's top-five playlist, then would be offered the opportunity to buy the long-form video on which the clip appears or the CD from which it came, and then would be given the option of buying tickets for the group's next performance in the area.[49] With regards to movies, an AT&T official described the system as making available in the subscriber's home "the entire contents of a videocassette rental store, 24 hours a day."[50]

In the early to mid-1990s, such alliances began to rapidly proliferate in a number of directions involving different facets of the interactive multimedia process. The alliances involved the core information and communications firms seeking to extend their power and influence into new technology realms. There may be a few new entrants as the need for specific technological devices and standards opens some niche markets, but the playing field is clearly slanted in favor of the established core firms. Indeed, it appears that there is once again much more coordination than competition among them. A partial list of joint ventures contemplated or announced in the early 1990s is revealing in this regard:

- an IBM and Rogers Communications Inc. eighteen-month test in Toronto using cable-TV lines to let business people send each other images, conduct video conferences, and work on the same spreadsheet
- an AT&T, US West, and TCI test of video on demand in Littleton, Colorado
- a TV Answer Inc. and Hewlett Packard Co. service to beam data laden radio waves to television sets in *a* tew major cities
- an Apple Computer Inc. and Toshiba Corp. plan to develop multimedia product that blends text, graphics, video, and sound for use by entertainment, education, and information services
- an initiative called First Cities, a multimedia alliance of eleven big computer and phone firms, including Apple, Tandem Computers Inc., US West, Bell Communications Research (Bellcore), Corning Inc., Eastman Kodak, IBM, North American Philips, and Southwestern Bell, aiming to develop and deliver interactive multimedia technology to 100,000 households in 1994
- an alliance between 3DO Co., Time Warner, and Matsushita to produce "interactive multiplayers," set-top controllers that allow users to play games, watch movies, listen to music, shop electronically, edit family videotapes, and so on
- an Intel Corp., Microsoft Corp., and General Instrument Corp. alliance; to develop a similar set-top device
- a Kaleida Labs Inc. (a joint software venture of IBM and Apple), Motorola Inc., and Scientific-Atlanta Inc. alliance to develop the software and hardware for delivering interactive and

multimedia services to homes through cable television networks

- an NBC, Nielsen Media Research, TCI, and Cablevision Systems Corp. alliance, called Interactive Network, to provide interactive TV programming and services, and
- an IBM and NBC joint venture to provide "news on demand."

Concerned about the proliferation of technological devices and standards, Time Warner and TCI, the two largest cable operators in the United States, announced a joint venture in 1993 to establish cable industry standards for the interactive multimedia systems of the future to be based upon "open architecture" that allows different hardware and software systems to communicate with one another. With 17 million of the 60 million U.S. cable households, the two companies provide enough purchasing volume to determine standards for the various components of these systems, particularly set-top converters, components inside the converter, and the computerised switches that direct movies, data, and voice through the networks.[51]

The logic of informational and cultural commodities and the logic of capital are driving these developments. These structural forces manifest themselves in the form of a consensus among the members of the hegemonic core of the capitalist class about the necessity and inevitability of new technologies. Core firms are worried about controlling the introduction and proliferation of new technologies so they do not jeopardise their oligopolistic status. Capitalists are attracted by the potential of investing in another Apple Computer, Microsoft, or TCI, success stories that propelled their major owners into the ranks of the super rich. John Hendricks, the creator of the Discovery Channel cable network and developer of a video-on-demand system called

Your Choice TV, argued that it is no more possible to stand in the way of video on demand than it was to stand in the way of cable television in 1975.[52]

For these reasons, interactive multimedia systems are another case of supply creating demand, very unlike the ideal models of a capitalist market system where demand determines supply. Indeed, consumers remain skeptical of these systems and reluctant to participate in the hype. Congress passed federal legislation rereg-ulating cable prices in the fall of 1992 in response to constituents' complaints about spiraling cable bills.[53] Only 44 per cent of subscribers surveyed by the Roper Organisation in 1993 felt that cable television was a good or excellent value for the money, and 33 per cent said the same about premium pay-cable channels.[54] An early 1992 survey by Family Opinion Inc. for the Conference Board asked members of 6,500 households to rate fifty widely used goods and services in terms of a "good," "fair," or "poor" value. Fresh poultry and videocassette rentals rated first and second, but pay-per-view TV bumped hospital charges as the worst buy on the list.[55] For this reason, both Veronis, Suhler & Associates, a New York investment bank, and the U.S. Department of Commerce concluded that pay-per-view would not have an immediate effect on home-video rental operations.[56] Nevertheless, the largest videocassette rental/retail operator in the United States, Blockbuster Entertainment Corp., is preparing for the eventual decline of the videocassette rental market, emphasising sales of prerecorded videocassettes; buying video retail stores in foreign markets where video on demand is a longer way off; entering into the music retailing business in the United States and Europe; buying a 48.2 per cent stake in the Spelling Entertainment Group, a television and motion picture production company; and joining the Viacom-Paramount alliance.

For owners of filmed entertainment copyrights, the new media promise to serve as valuable ancillary outlets in which they can cycle and recycle their intellectual property. If cable television and the VCR provide any guide to predicting future developments, which is precisely what this book seeks to do, the new communications technologies will eventually be brought into the marketing systems controlled by the dominant core firms. However, control over the use of film and video works remains problematic. With digital storage, transmission, and recording devices, it is possible to reproduce perfect copies of films and television programs. The next challenge to the filmed entertainment industry is how to capitalise on these new technologies without exacerbating the problem of unauthorised uses. Accordingly, for the filmed entertainment companies, it is imperative that they become partners in the various alliances that are developing and deploying these technologies, in order to ensure that they will include encryption, scrambling, and/or self-destructing mechanisms to prevent unauthorised uses and copying of copyrighted material. As the costs for filmed entertainment and information goods continue to rise, the temptation to seek ways to take a " free ride" by not paying for them also increases, especially given the high cost of of producing these goods in the first place.

The Economics of Filmed Entertainment

Another feature that economists note about informational and cultural products is that most of their production costs occur in producing the original version, whereas reproduction costs are relatively small. This makes for what Priest called "high investment-to-reproduction costs," that is, the creation costs of information divided by the cost of reproducing one unit of the good.[57] For example, the cost of producing an additional copy of an original feature-length film print might be $1,300, a mere fraction of the cost of producing the original, which for the major studios averaged $28.8 million in 1992.[58] Reproduction costs are relatively low because the raw materials (the movie set and equipment) and labor (actors, directors, technicians, etc.) that went into producing the original print do not have to be reassembled to reproduce another unit of the good (i.e., a copy of the original).

Thus, what makes information and filmed entertainment different from mass-produced tangible goods is what A. Allan Schmid called "the situation where the marginal cost of another use or user approaches or is zero (MC=0)."[59] Here we are concerned with the costs that additional consumers of the. product—either broadcasters, cable network operators, theater owners, or individual audience members—impose on the production, distribution, or exhibition of a particular film or program. For example, adding viewers to a broadcast audience adds nothing to the costs of producing and little to the costs of distributing a particular program but does raise income produced by the exhibition of the work as a result of higher advertising revenues. Similarly, filling the theater with additional consumers for a single showing of a feature film (until the house is full) adds nothing to the cost of that particular exhibition. This case is much like air transport of passengers where additional passengers add little to the cost of providing the service (i.e., until the plane is full). In contrast, the consumption of a private good, such as an automobile, is exclusive and therefore requires fixed expenditures for the production and distribution of an additional unit of that good in order to satisfy an additional consumer.

A motion picture can be bundled with a private, tangible good; for example, when placed on a videocassette. Serving an additional customer requires the assembly, taping, and distribution of an additional prerecorded videocassette, but the motion picture itself does not have to be reproduced. The nature of information goods to have high fixed costs and relatively low reproduction and distribution costs is the primary reason that copyright protection is required. Copyright seeks to stop pirates who can reproduce and distribute copies of information goods without paying the high fixed costs that went into producing the original and thus undercut the price set by the first "publisher." Copyright pro-tects an owner's exclusive rights to authorise any copying or derivative works so that fixed costs can be recovered and profits made.

In the case of information commodities, when any set of buyers (for example, theatergoers) pays enough to cover the original fixed costs, the additional sales to other sets of buyers (broadcasters, VCR rental shops, foreign distributors, etc.) constitute profits. Accordingly, it is logical for copyright owners of films to seek additional sales outlets for their property, either more theaters, new media, or new geographic markets, especially given the great profit potential of a "hit" film. However, the ability of copyright owners to extend their markets is restricted to available technologies for distribution and exhibition of filmed entertainment and by copyright laws that govern the uses of these technologies. Each communications technology also requires correlated marketing mechanisms for authorising use of copyrighted works and collecting for each use. The filmed entertainment industry uses new technologies in a marketing sequence that permits them to squeeze the most revenue out of each use of its product.

The Role of New Media Markets in Price Discrimination

According to economic analysts, another reason intellectual property markets have traditionally functioned inefficiently, even where exclusion is possible, is that owners of intellectual property have trouble establishing the exact price differentials that reflect the variations in the value of the information to distinct audiences.[60] For Priest, the "character of information to be non-monetizable" results from its intangibility and the problems of measuring the value of information. He defined "valuable" information as that which increases one's efficiency by increasing one's knowledge about a number of possible choices, thereby increasing one's probability of achieving positive outcomes. But because there are so many forms of information and so many potential outcomes, it is difficult for individuals or groups to determine specific values of any information. This is also complicated by the existence of free riders who, if possible, will not pay for information they value.

Priest's definition is too rationalistic in its assumption that people choose, for example, which motion picture to attend on the basis of the value of the information the film holds for them in future decision making.[61] McQuail noted that entertainment is typically consumed as an end in itself, for its immediate value, most often as an escape from a present "reality," with no particular thought to its future utility.[62] The decision about which motion picture to attend is based more often on prior experience with the medium, that is, a favorite star, director, genre, or the like, and can be predicted to a certain extent by such demographic characteristics as age, education, and income among other factors. Intellectual property owners attempt to capitalise on variations in demand among consumers, however genuine or created, to discriminate among them in terms of prices. The owners try to generate the highest net income that consumers as a whole are willing to pay for viewing or owning an individual work that was orginally captured on film or video.

In filmed entertainment markets such price

discrimination is rooted in the system of first- and sub-run theaters organised and controlled by the Hollywood majors during the studio era. Douglas Gomery stated that the five major film production-distribution companies, Warner Bros., Paramount, Twentieth Century-Fox, MGM, and RKO, developed this system to reduce risk and to ensure continuity of control.[63] The price-discrimination system served three basic purposes for the "Big Five" in this regard: It minimised the number of theaters they needed to own outright to control the industry; permitted the full and uninterrupted utilisation of their theaters; and helped keep transaction costs low.[64] Waterman suggested that the move toward television and away from the sub-run theater system was a trade-off of the higher pricing efficiency of the theater box office for the still lower distribution costs the electronic medium permitted.[65] Now this pricing efficiency has come to the television-based electronic media with pay-per-view and prerecorded videocassettes.

Price discrimination remains an essential feature of the current release sequence for motion pictures. The marketing cycle itself is made possible by copyright, which under U.S. law gives copyright proprietors exclusive rights to reproduction, adaptation, distribution, performance, and display. The fragmentation of the motion picture marketing sequence demonstrates how copyright is infinitely divisible and flexible enough to be applied to evolving technologies. Typically, the motion picture distribution process begins with theaters, which continue to play a crucial role in determining the value of the feature film in subsequent markets. Then, rights are made available for home video and pay-per-view cable, Television Receive Only (TVRO) or satellite systems, followed by pay-TV systems (HBO/ Cinemax, Showtime/The Movie Channel) and any subscription-TV services (microwave or satellite), then network television, back to pay-TV, and finally on to syndication to independent television stations, superstations (WTBS, WGN, WOR, etc.) and cable networks (USA, The Family Channel, Arts and Entertainment, etc.).

By 1991, after-theater markets accounted for 60 per cent of the revenues earned by U.S. filmed entertainment distributors.[66] Note that the less efficient means of distribution in terms of exclusion (e.g., broadcasting) appear at the end of the release sequence, confirming the decreasing value of this market in relation to more direct means of delivery and payment. This shows again that distinctions are developing between cable/pay-cable and broadcast television in terms of what and when programming will be available. It also shows how rights transfers have become increasingly complex from the days when theaters and broadcast television were the only outlets for owners of copyrighted filmed entertainment.

Not only has the typical release sequence for a theatrical feature film become more complex, it has also become a site of competitive struggle between sectors and firms that operate within or draw upon the filmed entertainment industry. For example, TCI announced a deal in May 1993 to invest $90 million in Carolco Pictures in exchange for the rights to three showings of up to four new Carolco movies on its pay-per-view network. These films were offered on pay-per-view the weekend before they were released for theatrical exhibition. TCI chose Carolco because of the event-like quality of its big-budget movies, such as *Terminator 2: Judgment Day*, *Total Recall*, and *Basic Instinct*. The announcement generated protests from theater owners, video dealers, and virtually every major studio. MGM, which invested $60 million in Carolco for worldwide distribution rights starting in 1994, announced it would not distribute the Carolco films released for pay-per-view before the theater "window," stating that the deal excluded movies already released to television. Warner Bros., Fox, Paramount, Disney, Tri-Star, MCA/Universal, and Orion echoed MGM with the sentiment that films should be seen on the big screen first.[67]

The National Association of Theater Owners (NATO) sent an open letter to the industry, stating that "NATO is dedicated to preserving the 'window' for the full and complete theatrical release of motion pictures. Destruction of this window as proposed in the recently announced TCI-Carolco deal is inimical to the interests of the entire filmed entertainment industry."[68] Several theater chains said they would not exhibit films that went to pay-per-view first, including Pacific Theaters (general partner of Time Warner), Loews Theaters (owned by Sony-Columbia) and the Cineplex Odeon Corp. (owned by Matsushita-Universal). The studios' resistance to the deal was based on the desire to maintain the theater box office, the most efficient system of exclusion and the outlet where the highest-value customers can be found, as the initial venue for feature films. Furthermore, their oligopolistic status was jeopardised by a powerful firm from another industry sector, TCI, and by a peripheral firm within their sector, Carolco, which had little to lose and much to gain by challenging the prevailing marketing structure.

Video dealers were similarly cool to the announcement, for it meant that pay-per-view would precede them in the feature film release sequence. In terms of the logic of efficient delivery, having pay-per-view precede videocassette release is probably not a concern shared by the filmed entertainment producer-distributors, except for concerns about people taping a pay-per-view movie in lieu of buying the prerecorded videocassette. Indeed, both video dealers and studio executives expressed concern about piracy of the films despite promises by TCI to scramble them.[69]

Videotaped copies of the film would threaten both theater attendance and video sales and rentals. The industry's experience has been, particularly with cable delivery systems, that given enough time and money inventive entrepreneurs can produce descrambling systems to render any copy-protection system irrelevant. The case again points out the contradiction between greater efficiency in terms of revenue take and the loss of control over intellectual property the new technologies introduce.

The Non-Depletability of Informational and Cultural Commodities

The release sequences for motion pictures and television programs take place in the context of rerelease sequences of motion pictures and television programs from film libraries. Copyright owners benefit from long-term legal protection that allows them to recycle their properties through existing as well as emergent media forms and to continue earning royalties. This results in broadcast of "classic" and "colorised" movies by local stations, superstations, and cable networks. Public television stations regularly feature "classic" films; Turner's superstation WTBS shows "colorised classics"; the American Movie Classics is a cable network that shows old movies twenty-four hours a day; and the Encore pay-cable channel features movies from the 1960s, 1970s, and 1980s. Additionally, the major filmed entertainment companies rerelease "classic" and older "hit" movies and television programs on prerecorded videocassettes (an example of the latter being CBS Video Library's "Star Trek Collector's Edition," available only on a subscription/approval basis). This ability to recycle filmed entertainment reflects another unique characteristic of information that economists have identified—its nondepletability.

Information is not depleted when it is consumed, unlike

other raw materials such as oil or coal. This means that copyright owners who release their works into the marketplace are competing not only with other new releases but also with all like products and media that have accumulated from past creativity and publication. This is not to suggest that old products necessarily compete with equal vigor, since marketing efforts are generally concentrated on new releases and most revenues on theatrical or videocassette releases are made in their first few weeks or months on the market. In this sense, informational and cultural products also require something like a "built-in obsolescence," another marketing strategy for dealing with information market imperfections. Marketing efforts are aimed at drawing attention to the latest releases and creating the impression that they must be seen immediately. The more a consumer is convinced of this the higher the price he or she is willing to pay for access and consumption.

Nevertheless, the rerelease of certain very popular movies or television programs may have built-in momentum when they reenter the market, making them attractive for investment purposes. And since their production costs are already amortised, they are cheaper to bring to the marketplace and thus constitute a risk-reducing mechanism for media capitalists that need to fill channel capacity. For example, Ted Turner bought the MGM/UA Entertainment Company in 1986 in order to acquire the broadcast and video rights to the MGM film library. His company also owns the rights to many of RKO's and Warner Bros.'s early films. The Turner company plays these films on superstation WTBS, with some 55 million subscribers in 1991, and the films also serve as the primary source of programming for another Turner cable network, TNT, which served some 50 million homes in 1990.[70] Turner's company used the film library to launch TNT Latin America, with 1 million subscribers in 1993, and combined its film and cartoon libraries to launch and program Turner Network Television Europe.

Many of the MGM films have also been put on videocassette (e.g., a set of four John Wayne "classics" and four Fred Astaire-Ginger Rogers videocassettes reproduced from the MGM film library have been advertised for mail-order sale on WTBS). The library includes *Gone with the Wind, Casablanca, 2001: A Space Odyssey, The Wizard of Oz,* and *Singin' in the Rain.* Media capitalist Ted Turner recognised the value of these products in terms of the surplus value their stars continue to produce, whether living or not. After acquiring the library, Turner remarked: "We've got Spencer Tracy and Jimmy Cagney working for us from the grave."[71]

Another example of the nondepletable value of some informational and cultural goods is the regular rerelease of Disney's animated feature films, not only on videocassette but also for theatrical exhibition. For example, Disney rereleased *Bambi* for theatrical exhibition in the summer of 1988. The film was originally made for $2 million in 1942 and after several rereleases has earned more than $100 million at the box office alone, demonstrating the income-earning potential of some copyrighted filmed entertainment works over the long term. Disney's strict management of its copyright in this case also shows the effectiveness of copyright and motion picture theaters as systems conducive to exclusion. It also demonstrates the importance of long-term copyright protection as granted by statute. By keeping *Bambi* locked up in its film vaults, Disney was able to demand that exhibitors charge top dollar at the box office and cancel all passes, matinee and bargain admissions, and free admission for children at drive-ins for the 1988 rerelease. Recognising the already existing market value of the "Walt Disney Classic" *Bambi,* Sears, McDonald's, and Walt Disney World correlated marketing efforts with the release of the video. Newspaper ads promoting the film in the theater listings encouraged consumers to go to Sears to "see the exciting Bambi collection of toys and apparel," to "stop into McDonald's for a Bambi Happy Meal featuring Bambi, Thumper, and friends," and to visit Walt Disney World when in Florida.[72] For Disney, this collaboration was also a way to cut advertising costs by getting others to participate in the expense. As Meehan noted, such merchandising efforts not only produce revenues from licensing fees but also contribute to the hype surrounding the film.[73] The increased hype makes the film a "must-see" cultural phenomenon and, in turn, increases the number of high-value customers who will attend its theatrical release.

The summer rerelease of *101 Dalmatians* in 1991 further confirmed the timeless value of Disney's animated library, with the film becoming the most successful animated reissue ever, earning just over $60 million in box-office gross. Disney spent about $5 million or so making 1,800 new prints of the film and advertising it. After splitting the box-office gross with exhibitors, Disney probably made about $20 million off the film.[74] However, the small profit from the 1992 theaterical rerelease of *Pinocchio* indicated that a film may become overexposed. *Pinocchio* was the first of Disney's animated classics to complete an entire rere-lease circuit: to theaters in 1984, to home video in 1985, to the Disney Channel in 1986, and then to theaters again. Disney officials discounted the possibility that the nine showings on the Disney Channel permitted massive copying by its subscribers, saying instead that the film was not given enough time to "breathe" and that they would keep the film in the vaults for a longer period before its next theatrical exhibition.[75] But it did became the best-selling video of 1993 when it was rereleased in that format, with 10.2 million units shipped to retailers. Disney planned a seventh theatrical rerelease of its first animated classic, *Snow White and the Seven Dwarves,* in the summer of 1993 while company officials insisted that the film would never be released on video. A little more than a year later, Disney released Snow *White* on video. William Bryan recalculated the total gross box-office receipts for a number of classic films since their initial release adjusting for inflation, population growth, and increased personal income. He estimated that *Snow White* would be the second highest all-time moneymaker at $6.2 billion, after *Gone with the Wind* ($6.7 billion). By these calculations, Disney's animated classics hold five of the top six positions in Bryan's rankings.[76]

The ability of filmed entertainment copyright owners to exploit their property within a wide range of ancillary markets means that they can be expected to invest more in the development of the product.[77] Similarly, investors in filmed entertainment would be attracted to those products that have potentially long shelf lives. Disney seems to have discovered a formula for producing this type of product with its animated feature films, reproducing the "classic" quality of its older films with *The Little Mermaid, Beauty and the Beast, Aladdin,* and *The Lion King.* Disney also lowers production costs in terms of story rights by using classic fairy tales that exist in the public domain.

Economies of Scale and of Scope

As we have seen, marginal costs of reproducing and distributing informational and cultural products approach zero (origination costs being high in comparison to reproduction and distribution costs). Accordingly, media capitalists can benefit from economies of scale in the production and distribution of such goods. This means that for a wide range of information and entertainment copyright owners have the incentive to find ways to increase the number of paying consumers of their product if they can employ efficient means of exclusion. Such an increase in the scale of operations results in a decrease in costs per unit of the good, thereby achieving economies of scale. However, in the pursuit of economies of scale, industry concentration seems to be inevitable, and this has significant implications when it comes to the diversity and range of informational and cultural goods that are produced and distributed.

Economists generally hold that the cure to concentration is the restoration of competition either through continued "breakthroughs" and product innovations or antitrust policy. A central theme of this book, however, is that technological breakthroughs and product innovations, though perhaps originating at the periphery, eventually get incorporated into the core. The problem with antitrust policy, as Guback has argued, is that market concentration is predominately defined by economists and policymakers according to the narrow dichotomy between monopoly capitalism and competitive capitalism.[78] Furthermore, the vertical reintegration of the filmed entertainment industry in recent years demonstrates that without governmental vigilance the normal tendencies within capitalism toward concentration will prevail. For example, the result of increased centralisation and concentration of theater chain ownership, often in the hands of the studios, is fewer films playing in more theaters at the same time. The films that get released on a massive, national scale are those with big budgets and big stars, usually produced by the major studios. The effect is to displace smaller-budget, independent, or foreign films from the theatrical shelf space.

Even though the majors generally produce fewer than half of U.S. feature films, it is primarily the economies of scale they have achieved at the level of distribution that gives them the power to determine what films the majority of U.S. and global audiences will see. In 1992, independents distributed fewer than ten of the top 100 films (in terms of gross box-office earnings) shown in U.S. theaters.[79] Of the top 300 movie releases during the period from 1986 to 1993, only eight came from distributors other than the seven majors and Orion Pictures.[80] There are many more film scripts written, proposals made, and films produced each year than are distributed. And fewer still receive the distribution effort of which only the majors are capable. If the majors are not interested in financing or distributing a "risky" film, it will be very difficult for it to get made and harder yet to get distributed. This was the case with *Glengarry Glen Ross,* a David Mamet drama starring Al Pacino and Jack Lemon that, despite the star-studded cast, required commitments from cable and video companies, a German television station, an Australian movie theater chain, several banks, and the film's independent distributor, New Line Cinema, for the film to be made.[81]

The major producer-distributors *do* produce their own films, help finance and distribute "independent" productions, and buy the distribution rights to completed films. They may exercise varying degrees of control over pictures they help finance. Normally, the major distributors own the copyrights to the movies they distribute. Only a producer-director of the stature of a James Cameron *(Terminator* and *Terminator 2: Judgment Day)* is able to retain ownership of his films, though he still requires backing from a major distributor to get the films made and distributed. In 1992, Cameron signed a five-year agreement with Twentieth Century Fox valued at about $500 million to produce twelve films, four of which he will direct.[82] In the deal, Fox gets the U.S. domestic distribution rights, including theatrical, video, and television outlets. The agreement demonstrates that power in the industry rests in the hands of the majors who are able to to extract rights in exchange for financing and distributing the films. In this manner, the handful of major distributors come to hold the most valuable filmed entertainment copyrights and/or related rights to the films that have big budgets and big stars and receive the big marketing push. The ownership of these rights serves as the basis of their oligopolistic control over filmed entertainment markets. It is evident too that oligopolistic control over filmed entertainment copyrights and distribution rights has permitted at least one of these firms to charge monopoly prices. In the 1980s, MGM/UA was charging one-third to one-half more than other filmed entertainment companies for licensing its films to broadcasters and cable networks, compelling Turner Broadcasting to acquire the MGM film library in order to cut licensing costs.[83] For the 3,650 MGM and United Artist films that the Turner company bought in 1986, Turner ended up paying $1.1 billion[84] but flow saves on licensing transaction costs each time the films are used by one of Turner's many media outlets.

Economists have identified a related characteristic of informational and cultural goods that also fosters economic concentration—economies of scope. Economies of scope arise when it costs less to produce several different products by the same firm because the firm draws from the same raw or intermediate product.[85] Costs are reduced as a result of this joint production. Again, Meehan's description of how Time Warner utilised the Batman character provides an excellent example of a media firm taking advantage of economies of scope. In this case, a single Time Warner-copyrighted character served as the vehicle for the production and sale by subsidiary corporations or licensees of a wide range of entertainment channels and consumer products (comic books, novelisations, toys, games, clothes, music soundtracks, music videos, videocassettes, etc.) and services (theatrical exhibition, pay-cable, pay-per-view, and network television). The Time Warner merger was specifically designed to further capitalise on economies of scope enjoyed by each company separately by bringing even more channels of media distribution under a single corporate umbrella. Intellectual property law defines and protects those derivative products and uses that are privately appropriable by a company such as Time Warner.

The impact of concentration is exacerbated by synergistic practices in which a single work spawns a variety of other copyrighted works and products, thereby extending the presence of a product into several different industries. Concentration of cultural industries, therefore, also increases the total amount of cultural space taken up by a handful of companies' products in the marketplace. Once more, the release of Warner Bros.'s *Batman* movie in the summer of 1989 is a case in point. The film prompted a "fad" that occupied our cultural space, from newspaper columns reviewing and celebrating the film to children's lunch boxes, clothing, linen, and toys. The entire apparatus gets revived and put into operation with each sequel. The ability of a single firm to focus our attention in such a way reflects enormous political and cultural power.

Risks in the Filmed Entertainment Business

Even with a variety of marketing mechanisms, restrictions on derivative uses, and a high degree of concentration resulting from economies of scale and of scope, private inefficiency (from the copyright owner's perspective) is inevitable and uncertainty and risk in information production are inherent.[86] This is because only some informational and cultural products that are published or released succeed in the marketplace and there is uncertainty as to which these will be. For example, of the average 350 or so films released each year in the United States, only ten or so will be major box-office hits. The higher the risks in terms of investment and the greater the uncertainties in terms of success, the higher the losses will be on unsuccessful projects, which are nevertheless a necessary cost of doing business. Since smaller firms are less able to handle such risks and uncertainty, they will go out of business or remain marginal. In this way, the inherent riskiness of informational and cultural production also fosters concentration.

Christopher Burns and Patricia Martin estimated that the major distributors, who generally have the better-selling products, distribute fewer than twenty films per year, of which only five will recover their costs at domestic theatrical box offices.[87] Two more films will recover their costs in the ancillary markets, foreign and domestic. Tino Balio concluded that over the years more than half of all motion pictures produced have lost money.[88] It is not the case, however, that the "distributor will hope to make a profit" as Burns and Martin suggested,[89] since the agreements between distributors and both the film producer and exhibitor generally guarantee the distributor a profit. Thus, it is the producer that faces a potential loss in the end. Balio found that in agreements between producers and major distributor-financiers, the latter typically take 50 per cent of the profits earned by the film and charge a distribution fee of 30-40 per cent of the gross revenues (which is guaranteed fixed income) for selling and marketing a picture worldwide.[90] Art Buchwald's lawsuit against Paramount Pictures for stealing his script idea titled *King for a Day* (made into the Eddie Murphy vehicle *Coming to America)* provided a revealing look at how creative accounting is used by the core firms to pass the risks off to the weaker participants in the marketplace.[91]

It is during bust periods of the common boom-bust cycle in the motion picture industry that the independents find themselves most squeezed and that the control of the industry by the major producer-distributors becomes most apparent. For example, the bust cycle beginning in mid-1988 claimed the bankruptcy of the De Laurentiis Entertainment Group; led to the buyout by Warner Communications of Lorimar Telepictures Corporations; caused the near bankruptcy of the Cannon Group; and exacerbated the financial problems for New World Entertainment Ltd. initially brought on by the October 1987 stock market crash. The film rights that each company held were sold or traded in an effort to fend off bankruptcy. The Cannon Group sold more than 2,000 titles, twenty-eight television series, and the Pathe historic newsreel archives to the Weintraub Entertainment Group Inc. for $90 million in cash and $4.3 million in stock, [92] De Laurentiis sold its 320-film library for $69 million to British financier Michael Stevens in order to pay off loans.[93] New World used its 150-film library as collateral for a bond swap in an effort to reduce its debt. The cochair of New World commented that bondholders were responsive to the deal because "they understood the value of the film library as collateral."[94] The use of filmed entertainment in this way underscores not only its primary function in capitalist society as a commodity but also the important role of copyright as the basis for such transactions.

The granting of copyright to protect original creators or independent producers does nothing to solve the problem of underproduction. Although U.S. copyright laws do protect "unpublished" works, only those products actually brought to the marketplace are able to generate exchange value and the income needed to recover negative costs. Like all the independents, Cannon and De Laurentiis were able to secure production financing but could not afford to compete with the majors as the costs of marketing and distribution continued to rise.[95] For such companies, copyright does little to increase their output or guarantee them income (reward) as theory would hold. Strict copyright laws, effective means of enforcement, and more efficient marketing systems may increase both investor confidence in intellectual property markets and incentive to invest therein. But with the prevailing high barriers to market entry, copyright laws and related mechanisms do nothing to enhance independent producers' access to distribution networks or the public's access to a diversity of informational and cultural products. On the contrary, to the extent that copyright permits the accumulation of filmed entertainment rights by a few companies, it enhances market concentration and inhibits access to and use of informational and cultural goods.

The Debate Over the Efficiency of Copyright

Given that economies of scale and of scope, strong copyright-based control of derivative uses, and the inherent uncertainty and risk in producing informational and cultural products all enhance the tendency toward concentration, it is clear that *social* efficiency, in terms of access to and use of informational and cultural products, is indeed threatened by private intellectual property rights. Social efficiency stems from the social nature of intellectual and artistic creativity. Besen stated the efficiency equation that economists construct in considering derivation from versus protection of copyrighted works:

> The creation of knowledge is a cumulative undertaking. An author, or scientist, or inventor, is more productive because of the activities of those who have come before him. If those who create cannot take advantage of the work of others, the process of creating intellectual property would be far less efficient. However, if this involves a

reduction in the return to earlier creators, the process of creation may be slowed. The problem is how to balance the need to permit building upon previous knowledge against the need to encourage creativity in the first place.[96]

The first half of the equation requires access and use and assumes that this will produce social efficiency through heightened creative output. The other half requires protection and controlled access and use in order to secure payment to the copyright owner, who may or may not be the actual creator. Nevertheless, the guarantee of remuneration provides at least the minimal security that investors need to risk their capital, though it does not necessarily provide the incentive for the actual creator to create. The incentive to create may be considered a natural propensity of human beings or it may come from the desire to make a contribution to society. It could be based on cultural values such as "love of learning," "goodness to others," "the work ethic," and so on.[97]

When information economists talk of the need to find a balance between creativity and access to information, they inevitably take economic reward as essential to stimulating creativity. The logical balance to achieve, in Besen's formula, is to "provide protection to the point where the value of the additional knowledge created equals the reduction in the value of the usefulness of the knowledge created by the restriction."[98] Similarly, the Office of Technology Assessment's report states the problem as the need to "determine precisely at what point rights to private use would maximise the joint welfare of users and producers [i.e., copyright owners]."[99] For Besen, achieving this balance is essentially the role of intellectual property law, which is necessary, since private efficiency does not always result in social efficiency. And, as the economics of information have shown, this is especially the case for markets in intellectual and artistic creativity.

Critics from within the economists' camp weigh this attempted balance to show that copyright may not in fact be the best approach to achieving either social or private efficiency. Denis Thomas, for example, questioned whether the limits on existing protection have already been passed and whether "the present limits are any incentive to the production of works of art."[100] If these questions cannot be answered, it may be necessary to reexamine copyrights from the view that the public has a "right to enjoy art more widely, more cheaply and with more advantage to themselves."[101]

The critical analysis from within the economic perspective has a long history. Thomas Macaulay, a British legal historian, in his speech to Parliament on a copyright bill in 1841, argued that "copyright is a monopoly, and produces all the effects which the general voice of mankind attributes to monopoly. The effect of monopoly generally is to make articles scarce, to make them dear, and to make them bad."[102] A minority report by Sir Louis Mallet in 1876 to the Royal Commission on Copyright followed this critique along similar lines, pointing out that a "limitation on supply by artificial causes, creates scarcity in order to create property. ... It is within this ... class that copyright in published works must be included."[103]

Another commonly cited economic critique of copyright is by Arnold Plant. He questioned whether the monopoly provided by copyright did indeed promote the creation of new ideas and works enough so as to offset the price of goods embodying intellectual property. Artificially high prices would result in the inefficient use of such ideas and works. Besen summarised Plant's argument this way: "Unless the gains from additional creation more than offset the inefficiencies from reduced use, the copyright and patent systems cannot be justified."[104] For Plant, the argument by advocates of copyrights in books had been made for centuries "as though book production were the conditioned response of authors, publishers and printers to the impulse of copyright legislation."[105] Thomas similarly questioned this correlation: "Does the ever-lengthening term of copyright protection enter [the artist's or author's] calculations very much, or indeed at all? Is it an inducement to give up one's means of livelihood and instead take up writing, painting, composing or design?"[106]

Stephen Breyer followed up on Plant's analysis in continuing the critique of copyright on its own economic terms.[107] He began by stressing that the performance of copyright in any particular sector varies and must be analyzed separately. In his analysis of the book trade then, Breyer found that the argument for copyright is weak given the criteria of efficiency. He argued that even without copyright the first publisher of a book retains significant advantages in terms of lead time that ought to discourage a second publisher of the title. In Breyer's view, copyrights in books could be replaced by a system based on advance orders and/or by the maintenance of a stock of extra copies by the first publisher for the purpose of deterring a second entrant.

Benjamin Kaplan brought a historical analysis to the same question of balancing copyright protection with derivation from published works.[108] In his second of three lectures he emphasised the freedom with which authors could borrow from other works—their plots, characterisations, settings, themes, and so forth— before copyright was firmly established in statutory form. He attributed the flourish of literary creativity that took place during the Elizabethan era in England to this freedom of appropriation and derivation. However, in Kaplan's view, the ever broadening scope of statutory copyright protection since then has inhibited or prohibited the same kind of free derivation from published works in terms of adaptation, abridgment, translation, dramatisation, and the like, thereby actually stifling creativity. Creativity in the postmodern age of electronic information, where derivation is possible in ever more countless numbers of ways, has exacerbated the tensions between exclusivity and access.

Although perhaps accepting the economic critique as reasonable, few economists or supporters of copyrights are willing to call for the abolition of copyright. Their support is based not so much on the fact that copyright has proven its efficiency, "but rather upon uncertainty as to what would happen if protection were removed."[109] Besen confirmed this view with his basic conclusion that "although private markets for intellectual properly cannot be expected to function efficiently, none of the alternatives is without its flaws."[110]

Therefore, economists acknowledge that intellectual property markets arc inefficient, in both private and social terms, and that the best that intellectual property law can do is attempt to maintain a balance between the inherently contradictory interests of copyright owners and the public of users. All contemporary analysts agree that new communications technologies are seriously and continuously upsetting this balance. New technologies make it easier to separate the content from the package in which it was first offered, "to copy an article without buying the magazine, to record a television program while zapping commercials, to download portions of a database."[111] The central question consistently is: Who should benefit from the new products and uses that emanate from new technologies, that is, "who pays fixed costs and who pays only marginal costs; or, if revenue exceeds total cost, who shares in the rents as among the various input suppliers and between producers and consumers"?[112] These issues are being decided in the marketplace, through labor negotiations, and also in the courts and Congress. However, those with market power have proven their success in significantly shaping the distribution of rewards generated by new technologies.

All the economists cited above agreed that given the inefficiency of intellectual property markets some forms of government intervention are necessary "in order to improve on the workings of the market."[113] Suggested policies range from minimum intervention to active government participation in information markets; from merely providing the legal definitions and protection of intellectual property rights (civil and criminal) to direct government subsidy to creators of intellectual and artistic products and to government production and dissemination of information itself.[114]

From Economics to Political Economics

As we have seen, current neoclassical economics has provided a complex, systematised analysis of the economics of information. The analysis falls short, however, due to its emphasis on a particular definition of efficiency. Since it has been shown that information markets function inefficiently and are prone to failure, the analyses and recommendations that economists put forward on any policy proposal for dealing with these markets can, at best, merely adjust who benefits from the rewards of intellectual and artistic creativity. These decisions concern the distribution and redistribution of property but do not question the system of private property itself. Economists therefore begin with the value-based judgment that private property is necessary to approach anything resembling economic efficiency in information markets. Their fundamental task is to determine and compare the efficiency of alternative systems of property based on their predictions of how individuals will behave within them. These predictions, too, are based on universal claims, for example "that economic actors pursue their own material well-being as best they can, given the constraints imposed by markets and ultimately by property law."[115] This assumption ignores those who produce intellectual and artistic goods lor other reasons.

The subjectivity of this supposed "scientific" analysis becomes obvious when, in the policy process, economists are employed by opposing interests to predict the outcome of various policy options and come up with entirely contradictory forecasts. Even then, the different analyses by the hired economists can generally only deal with the costs and benefits of the policy that are quantifiable. However, the positivistic and apparently empirical nature of economic analyses makes economists more forceful in the policymaking process than those making predictions or voicing concerns that are based more on an intuitive, philosophical, or even historical basis.

In their analysis of markets, economists also exclude all those transactions, or elements of transactions, that involve what Robert Babe and Conrad Winn called "nonproprietary. value" or "aspects of life considered to be worthwhile which are not, and perhaps cannot be, delimited and enforced by the state. Charity, love, and empathy are examples of attitudes or actions, unenforceable by law, yet considered valuable."[116] In the area of information economics, similar nonmarket characteristics have been identified that produce value above the actual cost and price of a "bit" of information ("positive externalities"). These are qualities of information that affect all aspects of our daily lives: its ability to produce wisdom, to reduce conflict, to encourage sharing relations, to promote democracy, to entertain, to promote employment and productivity, and so on—in general to raise the level of human welfare.[117]

Despite these commonly recognised nonmarket characteristics of information that make measuring the value of information all the more problematic, the tendency in economics is still to seek some way of measuring nonmarket values based on the criterion of efficiency. Priest identified the linkage between human welfare and information this way: "Human welfare is a product of individuals and groups achieving desired outcomes. Thus, *information is intrinsically related to human welfare* in that it inherently facilitates the achievement of outcomes."[118] It does this by contributing to the knowledge and understanding of groups and individuals of possible choices and outcomes. Yet from this assumption Priest again leads us to the central contradiction inherent in the concept and practice of copyright law. He concluded that property rights in information and human welfare can be "incompatible in a major way."[119] He then related information to freedom. In his definition, "freedom is the lack of restrictions on choices"[120] and information contributes to freedom because it increases the range of choices available to an individual or group. Consequently, for Priest, private property rights for information can conflict with freedom if they are used to inhibit access and use, whereas they may support freedom if they encourage increased creativity (another problematic assumption, as noted above).

The existence of tendencies toward increased market power and economic concentration is continuously revealed in the final analyses of information economcs, but it is never made the explicit focus of study. This is because economists concentrate too narrowly on competition while buying uncritically into the assumption that there is general equality in the marketplace. Radical political economy rejects this claim and makes power in the marketplace a central focus of study.

The Political Economy of the Filmed Entertainment Industry

The political economic analysis of various aspects of communications begins by situating the object of study within the context of capitalism or, using the Bowles and Edwards concept, within the context of the "social structure of accumulation."[121] Hence, it is an institutional analysis that considers relations within and among the institutions in the economic, political, cultural, and ideological domains and within which accumulation—the making and reinvesting of profits by individual capitalists or firms—occurs. It shares with conventional economics a focus on competition—the horizontal dimension of economics—where relations are based on voluntary exchange and where choice plays the predominant role.[122]

But economic relationships also involve power, and political economy goes beyond conventional economics by examining a vertical dimension: those aspects of market relations "in which power, coercion, hierarchy, and being a subordinate or superior come into play."[123] Finally, political economy adds a time dimension to the analysis of economics. It focuses on the way that economic systems have historically evolved; for example it sees capitalism as evolving through various stages. This is in contrast to the static approach of conventional economics in which time is frozen in order to take a snapshot view of the workings of markets and participants therein.

Political economy also does not claim to be "objective" or value-free, as no social theory can make that claim. "Economics inevitably involves values."[124] One of its normative claims, resembling conventional economics, is that markets and economies ought to function efficiently, "that for a given amount of productive inputs used in an economic system, the maximum output of useful goods and services is produced."[125] Unlike conventional economics, it considers the *usefulness* of the goods and services that are produced in the efficiency equation. This leaves most forms of advertising and military production, for example, out of the efficiency calculation. It also takes into account all inputs into production, paid for or not, including our natural environment, effort and health of the worker, and household labor.

Political economy adds two additional values to the analysis of economics. These are fairness (the extent to which the burdens and benefits of social production are shared equitably) and democracy (the extent to which citizens have opportunity of input into major decisions affecting society and civil rights and individual liberties). Bowles and Edwards concluded, after their analysis of the political economy of capitalism, that the system violates all three standards. Capitalism is not *efficient* because of the costs of unemployment, inefficient use of natural resources and waste of workers time and effort all of which are inherent to the system. Capitalism is not *fair* because inequalities begin at birth and because there is not equal pay lor equal work. Capitalism is not *democratic* because the citizenry does not control the economy. Major decisions that affect people's lives in serious ways are made by a handful of corporate owners and executives. These individuals lead not because they are chosen by the public, but because they own the capital goods necessary for economic production.[126]

These violations of political economy's standards can also be found on the industry level. In motion picture production, owners garner profits by controlling the means for filmed entertainment production and distribution, which allows them to extract surplus value. Workers within the production, distribution, and exhibition systems have no input into matters of strategic control over the operation of their employing firms. Under the work-for-hire doctrine, the efforts of workers in creating a film result in copyright ownership for the employer. Producers of filmed entertainment do not confront buyers of the product on equal terms, as the previous sections on the oligopolistic structure of the industry have already revealed. The relationship is one of exploitation. Consumers also do not receive fair treatment in the marketplace, as monopolistic structures in the industry facilitate the charging of monopoly prices. And there is much inefficient use of the medium of film, with market criteria largely determining what is to be produced. It seems legitimate to question the spending of as much as $100 million or more for the production, distribution, and marketing of major feature films in terms of taxing our society's budget for cultural creativity. Many more filmic visions could be available if these resources, as well as the training and technology to produce the films, were more broadly distributed.

Conclusion

Economists talk of concentration of intellectual property in relation to access and use. Political economists talk about several additional layers of concentration. They are motivated by concern not in the general sense of having a "free and efficient market" for filmed entertainment (or any other intellectual or artistic product), but by much more profound concerns. The structure of the filmed entertainment industry is crucial "because as a medium of communication, film sets before us images and ideas that influence us and our cultures."[127] Its global scale means that its influence on cultural life is variously felt by almost everyone on the planet.

It is not just a matter of economics; ideology and culture are also of concern here. Economic concentration is significant in shaping the art form. And at the basic level, filmed entertainment is produced within the capitalist social structure of accumulation in order to make a profit. Copyright serves as the mechanism by which this creativity is financed, produced, and privately appropriated. Accordingly, the industry remains owned and managed by the capitalist class, the ultimate measure of concentration. The result, as political economists of communications consistently point out, is that the views and accounts of the world held by the capitalist class and aligned class factions and groups are broadly disseminated and persistently publicised.[128] At the same time, the voices and groups that are most consistent in their challenges to the dominant groups lack economic power and resources to make themselves heard. Or they find their movements and messages captured and distorted through hegemonic media production practices. A commonly recognised influence is the need for commercial success in order to generate the revenues necessary to recover costs and make profits. This in turn narrows the range of material available in the mass media as market forces exclude all but the most commercially successful products.

The pervasiveness of "ruling-class views," hegemonic media practices, and the lack of alternative and critical views helps to maintain class inequalities and undemocratic social relationships. The state and the law play an important supporting role in this domination, and it is to these institutions that attention is turned in the following chapters.

NOTES

1. Thomas Jefferson, *The Portable Thomas Jefferson*, New York: Penguin Books, 1985, p. 530.
2. Stanley M. Besen, *New Technologies and Intellectual Property: An Economic Analysis*, Santa Monica, CA: Rand, 1987, p. 1.

3. W. Curtiss Priest, "The Character of Information: Characteristics and Properties of Information Related to Issues Concerning Intellectual Property," Washington, DC: Office of Technology Assessment, February 1985, p. 17.
4. Priest, p. 20.
5. Besen, p. 7.
6. Priest, p. 20.
7. Nicholas Garnham, *Capitalism and Communication*, Newbury Park, CA: Sage, 1990, p. 40.
8. Robert Sklar, *Movie-Made America: A Cultural History of American Movies*, New York: Vintage Books, 1975, p. 11.
9. Thomas Guback, "The Evolution of the Motion Picture Theater Business in the *1980s" Journal of Communication*, 37:2, 1987, pp. 60-77.
10. Robert C. Allen, "The Movies in Vaudeville: Historical Context of the Movies as Popular Entertainment," in Tino Balio (ed.), *The American Film Industry*, Madison: University of Wisconsin Press, 1985, pp. 57-82.
11. Tino Balio, "Part I: A Novelty Spawns Small Businesses, 1894-1908," in Balio (ed.), pp. 3-25, p. 20.
12. The 1909 Copyright Act applied to books; periodicals, including newspapers; lectures, sermons, addresses prepared for oral delivery; dramatic or dramatico-musical compositions; musical compositions; maps; works of art; models or designs for works of art; reproductions of works of art; drawings or plastic works of a scientific or technical character; photographs; prints and pictorial illustrations. 60th Congress, Sess. II, Chapter 320, Sec. 5(a)-(k). The act also granted the copyright owner the right to authorise translation, mechanical reproduction, and performance whether an author's permission was required in transforming a novel or a play into a film was not addressed until 1932, in MGM v. *Theatre Company* 59 E 2d (Ist Cir. 1932).
13. 62nd Congress, 2nd Sess., Chapter 356, Sec. 5(1),(m).
14. Both nations' public broadcast systems now must also compete with advertiser-supported television media. Traditionally, they have depended heavily on tax revenues, as licensing income regularly fails to produce sufficient funds for program production.
15. David J. Londoner, "The Changing Economics of Entertainment," in Balio (ed.), pp. 603-630, p. 622.
16. Mark Robichaux, "NBC Faces Loss from Olympics Pay-TV Plan," *Wall Street Journal*, June 15, 1992, pp. BI, B2.

17. Robichaux, p. B2.

18. Matt Stump, "Defending PPV" *Cable World;* November 30, 1992, pp. 31A-32A, p. 32A.

19. A standard form of bundling is to tie an information product to a private good to enhance the ability of excluding nonpayers (for example, the computer program sold with an operator's manual, a computer magazine subscription, and future updated versions of the program).

20. The Cable Communications Policy Act of 1984, Pub.L. 98-549, 98 Stat. 2770 (October 1984), Sec. 633(a)(l), (b)(l).

21. Public Law 98-549, Sec. 633(a)(l), (b)(2).

22. David Waterman, "Prerecorded Home Video and the Distribution of Theatrical Feature Films," in Eli Noam (ed.), *Video Media Competition,* New York: Columbia University Press, 1985, pp. 221-243, p. 233.

23. Besen, p. 17.

24. Coca-Cola Company, *1985 Annual Report,* p. 21.

25. Vincent Mosco, *The Pay-Per Society: Computers and Communication in the Information Age,* Norwood, NJ: Ablex, 1989, p. 27.

26. See Graham Murdock, "The 'Privatisation' of British Communications," in V. Mosco and J. Wasko (eds.), *Critical Communications Review 2,* Norwood, NJ: Ablex, 1984, pp. 265—290. Murdock believed that public broadcasting, particularly for low-income groups, would be increasingly affected by pay services. He feared that "the poor may well be disenfranchised twice over; once by their inability to pay for the new services, and once again by the reduced diversity of mainstream programming brought about by the combination of increased competition and mounting political pressures" to deliver mass audiences in order to justify costs (p. 282).

27. N. R. Kleinfield, "ESPN's Baseball-Rights Purchase: A Game-Saving Catch," *New York Times,* January 23, 1989, p. D8.

28. John Helyar, "Pay-Per-View Aims for Boxing Knockout," *Wall Street Journal,* January 24, 1992, pp. BI, B4.

29. "Will New Regulations Mean New Subscribers?" *Public Pulse,* April 1993, p. 4.

30. *Public Pulse,* p. 4.

31. "Commerce Growth Prediction," *Television Digest,* May 10, 1993, p. 11.

32. Stump, p. 31 A.
33. Of course the suggestion that broadcast television is free is false. In fact, the user pays for the costs of advertising through higher product prices, for both the manufacturer's recovery of advertising expenditures and the artificially high prices that result from advertising-based oligopolies. See Ben Bagdikian, *Media Monopoly* (4th ed.), Boston: Beacon, 1992, especially chapter 8, "The High Costs of Free Lunches," pp. 134-151. The cable industry, in an effort to counter broadcasters' claims that they provide "free TV," estimated that television advertising costs are passed on to consumers at an average of about $298 per TV household (Jay Arnold, "Cable Excess Say 'Free TV Ads May Mislead Viewers," *Centre Daily Times* [State College, PA], January 26, 1990, p. B5 [from the Associated Press wire service]).
34. 17 U.S.C. Sec. 109.
35. Marc Herman, "Rentals Reap Bulk of 1991 Vid Harvest," *Variety*, January 6, 1992, pp. 22, 104; 1992 figure cited from Paul Kagan Associates in Richard Turner, "Disney Leads Shift from Rentals to Sales in Videocassettes," *Wall Street Journal*, December 24, 1992, pp. 1, 30.
36. Turner, December 24, 1992, p. 30.
37. Walt Disney Company, *Annual Report*, 1992, p. 28.
38. Turner, December 24, 1992, p. 1.
39. Walt Disney Company, *Annual Report*, 1992, pp. 21, 23.
40. Turner, December 24, 1992, p. 1.
41. Andrew L. Yarrow, "Pay-Per-View Television Is Ready for Takeoff," *New York Times*, November 14, 1988, p. D9.
42. Stump, p. 31 A.
43. Matt Stump, "Hit Movies All the Time," *Cable World*, May 31, 1993, pp. 1A, 23A, p. 1A.
44. Matt Stump, "Adult PPV Programming," *Cable World*, November 30, 1992, p. 9A.
45. Matt Stump, "Warner Trying to Tie Its PPV Shelf Space to Box Office Revs," *Cable World*, May 31, 1993, pp. I A, 21 A, 23 A.
46. "Killen & Associates, Inc. $200 Billion Interactive TV Market Predicted for Consumer Electronics and Computer Suppliers by Year 2000," *Business Wire*, March 9, 1993.
47. Daniel Pearl, "Cox Envisions Global Pipeline for TV and Phone Signals," *Wall Street Journal*, March 3, 1993, p. B4.

48. Michael J. McCarthy, "Cox and BellSouth Discuss Venture in Electronic Ads," *Wall Street Journal*, June 7, 1993, p. B2.
49. Barry Layne, "Viacom Interacts with AT&T; Companies Confirm Plans to Test the Future in Northern California," *Hollywood Reporter*, June 3, 1993, pp. 4, 20.
50. Cindy Skrzycki, "AT&T Plans Trial Venture in Video," *Washington Post*, June 2, 1993, pp. FI, F4.
51. Mark Robichaux and Johnnie L. Roberts, "Time Warner, TCI Start Venture to Set Cable Standards," *Wall Street Journal*, June 4, 1993, p. B10.
52. Bill Carter, "Television: Scroll Through an Electronic List, and Pick the Program You Want to Watch at This Very Moment," *New York Times*, March 8, 1993, p. D7.
53. Cable Television Consumer Protection and Competition Act of 1992, Pub.L. 102-385, 106 Stat. 1460 (October 5, 1992).
54. *Public Pulse*, p. 4.
55. "Pay-Per-View TV Is Given Low Marks by Consumers," *Wall Street Journal*, February 16, 1993, p. B6.
56. Peter M. Nichols, "Home Video: Does Pay Per View Pay?" *New York Times*, July 2, 1992, p. C16; "Home Video Market Will Grow 5% in 1993, Commerce Dept. Predicts," *Video Week*, May 10, 1993, p. 4.
57. Priest, pp. 13-14.
58. David J. Jefferson. "Movie Making Cost. Record $28.8 Million in '92, Valenti Tells U. S. Theater Owners," *Wall Street Journal*, March 10, 1993, p.B6.
59. A. Allan Schmid. "A Conceptual Framework for Organising Observations on Intellectual Property Stakeholders," Washington, DC: Office of Ttechnology Assessment, February 1985, p.4.
60. Differentiated pricing exists lor other products and services. For example, automobiles biles are designed and produced to tit a variety of price ranges for different sets of buyers, and passenger airlines charge differentiated prices based on class of service and time frame within which the ticket is purchased.
61. Priest recognised this when noting at the outset that "music, movies and similar products that create synthesised experiences are part informational, part motivational and part consumptive" (p. 6).
62. Denis McQuail, "With the Benefit of Hindsight: Reflections on

Uses and Gratifications Research," *Critical Studies in Mass Communication*, 1:2, 1984, pp. 177-193.

63. Douglas Gomery, *The Hollywood Studio System*, New York: St. Martin's, 1986, pp. 15-18.

64. Gomery, pp. 17-18.

65. Waterman, p. 231.

66. Anne Gregor, "Entertaining Numbers: A Statistical Look at the Global-Entertainment Industry," *Wall Street Journal*, March 26, 1993, p. R16 (citing data from Veronis Suhler & Associates; Paul Kagan Associates; Wilkofsdy Gruen Associates).

67. Susan Ayscough, "Studios Join in Chorus of Disapproval on PPV," *Variety*, May 24, 1993, pp. 5, 18.

68. "MGM Balks at TCI-Carolco Pay-Per-View Deal," United Press International, May 7, 1993 (from LEXIS/NEXIS).

69. Peter M. Nichols, "Home Video: Like Art Imitating Life, Some Theatrical Releases May Follow Pay-Per-View," *New York Times*, May 6, 1993, p. C16.

70. Geraldine Fabrikant, "Some Promising Signs for Turner's Empire," *New York Times*, January 23, 1989, p. Dl; *Television and Cable Factbook*, Washington, DC: Warren Publishing, 1994, pp. G84, G85.

71. Stratford P. Sherman, "Ted Turner: Back from the Brink," *Fortune*, *July 7*, 1986, pp. 25-31, p. 28.

72. Newspaper ad for Country Fair Cinemas' showing of *Bambi* taken from the *Champaign-Urbana News Gazette* (Champaign, IL), July 15, 1988, p. A-12.

73. Eileen Meehan, "*Holy Commodity Fetish, Batman!* The Political Economy of a Commercial Intertext," in *The Many Lives of Batman: Critical Approaches to a Superhero and His Media*, R. E. Pearson and W. Uricchio (eds.), New York: Routledge, 1991, pp. 47-65.

74. Richard W. Stevenson, "30-Year-Old Film Is a Surprise Hit in Its 4th Re-Release," *New York Times*, August 5, 1991, pp. C9, C14.

75. Richard Turner, "Disney's 'Pinocchio' Re-Release Faces Struggle to Match Ticket Sales of 1984," *Wall Street Journal*, *July* 28, 1992, p. B3.

76. William Bryan, cited in "Cartoons Strike Back," *TV Entertainment Monthly*, March 1989, p. 5.

77. Besen, p. 23.

78. Thomas Guback, "Theatrical Film," in B. Compaine et al., *Who Owns the Media? Concentration of Ownership in the Mass Communications Industry*, White Plains, NJ: Knowledge Industries, 1979, pp. 179-249.

79. "Top Rental Films for 1992," *Variety*, January 11, 1993, p. 22.

80. Tom Graves, "Leisure-Time: Current Analysis," *Standard & Poor's Industry Surveys* November 1993, pp. LI-1,68, p. L23.

81. Bernard Weinraub, "The 'Glengarry' Math: Add Money and Stars, Then Subtract Ego," *New York Times*, October 12, 1992, pp. Cl1, C20.

82. Bernard Weinraub, "Fox Locks in Cameron with a 5-Year Deal Worth $500 Million," *New York Times*, April 22, 1992, p. C15; Thomas R. King, "'Terminator' Director Signed to Pact by Fox," *Wall Street Journal*, April 23, 1992, p. B5.

83. Fabrikant, January 23, 1989, p. D9.

84. Sherman, p. 29.

85. Priest, p. 27.

86. Priest, p. 29-30.

87. Christopher Burns and Patricia Martin, "The Economics of Information," Washington, DC: Office of Technology Assessment, April 1985, p. 11-19.

88. Tino Balio, "Part IV: Retrenchment, Reappraisal, and Reorganisation, 1948-," in Balio (ed.), pp. 401-447, p. 422.

89. Burns and Martin, p. 11-19.

90. Balio, "Part IV," p. 422.

91. Richard W. Stevenson, "Tinsel Magic:'Hit' Loses Millions," *New York Times*, April 13, 1990, pp. D1.D2.

92. Kathleen A. Hughes, "Cannon Sells Much of Its Film Library to Weintraub for Less Than Expected," *Wall Street Journal*, May 4, 1987, p. 18.

93. Roy J. Harris Jr., "De Laurentiis Entertainment Sets Film Accord," *Wall Street Journal*, March 16, 1988, p. 36.

94. Geraldine Fabrikant, "Talking Deals: New Lease on Life for New World," *New York Times*, September 29, 1988, p. D2.

95. Geraldine Fabrikant, "Blitz Hits Small-Studio Pix," *New York Times*, July 12, 1992, p. F7.

96. Besen, p. 44.

97. Priest, p. 60.
98. Besen, p. 45.
99. U.S. Congress, Office of Technology Assessment, *Intellectual Property Rights in an Age of Electronics and Information*, Washington, DC: U.S. Government Printing Office, April 1986 (hereinafter OTA Report), p. 204.
100. Denis Thomas, *Copyright and the Creative Artist*, London: Institute of Economic Affairs, 1967, p. 46.
101. Thomas, p. 46.
102. Quoted in Arnold Plant, "The Economic Aspects of Copyright in Books," *Economica*, 1:1-4, May 1934, pp. 167-195, pp. 170-171.
103. Quoted in Plant, pp. 193-194.
104. Besen, p. 11.
105. Plant, p. 167.
106. Thomas, p. 21.
107. Stephen Breyer, "The Uneasy Case for Copyright: A Study of Copyright in Books, Photocopies, and Computer Programs," *Harvard Law Review*, 84:2, 1970, pp. 281-351.
108. Benjamin Kaplan, *An Unhurried View of Copyright*, New York: Columbia University Press, 1967.
109. Breyer, p. 322.
110. Besen p. 60.
111. Burns and Martin, p. 1-7.
112. Schmid, p. 18.
113. Schmid, p. 51.
114. OTA Report, p. 169.
115. Robert E. Babe and Conrad Winn, *Broadcasting Policy and Copyright Law* , Ottawa; Department of Communications, Government of Canada, 1981, p. 28.
116. Babe and Winn, p. 19.
117. Priest, p. 39.
118. Priest, p. 41 (italics in original text).
119. Priest, p. 42.
120. Priest, p. 45.
121. Samuel Bowles and Richard Edwards, *Understanding Capitalism:*

Competition, Command, and Change in the U.S. Economy, New York: Harper and Row Publishers, 1985, p. 94.

122. Bowles and Edwards, p. 17.
123. Bowles and Edwards, p. 17.
124. Bowles and Edwards, p. 21.
125. Bowles and Edwards, p. 21.
126. Bowles and Edwards, pp. 375-381.
127. Guback, 1982, p. 250.
128. Graham Murdock and Peter Golding, "Capitalism, Communications, and Class Relations," in J. Curran, M. Gurevitch, and J. Woollacott (eds.), Mass *Communications and Society*, London: Edward Arnold, 1977, pp. 12-43, p. 15.

6 COMPULSORY LICENSES FOR CABLE RETRANSMISSIONS

Theories of the Capitalist State

This case study utilises theoretical tools drawn from radical and Marxist theories of the state and of law, approaches that take state intervention into the economy as an essential future of contemporary capitalism. Like the political economy of communications, Marxist- and radical-state theory can be divided into three distinct areas: (1) the relation between the capitalist class and the state; (2) the relation between the logic of capital and state policies; and (3) the class struggle and the state.[1]

As demonstrated elsewhere, the history and development of copyright, from book publishing through computer software, reflect the successive enclosure of intellectual and artistic creativity by those who own the means for producing and distributing creative products in tangible forms. This appropriation has been legitimated and facilitated by the capitalist state in the form of patent, trademark, and copyright laws. Consequently, the state is of crucial interest for understanding the institution of intellectual property.

In this case study I seek to bridge the three general areas of state theory in order to produce a more holistic analysis of the state's intervention into the economic domain.

The first of these, dealing with the relation between the capitalist class and the state, is often characterised as an "instrumental" approach, for it seeks to show how the ruling class is able to use the state as an instrument of domination. Marxists such as Miliband and power-structure analysts such as Domhoff have tried to identify the individual and institutional interlocks that constitute the social network of the dominant class, or power elite, and to show how the state is implicated in this system.[2] Instrumentalism tends to emphasise human agency at the level of consciousness; it remains near the level of surface appearances as it seeks to explain *how* members of the ruling capitalist class are consciously able to protect and extend their interests through the exercise of power in private (market) and public (governmental and nongovernmental) institutions.[3] The focus here is on the constitution of the ruling class, its control of the corporate sector (including media firms), its influence on the U.S. polity, and its relationship to state officials in the policymaking process.

The second general sphere of capitalist state theory draws attention to the relationship between the logic of capital and state policies. There are several variants within this theoretical field, including the structuralism of Poulantzas,[4] what Martin Carnoy called "logic of capital theory," and what Bob Jessop called "state derivationist theory."[5] The basic premise of these approaches is that the contemporary capitalist state emerged as a response to the continuing economic crises produced by contradictions inherent to the capitalist mode of production. They stress the unconscious, structural determinations that organise and shape human activity within the capitalist economy and the state, and they seek to penetrate the level of surface appearances to explain *why* the state intervenes into economic matters and *why* the objective structures that reinforce class domination and inequalities work as they do. Accordingly, structuralist-oriented theorists begin with an analysis of the capital accumulation process and its tendency toward crises. The state derives its form and function as it responds to market failures. The tendency toward systemic crises requires the state to continually intercede into economic matters in an effort to produce countertendencies by reorganising the processes of production, distribution, and consumption. Goran Therborn argued that the role of the state is to act as "the ideal collective capitalist," advancing the perceived interests of capital as a whole through "discriminatory management of monopolistic competition."[6]

Structuralism entails a higher level of abstraction than instrumentalism, as it seeks to theorise the particular "real concrete." For Mao, this constituted an effort to produce general knowledge of the "essence, the totality and the internal relation of things" by moving from an analysis of specificity to generality.[7] It is part of a larger attempt to escape empiricism and move closer to an understanding of the "real concrete" through interpretive theorising. Of particular importance to structuralism is how the logic of capital determines the motives and activities of the capitalist class within the state apparatus.

Critics of capital logic approaches find them too functionalist and essentialist in their orientation, particularly their assumption "that the interests of capital are always realised in the final analysis."[8] Giddens, for example, criticised structuralism for not adequately explaining why state officials themselves operate to reinforce the logic of capital, since they generally do not belong to the capitalist class.[9] On the one hand, certainly the vast majority of state workers do not belong to the capitalist class. On the other hand, those state officials who occupy the highest levels of government, the levels at which policy is determined, generally do belong to the ranks of what Domhoff called the "power elite." Power-structure analysts have clearly demonstrated these interlocks between the capitalist class and upper-level state officialdom.

Pluralists assume that there exist countless numbers of organised interest groups in society, including those representing capital and labor, and that these groups, or interests, compete on essentially equal terms preventing any one of them from holding permanent power or advantages. Though pluralists may concede that an upper class does indeed exist in capitalist society, they would not agree that it somehow dominates public opinion, policy planning, and policy-making or that it is able to hold absolute sway. From this perspective, the upper class is simply one more "interest group" competing for its share of the pie.

Both Domhoff and Miliband moved to refute this pluralist assumption of equal competition among various interest groups by empirically demonstrating ways in which the ruling class does, in fact, dominate public opinion, policy planning and policymaking, first through institutions outside of the state and then through those within it. Miliband argued that "business enjoys a massive superiority *outside* the state system ... in terms of the immensely stronger pressure which, as compared with labour and any other interest, it is able to exercise in the pursuit of its purposes."[10] This then is one aspect of ruling class domination of the policymaking process.

The privileged position of business, above its role as competing "interest group" in society, has been conceded by some pluralists. In what could be considered a defection from the ranks, Charles Lindblom acknowledged the increasingly dominant role of the corporate sector in social policy processes.[11] Similarly, Theodore Lowi recognised that "special-interest groups" have come to dominate policymaking with the effect of depriving government of its legitimacy.[12] Ironically, the report of President Ronald Reagan's Commission on Privatisation saw the privatisation movement as a significant reaction to the excess of "interest-group" politics.[13] The implication is that privatisation is in fact the very epitome of corporate dominance of policymaking, as the capitalist class, through privatisation, is capturing still more areas of human social activity for the purpose of commodifying them. In Domhoff's definition, domination means "the ability of a class or group to set the terms under which other classes or groups within a social system must operate," an ability that the ruling class in the United States possesses by virtue of its control over the use of capital.[14] Lindblom came to agree that this is indeed the basis for the privileged position of business in policymaking and even suggested that some reconsideration of pluralist thought is valid.

The structuralist-oriented approaches *do* provide sufficient explanations for why government officials tend to support and extend the long-term interests of the capitalist class as a whole. Therborn argued that state officials and workers constitute a "state managerial technocracy" that tends to perform its role as protector and promoter of capital due to its structural dependency upon the capital accumulation process from which the revenues for running the state are extracted. At the structural level, the state is dependent for its means of subsistence on the successful functioning of private capitalist enterprise. This is because the state does not control capital nor the processes of capital reproduction; these remain in the hands of individual capitalists. At the subjective level, state intervention into the economic sphere is the method whereby state officials attempt to "manage" the economy in an effort to keep their jobs and status but in ways that protect and promote the long-term interests of capital precisely because of the state's structural dependency on the private sector. However, since the state does not directly control capital, it can only indirectly intervene in the economy, and this intervention is typically "reactive," as the case studies in this book demonstrate.

Still, Giddens was correct when he criticised structuralist approaches for eliminating the human subject by reducing human individuals to bearers of structural determination. He posited instead a theory of structuration that resurrects Marx's dialectic between structural determination and human agency. This theoretical position points to the third general field of capitalist state theory, what Carnoy called "the class struggle theory" and Jessop labeled the "class theoretical position." This theoretical position stresses the dysfunctional, contradictory, and contingent nature of state intervention into the economy. Theories in this area see the state as a site of interclass and intraclass struggle. Accordingly, these approaches question the existence of both a unified ruling class and a lawlike logic of capital. They argue instead that the capitalist class, or a fraction thereof, must work in and through the state to maintain its dominant status and resist challenges arising from below.

Nevertheless, class struggle theorists do recognise that there is a "bias inscribed on the terrain of the [s]tate as a site of strategic action" that privileges the tactics of "some forces over others, some interests over others, some horizons over others, [and] some coalition possibilities over others."[15] Class struggle theories see the state as part of an ideological apparatus that serves to legitimate existing class relations by obscuring them. Mosco argued that through the interaction strategic for forces and state structures the state becomes a "vehicle for maintaining class power, without appearing to do so," precisely because of its structural bias toward capital.[16] Although the capitalist economic system works to isolate individuals from one another in the economic sphere by casting them as competitors in the marketplace, the ideological apparatuses—including the educational system, the media system, the legal system, the political system, and so on—work to reunify these competitive agents as a "people and nation" by posing as the site in which the general interests of the society, rather than class interests, are being pursued. Furthermore, the state appears as a mediator in a process of bargaining and compromise, masking the underlying inequality of access to and influence within the state.

The study of cable television in this chapter is largely a case of intraclass struggle. The discussion shows how various class factions or industry coalitions organised individuals inside and outside of the state apparatus in order to promote their interests through state action. The state was the site in which the cable; television, filmed entertainment, and broadcast industries struggled over control of a new intellectual property market. Jessop introduced the concept of the "hegemonic project" to describe the process by which the hegemonic class faction seeks to promote its long-term interests through mobilisation of state officials and relevant forces in "civil society" in support of its favored policies.[17] He argued that a hegemonic project is more likely to succeed if it can be linked up with the prevailing or emerging "accumulation strategy" or "mode of regulation," by which he means the particular form of the production, distribution, and consumption cycle operating within the capitalist economic system. The cable copyright case is exemplary, for it allows us to combine the instrumentalist, structuralist, and class struggle positions to explain the origin and evolution of the compulsory license for cable.

The question of whether cable retransmissions were protectable intellectual property under Title 17 revolved around how revenues from this new means of distributing filmed entertainment should be apportioned between the participating industries. This is the basic issue that must be dealt with each time a new communications technology is developed and deployed. My goals in this chapter are (1) to provide insight into the general conflict between new communications technologies and existing legal structures; (2) to examine the specific role of the upper class and the state (government and law) in copyright matters; and (3) to theorise the general nature of intellectual property conflicts, including the role of the state within the structure of the U.S. capitalist system.

Historical Background of the Cable Case

Cable television began in the late 1940s as "community antenna television"[18] (CATV) to bring better reception of local television broadcasts to community members or isolated communities in mountainous terrain. Although within the radius of a station's signals, these audiences needed more than rooftop antennas to pick up the local signals. The cable system captured broadcast signals via large antennas on mountaintops and simultaneously retransmitted them to its subscriber-households by cable. The first cooperative CATV system was established in Oregon (1949), and the first commercial system originated in Pennsylvania (1950). In 1952, there were seventy cable systems serving 14,000 customers.[19]

Cable television's growth was fueled further by the uneven national distribution of very high frequency (VHF) television broadcast stations that resulted from the Federal Communications Commission's (FCC) *Sixth Report and Order* in 1952.[20] Jeremy Tunstall reported that as a consequence of this allocation plan, the median number of VHF broadcast stations received by U.S. households by 1960 was four but that up to two-thirds could receive only NBC and CBS.[21] The FCC attempted to promote increased television options through development of ultrahigh frequency (UHF) broadcast stations. Congress supported this effort with legislation requiring that all television sets be manufactured with UHF tuners.[22] Private entrepreneurs who operated cable systems sought to remedy the situation by importing broadcast signals from distant markets by microwave.

There was little initial complaint by the three major broadcast networks and their local affiliates when cable simply improved local signal reception or imported those signals of the second and third networks not available over the air. According to Leonard Ross, broadcasters accepted the practice because "reception of three network signals had been too clearly established as a fundamental civil right, for protests [about distant-network signal importation] to be availing."[23] Eventually this new communications system, based on the combination of microwave and coaxial cable, began to undermine the filmed entertainment industry's copyright system, particularly in the area of television broadcast rights, as it threatened the rather orderly system by which filmed entertainment copyright owners licensed the product to broadcasters for local transmission.

The challenge to the television program rights system emerged in 1961, when a San Diego-based cable company (Southwestern Cable Co.) began importing the broadcast signals of the four Los Angeles VHF independents—KTLA (Channel 5), KHJ (Channel 9), KTTV (Channel 11), and KCET (Channel 13)—into San Diego County, despite the fact that San Diego had been served by the three networks on VHF-affiliate stations (the ABC affiliate, Channel 6, broadcast from Mexico) since 1952. Thus, even with this full complement of network stations, San Diegans showed that they were willing to pay for the increased viewing options offered by distant signal importation (DSI), especially those of a big-city market. The situation also seemed to indicate that stations in smaller markets, particularly independent UHF or new network-affiliated UHF stations (especially ABC affiliates), faced a serious competitive threat from broadcast signals imported from major markets.

The activities ol Southwestern Cable prompted a legal challenge as well resulting suiting ultimately in a landmark U.S. Supreme Court decision in which the Court recognised the FCC's regulatory authority over the cable television industry.[24] Midwest Television, owned by August C. Meyer, long a member of the Forbes 400 list of richest people in the United States until his death in 1992, initiated the challenge to free use of broadcast signals by cable operators. Midwest controlled the broadcast license for a VHF television station in San Diego and sought to limit the carriage of distant signals by Southwestern Cable on grounds that the importation of such signals fragmented the local broadcast market. Midwest claimed that audience fragmentation would result in reduced advertising revenues for local station by in turn forcing them to cut back or terminate service. It was a concern that spread quickly through the broadcast industry as cable systems proliferated. The broadcasters based their response on the claim that cable systems were engaged in "unfair competition," and sought help from the FCC. Copyright owners joined in with the claim that cable systems were infringing on their copyrights when they imported distant signals without authorisation, and sought judicial relief.

By 1962, there were 800 cable systems serving 850,000 subscribers.[25] It soon became apparent to FCC officials that cable, particularly DSI, had the potential to jeopardise their plans for the orderly development of UHF and their desire to see a competitive ABC television network. The networks and broadcasters played on this concern and argued that not only would DSI fragment their local audiences, it would especially impair the development of a viable independent UHF broadcast system. The argument sounded convincing to the FCC, though at that early point it had not been empirically demonstrated through econometric forecasting. Both broadcasters and filmed entertainment copyright owners also contended that DSI disrupted the system of exclusivity by which such programming had traditionally been marketed (a system in which broadcasters bought exclusive geographical rights to air motion pictures, television series, and individual programs based on a certain number of showings over a specific number of years).

The FCC's response reflected its dependency upon the broadcast industry. The relationship is offen cited as a classic case where a government agency had been "captured" by an industry as a result of its dependence upon the industry's health, expertise, and information—indeed upon the industry's very existence—to justify its own existence and regulatory functions. Therefore, it is not surprising that the FCC moved to shelter the industry from the so-called unfair competition posed by cable. In fact, the FCC had been slowly asserting its authority over cable since 1959.[26] In 1965, the FCC claimed regulatory jurisdiction over cable through the back door by using its recognised authority over the microwave communications links cable operators used in receiving and transmitting programming.[27]

The 1965 rules required cable systems leasing AT&T microwave facilities to carry all local broadcast stations (known as the "must-carry" rules) and to avoid duplicating local programming with distant-signal imports of the same program (known as the "network nonduplication" and "syndicated exclusivity" rules). In 1966, the FCC extended its regulation to cover all cable systems (claiming total authority on the basis of its role in maintaining an orderly broadcast system) and moved, without a hearing, to prohibit DSI into the top one hundred television markets (with approximately 87-89 per cent of all television households), finding that the importation would not be in the public interest.[28] The Supreme Court upheld the FCC's jurisdiction over cable television in *United States v. Southwestern Cable Company,* the case initiated by Midwest Television.[29]

In essence, the DSI restrictions constituted the FCC's response to broadcasters' complaints that cable operators had an "unfair competitive advantage" by not having to pay copyright royalties for retransmission of broadcast signals. For broadcasters, however, the issue of copyright infringement was just a subterfuge for attacking what they perceived as unfair competition, since broadcasters owned only a small fraction of copyrighted programming that was actually broadcast. The FCC rules sought to eliminate so-called unfair competition and preserve the system of exclusivity upon which television program marketing was based, not by imposing copyright liability on cable operators, which it had no authority to do, but rather by restricting cable operations. In effect, the 1966 rules froze the growth of cable television in the major markets and limited its growth to sparsely populated rural areas and small communities. The FCC granted few waivers in the three years following promulgation of the rules. Because FCC policies only partially protected the interests of broadcasters, as they did not deal with the copyright question, broadcasters continued to argue that the rules were insufficient to preserve territorial exclusivity and, more importantly, that competition remained "unfair," as broadcasters were still paying for programming while cable operators were not.

At the same time, the filmed entertainment copyright owners complained that their exclusive copyright control was being consistently eroded wherever cable systems were free to use local signals or import distant ones without authorisation. Although the syndicated exclusivity rules provided protection for specific programs in specific situations, they were not sufficient to prevent this general encroachment upon copyrights. Filmed entertainment copyright owners claimed that DSI undermined the value of their copyrights by bringing programs into markets for which licensing arrangements had not been secured. They argued that as the number of showings of a program or motion picture in an area increased, the price that could be charged for licensing a showing of that program or motion picture generally decreased.

From the filmed entertainment industry's perspective, the harm brought on by cable's DSI to their copyrights was twofold. First, copyright owners received lower prices for licensing their programming to broadcasters, since exclusivity could no longer be guaranteed. Second, due to the inability of filmed entertainment copyright owners to use federal copyright laws to prevent cable retransmissions, they were unable to collect royalties from cable operators for what they felt was clearly a commercial use. In the first instance, harm was a function of diminished income from existing markets, in the second, from potential revenues foregone. In addition to their mobilising the FCC, the filmed entertainment industry, the networks, and major broadcasters sought to remedy these instances of harm directly through participation in legislative proceedings, utilising what Domhoff called the special-interest process, and litigation. Policy-planning organisations also provided general assistance in the policy-planning process, outside and inside the state apparatus.

Efforts to Reform Copyright Law

The industrial struggle between the filmed entertainment industry and cable operators reflected larger conflicts between copyright owners and developers of new communications technologies. For years, copyright owners had urged Congress to revise the antiquated Copyright Act of 1909. Congress initiated this process in 1955, authorising the U.S. Copyright Office to conduct a program of studies of copyright issues. The Copyright Office issued its report in 1961, calling for a complete revision of the 1909 Act to account for new technologies.[30] Bills to revise the statute were introduced in the 88th Congress in the House (1964) and in the 89th Congress in both houses (1965). [31] The general position of the Motion Picture Association of America (MPAA) on copyright revision was naturally that

> the new statute must contemplate a future in which, instead of circulating several hundred 35mm prints successively among some ten thousand theatrical exhibition licensees of a picture, or 16mm prints for thousands of non-theatrical performances, the distributor may circulate electronic tape, wires, videodiscs, or other devices embodying the motion picture.[32]

Accordingly, the filmed entertainment industry approved of revisions that recognised its right to control all new uses of its copyrighted works made possible by new communications technologies.

In 1965, Arthur B. Krim, president of United Artists Corp., testified before a House subcommittee on behalf of the major television producer-distributors in support of legislation revising U.S. copyright law.[33] He noted that the fourteen companies he represented produced 75 per cent of the copyrighted material broadcast in 1965 and that fourteen additional companies would bring the total near 100 per cent. At the same time, he stated on behalf of the group strong opposition to any exemption of cable operators from copyright liability (an idea that was being floated at the time): "We believe that CATV operators should pay a fair compensation for the privilege of using our copyrighted property in the business for profit. There is no valid reason for carving out of the basic U.S. copyright statute a special exemption for commercial community antenna systems."[34]

None of the proposed hills contemplated a total exemption, but cable operators asked that one be included in the revisions. In a typical example of the "revolving door" between government and the private sector, former FCC Commissioner Frederick W. Ford came to House hearings representing the National Community Television Association (NCTA, made up of 620 CATV systems with 60 per cent of total subscribers in 1965).[35] He argued that the function of cable television was exactly the same as the home viewer's antenna, the master antennas on apartment buildings, or those serving housing subdivisions and thus did not "perform" copyrighted works but simply made a legal secondary use. In this regard Ford argued: "Once the copyright proprietor has authorised a dissemination of his work, Congress has recognised that the proprietor's control over that dissemination should cease and the public interest can best be served by giving the public access to the disseminated work free from further copyright restrictions."[36]

Ford based this claim on the first-sale doctrine, found in section 27 of the 1909 Act, in which Congress determined that publishers could not prevent resales of individual copies of books. He added further that the larger audiences that cable produced would ultimately benefit copyright owners from increased advertising revenue. Copyright owners recognised this potential and did not seek to prohibit cable's development (toward which broadcasters may have been more inclined given cable's direct competitive threat); they simply wanted cable operators to be good customers and pay for the use of the copyrighted works in retransmitted broadcasts.

The cable industry also argued that its lack of control over broadcast programming content made any process of licensing a technical impossibility. As passive recipients of the broadcaster's scheduled programming, cable operators had to take what was transmitted. Sudden program changes would always make cable operators potential infringers of copyrights since they would be unable to secure clearances sufficiently in advance. Cable television representatives challenged broadcasters or copyright owners to come up with a workable system that would make copyright clearances possible and prevent such unintended infringement. They further dramatised this problem by stressing that hundreds of cable systems would have to obtain permissions for hundreds of hours of programming if retransmissions became protectable under copyright law. The filmed entertainment industry responded that obtaining permissions was already routine for broadcasters and that, indeed, the concentration of program copyrights in a few hands had reduced the number of suppliers with whom cable operators would have to deal. It is rather ironic to see copyright owners arguing here that concentration can be a good thing. Because of this concentration, however, the cable industry feared that filmed entertainment copyright owners would use their superior corporate power and their copyright monopoly to demand monopoly prices from the weaker cable industry.[37]

Broadcasters called for a revised copyright law incorporating Cable Retransmission rights to be implemented in conjunction with the regulatory protection already provided by the FCC. On this issue, they were represented by the Association of Maximum Service Telecasters, Inc. (MST), an organisation composed of 160 commercial and "educational" VHF and UHF broadcasters.[38] MST was concerned mainly about broadcasters' ability to maintain the system of territorial exclusivity for licensed television programming and motion pictures, particularly in the face of DSI Broadcasters felt that the nonduplication rules of the FCC were limited in their ability to sustain the system of exclusivity, especially since the rules applied only fifteen days before and after a local broadcast of a program. They therefore supported copyright liability for cable in general and sought the right to bring action against an infringing cable operator in cases where their exclusive agreements were violated. In essence, broadcasters wanted the right to authorise further retransmission of the broadcast signal, that is, a copyright on the broadcast itself. With this right they could prevent the importation of distant signals into their markets and exportation of their signals to distant broadcast markets. They continued to push for a copyright on the broadcast, but Congress would not accommodate them on this point since, theoretically, the airwaves belong to the public.

In response to the cable industry's demand for some type of workable copyright proposal for cable, CBS proposed to Congress that broadcasters serve as the copyright clearance source for cable.[39] This would have required in turn that copyright owners grant broadcasters the right to make such authorisations, which copyright owners were reluctant to do, again, because it implied a loss of control over the use of their copyrighted programming. In CBS's view, this system would resolve the mechanical difficulties in administering a cable copyright. Cable operators doubted that broadcasters, as their primary competitors, would deal in good faith under such a plan and, indeed, could use such control to drive them out of business.

The Compulsory License Proposal

While Congress worked on a copyright revision, litigation on the question of copyright liability for cable was pending. On May 23, 1966, the U.S. District Court for the Southern District of New York determined in *United Artists Television, Inc. v. Fortnightly Corp,* that cable retransmission of broadcast signals constituted a "multiple performance" and hence infringed filmed entertainment copyrights.[40] The decision was a serious blow to cable operators, who had based their case for a statutory copyright exemption on the argument that cable retransmission was not a performance. Consequently, when representatives of the cable industry returned to testify on copyright revision before the 89th Congress in 1966, they submitted the proposal out of which the resolution to the conflict eventually emerged.

NCTA president Ford conceded that under the district court's ruling cable systems were now liable for copyright infringement for the retransmission of programs contained in original broadcasts.[41] Additionally, the copyright revision bill constituting S. 1006, on which Ford was testifying, sought to establish full copyright liability for cable retransmission. For this reason, cable operators offered a compromise to copyright owners and broadcasters in the form of a compulsory license. The compromise seemed essential to cable operators who were suddenly fighting to safeguard their very existence.

More precisely, they asked Congress for a copyright exemption for those programs contained in must-carry broadcast signals since the FCC required them to carry these signals regardless of copyright considerations. The cable operators announced their willingness to seek a license from copyright owners for programming contained in imported signals. However, they asked for a compulsory license for DSI into areas that were "underserved" by regular broadcast service, that is, "areas that have no service of their own, or that have an inadequate number of signals."[42] They believed that in such cases, where there were fewer than three network affiliates and one independent station, the "public interest" was best served by legislation facilitating DSI. Accordingly, for this situation, they asked Congress to grant them a compulsory license and establish a "reasonable" royalty fee by statute. They figured Congress would give them a better rate than the copyright-owning oligopoly. Finally, they were ready to compete head-to-head for copyright licenses in markets where broadcast television service was ample.

The compulsory license for cable first emerged for public discussion in the Senate hearings of 1966, not at FCC panel discussions in March 1971, as Leonard Ross has claimed.[43] It surfaced because cable operators sensed regulatory, judicial, and legislative momentum shifting against them. In these same hearings before the Senate Subcommittee on Patents, Copyrights, and Trademarks, broadcast and copyright owners categorically rejected any type of compromise. The National Association of Broadcasters (NAB) saw the compulsory license idea as a serious threat to its members' ability to maintain a viable system of license exclusivity. It asked again for the right to authorise retransmission of local transmissions by CATV and demanded that the FCC hold firm its ban on distant-signal importation. The NAB reiterated that cable threatened UHF broadcasters even in those areas considered "underserved" and in which the NCTA sought a compulsory license.[44]

Copyright owners were emphatically opposed to any notion of a compulsory license. Their view was that "it would be extraordinary for the Senate to compel a property owner to sell his property without having the opportunity to having pricing reach its own level in the marketplace."[45] Attorney Louis Nizer spoke on behalf of the MPAA and the Association of Motion Picture and Television Producers, stressing again that cable systems would have no problem dealing with the thirty or so television and motion picture distributors.[46] At the same time, he maintained that cable systems would confront a very competitive program distribution market that would prevent monopoly pricing. Edwin M. Zimmerman, acting assistant attorney general of the Department of Justice Antitrust Division, highlighted the contradictory nature of this claim. He noted that "ownership and control of copyrights is highly concentrated in the networks, movie studios, and other television producers" and that with this monopoly power "the networks or other large copyright holders might withhold permission to rebroadcast programs and thereby seek to reserve the CATV market for themselves."[47] Fearing this "anticompetitive" outcome, the Department of Justice asked the Senate subcommittee to postpone legislation imposing full copyright liability on cable systems. The Department of Justice was not ready to accept the copyright owners' claims that extension of its copyright monopoly to encompass new technologies was natural and inevitable. In its view, access to information and culture may require limits on copyright owners' exclusive control over derivative uses of their property.

Charlton Heston came to the hearings on S. 1006 as president of the Screen Actors Guild (SAG), establishing a tradition of union participation in many subsequent hearings on copyright legislation concerning new technology and the filmed entertainment industry.[48] In his testimony, Heston came out in support of copyright liability for cable, arguing that it would benefit especially those 16,000 SAG members who earned on average less than $3,000 per year. Heston claimed that through union contracts actors would ultimately be rewarded for their creativity as copyright royalties trickled down. Heston's testimony reflects a situation in which employees support their employers' efforts to extend the private appropriation of socially based creativity because their wages are tied to royalties. In the process, the antagonistic relationship between capital and labor becomes obscured, whereas the antagonistic relationship between individuals and the community are emphasised (i.e., private appropriation from the socially constituted intellectual commons). Actually, Heston did identify the former antagonism quite clearly but not, obviously, its essential basis in capitalism:

> The heart of this entire system, of course, is the protection which the owner of the film has under the copyright laws. To our regret, copyright laws do not extend to cover actors and similar creative artists. So whatever derivative rights we have are precisely that, derivatively obtained. And if the film companies and television networks are deprived of any part of the property protection that they now have under copyright laws, the members of the Screen Actors Guild will suffer a loss in earnings.[49]

SAG stood for full copyright liability for cable retransmission. It has taken this position on subsequent contests over who should benefit from new derivative uses; for example, it supported legislation for a royalty mechanism for off-air home-video recording in the early 1980s.[50]

The Supreme Court's Ruling in Fortnightly

When the U.S. Court of Appeals affirmed the decision of the lower district court in *Fortnightly,*[51] it appeared inevitable that cable operators would have to sit down with copyright owners to negotiate the terms of the cable copyright. Surprisingly, the U.S. Supreme Court reversed the decisions of the lower courts by a vote of 5 to I.[52] As in the district court's opinion, the Supreme Court's decision hinged on the question of whether Fortnightly "performed" United Artists' copyrighted works. United Artists contended that by picking up and retransmitting broadcasts containing its copyrighted works, Fortnightly infringed its exclusive rights under sections l(c) and (d) of the Copyright Act of 1909 to "perform ... in public for profit" nondramatic literary works and to "perform ... publicly" dramatic works. Fortnightly defended on the grounds that cable retransmission was not a public performance. The conflicting claims resulted from the fact that, understandably, the Copyright Act did not contemplate "performance" by technology that did not exist when it was enacted.

The Supreme Court had considered retransmission of radio broadcasting and the general question of what constituted a "performance" in *Buck v. Jewell-LaSalle Realty Company* (1931).[53] In this case, a hotel owner retransmitted, by wire, radio broadcasts from a central radio to individual rooms within the establishment without authorisation of the music copyright owners whose works were contained in the broadcasts. Under the "multiple performance" doctrine, the Supreme Court held that this use of copyrighted work was an infringement. In *Fortnightly,* the copyright owner (United Artists) argued that the retransmission of television broadcasts by cable to subscribers was analogous to the situation in *Jewell-LaSalle.* The Supreme Court rejected this case as holding precedent and, in a decision described as "a surprisingly unsophisticated analysis of the functions of the cable television system,"[54] found that cable retransmission of broadcasts did not constitute a "performance" within the meaning of the 1909 Act.

In reaching its decision, the Court questioned whether cable television acted as "broadcaster" or "viewer," considering the former an active performer (selecting, producing, and propagating programs) and the latter a "passive beneficiary." It concluded that "when CATV is considered in this framework ... it falls on the viewer's side of the line. Essentially, a CATV system no more than enhances the viewer's capacity to receive the broadcaster's signals; it provides a well-located antenna with an efficient connection to the viewer's television set."[55] From the Court's perspective, the only difference between the antenna system of the viewer and the cable operator was that "in the case of CATV . . . the antenna system is erected and owned not by its users but by an entrepreneur".[56] Upon recognising this distinction, however, the Court should have realised the error of its ways. It is clear that cable system operators garner profit from the use of copyrighted filmed entertainment works. If the Court was to maintain consistency with the logic of intellectual property, such commercial use of copyrighted works by cable operators would require that a portion of their profits be.passed on to those who own those works. However, as critical legal studies have so correctly recognised, the outcome of litigation is fraught with such contradictions and inconsistencies. The Court had the choice of following *Jewell-LaSalle,* in which the commercial nature of the use was essentially analogous to cable retransmission; or it could take into account new technological realities and bring the concept of "performance up to date. It did neither, following instead the reasoning of Cable Operators—that they were like viewers, not broadcasters, and therefore did not perform the copyrighted works.

The Court clearly recognised that there was more at stake in this case than simply an interpretation of the nature of "performance," though Schmid argued that by basing the decision on this question it "miss[ed] the essential definition of the MC=0 [marginal cost equals zero] situation."[57] He explained: "Arguments over definition are really policy arguments over who gets to capture the values created by a new use (transformation) of content in a different new media where these new uses add nothing to the original cost of the content."[58] The policy question then becomes How far do the rights of copyright owners "extend beyond the recovery of fixed costs to include more of the total value created by the transformed product"?[59] Like the officials from the Department of Justice's Antitrust Division, the Court's majority did not see the extension of copyright to encompass new technology as necessary or inevitable.

This case highlights the crucial role of the state in determining the limits of private property. Such limits are built into intellectual property law (fair use,' periods of duration, compulsory licenses, etc.) to meet policy goals of facilitating public access to intellectual and artistic creativity. Filmed entertainment copyright owners typically respond that given the risks inherent in producing their works they are entitled to compensation from any subsequent uses. Obviously, the individuals who operate within the institutions of the state apparatus do not assent to this argument every time and consequently produce contradictory decisions as in *Fortnightly*.

Nevertheless, members of the Court were aware of the profound implications of the case, particularly for copyright owners, cable operators, and consumers and more generally for the future growth of cable television. As Justice Abe Fortas indicated in his dissent, the decision had the potential to make or break cable as an independent means of communication. Given the importance of the case for cable's future, the Court drew its decision narrowly, refusing to accommodate the various competing considerations of copyright, communications, and antitrust policy that it believed ought to be up to Congress to resolve. The decision to maintain the status quo (i.e., no copyright liability for cable) looks like an attempt by the Court to force Congress into settling the matter in a comprehensive way. In his dissent, Justice Fortas again tipped the majority's hand when he warned of the dangers in waiting for legislation: "Important economic values are at stake, and it would be hazardous to assume that Congress will act promptly, comprehensively, and retroactively."[60]

The *Fortnightly* decision was nevertheless limited in scope. It applied only to the retransmission of local broadcast signals, not to DSL. By leaving this question temporarily unresolved, neither the FCC nor Congress rushed to alter the situation as it had stood since the FCC's *Second Report and Order.* The FCC continued to require waivers for DSI but granted few, thereby maintaining the freeze on cable's growth. The copyright revision process in Congress ground to a halt; the result was a standoff between the Senate Judiciary Committee's copyright panel, representing most strongly the pro-cable forces and the Senate Commerce Committee's communications subcommittee, which represented the probroad cast elements. Efforts at negotiated settlements between industry sectors were held up due to fear of antitrust action "and, more importantly, by each side's willingness to try its luck in the political arena."[61] The executive branch joined the fray at this point, as did policy groups outside of the state apparatus, in attempts to break the stalemate produced by the contradictory actions of legislative, judicial, and administrative institutions and the uncompromising stances of the industry sectors.

Intervention by the Policy-Planning Network

In terms of the class struggle theory of the state, breaking the impasse required the constitution of a hegemonic power bloc in order for the long-term interests of capital to prevail. The primary long-term interest at this point in time, from the perspective of capital as a whole, was the preservation of the integrity of intellectual property rights in the face of new communications technology. Clearly, the Supreme Court's decision in *Fortnightly* threatened this integrity by allowing for-profit use of copyrighted programming without authorisation of or compensation to copyright owners. Capital as a whole had another long-term interest regarding communications policy, which was to see the demolition of regulatory barriers protecting the monopoly positions of dominant companies (e.g., AT&T, CBS, and NBC). Indeed, the major policy-planning groups soon began advocating the deregulation of television and cable to reduce the power of the networks. This was part of a larger effort to generate more (oligopolistic) competition in the communications industries in order to promote the development of goods and services necessary for U.S. capital to enter the so-called Information Age. In instrumentalist terms, the constitution of this bloc required the active participation of superior forces rooted in the corporate community and policy-planning network that could transcend the particular and limited interests of broadcasters, copyright owners, and cable operators that produced the deadlock.

Monroe Price estimated that by 1974 the expenditures for funding research on cable by government and foundations probably exceeded $5 million.[62] The initial government-sponsored report came from the 1968 Rostow Task Force on Telecommunications Policy. Next came the Sloan Commission's report on cable communications, which is of particular interest to this case study. The Alfred P.

Sloan Foundation commissioned the study in June 1970 with a grant of $500,000 when activity on the cable copyright issue was still stalled. Reflecting the sociopolitical context of the late 1960s, the commission was particularly interested in the potential of cable to be the technological "fix" for turmoil in the inner cities. The commission serves as a significant illustration of the role of foundations and the power elite in the policy-planning process as evidenced by its membership and commissioned papers.[63]

The report itself is also an interesting cultural document with its "blue sky" proposals lor solving social ills by enhancing communications through technology. Cable television was heralded for its potential use in the political process, the delivery of health services, the control of nonmedical uses of drugs (all critical problems in inner cities), and, with more caution on the part of the commission, for low-cost point-to-point television transmissions, the delivery of any book from a library from any continent, and cooking dinner, washing windows, and tending babies.[64] The commission's top-down vision of policy implementation (a function of its elitism) and its failure to consider the history of technology, particularly of communications technology, is also typical. However, the report successfully equated the viability of cable television with the general interest of the people and nation.

The commission recommended allowing cable operators and broadcasters (including UHF) ta battle it out in the marketplace, thereby permitting the development and growth of pay-cable television and the elimination of restrictions and conditions for cable's use of over-the-air programming. These policy recommendations basically sought the creation of an open market for the procurement and retransmission of television programming. In the commission's view, this would make the DSI problem insignificant. This was based on the belief that copyright owners went along with exclusivity not because they believed that it maximised revenues but in order not to "risk their oligopolistic customers' wrath by abandoning a practice with advantages for the customers and no disadvantages for them."[65] To appease broadcasters, the commission recommended, therefore, that cable operators pay a copyright fee to copyright owners and a packaging fee to the broadcaster in the case of cable retransmission. Otherwise, the cable operator could buy programming in the second-run market and repackage it on the system's own channels.

The compulsory license received some legitimacy in a report that Leonard Ross of Harvard Law School submitted to the commission. This policy option steadily gained legitimacy from the cable industry's continuing claim that the high transaction costs associated with the process of negotiating and contracting for the rights to use copyrighted filmed entertainment programming by the more than 2,500 cable systems would make cable retransmission an unprofitable venture.[66] The compulsory license was proposed, therefore, as a mechanism to reduce these high transaction costs.[67] Given that the powerful broadcast industry would not give up its system of exclusivity and that copyright owners were not inclined to force it to, the compulsory license option was more realistic than the proposal by the Sloan Commission that exclusivity be sharply curtailed.

The following is a summary of the positions held by the three industry sectors at the point of impasse (circa 1970). Despite the fact that cable operators were exempt from copyright liability for retransmission of local broadcasts as a result of *Fortnightly,* cable's growth was still inhibited by the FCC's restrictions on DSI. Its potential for importing signals from distant markets (especially Los Angeles, Chicago, and New York) to most other markets was restricted by FCC rules. The networks liked seeing cable as simply a supplementary service for "filling in" network and educational broadcast services in underserved areas. The FCC also preserved the broadcast industry's system of syndicated exclusivity through regulation. Broadcasters had convinced the FCC that without exclusivity their local audiences would shrink to the point of threatening their very existence. They continued to complain about the "unfair" competition afforded to cable operators who did not have to pay royalties for the use of television programming.

Copyright owners continued to insist on full copyright liability but were especially adamant that cable be kept out of the top fifty markets from which the bulk of their licensing revenues were derived. They persisted in their rejection of a compulsory license for cable that represented, in their view, a loss of control over private property. They also feared they would have to lower prices on their licenses if they could not guarantee broadcasters exclusivity. At the same time, however, since they were receiving no remuneration from cable operations a compulsory license did seem better than nothing, though this was not conceded in public.

As noted, cable operators were prepared to accept a compulsory license in exchange for the FCC's easing of DSI restrictions. The courts had yet to decide the question of copyright liability for DSI, which was pending in *Teleprompter Corp. v. CBS, Inc.*[68] (an important case discussed in more detail below), but waiting for a court decision was clearly too risky. There was always the threat that should the courts decide against them, cable operators would have to pay enormous sums in back royalties. Thus, cable operators had the most to gain from resolution of the copyright conflict, and copyright owners would gain if they could secure remuneration for this use of their property. Broadcasters benefited most from the status quo, although all were not entirely equal in the intensity of their opposition to the cable industry, since of the one-half of all cable systems owned by communications companies in 1971, 30 per cent belonged to broadcasters (12 per cent were owned by newspaper companies and other publishers and 5 per cent by phone companies).[69] In any case, resolution of the conflict was essential for copyright revision to proceed.

Clearly, copyright revision was important to many other sectors of the informational and cultural industries, and certainly pressure from these emerging groups (e.g., publishers, computer companies, and information service industries) made state officials eager to break the stalemate. The issue therefore came to the attention of officials at the highest levels of the executive branch, including President Richard Nixon. Accordingly, the administration moved to forge a compromise.

The "Consensus Agreement" and the FCC's 1972 Cable Rules

Efforts to resolve the cable copyright issue at the executive level began with a "Letter of Intent" from FCC chair Dean Burch (former chair of the Republican National Committee), informing Congress of proposal FCC modifications to the 1966 cable regulations that aimed to clear the way for a compromise between interested parties.[70] Burch claimed that modifications would ultimately facilitate passage of the copyright revision by Congress. To this end, he joined Clay T. Whitehead, director of the newly established Office of Telecommunications Policy (OTP), at the White House for a series of negotiations between cable operators, broadcasters, and copyright owners. Out of these negotiations the "Consensus Agreement" emerged and was signed in November 1971 by the NCTA, the NAB, and the Committee of Copyright Owners.[71]

The Consensus Agreement preserved the system of exclusivity between copyright owners and broadcasters in the top fifty broadcast markets (with 75 per cent of all households) but limited the periods of exclusivity to one to two years depending on program type in the second fifty markets. Maintaining the system of exclusivity thus conformed closest to the interests of the broadcast and copyright industries, particularly with its extensive restrictions in the top fifty markets, where the bulk of revenues for program suppliers were derived and where new UHF stations were largely concentrated. The FCC's objective in retaining exclusivity rules was "to establish viewer loyalty for the local station."[72] But this prevented cable systems in the top fifty markets from offering much more than clear reception of local signals. This was not enough to make cable attractive to subscribers to promote growth in these markets. In the second fifty markets, cable systems could often add a considerably greater choice of signals than was available over the air, thereby giving cable growth some impetus in these markets.

Together, the DSI restrictions and exclusivity rules continued to protect broadcasters against the "competitive advantage" held by cable operators who had yet to pay any copyright royalties. Consequently, the Consensus Agreement permitted a limited expansion of cable television but was still strongly biased toward broadcast interests. The NCTA, testifying at copyright revision hearings before the Senate Subcommittee on Patents, Copyrights, and Trademarks in 1973, revealed that it had been intimidated into accepting the agreement by the Nixon administration and the OTP. The choices left were either the continuation of the FCC's "freeze" or the "equally unattractive possibility of extensive and unproductive congressional hearings."[73] The Nixon administration held early in its tenure that cable should serve as a supplement to broadcast television, not as a competitor.

The Consensus Agreement did provide for the compulsory license that the cable industry sought. It committed copyright owners and broadcasters to support cable television copyright legislation and to seek its early passage. The agreement also committed copyright owners and cable operators to sit down and negotiate a schedule of fees covering the compulsory license that could be included in the new copyright statute. If such an agreement could not be reached in private then legislation would provide for compulsory arbitration. This proved to be the next sticking point in the copyright revision process. Cable operators put forward figures between 1 and 5 per cent of their annual gross earnings and commissioned economists to demonstrate that anything higher would jeopardise profitability.[74] Copyright owners suggested a figure averaging 16 per cent and also employed economists to show that this was fair and affordable for cable operators.[75]

Despite the Consensus Agreement and the promise of all parties to support early passage of a copyright revision, the cable copyright issue was once again stalled. The momentum toward resolution of the issue shifted in favor of cable operators in 1974 as a result of the issuance of an executive-level report on cable and the Supreme Court's decision in *Teleprompter*.

Report of the Cabinet Committee on Cable Communications

The Cabinet Committee on Cable Communications released its report to the president in January 1974 through the OTP. Nixon formed the committee in 1971 to "come to grips with cable communications in order to avoid the social, economic, and regulatory instability that this technological innovation could cause."[76] At that time, as the quote implies, Nixon was clearly biased in favor of the broadcast industry. However, the tone of the report as released in 1974 took aim at the broadcast industry and the monopoly privileges conferred upon it by FCC regulation, much more in line with the particular interests of the rising hegemonic faction of capital, that is, the large information providers and users. The report rejected the FCC's perspective that cable was simply an extension of the broadcast industry and that the latter's interests were therefore always primary, stating that cable "has the potential to become an important and entirely new communications medium, open and available to all."[77] The report stressed the urgency of federal action on this issue given the emergent "postindustrial'" society in which cable television could play a vital role.[78] It also underscored the connection of cable to several major national industries including electronic data processing, telephone, television and radio broadcasting, the motion picture and music industries, and communications satellites.[79]

The report couched the necessity of curbing excessive governmental power and excessive concentrations of private economic power in terms of traditional rhetoric on democratic decision making and access to information. However, beneath this rhetoric lurked the goal of "deregulation," that is, the shifting of policy and decisionmaking regarding communications out of the hands of the partially accountable public sphere and into the hands of the private sphere of capital. The social unrest of the 1960s had resulted in intolerable levels of public insurgency into state apparatuses for many in the upper class and corporate community. Robert Horowitz argued that "more than any other factor, it was the growth of regulation which prompted the business political counterattack."[80]

Consequently, the Nixon and Ford administrations began seeking to reverse many of these gains. Willard Rowland placed the beginning of the communications deregulation trend precisely at this time.[81] In the mass communications field alone, counterreform included halting the progress of the public access mandate to the electronic media achieved through the fairness doctrine in CBS v. DNG;[82] striking down mandatory access to cable in FCC v. Midwest Video Corp,;[83] a general weakening of the public's right to challenge broadcast licenses; and increasing regulation of broadcast content deemed "indecent" as well as "obscene."'[84]

Coupled with this counterretbrmism came the effort to break down the monopoly privileges of entrenched communications companies, primarily AT&T, IBM, and the broadcast networks. With regards to AT&T, Daniel Schiller has shown that deregulation was intended to force this public monopoly to shift its focus from voice-telephone service to U.S. households to the telecommunications needs of big business.[85] In his view, the inner group of the corporate community recognised the need to inject some competition into communications sectors to preserve and promote U.S. hegemony in the shift to an information-based global economy. The cabinet committee report was an early statement reflecting this view, particularly in addressing cable and broadcasting. It recommended that telephone companies be prohibited from operating cable systems in the same areas in which they provided common carrier services but not be banned outright from cable ownership.

Additional elite policy statements are found in the report of the Committee on Economic Development's

Research and Policy Committee[86] and the research papers of Gerald Ford's Domestic Council Review Group on Regulatory Reform published by the American Enterprise Institute for Public Policy Research.[87] One of the Domestic Council's research papers on cable deregulation took the following positions:

1. Cable television does not offer an immediate threat to the general public: it will not in the foreseeable future drive over-the-air broadcasting out of business. Instead, it does offer the prospect of giving its subscribers substantially more entertainment options than they now possess.
2. Cable television does pose an economic threat to broadcasters, but only because it threatens a monopolistic position. More competition will result in lower profits for the television industry, and consequently the value of television licenses will fall. But these effects will not be great enough to cause a wholesale reduction in the number of broadcasting stations.[88]

The cabinet committee devoted only two paragraphs out of fifty pages of text to the cable copyright issue. Thus, by early 1974, when the report was released, the issue appeared essentially resolved except for the details. It recommended that cable operators pay for use of copyrighted programming (as did all other media) and be held for full copyright liability for retransmission of broadcasts. It concluded that "given the reasonable expectations created by current regulatory policy, the cable operator should be entitled to a non-negotiated, blanket license, conferred by statute, to cover his own retransmission of broadcast signals."[89]

Thus, the policy option for resolving the cable copyright question had been essentially determined within the policymaking process, whereas Congress had yet to act. Disagreements over the specifics of this policy option continued to hold up such legislation. The final push therefore came from the Supreme Court.

The Supreme Court's Teleprompter Decision

The *Teleprompter* litigation again reflected the ambiguity surrounding new communications technology and copyright. The federal district court in this case, relying on *Fortnightly,* dismissed the CBS claim that cable operator Teleprompter infringed its copyrights by importing the broadcast signals of a CBS affiliate for retransmission to subscribers.[90] The U.S. Court of Appeals reversed the district court's decision.[91] It distinguished the case from *Fortnightly,* which it recognised as applying only to local broadcast signals, not DSL. Cable operators *did* function as viewers in the *Fortnightly* case because, like home viewers, they simply used their antennas and cables to improve local broadcast signal reception. However, in the case of DSI, the cable operator delivered the broadcast signal to a new audience via microwave. This factor of bringing the signal into a market where it was not ordinarily receivable constituted a performance under the appeals court's interpretation of the 1909 Copyright Act. Accordingly, Teleprompter infringed CBS's copyrights. On this point, the Supreme Court reversed (on a vote of 6 to 3), holding that the distance between the broadcast station and the viewer was irrelevant in determining whether retransmission was a broadcaster or viewer function; cable retransmission was a viewer function.[92]

The Court's decision in March 1974, the increasing hostility of the Nixon administration toward broadcasters, and the emerging deregulatory mood put copyright owners and broadcasters in a position where they had to compromise. Despite the tact that cable operators won in the *Teleprompter* case, they could not hope to break out of the FCC's regulatory grip, which kept them out of the top fifty markets, unless they did in fact pay copyright royalties. Additionally, the policy-planning reports all insisted that cable operators pay for the programming content that they used. Finally, to remain consistent with the logic of intellectual property law, the state had to require that users of new communications technologies obtain authorisation from and pay remuneration to the copyright owners of the works they utilised. Consequently, the Copyright Act of 1976 included for the first time photocopying, computer and information systems, audiotape recording, and cable television systems.[93]

Although it can be argued that the resulting compulsory license demonstrates the contradictory and contingent nature of policy outcomes because it took rights negotiations out of the marketplace and brought them within the domain of the state, it can be countered that the law was nevertheless determined by the logic of copyright. The cable copyright ratified and extended the rights of filmed entertainment copyright owners, putting them in the position to achieve market dominance over a new media sector. This is precisely the pattern the case studies in this book demonstrate time and again.

The Law of Copyright and the Logic of Capital

Copyright owners were happy finally to be receiving some compensation for cable operators' use of their property. In 1987, they collected $140 million from cable operators under the compulsory license.[94] Nevertheless, copyright owners complained that CRT rates were lower than those they could achieve in the marketplace, despite the fact that the compulsory fee paid by cable systems is indexed and periodically has been increased. In 1988, the National Telecommunications and Information Administration

(NTIA) called for the repeal of the compulsory license in a report on video program distribution and cable television.[95] The report found that cable operators paid less than 2 per cent of their gross revenues to copyright owners and that such preferential treatment was no longer justified. It recommended that cable operators enter into market-based contracts with program suppliers. Early in 1990, the FCC voted to recommend to Congress that it abolish the compulsory license as a move to benefit consumers, broadcasters, and cable programming services.[96]

Meanwhile, the increasing concentration of cable systems into the hands of multisystem operators (MSOs) substantially weakened the argument that the compulsory license was necessary in order to keep transaction costs at a manageable level. The NTIA reported that in December 1987 the top ten MSOs controlled 60 per cent of all subscribers.[97] It found that the leading MSO, Tele-Communications Inc. (TCI), with 10.9 million subscribers, captured 23 per cent of the market in 1987.[98] Its programming stakes in 1988 included American Movie Classics (50 per cent), Black Entertainment Television (14 per cent), Discovery Channel (49 per cent), Prime Time Tonight (35 per cent), QVC Network Inc. (27 per cent), Think Entertainment (38 per cent), and Turner Broadcasting System Inc. (22 per cent).[99] The Time-Warner merger brought together the second and sixth largest cable system operators, giving the conglomerate a combined share of 5.5 million basic subscribers in 1989, which grew to 6.8 million by mid-1993.[100] Early in 1995, Time Warner announced plans to acquire Cablevision Systems, the sixth largest MSO, which would bring the company's total number of subscribers to 11.5 million.[101]

Consequently, the transfer of copyrights simply requires negotiations between two oligopolistic industries: cable MSOs and filmed entertainment. Given increasing vertical integration of program suppliers with cable operators, the rights transfers can take place within the same corporate structure. Part of the logic of the Time-Warner merger itself was to reduce such transaction costs. Accordingly, the demise of mom-and-pop cable systems also signaled that transaction costs for securing copyrights from copyright owners were no longer prohibitive. As large MSOs came to control programming through equity interests or through exclusive contracts, they were also able to thwart potential competition from providers of alternative delivery systems, such as satellite or microwave, thus preserving their local monopoly status.

The changed conditions of the late 1980s led copyright owners to begin pushing more strongly for the repeal of the compulsory license.[102] Broadcasters also supported repeal on the grounds that the compulsory license constituted an "unfair subsidy" to the cable industry. Additionally, they resurrected demands for copyrights on the broadcast signal itself through some type of "retransmission consent" mechanism. However, they expressed willingness to retain the system in exchange for codification of the FCC's must-carry rules—the requirement that cable companies carry local broadcast signals—after the rules were found unconstitutional by the courts in 1985 and 1987.[103] Broadcasters began to worry that without such legislation cable operators would drop local broadcast stations, with whom they compete for advertising dollars.[104]

Thus, policies that sought to encourage the growth of cable and weaken broadcasters' oligopolistic power permitted the industry to become a competitive threat to over-the-air broadcasting. This outcome again demonstrates the reactive role of the state within the economic sphere. The contradictory tendencies within capitalism promote endless crises of accumulation to which the state can only react through minimal intervention into the marketplace.

Despite the best efforts of state officials, a competitive market remains a chimera given the inherent tendency within capitalism toward concentration.

The shift from one dominant media sector—broadcasting—to the emerging cable oligopoly prompted state officials to reconsider cable deregulation, partly because broadcasters still retained enough influence in the late 1980s to affect policy agendas and partly because of public outcry over the cable industry's monopolistic practices. Developers of alternative program delivery systems also demanded action. Much of the cable industry's growing power could be traced to the Cable Communications Policy Act of 1984, which virtually eliminated municipal and state regulation of cable rates upon taking effect in 1987.[105] Price deregulation gave cable operators a green light for raising their rates. A study by the General Accounting Office (GAO) reported that average basic cable rates rose 43 per cent, from $11.14 to $15.95 per subscriber, between November 30, 1986, and December 31, 1989, roughly three times as much as the Consumer Price Index.[106] By 1991, cable rates had increased 56 per cent in the five years subsequent to rate deregulation, according to the GAO.[107] Subscribers also complained about poor service despite soaring hookup and maintenance fees.

The growing pressure emanating from broadcasters, satellite and microwave companies, and consumers had prompted two FCC proceedings and the introduction of fourteen bills in Congress regarding cable reregulation by 1990. It took Congress another two years to pass the Cable Television Consumer Protection and Competition Act of 1992 in an attempt to reregulate cable rates and services.[108] As implied by its title this legislation was intended to significantly roll back the subscription prices and service fees by mandating "fair" pricing guidelines and to interject competition into the program delivery market place by requiring the vertically integrated MSOs to license their programming to alternative delivery systems. By the mid-1990s, cable subscribers had seen little change in their bills and alternative delivery systems remained marginal.

The law did not repeal the compulsory license for cable, as recommended by certain federal agencies and demanded by the filmed entertainment industry. However, it did confer a copyright on broadcast signals by granting local broadcasters the right to demand retransmission consent from cable operators for carrying their signal. Following the logic of copyright, the law permitted broadcasters to demand payment for the use of their broadcast signals for the first time. As Congress debated this provision, cable operators argued that it would add up to $1 billion to their programming costs, which they naturally would have to pass on to subscribers. To temper this possibility, the Act allowed local broadcasters to forego charging cable operators retransmission consent fees in exchange for promotions, advertising time, or preferential channel positioning. In essence, Congress overrode court restrictions on the must-carry rule by making it "voluntary."

The filmed entertainment industry vehemently opposed the retransmission consent provision, arguing that it permitted broadcasters to gain economic benefits from programming to which it held the rights. Broadcasters countered that they were simply being remunerated for the added value generated by packaging programming into the broadcast schedule. Furthermore, broadcasters had already paid for programming upon licensing it, as had cable operators through the compulsory license mechanism. Thus, the filmed entertainment industry, when demanding a cut of the retransmission fees, hoped to be paid twice for the same programs. The industry was thwarted in its try for two bites at the apple. Ultimately, the retransmission consent provision strengthened the position of core-firm broadcasters and underscored the oligopolistic power of the cable industry. The largest cable firms announced that they would simply refuse to pay any retransmission consent fees. This prompted a letter from Senator Daniel K. Inouye (D-Hawaii) to the Department of Justice and the Federal Trade Commission asking them to investigate the "tactical and semantic uniformity" and "parallel strategies" of cable operators subsequent to the passage of the Act.[109]

Instead of paying retransmission fees, the largest cable operators entered into contracts with three of the four major networks, whereby the MSOs agreed to carry the networks' newly established cable channels. The agreements gave Fox, ABC, and NBC immediate entry into cable programming ahead of other potential cable network providers. The deals also demonstrated expanding recycling and synergistic practices among major media conglomerates. Fox launched the FX channel specialising in network syndicated programming from the 1970s and early 1980s, ABC/Capital Cities spun off ESPN2 from ESPN, and NBC proposed three new networks: America's Talking, an all-talk show format; SportsChannel, a joint venture with Liberty Media Corp. and Cablevision Systems; and a Latin American Spanish-language news service. The two largest cable operators, TCI and Time Warner, allegedly thwarted CBS's effort to launch a news channel clue to their stakes in the Turner system's CNN and Headline News services.[110] Ironically, it was CBS CEO Laurence Tisch who was credited with being the major impetus behind passage of the retransmission consent provision.[111] Consequently, the majority of cable networks are directly or indirectly controlled by core broadcasters, MSOs, and filmed entertainment producers.

The power-structure analysis, particularly with its focus on lobbying and electoral processes, provides sufficient explanations for why Congress passed the 1992 Cable Act in the face of opposition from cable operators and Hollywood. Despite the cable industry's encroachment on the economic and political power of broadcasters, the latter retained significant residual influence in Washington through its lobbying arm, the National Association of Broadcasters. More importantly, broadcasters continued to exercise significant political power due to their pivotal role in electoral processes. Clearly, the retransmission consent provision constituted a valuable gift to local broadcasters whose control of access to the public via the airwaves could not be ignored by Congress. Electoral strategies also prompted Congress to pass the "consumer protection" portion of the bill as a response to complaints by cable subscribers. Thus, when President George Bush vetoed the bill, Congress handed him his first veto override in thirty-five attempts.

In class theory terms, the 1992 Cable Act reflected the intervention of consumer reform groups, particularly the Consumer Federation of America, into the state system for purposes of curbing the excesses of monopoly. However, this intervention hardly constitutes qualification as "class struggle," for it remained well within the confines of the logic of capital. In sum, the 1992 Cable Act was a short-term fix for market failure brought about by capital concentration. In opposing the Act, the Bush administration more closely reflected the long-term interests of capital as a whole. Its position was to open up the telecommunications marketplace to more "competition," primarily the telephone companies. Although the administration was thwarted in this effort, structural forces continued to propel the telecommunications sector toward further integration and concentration. Accordingly, it is the logic-of-capital analysis of the state that holds the strongest explanatory power for interpreting and predicting cable's evolution.

Continuing developments in the telecommunications sector suggest that industrial, technological, and institutional forces are outrunning the ability of state officials to establish "coherent" policies. Cable firms are moving into telephone services, telephone companies are beginning to offer video services, and software providers are becoming increasingly integrated into both sectors. At the same time, regulatory barriers that prohibited cable and telephone companies from entering into one another's businesses have been challenged and slowly repealed.

For some major companies, the pace of repeal has not be been rapid enough and they have signaled their dissatisfaction with state officials and agencies by engaging in investment strikes. In early 1994, Bell Atlantic—TCI announced that its proposed merger had been called off, Southwestern Bell and Cox Enterprises called off a joint venture in cable television, and AT&T and McCaw Cellular Communications called time-out on their proposed merger (a deal that eventually went through). Commenting on these failed deals, Marc L. Fiedler, vice president of BellSouth Corp., confirmed the connection between state regulation and the investment strike in stating: "There's a lot of uncertainty about regulatory treatment, and in the face of all that uncertainty, it's difficult to make big financial commitments."[112] Nevertheless, mergers and buyouts on smaller scales have continued unabated and all industry officials agree that convergence is pending. Congress sought to smooth the grade for pavement of the information superhighway by introducing legislation in midsummer 1994, lifting many of the restrictions on market entry by telephone companies into other lines of business. As demonstrated, capitalist owners of core communications firms are most likely to control this highway as well as the traffic running on it.

Conclusion

This case study considers the first challenge to the filmed entertainment copyright system. It demonstrates the ambiguity surrounding the introduction of new communications technologies in the single area of copyright law. Similar ambiguities exist across an entire range of economic, political, and social institutions producing tensions and conflicts that then shape how the technologies are adopted and developed. The clash of new communications technology and the institution of intellectual property is a valuable area of study for revealing how the structure of capitalism is reproduced and what roles the state and law play in this process. The tensions produced by new technologies are themselves manifestations of in terclass and intraclass struggles.

The central question to be resolved in the cable case was: Who should benefit from the introduction of this new means of distributing broadcasts? Cable television therefore did not evolve as a system bringing alternative means of communication or programming. Cable entrepreneurs simply inserted themselves into the existing distribution system for filmed entertainment programming and profited handsomely for improving the efficiency of broadcast television in reaching its audiences. They had to struggle against the hegemony of the broadcast industry and the demands by copyright owners that they be compensated for this commercial use. There was no mandate for state institutions to maintain the hegemony of television broadcasting, though this power did allow the industry to preserve its position in the face of the cable television challenge for some time. However, the larger interests of capital as a whole did require a reconstitution of the hegemonic friction of the capitalist class. As a result, broadcasters and AT&T lost some of their regulatory-based monopoly power in the face of the greater structural necessities of the capitalist class. This demonstrates that regulatory agencies can exercise a relative autonomy as well. The FCC was able to loosen the bonds of "captivity" imposed by broadcasters as it began promoting the larger interests of capital as a whole.

The law and nature of intellectual property are essentially based in capitalism. Here the options of the state apparatus were even more limited. Despite the contradictory nature of the policymaking, legislating, and litigating processes, the pressures and limits imposed by capitalism determined the outcome that cable-operators ultimately be held liable for retransmission of copyrighted filmed entertainment. The form that the liability would take was a matter of negotiation and struggle between individuals, institutions, and industries. This case study shows how the adoption and development of new communications technology can be contingent but still determined by economic structures. This is particularly the case where private property rights are concerned, since they are essential to the definition of capitalism.

NOTES

1. Martin Carnoy, *The State and Political Theory*, Princeton: Princeton University Press, 1984, p. 210.
2. Ralph Miliband, *The State in Capitalist Society*, New York: Basic Books, 1969; G. W. Domhoff, *Who Rules America Now?* Englewood Cliffs, NJ: Prentice-Hall, 1983; and, *The Power Elite and the State: How Policy Is Made in America*, New York: Aldine de Gruyter, 1990.
3. The descriptions of instrumentalism and structuralism are adapted from Vincent Mosco, *Pushbutton Fantasies: Critical Perspectives on Videotex and Information Technology*, Norwood, NJ: Ablex, 1982.

4. Nicos Poulantzas, *Classes in Contemporary Socialism*, London: New Left Books, 1975; *Political Power and Social Classes*, London: New Left Books, 1975; *State, Power, and Socialism*, London: New Left Books, 1978.
5. Bob Jessop, *The Capitalist State*, New York: New York University Press, 1982; *State Theory: Putting the Capitalist State in Its Place*, University Park, PA: Pennsylvania State University Press, 1990.
6. Goran Therborn, *What Does the Ruling Class Do When It Rules?* London: Verso, 1980, p. 89.
7. Mao Tse-Tung, "On Practice: On the Relation Between Knowledge and Practice," in A. Mandel (ed.), *Four Essays on Philosophy*, Peking: Foreign Language Press, 1966, pp. 1-20, p. 5.
8. Jessop, 1990, p. 37.
9. Anthony Giddens, *Power, Property, and the State: A Contemporary Critique of Historical Materialism*, Berkeley: University of California Press, 1981.
10. Miliband, p. 146.
11. Charles Lindblom, *Politics and Markets: The World's Political Systems*, New York: Basic Books, 1977.
12. Theodore Lowi, *The End of Liberalism: Ideology, Policy and the Crisis of Public Authority*, New York: Norton, 1969.
13. President's Commission on Privatisation, *Privatisation: Toward More Effective Government*, Washington, DC: U.S Government Printing Office. 1988, p. 233.
14. Domhoff, 1983, p. 150.
15. Jessop, 1990, p. 10.
16. Vincent Mosco, *The Pay-Per Society: Computers und Communication in the Information Age*, Norwood, NJ: Ablex, 1989, p. 102.
17. Jessop, 1990.
18. Parsons revealed that cable operators deliberately used the label "community antenna television" as a rhetorical device in the struggle to avoid copyright liability for broadcast retransmissions. See Patrick Parsons, "Defining Cable Television: Structuration and Public Policy," *Journal of Communication*, 39:2, 1989, pp. 10-26.
19. The Cabinet Committee on Cable Communications, *Cable: Report to the President*, Washington, DC: U.S. Government Printing Office, 1974, p. 10.

20. Federal Communications Commission, *Sixth Report and Order*, 41 FCC 148'(1952).
21. Jeremy Tunstall, *Communications Deregulation: The Unleashing of America's Communications Industries*, Oxford, UK: Blackwell, 1986, pp. 121, 125.
22. *All-Channels Receiver Act, U.S. Code* 1982, Title 47, sections 303, 330, July 10, 1962.
23. Leonard Ross, *The Copyright Question in CATV*, New York: Sloan Commission on Cable Communications, April 1971, p. 2.
24. *United States v. Southwestern Cable* Co., 392 U.S. 157 (1968).
25. Cabinet Committee on Cable Communications, p. 10.
26. Federal Communications Commission, *In re Inquiry into the Impact of Community Antenna Systems, Television Translators, Television "Satellite" Stations, and Television "Repeaters" on the Orderly Development of Television Broadcasting*, 26 FCC 403 (1959).
27. Federal Communications Commission, *First Report and Order on Microwave-Served Community Antenna Television*, 38 FCC 683 (1965).
28. Federal Communications Commission, *Second Report and Order on Community Antenna Television*, 2 FCC 2d 725 (1966).
29. *United States v. Southwestern Cable Co.*, 392 U.S. 157 (1968).
30. U.S. Register of Copyrights, *Report on the General Revision of the U.S. Copyright Law*, 87th Cong., 1st Sess., Washington, DC: U.S. House Judiciary Committee Print, 1961.
31. U.S. House, Judiciary Committee, Subcommittee No. 3, *Copyright Law Revision*, Hearings on H.R. 4347, 5680,6831, 6835, May 26-September 2,1965,89th Cong., 1st Sess., Washington, DC: U.S. Government Printing Office, 1965; U.S. Senate, Committee on the Judiciary, Subcommittee on Patents, Copyrights, and Trademarks, *Copyright Law Revision—CATV*, Hearings on S. 1006, August 2-25, 1966, 89th Cong., 2nd Sess., Washington, DC: U.S. Government Printing Office, 1966.
32. U.S. House, *Copyright Law Revision*, Motion Picture Association of America, "Memorandum by the Copyright Committee of the Motion Picture Association of America, Inc., on H.R. 4347," pp. 987-1046, p. 1002.
33. Krim represented Allied Artists Television Corp.; Danny Thomas Enterprises, Inc.; Desilu Productions, Inc.; Embassy Pictures Corp.; Independent Television Corp.; Metro Goldwyn-Mayer, Inc.; Wolper Productions; Screen Dems, Inc.; Seven Arts Productions Inc.;

Twentieth Century Fox Television, Inc.; United Artists Television, Inc.; Universal Pictures, Inc.; Walt Disney Productions, Inc.; and Warner Bros. Pictures, Inc. (U.S. House, *Copyright Law Revision,* Testimony of Arthur B. Krim, President, United Artists Corp., pp. 1332-1353).

34. U.S. House, *Copyright Law Revision,* p. 1334.

35. U.S. House, *Copyright Law Revision,* Statement of Frederick W. Ford, National Community Television Association, Inc., pp. 1241-1255. Just a year earlier Ford spoke as FCC Commissioner to the NCTA at its annual convention in Philadelphia, sounding the death knell for local broadcasters in the face of the CATV challenge. See text of speech, "Television: Divided or United—Some Problems in Television Growth," in U.S. House, *Copyright Law Revision*, pp. 1341-1349.

36. U.S. House, *Copyright Law Revision,* p. 1247.

37. Although most cable operations were "mom-and-pop" affairs, some of the major communications interests, including broadcasters, were entering into the business. Among these were: Western Union Telegraph Co. (owner of 12 per cent of Teleprompter Corp.'s stock), RKO General (a wholly owned subsidiary of General Tire and Rubber), Cox Broadcasting, Storer Broadcasting, Westinghouse, General Electric, Time, Inc., Meredith-Avco Corp., and numerous others in the investment, publishing, broadcasting, and allied communications and electronics field. See U.S. House, *Copyright Law Revision,* Letter from Lawrence S. Lesser to Herbert Fuchs, Counsel (July 21, 1965), pp. 1375-1377.

38. U.S. House, *Copyright Law Revision,* Statement of Ernest W. Jennes, Association of Maximum Service Telecasters, Inc., pp. 1223-1231.

39. U.S. House, *Copyright Law Revision,* Letter from Columbia Broadcasting System, Inc. to Hon. Edwin E. Willis, Chair of Subcommittee No. 3, pp. 1892-1893.

40. *United Artists Television, Inc. v. Fortnightly Corp.*, 255 F. Supp. 177 (S.D.N.Y.), *aff'd,* 377 F.2d 872 (2d Cir. 1967).

41. U.S. Senate, *Copyright Law Revision—CATV,* Statement of Frederick Ford, National Community Television Association, Inc., pp. 84-89.

42. U.S. Senate, *Copyright Law Revision—CATV,* p. 87.

43. Ross, p. 16.

44. U.S. Senate, *Copyright Law Revision—CATV,* Statement of Douglas

A. Anello, General Counsel of the National Association of Broadcasters, pp. 109-113.

45. U.S. Senate, *Copyright Law Revision—CATV*, Statement of Arthur B. Krim, President, United Artists, pp. 167-191, p. 187.
46. U.S. Senate, *Copyright Law Revision—CATV*, Statement of Louis Nizer, General Counsel, Motion Picture Association of America, pp. 191-195.
47. U.S. House, *Copyright Law Revision*, Statement of Edwin M. Zimmerman, Acting Assistant Attorney General, pp. 211-215, p. 212.
48. U.S. Senate, *Copyright Law Revision—CATV*, Statement of Charlton Heston, President, Screen Actors Guild, pp. 205-210.
49. U.S. Senate, *Copyright Law Revision—CATV*, p. 206.
50. U.S. House, Committee on the Judiciary, Subcommittee on Courts, Civil Liberties, and the Administration of Justice, *Home Recording of Copyrighted Works—Part 1*, Hearings on H.R. 4783, H.R. 4794, H.R. 4808, H.R. 5250, H.R. 5488, and H.R. 5705, April 12-14, June 24, August 11, September 22, 23 1982, 97th Cong., Ist and 2nd Sess., Washington. DC: U.S. Government Printing Officc, 1983, Statement of Clint Eastwood, pp. 115-116.
51. *Fortnightly Corp. v. United Artists T,elevision. Inc.*, 377 E.2d 872 (2d Cir, 1967).
52. *Fortnightly Corp. v. United Artists Television, Inc.*, 392 U.S. 390 (1968).
53. *Buck v. Jewell-LaSalle Realty Co.*, 283 U.S. 191 (1931).
54. Susan C. Greene, "The Cable Provisions of the Revised Copyright Act," *Catholic University Law Review*, 27:2, 1978, pp. 263-303, p. 270.
55. 392 U.S. 390, 399.
56. 392 U.S. 390, 400.
57. A. Allan Schmid, "A Conceptual Framework for Organising Observations on Intellectual Property Stakeholders," Washington, DC: Office of Technology Assessment, February 1985, p. 23.
58. Schmid, p. 23.
59. Schmid, p. 20.
60. 392 U.S. 390, 404.
61. Ross, pp. 7-8.

62. Monroe E. Price, "The Illusions of Cable Television," *Journal of Communication*, 24:3, 1974, pp. 71-76, p. 73.
63. Sloan Commission on Cable Communications, On *the Cable: The Television of Abundance*, New York: McGraw Hill, 1971. The members of the Sloan Commission on Cable Communications included members or representatives of the "power elite" as defined by Domhoff: Edward S. Mason, Chairman, Dean Emeritus, Graduate School of Public Administration, Harvard University; Ivan Allen Jr., former Mayor of Atlanta; John F. Collins, former Mayor of Boston; Lloyd C. Elam, President, Meharry Medical College; Kermit Gordon, President, Brookings Institution; William Gorhan, President, Urban Institute; Morton L. JankJow, Attorney with Janklow and Traum, New York; Carl Kaysen, Director, Institute for Advanced Study, Princeton, New Jersey, Edward H. Levi, President, University of Chicago; Emanuel R. Piore, Vice President and Chief Scientist, IBM Corporation; Henry S. Rowen, President, Rand Corporation; Frederick Seitz, President, Rockefeller University; Franklin A. Thomas, President, Bedford-Stuyvesant Restoration Corporation; Patricia M. Wald, Attorney with the Center for Law and Social Policy, Washington, DC; Jerome B. Wiesner, President, Massachusetts Institute of Technology; James Q.Wilson, Professor of Government, Harvard University (Appendix F, pp. 251-252).
64. Sloan Commission, pp. 4, 9.
65. Sloan Commission, p. 14.
66. The transaction costs of information are "the additional costs incurred by the producer in appropriating the value of information" (W. Curtiss Priest, "The Character of Information: Characteristics and Properties of Information Related to Issues Concerning Intellectual Property," Washington, DC: Office of Technology Assessment, 1985, p. 36).
67. Wendy Gordon, "Fair Use as Market Failure: A Structural and Economic Analysis of the Betamax Case and Its Predecessors," *Columbia Law Review*, 82:7, 1982, pp. 1600-1657.
68. *Teleprompter Corp. v. CBS, Inc.*, 415 U.S. 394 (1974).
69. Sloan Commission, p. 32.
70. Federal Communications Commission, *Commission Proposals for Regulation of Cable Television*, 31 FCC 115 (1971) ("Letter of Intent" to Congress).
71. Federal Communications Commission, *Cable Television Report and Order*, 36 FCC 2d 143 (1972) (Appendix D, pp. 285-286).

72. Federal Communications Commission, 1972, p. 185.
73. U.S. Senate, Judiciary Committee, Subcommittee on Patents, Copyrights, and Trademarks, *Copyright Law Revision,* Hearings on S. 1361, July 31 and August 1, 1973, 93rd Cong., 1st Sess., Washington, DC: U.S. Government Printing Office, 1973, Letter from David H. Foster, NCTA, to Sen. John McClellan, August 1, 1973, pp. 639-640.
74. U.S. Senate, *Copyright Law Revision,* Hearings on S. 1361, Bridger M. Mitchell and Robert H. Smiley, "Cable Television Under the 1972 FCC Rules and the Impact of Alternative Copyright Fee Proposals: An Economic Analysis," pp. 426-485.
75. U.S. Senate, *Copyright Law Revision,* Hearings on S. 1361, Robert W. Crandall and Lionel L. Fray, "The Profitability of Cable Television Systems and Effects of Copyright Fee Payments," pp. 317-376.
76. The Cabinet Committee on Cable Communications, p. 3. Committee members included: Robert H. Finch; Leonard Garment; Herbert G. Klein; Peter G. Peterson (Secretary of Commerce); Elliot L. Richardson (Secretary of Health, Education, and Welfare); George Romney (Secretary of Housing and Urban Development); Clay T. Whitehead.
77. Cabinet Committee on Cable Communications, p. 13.
78. Cabinet Committee on Cable Communications, p. 13.
79. Cabinet Committee on Cable Communications, p. 14.
80. Robert Horowitz, *The Irony of Regulatory Reform: The Regulation of American Telecommunications,* New York: Oxford University Press, 1989, p. 82.
81. Willard Rowland, "The Further Process of Reification: Continuing Trends in Communication Legislation and Policymaking," *Journal of Communication,* 34:2, 1982, pp. 114-136.
82. *Columbia Broadcasting System, Inc. v. Democratic National Committee,* 412 U.S. 94 (1973).
83. *Federal Communications Commission v. Midwest Video Corp.,* 440 U.S. 689 (1979).
84. *Federal Communications Commission v. Pacifica Foundation,* 438 U.S. 726 (1973).
85. Daniel Schiller, *Telematics and Government,* Norwood, NJ: Ablex, 1982.
86. Committee for Economic Development, Research and Policy

86. Committee for Economic Development, Research and Policy Committee, *Broadcasting and Cable: Policies for Diversity and Change*, New York: Committee for Economic Development, 1975.

87. American Enterprise Institute, *Deregulation of Cable Television: Ford Administration Papers on Regulatory Reform*, Paul MacAvoy (ed.), Washington, DC: American Enterprise Institute for Public Policy Research, 1977.

88. American Enterprise Institute, *Deregulation of Cable Television*, S. M. Besen, B. M. Mitchell, R. G. Noll, B. M. Owen, R. E. Park, and J. N. Rosse, "Economic Policy Research on Cable Television: Assessing the Costs and Benefits of Cable Deregulation," pp. 45-87, p. 54. Those familiar with communications policymaking will recognise the high profile of these economists in the policy-planning process. Since the mid-1970s, they have produced and presented much of the economic reasoning fed into the policy-planning process in support of deregulation.

89. Cabinet Committee on Cable Communications, p. 39.

90. *Columbia Broadcasting System, Inc. v. Teleprompter Corp.*, 355 F. Supp. 618 (S.D.N.Y. 1972).

91. *Columbia Broadcasting System, Inc. V. Teleprompter Corp.*, 476 E2d 338 (2d Cir-1973

92. *Teleprompter Corp.*, v. CBS, Inc., 415 U.S. 408 (1974).

93. The compulsory license for cable appears in section 111 of the 1976 Act. Cable systems are exempt from copyright liability but must, in turn, pay royalties determined by statute to the Copyright Royalty Tribunal (CRT) (also established in the Act in section 801). Under section 11l(d)(2)(B), fees are based on the gross receipts of a cable system for those nonnetwork distant signals it retransmits as part of its basic tier. Under section 111 (d)(4)(5), programming carried on local or network broadcast signals is largely exempt from copyright liability. The fees collected by the CRT are distributed among copyright owners in filmed entertainment, broadcasting, music, and sports.

94. Data from Copyright Royalty Tribunal cited in U.S. Department of Commerce, National Telecommunications and Information Administration, *NTIA Telecom 2000: Charting the Course for a New Century*, 1988, p. 554.

95. U.S. Department of Commerce, National Telecommunications and Information Administration, *Video Program Distribution and Cable Television: Current Policy Issues and Recommendations*, Washington, DC: U.S. Department of Commerce, June 1988.

96. Federal Communications Commission, *In the Matter of Compulsory License for Cable Retransmission*, 4 FCC Red 6711 (1989).

97. *Video Program Distribution*, Attachment 2, p. 6.

98. *Video Program Distribution*, Attachment 2, p. 6.

99. Tele-Communications Inc., *Annual Report*, 1988.

100. Tom Graves, "Leisure-Time: Current Analysis," *Standard & Poor's Industry Surveys*, November 11, 1993, pp. L1-L68, p. L3.

101. Geraldine Fabrikant, "Time Warner Agrees to Acquire Cablevision," *New York Times*, February 8, 1995, pp. Dl, D18.

102. Dennis Wharton, "Cable Takes Some Lumps on Capitol Hill; Solons Warn Regulation Is Coming," *Variety*, November 22, 1989, p. 88.

103. *Quincy Cable Television v. Federal Communications Commission*, 768 F.2d 1434 (D.C. Cir. 1985); *Century Communications Corp. v. Federal Communications Commission*, 835 F.2d 292 (D.C. Cir. 1987).

104. Cable operators were taking in an estimated $600 million for local advertising by 1990 (Richard Huff, "Cable: As Program 'Gatekeeper' in Half of U.S., Cable Systems Emerge as Growing Force in TV," *Variety*, October 11, 1989, p. 103).

105. *The Cable Communications Policy Act of 1984*, Pub.L. 98-549, 98 Stat. 2770 (October 1984).

106. U.S. General Accounting Office, *Telecommunications: 1990 Survey of Cable Television Rates and Services*, Gaithersburg, MD: U.S. General Accounting Office, June 1990.

107. U.S. General Accounting Office, *Telecommunications: 1991 Survey of Cable Television Rates and Services*, Gaithersburg, MD: U.S. General Accounting Office, July 1991.

108. *Cable Television Consumer Protection and Competition Act of 1992*, Pub.L. 102-385, 106 Stat. 1460 (October 1992).

109. Mark Robichaux, "Senator Urges Antitrust Probe of Cable," *Wall Street Journal*, August 10, 1993, pp. BI, B6.

110. Bill Carter, "CRS Fails to Get Pay from Cable," *New York Times*, September 28 1993, pp.D1, D5. pp. D1.D5.

111. James P. Mooncy, "Watch Cable TV Rates Rise," *New York Times*, September 18 1992, p. A35.

112. Edmund L. Andrews, "Ruts in Data Highway," *New York Times*, April 7 1994, pp. D1, D6.

7 THE LAW OF INTELLECTUAL PROPERTY: THE VIDEOCASSETTE RECORDER AND THE CONTROL OF COPYRIGHTS

Another challenge to the filmed entertainment copyright system emerged with the sale of videocassette recorders (VCRs) to the home consumer in late 1975. For the first time, this new technology made it possible for consumers to buy or rent copies of movies, to tape and build home libraries of television programs and movies, and to watch them at times of convenience. Although providing more flexibility to users of audiovisual media, the VCR once again meant a certain loss of control for copyright owners over their copyrighted works. Along with technologies such as photocopiers, audiocassette recorders, and computers, VCRs made the use and reproduction of copyrighted works possible on a massive scale, often without compensation to the copyright owner.

With few exceptions, copyright is based on an owner's ability to have exclusive control over the use of his or her product. This exclusive control is what protects the exchange value of the copyrighted work in the intellectual property marketplace. Traditionally, copyright owners have chosen when and where to exploit their copyrighted property to achieve what they hope will be a profitable return on their investments. Where reproductive technologies erode this exclusive control, the exchange value of the copyright is reduced as more people will be able to make use of the property without payment. Accordingly, copyright owners seek mechanisms in the marketplace, the court system, or the legislature that will allow them to capitalise on the uses of their property that new technologies afford.

Here we have examined the responses of filmed entertainment copyright owners, as manifested particularly in the courts and Congress, to the emergence and proliferation of the VCR. The primary focus here is on the emerging use of VCRs to record broadcast television programming and to play rented and purchased filmed entertainment, mainly produced by the major Hollywood studios. The incorporation of this new technology into the hands of core firms is now largely completed as filmed entertainment companies have shifted their efforts to exploit the VCR from the legal and legislative realms, in which they were increasingly frustrated, to the marketplace. Consequently, like the cable case the technology emerged as a challenge to the filmed entertainment copyright system yet ultimately became incorporated into the industry's distribution system. Furthermore, the industries that introduced these technological challenges—cable operators and VCR manufacturers—have also become important and profitable sectors in the communications system, especially as they have integrated with software providers (e.g., Sony and Columbia Pictures, Matsushita and Universal Pictures, Toshiba and Time Warner, and Philips N.V. and Gramercy Pictures).

In this chapter we spotlight the VCR as a means of demonstrating the utility of critical legal studies (CLS) for analysing the relationship between new communications technologies and law. The specific focus is on the Betamax case, in which the Walt Disney Company and Universal

City Studios sued the Sony Corporation for copyright infringements by VCR owners who taped television broadcasts.[1] Not satisfied with judicial proceedings alone, the major Hollywood television producers also sought to address the VCR's challenge to their copyrights in Congress through a series of "home recording acts." As with the cable case, Congress found itself reacting to the decisions of the courts. The participation of executive and administrative agencies was marginal in this case except for the Department of Justice and the U.S. Copyright Office.

The case study presented in this chapter illustrates both intraclass conflict (between different factions of the capitalist class) and conflict between copyright owners and the "public of users."[2] However, as in the cable case, there was very little participation by the public of users in resolving these conflicts. Various factions of capital battled at the intraclass level with each side invoking the rhetoric of the "public interest," "freedom of speech," and "access" in order to legitimise their cause. As with every other new communications technology, the promoters of the VCR hailed it with Utopian rhetoric. But rather than significantly expanding the realm of democratic communications, the VCR, like the communications technologies that preceded it, ended up strengthening the dominance of capital over the media system.

Critical Legal Studies and the Law of Copyright

Marxist and critical legal studies can be divided into the same three general fields that have been laid out for political economy and capitalist state theory. An instrumental approach to the role of law in capitalist society begins, at the very basic level, by identifying the class background and social status of judges, their interlocks with power-structure institutions, and their general ideological orientation. This is also an important first step in rejecting the formalism and objectivism upon which modern legal thought is based. In questioning whether Western-type judicial systems are "independent" from the economic and political domains, Miliband argued that judges themselves "are by no means, and cannot be independent of the multitude of influences, notably, class, origin, education, class situation and professional tendency, which contribute as much to the formation of their view of the world as they do in the case of the men [and women]."[3] In this regard, he noted that judicial elites, like other state elites, are drawn mainly from the upper and middle layers of the social stratification system. For example, a survey of the incomes of federal judges by the Associated Press in 1987 found that few jurists relied solely on their salaries for income (ranging from $89,500 to $115,000 per year) and that the majority held six-figure investment portfolios in real estate, securities, and stock.[4]

Like corporate executives and other upper-level state officials, those who may have started out at lower social stations have clearly come to belong to the power elite by the time they reach the bench. David Kairys, arguing against a more deterministic structuralist view of law, stressed that judges are people too; that "like the rest of us, [they] form values and prioritise considerations based on their experience, socialisation, political perspectives, self-perceptions, hopes, fears, and a variety of other factors."[5] According to James Lardner, the personal belief system of Warren Ferguson, the presiding federal district court judge in the Betamax case, strongly influenced his decision to reject the infringement claims by Universal and Disney.[6] His written decision was heavily relied upon by the Supreme Court in arguing its holding.

Appointed to the bench by Lyndon Johnson, Ferguson initially came off as a stern upholder of law and order.

However, after the death of his son in Vietnam, he became increasingly skeptical about government intrusion into people's daily lives. Throughout the trial, he was actively critical of the idea that filmed entertainment companies or the government, through the copyright mechanism, should be in control of what people watched on television and when. Judge Ferguson often engaged in cross-examination of witnesses himself, revealing early in the trial, with his questioning of Disney chair Donn B. Tatum, a dislike of the implications of a decision that would involve the government determining how VCRs could be used. He also placed the burden of proving harm on the plaintiffs and maintained a strict definition of harm as actual losses suffered from the alleged infringing uses. To this end, he refused to accept the claims of advertisers, who were enlisted on behalf of the plaintiffs, when they tried to show that home taping of broadcasts would reduce the value of advertising time and thus the prices filmed entertainment copyright owners could charge for their programming.

To go beyond such a subjective and surface-level account of judicial decision-making requires consideration of the institutional socialisation of jurists. Miliband emphasised the common professional legal background of most judges that produces individuals "whose ideological dispositions are traditionally cast in a highly conservative mold."[7] Bagdikian noted the remarkable fact that by 1980 conservative foundations had paid for fully one-fifth of the entire federal judiciary to travel to Miami (all expenses paid) so they could take courses in the laissez-faire doctrine of Milton Friedman.[8]

Kairys also underscored that judges share common backgrounds from their law school experiences and from typically practicing commercial forms of law. These ideological influences enter the process of legal decision making and produce results that are not totally random. Countering the claims of poststructuralist state and legal theorists who stress the contingent nature of policy and law, Kairys argued that legal rulings demonstrate a patterning and consistency in the ways they categorise, approach, and resolve social and political conflicts.[9]

The central and most uniform conservative influence in the judicial process, again as in the case of state officials in government, is common agreement on the basic economic, social, and political arrangements of capitalist society. Even the most progressive judges do not cast their decisions in a way that disrupts or questions the fundamental social order. Indeed, as Miliband pointed out, in times of social crisis judges will see it as their distinctive duty to reinforce or reestablish this order.[10] Such was the case during the presidency of Salvador Allende Gossens in Chile (1970-1973), when the courts consistently nullified legislative efforts of the Unidad Popular to recast the bourgeois order in forms more consistent with socialist ideals. Similarly, it is inconceivable that a judge in the United States would ever base his or her decision in a copyright infringement case on a Proudhonian notion that "intellectual property is theft."[11]

Miliband also contended that in capitalist countries judges "have generally taken a rather poor view of radical dissent, and the more radical the dissent, the greater has been judicial hostility to it."[12] In dealing with cases of dissent that challenge state authority elsewhere in the system, Miliband added that judicial discretion has "tended to be used to support rather than to curb the attempts which governments and legislatures have made at one time or another to contain, subdue or suppress views and activities."[13] This is not to minimise those occasions when the courts have tempered state intolerance but rather to underscore the dominant tendencies within the judicial system toward the suppression of radical challenges to the social order. Miliband concluded:

> The judicial application of the law and judicial acceptance of the repressive efforts of governments and legislatures do not simply constitute "neutral" discharge of the judicial function; they constitute a *political* act of considerable significance and provide these governments and legislatures with a precious element of additional legitimation.[14]

This general bias against dissent is complemented by and indeed rooted in the more consistently displayed bias by the judiciary in favor of "privilege, property and capital."[15] This brings us to the second general field of critical perspectives on the law that considers the relationship between the logic of capital and capitalist legal structures. The formal rules that judges are supposed to follow in reaching decisions in particular areas of litigation are biased toward the protection of the capitalist economic system. For example, in the Betamax case study that follows, the application of the fair use doctrine to the home-taping question revealed that the four-part test used to determine fair use is biased toward protecting the economic rights of copyright owners against the rights of access and free use of copyrighted material. Therefore, not only are judges themselves ideologically biased toward the protection of private properly rights, so are the formal rules that they are required to apply. CLS emphasises that in all these ways the law is not separate from nor above politics, economics, culture, values, or the particular ideological dispositions of judges; it is "simply politics by other means."[16]

The doctrine of legal formalism that dominates mainstream law and practice posits law as a body of intelligible and "impersonal purposes, politics and principles" that forms "a gapless system of rules" from which legal reasoning and subsequent decisions are derived.[17] These rulings come after "objective" hearings where evidence is presented according to certain procedures, and out of the process "truth" ultimately emerges. In combination with the doctrine of objectivism, law is held to be an apolitical realm for the exercise of state authority. The decisionmaking-process itself supposedly guarantees that law remains above politics. Its attributes include "judicial subservience to a Constitution, statutes and precedent; the quasi-scientific, objective nature of legal analysis; and the technical expertise of judges and lawyers."[18] By applying the process to a particular legal question, "any reasonable and fair judge will reach the 'correct' decision."[19]

CLS rejects this "idealised model" of law by stressing the inconsistency in the application of legal doctrine, evidenced by the wide range of choices and outcomes that are possible in any particular case. Ideologically, jurists participate in the perpetuation of this "idealised model" by claiming that through the neutral application of law and precedents they are able to bracket out political influences in coming to and rendering their decisions. This allows the legal system to be particularly oppressive when laissez-faire economism serves as the basis of decision-making. The law and economics school reifies the market and the maximisation of choice as the normative standard by which law and politics are to be determined—a process in which Roberto Unger claimed "the analytic apparatus ... gets mistaken for a particular empirical and normative vision."[20] This normative vision serves to reinforce the capital accumulation process while becoming conceptually obscured by the "formal analytic notion of allocational efficiency."[21]

Cases in which the courts address economic issues starkly reveal the structural tilt of the legal terrain toward capital. Demonstrating this, Edelman provided an interesting discussion of how French jurists rejected copyright protection for photographs in the nineteenth century by holding that taking a picture did not involve any creative activity by the photographer and that the "reality" being photographed belonged in the public domain and therefore could not be appropriated as private property.[22] However, the courts reversed this decision when photography became filmmaking and thus a significant economic sector requiring state protection of property rights.

The structuralist orientation of logic-of-capital approaches seeks to explain the ideological role of law in legitimising class oppression by highlighting the split between the public sphere of politics and the private sphere of economics. With law appearing neutral, objective, and quasi-scientific, the judicial process in turn"lends a broader legitimacy to the social and power relations and ideology that are reflected, articulated, and enforced by the courts."[23] As the apparent democratic processes (e.g., universal suffrage, freedom of speech and assembly, etc.) in the political region serve to legitimise class rule, legal objectivism and formalism serve the same purpose in the judicial realm. The source of law's great power, according to Unger, is that "it enforces, reflects, constitutes, and legitimises dominant social and power relations without a need for or the appearance of control from outside and by means of social actors who largely believe in their own neutrality and the myth of legal reasoning."[24] Accordingly, law is a vehicle for gaining the consent or acquiescence of dominated groups and classes to the existing economic and social order while helping to legitimise the dominance of the capitalist class as part and parcel of ruling-class hegemony. Following Louis Althusser, Edelman argued that law functions as part of the ideological apparatus, not just the state apparatus, by constituting human subjects in the form of law. Along with ideology, law can be seen as an imaginary representation of the human subject's relation to his or her conditions of existence.

Isaac Balbus asked why citizens support this legal order when its primary function is to maintain their own domination.[25] His answer is derived from developing a homology between commodity fetishism as posited by Marx and legal fetishism. In the process of fetishizing law, "the legal order appears not as an object of rational choice undertaken by autonomous subjects, but rather as an autonomous subject itself, whose very existence requires that individuals 'objectify' themselves before it."[26] In this way, individual human subjects forget that law is a social creation, constituted through collective human activity, and deny themselves the possibility of abolishing law as a dominating structure so constituted.

When law is fetishized and, indeed, becomes personified (i.e., it takes on human characteristics), the "relative autonomy" of law is established. However, this "relative autonomy" is from social actors who have reified the law; autonomous from members of both dominant and dominated classes. The law is not relatively autonomous from the capitalist system within which these social actors participate. Following Poulantzas,[27] Balbus concluded that the relative autonomy of law from social actors, including the capitalist class, is necessary for the "reproduction of the overall conditions that make capitalism possible, and thus its capacity to serve the interests of capital as a *class*."[28]

Like Poulantzas, Balbus readily admitted that the growing role of the state in the economy is breaking down the separation between the economic and ju-ridico-political regions. This signals

> an erosion of the rule of Law and the emergence of less formalistic, more instrumentalist and technocratic modes of social and political control; the Law as universal political equivalent gradually gives way to a series of relatively *ad hoc techniques* which, by their very nature, recognise specific interests and specific social origins.[29]

Thus, under monopoly capitalism—as opposed to competitive capitalism, under which law had greater relative autonomy from the capitalist class—law increasingly has become an explicit instrument of class rule as well as a site in which dominated classes can exercise opposition. Law, like the state, becomes a realm within which the class struggle takes place precisely because of growing involvement with economic matters. The degree to which the dominant class finds the judicial system rigged in its favor, either instrumentally or structurally, is now the central debate within GLS. The third general field of critical approaches to law emphasises the law as a site of such struggles.

Unger identified law as a realm of opportunity for the reshaping of human existence. This theory is founded upon the view that different areas of social activity can be recombined with the elements of other systems in a process of continual, collective economic, political, cultural, and social experimentation. This requires people to understand "society as made and imagined rather than as merely given in a self-generating process that . . . unfold[s] independently of the will and the imagination."[30] Accordingly, members of a society can always violate the generative rules of their mental and social constructs and put other rules and constructs in their place that are less alienating or dominating. Unger recommended this course as a middle ground between incremental reform and radical revolution, that is, popular insurrection with total social transformation, a process he called "revolutionary reform." In the realm of law, revolutionary practice utilises the contradictions found within the social system to find "alternative ways of defining collective interests, collective identities, and assumptions about what is possible."[31]

Unger follows the strand of GLS based upon postmodernism and poststruc-turalism that emphasises the contingency and "indeterminacy" of human history. These approaches begin with the rejection of any concept of capitalism as a social totality with its own internal logic. The adoration of the human subject found in such approaches often leads to an abandonment of any notion of determining structures in social life. In radically rejecting functionalism and Marxism, these approaches posit that "none of [the regularities] in social life are *necessary* consequences of the adoption of a given regime of rules."[32] The use of the concept of capitalism, in this view, is devoid of any analytical or explanatory power or purpose. The distinction between different regions (e.g., economics and law) cannot be made; they are "simply cross-cutting slices out of the same organic tissue."[33] To do so, as do instrumentalists and structuralists, is to reify these structures analytically. This is "meaningless, since what we experience as 'social reality' is something that we ourselves are constantly constructing."[34]

Accordingly, adopting this poststructuralist approach will influence one's methodology: "One would no longer be inclined to look for 'scientific' or 'pos-itivist' explanations of how the world works in large-scale theories of historical interrelations between states, societies, and economies";[35] instead one would actually be attempting to knock down such theories. The research orientation suggested by Robert Gordon is to follow Foucault,[36] to look for practices of domination in the "smallest, most routine, most ordinary interactions of daily life."[37]

Although this locus on the level of daily life is indeed useful and necessary, for this is where we experience domination most directly, it ends up being incomplete and thus politically futile because those very structures whose existence poststructuralists deny *do exist* and *do extend* their reach down into this very level. Capitalism, racism, sexism, and imperialism penetrate and shape behavior at the interpersonal, intergroup, national, and international levels. Consequently, these structures of domination cannot be confronted at the microlevel alone. For example, the logic of capital shapes informational and cultural policy in a way that preserves the system of private appropriation and ownership of intellectual property and artistic creativity, a system that in turn determines the form and content of such creativity. The effect of this logic is to make participation in the production of and access to intellectual and artistic works consistently undemocratic.

The poststructuralist approach becomes voluntaristic with its one-sided, non-dialectical focus on humans as determining. It returns to a form of pluralism with its emphasis on contingency and indeterminacy. It fails to recognise, as power-structure research has shown, that dominant classes are generally able to determine particular outcomes in policymaking and legal decisionmaking by virtue of their economic, political, and ideological power. Of course, the specific forms and functions of the state and law do vary in accordance with the structural dynamics of the economic system. Thus, in each historical epoch it is possible to identify "substantial congruence" between material relations in society and the legal and state systems.[38]

The class theoretical position remains useful when not

taken to its poststructuralist extremes. Certainly, the particular forms of state and legal systems are not precisely determined nor inevitable because human beings do indeed create and re-create these structures, primarily within the context of class struggle. Again, it is useful to return to the concept of the hegemonic project to remind us that hegemony is never total and that it must constantly be renewed by dominant classes or groups in the face of never-ending challenges from below. How filmed entertainment copyright owners responded to the challenge to their property rights brought about by the introduction of the VCR is the focus of the case study that follows.

The Betamax Case

Sony Corporation introduced the Betamax VCR, the first mass-produced home-video taping system, in the fall of 1975. Sony's advertising agency, Doyle Dane and Bernbach (DD&B), brought the new technology to the attention of Sydney Sheinberg, president of MCA/Universal, by sending him a proposed advertising sketch. The advertisement boasted that the new machine made it possible to watch both *Columbo* and *Kojak,* two Universal productions aired at the same time on competing channels. With the Betamax it was possible to watch one "live" while taping the other for later viewing. The people at DD&B thought, perhaps naively, that Universal would be delighted that both of its programs could now be viewed by the television audience. However, in November 1976 Universal and Disney brought a copyright infringement suit in federal district court against Sony, Sony Corporation America, DD&B, several Betamax retailers, and an individual home taper, William Griffiths.[39]

Although the suit against Griffiths was a "friendly" one, Universal and Disney alleged that he was liable for copyright violations for making unauthorised copies of the plaintiffs' programs, which he had taped off the air using his Betamax. The plaintiffs were not after Griffiths but rather Sony, DD&B, and Betamax retailers, alleging that the defendants engaged in contributory infringement of copyrights when they intentionally marketed and sold VCRs with knowledge they would be used for infringing purposes. The plaintiffs sought relief in the form of damages, an equitable accounting of profits, and an injunction against the manufacture and marketing of the Betamax VCR within the United States.

The motivations of Universal in initiating the case (and asking Disney to join in) were twofold: One was Universal's commitment to a videodisc player (DiscoVision), on which it held all the major patents; the other was protecting its copyrights in the face of new technologies. The first motivation is thus rooted in short-term corporate interests in the profitable development and marketing of a new home-consumer product. The Betamax VCR competed directly with the videodisc plus had the additional (and ultimately decisive) feature of being a recorder and not just a player.

The second motivation was rooted in the copyright question. Here was another technology that disrupted the system of exclusivity in the marketing and distribution of filmed entertainment programming. Universal's Sheinberg perceived a serious long-term threat to the integrity of the institution of copyright when millions of U.S. households contained VCRs and used them to tape and build libraries of copyrighted programming. Thus, it was not that any immediate or actual harm was evident to Sheinberg but that such an encroachment on copyright had to be stopped or regulated to prevent further loss of control over copyrights brought on by continuing technological challenges. Sheinberg's recognition of and concern about the threat posed by the VCR reflected his ability to see beyond immediate corporate interests (ignoring now his interest in Disco Vision) and perceive the long-term interests of capital as a whole. He reported to Lardner that no other filmed entertainment company executives or owners seemed to share his passion for the Betamax issue, a reflection of what he identified as "a constant problem in this industry: that most people in high places are not worried about what might happen ten years down the road—they're worried about getting to the Polo Lounge."[40]

Accordingly, the long-term necessity of protecting and extending the institution of intellectual property in the face of new technology provided the primary motivation behind the suit. This does not mean that all new uses of the VCR would indeed be incorporated into the intellectual property system, as we shall see in this case. However, the general logic underlying the copyright system drives copyright owners to seek compensation from all new forms of use. The logic of copyright also determines that intellectual property owners consistently realise such compensation.

The cable case provided the groundwork and terms of struggle upon which the filmed entertainment industry could base its response to the VCR copyright question, although there were some unique twists in this case. Universal solicited Disney's participation in the suit because of the latter's record for avidly going after infringers of its copyrights. At that time, it seemed to Disney that there was no alternative to an injunction on the manufacture and/or sale of the Betamax in the United States. The injunction was essential to Disney for maintaining its rerelease system for classic films in theaters and television broadcasts, exactly the kinds of films that people want to tape and keep in their video libraries. The first witness at the trial was Donn B. Tatum, then chair of Disney. He testified that the VCR threat was very real to the company, as evidenced by Disney's refusal to allow the QUBE cable system in Columbus, Ohio, to show *Mary Poppins* and *The Jungle Book* since among the 1,000 or so subscribers there were about a dozen VCR owners.[41] Tatum's testimony did not help the plaintiffs' cause. First, the Betamax case did not challenge home taping from cable television. Second, Tatum could not show any specific economic harm to Disney's copyright. He could only suggest that the harm came as a result of foregone revenues as Disney felt compelled to withhold its programming from the cable outlet.

Judge Ferguson, in the decision for Sony three years later, found that home taping was a fair use of copyrighted material since "home recording is done by individuals or families in the privacy of their own homes for use in their home [and] the material copied has been voluntarily sold by the authors for broadcast over the public airwaves to private homes free of charge."[42] The judge's emphasis on the private nature of the copying is clear from this statement. He also pointed out that home use of the VCR increased access to television programming and therefore met the public interest criterion of copyright law. Access is, after all, one of the underlying tenets of copyright law as evidenced by the fair use doctrine. The fair use doctrine evolved historically through copyright litigation to permit certain types of uses of copyrighted works without authorisation of or compensation to the copyright owner. It traditionally applied to scholarship, teaching, news gathering, and parody—generally noncommercial and educative purposes—in order to enhance access to copyrighted works and limit the monopolistic privileges granted by copyright. Ferguson extended fair use into new territory when he decided that an individual's private copying of entertainment for purposes of convenience was a fair use. The decision, therefore, found Sony not liable for contributory infringement. Additionally, Judge Ferguson found that since Sony maintained no direct supervision over the use of the Betamax by those who purchased it there could be no liability on Sony's part.

In the view of one legal analyst, the decision was based,on the judge's concess as to how the practical issues of compensation would be handled had he decided in favor of the plaintiffs and "a deep-seated reluctance on the part of the judiciary to stand in the way of technological experimentation and advance, rather than by directly applicable legal precedent derived from cases and statutes."[43] However, legal precedent was not all that clear, and statutory treatment of uses of reprographic technology in this manner was nonexistent. The Supreme Court had only once before dealt with a case involving reprographic technologies, in *Williams & Wilkins Co. v. United States,* where the issue was use of photocopiers.[44] Consequently, legal formalism broke down in this case and Judge Ferguson's decision reflected personal, ideological, and practical factors.

The Williams & Wilkins Case

The Xerox Corporation introduced copiers for general office use in 1960, a technology that dramatically improved the copying of documents in comparison to carbon paper and mimeograph machines. Xerox held patent monopolies on "xerography" until the mid-1970s, when it settled an antitrust suit filed by the Federal Trade Commission that required the company to give competitors licenses for its office-copier patents. As the photocopy machine became increasingly available, it foreshadowed what was to come with audiocassette recorders, VCRs, home satellites, and home computers in terms of the public of users' ability to have greater access to and cheaper use of copyrighted materials.

The *Williams & Wilkins* case involved a suit brought by a publisher of medical journals against the National Institutes of Health (NIH) and the National Library of Medicine (NLM), two nonprofit organisations of the federal government. These organisations provided photocopies of articles from various academic journals requested by its research staff. Of significance is the infringement claim against public sector institutions rather than the corporate sector even though the extent of such copying practices had become quite common among the latter. Thus, Williams & Wilkins attacked public appropriation of copyrighted works in order to preserve the integrity of its copyrights. By making the public sector appear parasitical, the suit obscured the fact that vast amounts of scientific research and information are produced and made available due to public funding.

Nevertheless, the Court of Claims majority found that the photocopying done by the NIH and the NLM was a fair use for two reasons: First, there was a lack of evidence by the plaintiff that it was or would be harmed substantially by these photocopy practices; second, medicine and medical research would be injured by holding these practices an infringement and that it was inappropriate to "place such a risk of harm upon science and medicine."[45] Since the ruling predated the 1976 copyright revision, the court did not apply the four-part test for determining fair use subsequently codified in section 107 of the Act. But in attempting to follow judicial precedent for making judgments of fair use, the court did stress that:

1. The NIM and the NLM are nonprofit institutions, devoted solely to the advancement and dissemination of medical knowledge, and that the photocopy service was not an attempt to

profit or gain financially but to better carry out their knowledge disseminating purposes;

2. The scientific researchers and practitioners who requested the copies of journal articles did so for their own personal use in their scientific work; and
3. The entire purpose of both sides—library and scholar—is scientific progress.

The court concluded that there had been "no attempt to misappropriate the work of earlier scientific writers for forbidden ends, but rather an effort to gain easier access to the material for study and research."[46] In the court's view, the amount of copying did not seem "excessive or disproportionate." The majority's decision appeared to be grounded in philosophical principles but actually seems to be based on practical questions as to how use of photocopiers could be monitored and royalty fees collected. This is revealed in the court's appeal for help from Congress.

In a statement that seems to emanate regularly from the judiciary with regard to copyright cases, the court urged Congress to consider the issue and fashion more precise statutory guidance for the courts to follow:

> The truth is that this is now preeminently a problem for Congress: to decide the extent of photocopying that should be allowed, the questions of a compulsory license and the payments (if any) to copyright owners, the system for collecting those payments . . . the special status (if any) of scientific and education needs.. . . The choices involve economic, social and policy factors which are far better sifted by a legislature. The possible intermediate solutions are also of the pragmatic kind legislatures, not courts, can and should fashion.[47]

The implication is that the courts should not make policy, keeping with the myth that the law is above politics.

Even though the narrow scope of questions arising in litigation typically makes it difficult for the judiciary to affirm or fashion broad policy, the interplay between the courts and the legislature ultimately does shape policy outcomes. Therefore, in this case the court quickly added that its decision was narrow in scope and was not meant to apply "to dissimilar systems or uses of copyrighted materials by other institutions or enterprises, or in other fields, or as applied to items other than journal articles, with other significant variables."[48] It felt obligated to follow the "canon of judicial parsimony, being stingy rather than expansive in the reach of [the] holding."[49] However, the ruling's effect did have broad implications, for it compelled Congress to specifically address and codify the fair use doctrine in the 1976 Copyright Act. Like the Supreme Court decision in *Teleprompter v. CBS*, which dismissed copyright liability for cable operators, the *Williams & Wilkins* ruling appears to violate the logic of copyright. However, the effects of both rulings ultimately prompted legislation preserving the integrity of copyright in the face of technological challenges to it.

In his dissent to the *Williams & Wilkins* decision, Chief Judge Robert E. Cowen wrote that making the copyright proprietor prove the degree of injury flew in the face of legal precedent due to the difficulty of demonstrating such harm. In his view, case law established "that proof of actual damage is not required, and the defense of fair use may be overcome where potential injury is shown."[50] Thus, Cowen felt that the second definition of harm—potential revenues foregone from new communications technologies—need only be alleged, a point later made by Justice Harry Blackmun in his dissent in *Sony v. Universal.* Williams & Wilkins tried to show potential economic harm by asserting that the libraries' photocopy services deprived them of subscriptions. In essence, this charge privileges economic rights over social rights, for claims of foregone revenues are much more tangible conceptually, even if not precisely demonstrable, than claims that copyright monopolies may suppress access to informational and cultural, works, thereby harming the public good. Cowen's dissent revealed the tilt of the legal terrain of copyright toward the economic rights of capital and against the moral claims of the public good.

Although the Supreme Court reviewed the *Williams & Wilkins* case in 1974, it split evenly in its decision 4 to 4,[51] thereby affirming the lower court's decision. The tie vote left the lower court's decision without value as precedent. This made the case inapplicable in the Betamax case, broadening the range of potential outcomes on the question of home videotaping. Additionally, the kinds of uses the two courts had to determine as fair or not are very different. To understand the difference, it is necessary to briefly consider the fair use doctrine.

The rights embraced in copyright include:

- the right to reproduce the work in copies
- the right to distribute those copies
- the right to prepare derivative works (such as translations and dramatisations) based upon copyrighted works
- the right to perform or display the work publicly

These rights are codified in section 106 of the 1976 Copyright Act and are conditioned and limited by the specifications of sections 107 to 118.

The copyright owner's rights have never been entirely exclusive. For example, limits on duration of copyright coverage have existed since the first modern copyright law was passed in England in 1709. Once these expire, the copyrighted work passes into the public domain. This qualification on the copyright owner's exclusivity is just one of many created to safeguard the public's access to literary and artistic creations. Another exception is the compulsory license that gives the public guaranteed access to copyrighted works embodied in or distributed through various media while at the same time providing compensation to the copyright owner. Compulsory licenses are used for jukeboxes, reproduction of phono-records previously published, public broadcasts of nondramatic music, and published pictorial, graphic, and sculptural works, as well as for cable retransmission of radio and television programs. The compulsory license is applied in situations where market transactions between copyright owners and users are deemed unfeasible due to high transaction costs.

The fair use doctrine is another exception to the exclusivity of copyright. It is a well-established judicial "rule of reason" designed to permit access to and use of copyrighted material despite the copyright owner's monopoly. Congress codified the doctrine in section 107 of the 1976 Act, thereby making it a statutory right. This section states: "The fair use of a copyrighted work, including such use by reproduction in copies or phonorecords or by other means specified [by section 106], for purposes such as criticism, comment, news reporting, teaching (including multiple copies for classroom use), scholarship, or research is not an infringement of copyright." Congress was reluctant to give the courts further guidance in determining fair use, preferring to let it be defined on a case-by-case basis. With this sentiment, Congress recognised the futility of legal formalism in the face of the fast pace of technological change.

The list of fair uses in section 107 refers to those that have traditionally been seen as "productive": copyrighted work that leads to the creation of additional information and knowledge. The advancement of science and medicine in the *Williams & Wilkins* case was clearly the type of "productive" use that the doctrine may exempt from copyright liability. The question of fair use in home recording of television broadcasts clearly does not fit this traditional standard. Home tapers of television broadcasts engage in the practice in order to time-shift programming for viewing at a more convenient time, and the bulk of the programming that is recorded is entertainment. Judge Ferguson's expansion of the fair use doctrine beyond its traditional boundaries and his strict definition of harm as actual revenues lost from infringing activity became the key points of deliberation in the appeal by copyright owners.

The Court of Appeals Decision in the Betamax Case

The U.S. Court of Appeals reversed the lower court, found home taping of broadcasts an infringement, and sided with the plaintiffs on nearly all other counts. The three-judge appellate panel held, in October 1981, that off-the-air recording— even for private, noncommercial purposes—was an infringement.[52] The court was convinced "that the fair use doctrine does not sanction home-video recording"[53] because it was not a "productive" use in the same manner as educational, news reporting, or study situations. Instead, the court considered home recording an "intrinsic" use. It reached this conclusion after applying the four-part fair use test provided in section 107.

The first factor to take into account in the four part test is the purpose and character of the use, including whether such use is of commercial nature or is for nonprofit educational purposes. The court did not find this the case in home recording of television broadcasts. It stated: "The fact that the 'infringing' activity takes place in the home does not warrant a blanket exemption from any liability."[54] Nor did the court find merit in the claim that First Amendment concerns supported such use or the claim that the First Amendment somehow constitutionally superseded copyrights. Taking a firm stand on copyright as an economic right, the court declared: "The First Amendment is not a license to trammel on legally recognised rights in intellectual property."[55]

The second factor considered in the fair use test is the nature of the copyrighted work. In the opinion of the appeals court, "If a work is more appropriately characterised as entertainment, it is less likely that a claim of fair use will be accepted."[56] Thus, following the logic begun with the first factor, the court assumed that most tapes made by home users would be of programming for intrinsic and entertainment purposes. In the judges' opinion, this counted against a finding of fair use. However, by demonstrating a bias toward news and public affairs programming, the court missed the point that entertainment *is* information and provides much of the cultural raw materials from which we draw our perspectives on and knowledge of the world. Indeed, much news and information programming is itself often meant to be "entertaining," particularly within advertiser-supported media. An access mandate requires rejecting such categories as scholarly, newsworthy, informative, or entertaining, as all are essential for constituting our social "reality." To this end, the appeals court ignored the findings of the Supreme Court in *Burstyn v. Wilson*, which extended First Amendment protection to motion pictures.[57] In that case, the Supreme Court declared that motion pictures are "a significant medium for the communication of ideas" and that their importance is not lessened by the fact that they are intended to "entertain as well as inform."[58]

The third factor in the fair use test concerns the amount and substantiality of the portions used in relation to the copyrighted work as a whole. The court determined that this factor clearly weighed in favor of the plaintiffs and against a finding of fair use. Citing the district court decision, the court declared that usually home taping of broadcasts involves copying the whole work.[59] The court again stressed copyright as an economic right and "the notion that copyright is a property interest and that it is impermissible, in the vast majority of cases, to 'appropriate' the copyrighted material without the owner's consent."[60] The court assumed that the appropriation of a work in its entirety "typically precludes a finding of fair use."[61]

When considering the final factor—the effect of the use upon the potential market for or value of the copyrighted work—the district court had ruled against the studios because they failed to provide sufficient evidence of actual economic harm. The appeals court disagreed, recalling the views of the dissenters in *Williams & Wilkins* that to make plaintiffs prove actual economic damage is "simply too great a burden to impose," that it is necessary only to demonstrate a tendency toward economic harm.[62] For the court to find home recording an infringement, it was enough for the plaintiff-appellants to show that when putting copies of their works on the market they would have to compete with the appropriated versions, thus reducing potential sales. The appellate panel concluded on this point that home users obviously found an economic benefit in having control over access to copyrighted works. Accordingly, "the copyright laws would seem to require that the copyright owner be given the opportunity to exploit this market."[63]

Upon its review of the district court's decision and of the fair use doctrine as codified in copyright law, the appeals court found that the lower court failed to "correctly" apply and interpret the law. As CLS has shown, such an assertion simply cannot be made, since there is no such thing as a "correct" or "true" decision. Despite the four-part test that is somehow supposed to lead the judiciary through a proceeding to the "correct" decision, the different factors themselves are susceptible to differing interpretations, as the Supreme Court decision in this case demonstrates.

Nor is it possible to know the "true" intent of Congress when it fashioned a particular statute or fragment thereof. The appeals court found no congressional intent to create a blanket home-use exemption to copyright protection. Actually, Congress did not determine one way or the other on the matter of home recording for private use. Thus, it is possible to say either that Congress did not specifically prohibit such a use or that Congress did not specifically permit such a use. The appeals court did find a quote in a Senate report that stated: "Isolated instances of minor infringements, when multiplied many times, become a major inroad on copyright that must be prevented."[64] Preventing home recording for private use first required a finding that it was indeed an infringement. If it was found to be a fair use, it was not an infringing use. The point is, the intent of Congress on this matter was simply not clear.

The decision of the appeals court is significant for a couple of reasons. First, it exemplified the philosophy underlying copyright in a capitalist economic system. From this court's perspective, copyright is a property right that demands government protection. Some public uses of copyrighted works without economic compensation are considered unlawful appropriation even if they are noncommercial uses. For the appeals court, one such use was off-air recording of television broadcasts. "Copyrightists" across the United States celebrated the decision for its "return to 'basics' and a reaffirmation of the 'traditional' ideas of fair use."[65] Scholars of copyright law, publishers, computer software developers, music recording companies, and the filmed entertainment industry were all pleased with the decision despite the very large question of what would happen to the hardware that employed this software and how uses of the hardware would be policed. It was easy enough lor the appeals to reverse and remand the decision to the court since it did not have to fashion the relief. In any event, easy resolution of the issue in a national context would not be forthcoming; the rapid growth in the number of VCR households (and thus the number of potential infringers) increasingly complicated the matter of fashioning such relief.

The second significant point of the appeals court's decision was that it prompted immediate action on the legislative front. Suddenly, one of the main uses for which people were buying Betamaxes was ruled illegal, and it was natural that Congress began hearing from its constituents. Indeed, the hundreds of thousands of home videotapers in the West could now be held liable for copyright infringement whenever they taped television broadcasts. Political cartoonists and columnists had a field day with images and descriptions of "video police," dressed up like German SS officers, seeking out home tapers and confiscating tapes and Betamaxes. Obviously, the members of Congress also were hearing from major electronic industry lobbyists worried about the impact of the decision on the sale of this new communications technology.

The "Home Recording" Acts

While Sony took its appeal to the Supreme Court, Congress became the main arena of activity. There were two basic types of bills introduced in Congress to deal with the home-taping issue. One type, which dealt with the problem of mass infringement only, aimed specifically to exempt all private, noncommercial videotaping from copyright liability. A typical bill with this intent was H.R. 4783, introduced by Rep. John Duncan (R-Tenn.) in the House in October 1981, immediately after the Court of Appeals decision in the Betamax case,[66] to amend Title 17 of the U.S. Code to exempt the home recording of copyrighted works on home-video recorders from copyright infringement. Under the terms of the bill, home taping was not an infringement if (1) the recording was made without any purpose of direct or indirect commercial sale; and *(2)* the recording was to be utilised exclusively in a private home. This was the kind of legislation sought by the manufacturers and importers of VCRs and videocassettes (a coalition of U.S. and Japanese companies) supported through their lobbying organisations—the Home Recording Rights Coalition (HRRC) and the Electronic Industries Association (EIA).[67] The consumer electronics industry formed the HRRC in direct response to the appeals court's ruling.

The filmed entertainment industry developed and advanced the other main type of legislation for selected members of Congress to introduce on its behalf. The bill was supported by a broad coalition of copyright owners and others dependent on copyrights calling themselves the Coalition to Preserve the American Copyright.[68] Rep. Don Edwards, a liberal Democrat from California, where the filmed entertainment industry is an important economic sector, introduced the copyrightists' version of a home recording act in early 1982.[69] Sen. Charles Mathias (R-Md.), who had been approached because of his reputation as the Senate's leading copyright authority and defender of intellectual property rights, introduced a similar version of this bill in the Senate in early 1983.[70] Sen. Alan Cranston, also a liberal Democrat from California, cosponsored the

Senate home recording acts. The preamble to H.R. 5705 identifies the dual though contradictory function of copyright in the U.S.: "This system benefits both the creators of intellectual property and the consuming public—the creators by providing fair compensation and thereby the incentive to create new works, and the consumer by assuring a rich and ever-increasing variety of works from which to choose." The text of the bill continued with the assumption that in order to stimulate intellectual and artistic creativity "copyright owners should receive fair compensation for their creative endeavors and the use of their property." Next it identified the home recording of musical works, sound recordings, motion pictures, and other audiovisual works on audio recorders and VCRs as an infringement under section 106(1) of the Copyright Act. After declaring such use an infringement, it went on to exempt the copying of such works "by individuals who make audio and video recordings in the home for private use." However, this exemption was tied to a compulsory license established for importers and manufacturers of recording devices and videotape whom the bill determined commercially benefited from such infringement.

The Mathias-Edwards proposals thus tied the exemption of home taping to a compulsory license and statutory royalty fee to be established by the Copyright Royalty Tribunal (CRT). The proposal for a compulsory license for VCRs and tapes was first presented by Sony Corp. of America's (Sonam) president, Harvey Schein, to MCA/Universal's president, Sidney Sheinberg, over lunch a few days after the original suit was filed in 1976. At that time, Sonam's Schein suggested that the filmed entertainment industry and Sony form a committee to approach Congress to consider attaching a royalty fee to the machines and cassettes.[71] Sheinberg chose to take his chances in court instead. Sheinberg had no choice but to accept the idea after the introduction of the home recording bills that sought to exempt home taping. This situation reveals how much legislation actually originates in the corporate sector—in the boardroom, over lunch, in the policy-planning network—then makes its way to Congress for consideration. The compulsory license for VCRs and videocassette tapes did indeed have such a beginning.

As we saw in the cable case, the compulsory license is a mechanism usually established by Congress to deal with the massive and widespread use of copyrighted materials. Costs of transaction, detection, and enforcement are so high as to make these normal means for upholding copyrights unworkable since each individual infringement constitutes a mere fragment of the total level of infringing activity. Thus, the amount of harm inflicted by a single infringement is not worth the effort to collect damages. The compulsory license maintains the integrity of intellectual property by recognising the use as an infringement and then extending a blanket exemption to the users in exchange for a royalty fee.

Copyright owners do not like such an arrangement because it takes copyright contracting out of the marketplace and puts it into the hands of government or private administrative agencies. If copyright owners have choice, they choose the latter. An organisation such as the American Society of Composers, Authors and Publishers (ASCAP) produces economies of scale in collective enforcement of rights to deal with the situation where losses from any single infringement are generally small. Private, home copying has the additional characteristic of being difficult to enforce since it takes place inside the home and is neither identifiable nor countable. At hearings on the different House bills dealing with the issue, then Register of Copyrights David Ladd described the problem and proposed solution best: "It is impossible to insert the 'box office' anywhere between the copyrighted work and the taper; and therefore an indirect measurement—i.e., a measurement of materials, the machines and tapes—becomes the only feasible 'meter' for copying."[72]

Schein's idea of a levy on recording equipment was already in effect in the Federal Republic of Germany. German copyright law (Article 53[5]) mandated taxes on audio recording equipment based on a rate negotiated by manufacturers and importers of the machines and music collecting societies. Austria adopted a similar system in 1980 (Article 42[5]), though the tax is levied on the blank tapes rather than the hardware. The proceeds of the tax are channeled variously back to copyright owners or other cultural production organisations. When the proposal emerged in the U.S. Congress, witnesses for the proroyalty copyright owners pointed to these two systems as working models. However, neither had been applied to VCRs or blank videocassettes.

Sen. Mathias persuaded Jack Valenti, president of the MPAA, not to prescribe specific royalty rates in the legislation itself but rather to leave it up to the CRT. Filmed entertainment copyright owners were dissatisfied with the royalty rate established under the cable compulsory license. Yet, as in the cable case, the choice of the copyright owners was a statutory fee or nothing. The figures that Valenti proposed in congressional hearings ran at $50 per machine and at $1-$2 per tape. This was at the time when VCRs began at $700 at discount prices and blank tapes began at $12. Had these figures been adopted they would have constituted an increasingly significant proportion of the purchase price of the VCR and tapes as prices dropped. The proposed royalty legislation intended to grant the CRT the authority to determine the royalty fee on the equipment and tapes, which was to be paid by manufacturers and importers. The royalties that the CRT collected were to be distributed on the basis of audience ratings and program schedule sampling, since there was no way to determine what home tapers actually recorded. This mechanism would obviously have been problematic, as the ratings system itself is rife with imprecision, and there is no necessary correlation between a program's high ratings and the likelihood of that program being taped.

Valenti testified first at the House hearings on the proposed bills.[73] He called attention to the industry's economic structure and performance in order to stress the "high risk" involved in motion picture production, including the general trend toward higher negative, advertising, promotion, copying, and distribution costs; the fact that eight out of ten films do not retrieve their investment from theatrical exhibition; and that six out of ten films do not retrieve their total investment.[74] Valenti claimed that these factors underscored the significance of the ancillary markets after theatrical distribution. According to Valenti, home taping on VCRs posed threats to these ancillary markets in a number of ways:

- To prerecorded videocassette sales, as people no longer purchased them at $60-$80 when they could record two to three full-length movies at home on one blank tape costing as little as $8;
- To pay-TV and cable markets, as people swapped tapes with their subscriber friends instead of taking the service themselves;
- To network and syndicated television markets, as the ability of tapers to erase (zap) or fast-forward (zip) through commercials undermined advertising revenues for broadcasters, thus reducing the price filmed entertainment companies could ask when licensing them;

- Again to the networks in particular, as prime-time audiences diminished as people watched commercial-free VCR material; and
- To revenues from theatrical rentals, as people stayed home to watch taped movies on VCRs rather than at the theater.

In an argument reminiscent of the debate surrounding the rise of cable television, Valenti predicted that the end result of the above harm to ancillary markets would be a deterioration in "free" television as it was left to the poor and elderly who could not afford cable and VCRs. Strong copyright protection was essential for all of these markets to be viable for the film industry.

Valenti also underscored the marginal position of many of the workers in the filmed entertainment industry in an effort to elicit sympathy from Congress for the proroyalty forces (which included the talent and craft guilds and unions). He spoke for "the many thousands of men and women organised in guilds and unions who are the backbone of the American film industry."[75] Valenti's rhetoric implied that the royalty on VCRs and tapes was being sought on behalf of workers rather than on behalf of filmed entertainment company owners. With regard to the industry's employees Valenti declared: "It is these people who must depend on the basic health of their industry for economic security. And it is these people who would benefit from copyright royalty mechanisms as a result of contractual agreements with film producers."[76]

The unions and guilds sent their own representatives to support the royalty fee but admitted that they would benefit only through the trickle-down of the returns to the copyright owners. Clint Eastwood, a successful and wealthy actor-producer-director, showed up at the House hearings to speak for actors.[77] Charlton Heston and Beverly Sills appeared at the Senate hearings. The irony of stars like Heston (in the cable case and this case), and Eastwood speaking on behalf of "poor starving actors" is self-evident, Gene Allen, vice president of the International Alliance of Theatrical Stage Employees (IATSE), succinctly described the powerless situation of workers in the industry (indeed all workers in a capitalist system): "Unless there is incentive for the producer to make the product, our people are not going to work."[78] Again, as in the cable case, the real revolutionary challenge to copyright was not made, by either workers or the public of users, that is, there was no discussion or effort on the part of workers to reappropriate their alienated labor nor on the part of the public of users to resurrect the intellectual commons by rejecting private appropriation in the first instance. There are some questionable assumptions underlying the position of the proroyalty forces as well. One was that, without economic incentive, artistic and intellectual production would automatically cease, and consequently social progress would be brought to a halt. But there must be more to the human impulse to create art and literature than simply an economic stimulus. This may, or may not, be the case in the context of capitalist society in which the sale of one's labor is necessary for survival. In this context, artistic and intellectual endeavors by actual creators are indeed a means for acquiring economic reward in the end, even if minimal in the typical case (the reward is from wage labor rather than ownership of copyright). It is questionable whether individuals pursue careers in artistic and intellectual activities on the basis of economic motivations when unemployment in these sectors runs so high. It is more plausible to assume that economic incentive appeals to the capitalists who invest in these activities and who would not invest if the potential for a profitable return on their investment did not exist. If the economic incentive were removed, *people* would still "produce" art and literature, but capitalists would not invest in the creative process.

Debates over the Effects of Home Taping

Much of the debate between the proroyalty and the protaping forces centered on the question of "time-shifting" and "librarying." Many of Valenti's predictions above centered on the notion that VCR owners kept the tapes of broadcasts to build "libraries." Once people have television programs and motion pictures in their libraries, they would not tune in to their rebroadcast. MPAA-commissioned research presented to Congress found that VCR owners owned many more video-cassettes than needed for just time-shifting and thus concluded that they were indeed building libraries.[79]

The protaping lobbyists claimed that the major advantage and use of the VCR is for time-shifting—the recording of television programs for later viewing at a more convenient time. They commissioned research that generally backed the claim that this was the primary use of VCRs. Clearly, time-shifting increases television viewers' ability to gain some control over the scheduling of television programs. Former FCC chair Charles Ferris, testifying on behalf of the HRRC, predicted that the VCR would result in increased diversity in television programming as late hours could be filled with a variety of material that individuals could tape for viewing at more convenient times. Indeed, both sides invoked the "diversity" argument, with the protaping forces predicting the VCR would increase diversity and the proroyalty forces forecasting decreased diversity with increased home taping. The history of U.S. entertainment and communications policymaking is filled with such rhetoric, and the various industries have repeatedly failed to deliver such increased diversity. As the political economy of communications has pointed out, much of the failure by media industries to deliver diversity is a result of the market structure within which they operate, particularly their emphasis on mass audiences.

The HRRC also argued that the royalty system proposed by the copyrightists was a system of double compensation to copyright owners, as cable operators had charged in the cable case. Copyright owners were paid once when they licensed their works to broadcasters for delivery of filmed entertainment to their audiences free of charge (this is not to ignore the charges to consumers embedded in goods and services to recover advertising expenditures or the cost of the TV set). The HRRC argued that if an individual could view the program as it was being broadcast for free so should the home taper who was merely recording for the purpose of viewing the program later. To charge a royalty fee for this use implied a windfall for copyright owners through double compensation. Accordingly, the HRRC maintained that if copyright owners wanted to control the use of their products, they simply ought not make them available to broadcast or pay television.[80]

Two additional features of the Mathias-Edwards-type bills are worth briefly mentioning. The first was their application to home audiotaping. The second was their repeal of the first sale doctrine. The filmed entertainment copyright owners found a naturalally in music publishers and record producers. Since the late 1970s, the music recording industry had complained that home audiotaping was seriously eroding its income. Unlike the filmed entertainment copyright owners, who were unable to show evidence of actual harm from home taping, the music industry was able to show that revenues from phonograph records and tapes had flattened out since 1978 after a long period of large and steady growth. Music publishers and producers blamed the lull on the mass proliferation of audiocassette recorders during the same period and the increase of off-the-air taping or the borrowing of phonograph records for taping. A representative from the Recording Industry Association of America (RIAA), in testimony to the House subcommittee considering this legislation, estimated the displaced sales from home taping cost the industry $1 billion per year.[81]

Both the RIAA and MPAA argued that home taping siphoned off revenues from the big hit and in so doing jeopardised the ability of filmed entertainment and music producers to channel these revenues into efforts that are riskier and not as profitable. The revenues from the hits are essential, they said, for maintaining the diversity in talent and art forms needed to satisfy the interests of "minority" audiences (audiences with special interests, tastes, lifestyles, and so forth). In essence, these representatives of capital were threatening an investment strike unless the state was willing to protect and extend their copyright monopoly. They demanded a compulsory license for manufacturers and importers of recording equipment, which they claimed was necessary to ensure the continued income for promoting diversity in intellectual and artistic creativity. The threat underscores the degree of control that media capitalists have over the production of information and culture and the lack of influence of unprofitable audiences. This control by media capitalists is based on ownership of the means of intellectual and artistic production, whereas the minority audiences' lack of influence stems from the system's commercial for-profit nature.

The protaping lobbyists questioned the RIAA's claim that deteriorating business conditions were related to home taping. They saw it rather as a factor of the general economic recession of the late 1970s and early 1980s, the lack of hits by big name artists, changing audience demographics (due to a smaller cohort of teenagers), and rising prices for recordings. Such claims and counterclaims were typical of the intense lobbying efforts surrounding these bills and ranged from the purely speculative to empirical surveys by public opinion firms of home recording use and econometric analyses by economic consultants of filmed entertainment and recording markets.[82]

The Pursuit of Special Interests

The prominent role of economists and opinion pollsters in this case is in remarkable contrast to the way the special-interest process functioned when the cable copyright question was first debated in Congress and only industry representatives and their lawyers appeared on the record. It demonstrates how empirical social science has become a significant part of politics and policymaking. Thus, Alan Greenspan, current chair of the Federal Reserve, testified on behalf of the recording industry at the Senate hearings on the home recording acts.[83] In addition, two prominent lawyers added their legal treatises to the House proceedings. Laurence H. Tribe, professor of constitutional law at Harvard University, produced a report for use by the MPAA entitled "Constitutional Law on Copyright Compensation"; and Melville B. Nimmer, noted professor of copyright law at UCLA's law school, produced a report entitled "The Legal Status of Home Audio Recording of Copyrighted Works."[84] Nimmer refused to align himself with any industry segment or coalition, but his conclusions came down strongly on the side of the proroyalty forces. Tribe argued that exempting home tapers from infringement was a violation of the Fifth Amendment, which prevents the state from taking private property without just cause and compensation.

The participation of noted legal scholars in the legislative process is just one more illustration of CLS's refutation of the claim that law is above politics. Indeed, the boundaries between legislative and judicial realms have become in wishing to influence policymaking. Like expert economists who stake their credibility on econometrics in making their predictions, legal experts stake their claims on formalism, rooting their findings in judicial precedents and congressional intent. Remarkably, private interests seeking to support one point of view or another are readily able to find economists and lawyers to back them up.

The second key feature of the Mathias-Edwards bills was their attempt to narrow the scope of the first sale doctrine through a "fair marketing" amendment. The first sale doctrine originated in the 1909 Copyright Act (section 109[a]) and provided that anyone who purchased a copy of a copyrighted work was entitled to sell or otherwise dispose of the possession without the permission of the copyright owner. This provision has permitted the rental of prerecorded videocassettes without the permission of or compensation to the copyright owner. All the major motion picture producer-distributors had entered the home-video market by the end of 1981 and found that the rental market seriously undermined their efforts to sell prerecorded videocassettes. The fair marketing amendment (section 6 of the proposed home recording acts), first proposed to Congress by Twentieth Century Fox, sought to condition the rental, sale, or lending of a phonorecord or prerecorded videocassette upon the copyright owner's authorisation. The motion picture producer-distributors felt that this was just one more form of commercial use of their intellectual property for which they were entitled compensation.

Hearings on the home recording acts were conducted until late 1983, and at all the sessions there was speculation on how the Supreme Court would rule in the Betamax case (the Court had recently agreed to hear Sony's appeal).[85] The parties interested in "preserving the U.S. copyright system" urged Congress to follow through with the proposed legislation, since the Supreme Court would hardly resolve all of the different issues involved (the provisions for audiotaping, for taping from cable and subscription television, the ban on duplication of prerecorded videocassettes, and the modification of the first sale doctrine). At the same time, both the protapers and the copyrightists circulated actively in the opinion-shaping network, taking part in panel discussions and appearing before the Congressional Arts Caucus, the National Association of Attorneys General, and the International Television Association; and on the Cable News Network, Larry King's radio show, and CBS's "Morning News."[86] A notable number of former government officials—from cabinet members to presidential aides to retired members of Congress and others—were involved in the process, making notable amounts of money.[87]

The Copyright Committee of the American Bar Association voted in favor of the narrowing of the first sale doctrine but decided to table taking a position on legislation for home-taping royalties.[88] But because no consensus could be forged among the different factions of the corporate community involved in this case, and because of the equally ample resources and power at the disposal of both sides, Congress refused to act on the proposed legislation. Besides having to contend with a fragmented power bloc, Congress faced the wrath of the ever growing share of the public owning and using VCRs (over 4 million units had been sold by manufacturers to retailers by the end of 1983).[89] As in the cable case, where activity in Congress became stalled due to its indecisiveness, Congress again let the Supreme Court make the next crucial move.

There was one minor victory for copyright owners to come out of this flurry of activity. Both the Senate and the House followed up the home recording acts with hearings on the copyright issues surrounding audio and video rental operations.[90] The hearings culminated with legislation that made the rental of audio recordings without permission of the copyright holder an infringement. One reason that Congress acted on the audio rental issue but not video rental is that video rental shops were already widely established and held significant lobbying clout. By contrast, there were only a handful of phonograph record and tape rental shops, and growth of these could easily be halted without much opposition to the legislation. Accordingly, Congress repealed the first sale doctrine as it applied to audio records and tapes with the record rental amendment, which took effect in October 1984.[91]

The record rental amendment sought to curb the growth of musical recording rental operations. The House report on the legislation concluded that the "nexus of commercial record rental and duplication may directly and adversely affect the ability of copyright holders to exercise their reproduction and distribution rights under the Copyright Act."[92] It therefore prohibited the renting, leasing, or lending of phonorecords without the authorisation of the copyright owner. The Senate report supplied the rationale for the law, again basing it on an appeal to "diversity."[93] The report concluded that record rentals were ultimately detrimental to consumers when they resulted in reduced sales revenues that in turn would produce two adverse consequences: one, higher prices for purchasers of records ("those honoring copyright laws"); two, it would affect musical creativity by forcing the recording industry to "retrench," "reduce risk," and be "less willing to take a chance on unknown artists and songwriters or to experiment with innovative musical forms."[94] The underlying intent of the legislation was to give control of distribution rights back to copyright owners of musical works that were usurped by the first sale doctrine, the record rental concept, and the millions of au-diorecording devices in the hands of the public of users.

The arrival of compact discs and digital taping systems added a special urgency to this particular legislation because their digital quality make them ideal "master recordings." However, the House report noted that with regard to other recording technologies and issues, this particular bit of legislation held "no precedential value."[95]

The Supreme Court Decision on Home Recording Rights

Indicative of the importance of the Betamax case, the Supreme Court heard arguments twice in response to Sony's appeal. In January 1984, the Court voted 5 to 4 to overturn the appeals court's decision. It held that the sale of VCRs to the general public did not constitute contributory infringement and that home recording of copyrighted programs from commercial television for purposes of time-shifting was a fair use. [96] Justice John Paul Stevens, who wrote the majority opinion, found the district court's decision quite convincing and cited it frequently.[97] In a significant recognition of the First Amendment dimensions of copyright law, the court found noncommercial home taping a use that "served the public interest in increasing access to television programming, an interest that 'is consistent with the First Amendment policy of providing the fullest possible access to information through the public airwaves' [citing the district court opinion]."[98] The Court recognised that "access is not just a matter of convenience, as plaintiffs have suggested. Access has been limited not simply by inconvenience but by the basic need to work. Access to the better programs has also been limited by the competitive practice of counterprogramming."[99] The "free" broadcast of the programming to the public and the noncommercial, private nature of home VCR recording and use convinced the district court that this activity was a fair use. The Supreme Court agreed and to that extent also held that Sony was not liable for contributory infringement.

The Court identified the many noninfringing uses that the Betamax had as well, for example home videomaking. The Supreme Court also stressed that an injunction against the sale of the Betamax would deprive VCR users of the ability to tape noncopyrighted material or material whose owners consented to the copying. The latter group included religious, educational, and sports program producers who had initially testified for the district court that they had no objection to home taping for private, noncommercial use. In the majority's opinion, "The sale of copying equipment, like the sale of other articles of commerce, does not constitute contributory infringement if the product is widely used for legitimate, unobjectionable purposes, or indeed, is merely capable of substantial non-infringing uses."[100] The Supreme Court cited specifically the testimony of Fred Rogers of *Mister Rogers' Neighborhood*, who felt that VCRs provided a useful function in allowing families to record and view children's programs at times more convenient to them.[101] With regard to infringing uses, the Court could not find Sony liable since the only contact between it and the VCR user was at the moment of sale.[102] Sony could not be held responsible for the infringing uses of the Betamax since it had no control over the use of the Betamax by its consumers.

In determining private home taping of television broadcasts a fair use, the Supreme Court applied the four-part fair use test and found that economic harm to the potential market for or value of the respondent's copyrighted works from time-shifting was minimal. The appeals court had felt that home taping was not a fair use because it was not a productive use (i.e., not educational or scholarly). The Supreme Court disregarded this distinction and focused instead on that part of the first factor that asks whether the use was commercial or not. It thereby went with the expanded notion of fair use proposed by the district court that certain noncommercial uses are exempt. In the majority opinion, fair use does not have to entail an educational purpose. What is more important is whether the use is commercial. This finding remains one of the most significant holdings of the Betamax case.

The Court collapsed factors two and three of the fair use test, recognising "the nature of the copyrighted work" as a "televised copyrighted audiovisual work," Time-shifting merely enabled the viewer to see a program that the viewer had been invited to watch in its entirety for "free." Thus, the fact that viewers taped the entire program did "not have its ordinary effect of militating against a finding of fair use."[103] The Court avoided any distinction as to the type of copyrighted work in terms of information versus entertainment. The appeals court found that most programs recorded on VCRs were entertaining in nature and therefore not a fair use in terms of advancing education and scholarship. It also felt that copying an entire work was generally proscribed under traditional findings of fair use. In finding home taping a fair use, the Supreme Court therefore *did* have to significantly extend the traditional boundaries of fair use established in case law.

In considering factor four (the effect of the use upon the potential market for or value of the copyrighted work), the Supreme Court held that the burden of proof of harm lay with the copyright owners and that they had failed to demonstrate any effect of home taping on the potential for or the value of the copyrighted work. Accordingly, the Court's majority found no need to prohibit the use when it did not affect the "author's incentive to create."[104] Justice Stevens invoked the access-to-information mandate when he maintained that the "prohibition of such noncommercial uses would merely inhibit access to ideas without any countervailing benefit."[105] Thus, in the majority opinion, a use of a copyrighted material for commercial purposes permitted the presumption of economic harm and would not be a fair use. "But if it is for noncommercial purpose, the likelihood [of economic harm] must be demonstrated."[106]

Universal and Disney admitted that to date they could not show actual harm to the value of their copyrights. Their arguments for potential economic harm were based on the notion of loss of control over their copyrighted works and their ability to engage in price discrimination in various ancillary markets. Judge Ferguson was the first to reject Valenti's predictions of potential harm cataloged above, and the Supreme Court majority concurred. As Judge Ferguson had pointed out, these arguments were based "on speculation about audience viewing patterns and ratings ... a 'black art' because of the significant imprecision involved in the calculations."[107] Thus, the copyright owners failed to show either actual or potential economic harm, which weighed against a finding of infringement and in favor of a finding of fair use.

Justice Blackmun's dissent was based primarily on factor four—the question of economic harm. To him, the potential economic harm was self-evident. VCR owners and users did in fact find commercial value in the use of these devices. It allowed them to record programs and watch them at more convenient times, which is why they bought tapes and recorders in the first place. Blackmun concluded that VCR users would undoubtedly "be willing to pay some kind of royalty to copyright holders. The Studios correctly argue that they have been deprived of

the ability to exploit this sizable market."[108] The benefits that VCR owners derived from using these devices were only exploitable by the manufacturers and importers. Blackmun believed that copyright owners deserved a cut from the revenues produced by this new use of their property. The copyright owners convinced him of the economic harm of VCR use by simply "showing that the value of their copyrights would increase if they were compensated for the copies that are used in the new market."[109]

Journal publishers made the same argument in *Williams and Wilkins.* They felt deprived of deserved compensation from the copying of their copyrighted works in which the researchers obviously found an economic utility, since they did not have to subscribe to the journals to acquire the articles. Thus, the publishers lost out on potential subscribers. In Blackmun's approach, this is a sufficient showing of potential economic harm and negates any claims of fair use.

In his consideration of the first factor of the fair use test, Blackmun repeated the same argument made by the appeals court in finding home taping an "intrinsic" use rather than a productive use and therefore not a fair use. Home taping was not the type of use "for socially laudable purposes" that the fair use doctrine sought to protect, as opposed to, say, photocopying journal articles for purposes of furthering medicine and science. In terms of legislative intent, Blackmun concluded "neither the statute nor its legislative history suggest any intent to create a general exemption for a single copy made for private or personal use."[110]

With the Supreme Court's Betamax decision, the efforts of copyright owners to impose levies on VCRs and blank

videocassettes came to an end. As this case study demonstrates, the divisions among factions of the capitalist class made reaching a consensus on the issue virtually impossible. Additionally, VCRs proved to be important generators of revenue for the filmed entertainment industry from the sale of prerecorded videocassettes to rental shops and directly to consumers. The outcome of the Betamax case was apparently contingent in terms of the logic of copyright but turned out to be largely irrelevant in terms of judicial precedence and its effects on the filmed entertainment industry's revenues. It is enough to conclude this case study with the point that the filmed entertainment industry decided to tolerate home taping for time-shifting purposes and to channel its political efforts into continuing the call for narrowing of the first sale doctrine and legislation requiring VCR manufacturers to insert antitaping devices to halt back-to-back copying of prerecorded videocassettes.[111] In addition to continuing legislative and technological strategies, the filmed entertainment industry successfully consolidated its control over the VCR by incorporating the new technology into its market structure, thus once more thwarting the challenge to its copyright system.

"Fixing" the Marketplace

Though it seems that the filmed entertainment industry suffered a setback in the Betamax case, the Supreme Court's decision had only minimal effects, if any, on the value of its copyrights. Furthermore, the case provided little in terms of legal precedent in subsequent copyright litigation. Finally, once the VCR reached household saturation, it became apparent that people used them much more to watch rented movies than for time-shifting. An A. C. Nielsen survey reported in 1991 that VCR owners spent one and a half hours per week, only 3 per cent of their total television viewing time, watching programs they had recorded.[112] By that time, the major Hollywood studios discovered that

the VCR could be a source of significant revenues, despite the first sale doctrine and various forms of piracy.

By early 1993, 77 per cent of U.S. television households contained VCRs. As the number of VCR households increased, the filmed entertainment industry shifted its priorities from the video rental marketplace to sales of videocassettes direct to consumers (known as "sell-through" in industry parlance). By 1990, sales of videos to consumers surpassed sales to rental outlets. In 1992, the major Hollywood studios earned $2.5 billion from sell-through videos versus $2 billion from video rental outlets.[113] As reported, the six active major studios—Disney, Warner Bros., Twentieth Century Fox, Columbia, Paramount, and Universal—accounted for 77 per cent of the total revenues earned from videocas-sette sales in the North American market.[114] The U.S. Department of Commerce predicted that home-video retailers would earn between $12 billion and $18 billion from video rentals and sales in 1993.[115]

The clear leader of the home-video rental/retail sector is Blockbuster Video, which had 4,000 video stores by the end of 1993.[116] This market dominance has given Blockbuster significant clout in determining what is made available to video renters and purchasers. Charges of censorship by Blockbuster emerged when it refused to carry Woody Allen's *Shadows and Fog* while Allen was involved in a highly publicised custody battle with Mia Farrow. The conservative Blockbuster corporation denied assertions that the decision not to carry the video was based on moral principles, claiming instead that it was market based.[117] Bagdikian points out that this defense is commonly used when a particular media product is excluded from the marketplace in order to disguise situations where the product in question runs contrary to the personal politics of the owner or governing board of the media corporation.[118] Blockbuster also refuses to carry movies that receive an NC-17 rating from the Classifications and Ratings Board of the Motion Picture Association of America. Critics have charged the board with being biased against independent and international film producers by giving them stricter ratings; of being more tolerant of explicit violence than sex or profanity; and of being racist when giving more rigorous scrutiny to films with black themes or actors.[119] Here again we see the effects of monopolistic power in limiting the range and diversity of products in the media marketplace.

The growth of the sell-through market reflects the strategies of the major video distributors to distinguish titles for sale to rental outlets versus those marketed for direct purchase by consumers. Titles intended for the rental market are usually priced at $100 retail ($70 wholesale), whereas those aimed at the sell-through market have a suggested retail price of less than $20. The film's producer-distributor usually keeps about 55 per cent of the retail price of a video.[120] This pricing strategy reflects the filmed entertainment industry's efforts to cope with the first sale doctrine, which denies it a cut of rental revenues. By charging higher up-front prices to video rental outlets, the industry can control the videocassette release "window" to some extent. Another strategy along these lines is to first release a video at the higher retail price and then rerelease it for sell-through, as Orion did with *Silence of the Lambs,* which was originally sold to dealers for $99.98 and later direct to consumers for $19.98.[121] This strategy follows the price discrimination tactics long practiced by the industry to take advantage of "high-value" customers. This recalls that highlighted Disney's efforts to control the ancillary market, from theaters to home video, by creating artificial scarcity for its classic animated movies. Imitating the Disney system, Turner Home Entertainment released a fiftieth-anniversary edition of *Casablanca* after rereleasing the film for theatrical exhibition a couple months earlier.[122]

Another strategy for encouraging the growth of the sell-through market involves various tie-ins with a wide variety of consumer products. By involving other companies in the marketing and promotion of a video, the filmed entertainment industry can lower costs and gain exposure in supermarkets and other mass outlets. For example, the regular edition of *Casablanca* was list-priced at $24.98 but consumers could get $5 off with a rebate coupon from Taster's Choice coffee.[123] Turner enlisted four sponsors for its sixtieth-anniversary reissue of *King Kong:* Delta Airlines, the New York Hilton, the City of New York, and Universal Electronics. All four companies placed advertisements on the home video in exchange for helping to defray the costs of promoting *King Kong* in stores.[124] Placing advertising on home videos has become common practice as both the filmed entertainment industry and advertisers seek to exploit this new medium. Other notable promotional tie-ins included *Hook* with Ocean Spray and Breck shampoo; *Wayne's World* with Nestle's Butterfinger candy bar; and *Fried Green Tomatoes* with Mary Kay cosmetics, a brand featured in the movie itself.[125] Orion pioneered the sale of videos through fast-food outlets in a deal with McDonald's to sell *Dances With Wolves* at less than $8 between Thanksgiving and Christmas in 1992. The deal came after Orion had sold some 600,000 videos to rental outlets for $99.98.[126] The movie was again released in early 1993 to video retailers and discount department stores at a suggested retail price of $14.98.

The result of the video industry's focus on the big hits has been to reduce the range of titles available at video outlets. One video dealer admitted that due to the necessity of buying more copies of few hits, his selection had narrowed significantly.[127] Similarly, the sales of videos by black directors or with black casts lag behind those of other videos with comparable box-office grosses or other genre-specific movies.[128] The increasing incursion of chain video retailers has had the same effect on media diversity as in other retail media sectors, from book publishing,[129] to newspaper publishing,[130] to sales of musical recordings.[131] Consequently, a handful of companies control the production, distribution, and sale of filmed entertainment videos. In sum, the VCR, like cable, has become one more morsel in the large media conglomerate food chain. How this has occurred at the international level is the focus of the next chapter.

NOTES

1. *Universal City Studios, Inc. v. Sony Corporation of America*, 480 F. Supp. 429 (C.D. Cal. 1979); *Sony Corporation of America, Inc. v. Universal City Studies, Inc.*, 659 F.2d 963 (9th Cir. 1981); *Sony Corporation of America, Inc. v. Universal City Studios, Inc.*, 464 U.S. 417 (1984).
2. "Public of users" is a term to describe the private use of reproductive technologies to copy and make use of copyrighted material, for example, home taping and playback of broadcasts (television and radio), reproduction of prerecorded phonograph recordings and videocassettes, photocopying of published printed works, copying of computer software, etc. This is use of copyrighted works for private, noncommercial purposes, including scholarly and educational uses permitted under the fair use doctrine.
3. Ralph Miliband, *The State in Capitalist Society*, New York: Basic Books, 1969, p. 138.
4. The Associated Press, "Survey of Judges' Income," *Christian Science Monitor*, June 6, 1989, p. 8; The Associated Press, "Most Judges Earn More Off Bench, Study Says," *Chicago Tribune*, June 5, 1989, p. 4.
5. David Kairys, "Introduction," in D. Kairys (ed.), *Politics and Law*, New York: Pantheon Books, 1982, pp. 1-7, p. 5.
6. James Lardner, "Annals of Law: The Betamax Case—1,2," *New Yorker*, April 6, 1987, pp. 45 *ff.*, and April 13, 1987, pp. 60 *ff.*
7. Miliband, p. 138.
8. Ben Bagdikian, *The Media Monopoly* (4th ed.), Boston: Beacon, 1992, p. 50.

9. Kairys, "Introduction," p. 5.
10. Miliband, pp. 141-142.
11. Pierre Joseph Proudhon, *What Is Property? An Inquiry into the Principle of Right and Government*, New York: Dover Publications, 1970, pp. 393-397.
12. Miliband, p. 142.
13. Miliband, p. 142.
14. Miliband, p. 143.
15. Miliband, p. 143.
16. David Kairys, "Legal Reasoning," in D. Kairys (ed.), *Politics and Law,* New York: Pantheon Books, 1982, pp. 11-17, p. 17.
17. Roberto Unger, *The Critical Legal Studies Movement*, Cambridge, MA: Harvard University Press, 1986, p. 1.
18. Kairys, "Introduction," p. 1.
19. Kairys, "Introduction," p. 2.
20. Unger, p. 12.
21. Unger, p. 12.
22. Bernard Edelman, *Ownership of the Iinage: Elements for a Marxist Theory of Law,* Boston: Routledge and Kegan Paul, 1979.
23. Unger, p. 4.
24. Unger, p. 5.
25. Isaac D. Balbus, "Commodity Form and Legal Form: An Essay on the 'Relative Autonomy' of the Law," *Law and Society Review,* 11:3, 1977, pp. 571-588
26. Balbus, p. 583.
27. Nicos Poulantzas, "The Problem of the Capitalist State," in R. Blackburn (ed.), *Ideology in Social Science,* New York: Vintage Books, 1973, pp. 238-262.
28. Balbus, p. 585 (italics in original text).
29. Balbus, p. 586 (italics in original text). Balbus does note that the trend is by no means complete nor entirely uncontradictory.
30. Unger, p. 108.
31. Unger, p. 111.
32. Robert W. Gordon, "Critical Legal Histories," *Stanford Law Review,* 36:1-2, 1984, pp. 57-125, p. 125 (italics in original text).
33. Gordon, 1984, p. 124.

34. Robert W. Gordon, "New Developments in Legal Theory," in D. Kairys (ed.), *Politics and Law,* New York: Pantheon Books, 1982, pp. 281-293, p. 287.
35. Gordon, 1982, p. 290.
36. Michel Foucault, *Discipline and Punishment: The Birth of the Prison* (trans. Alan Sheridan), New York: Pantheon Books, 1977.
37. Gordon, 1982, p. 290.
38. Allan Hutchinson and Patrick J. Monahan, "Law, Politics, and the Critical Legal Scholars: The Unfolding Drama of American Legal Thought," *Stanford Law Review,* 36:1-2, 1984, pp. 199-245, p. 225-226.
39. 480 F. Supp. 429 (CD. Cal. 1979).
40. Lardner (Part 1), p. 50.
41. Lardner (Part 1), p. 57.
42. 480 F. Supp. 429, 450.
43. H.J. Hipsh, "The Betamax Case and the Breakdown of the Traditional Concept of Fair Use," *Communications and the Law,* 2:4, 1980, pp. 39-48, p. 40.
44. *Williams and Wilkins Co. v. United States,* 487 F.2d 1345 (U.S. Ct. of Claims, 1973), *aff'd per curiam,* 420 U.S. 376 (1975).
45. 487 F.2d 1345, 1354.
46. 487 F.2d 1345, 1354.
47. 487 F.2d 1345, 1360.
48. 487 F.2d 1345, 1362.
49. 487 F.2d 1345, 1362.
50. 487 F.2d 1345, 1368.
51. Blackmun did not participate in the decision due to conflict of interest.
52. 659 F.2d 963 (C.D. Cal 1979).
53. 659 E.2d 963, 921.
54. 659 E2d 963, 971.
55. 659 E2d 963, 972.
56. 659 E2d 963,972.
57. Burstyn *v. Wilson, 343* U.S. 495 (1952).
58. 343 U.S. 495, 501-502.

59. 659 E2d 963, 973.
60. 659 E2d 963, 973.
61. 659 E2d963, 973.
62. 659 F.2d 963, 974.
63. 659 F.2d 963, 974.
64. 659 F.2d 963, 977.
65. Lardner (Part 1), p. 69.
66. U.S. House, H.R. 4783, 97th Cong., 1st Sess., October 20, 1981.
67. The members of the HRRC included RCA (which held the largest distributor share of the U.S. VCR market), General Electric, 3M, Dupont, Sony Corp. of America, Matsushita, JC Penny, Sears and Roebuck, and the trade organisations Electronic Industries Association, American Retail Federation, and the National Retail Merchants Association.
68. Among supporters of the bill were the MPAA, made up of:

    Columbia Pictures Industries, Inc.

    Walt Disney Productions

    Embassy Communications

    Filmways Pictures

    Metro-Goldwyn-Mayer Film Co.

    Paramount Pictures

    Twentieth Century Fox Film Corporation

    United Artists Corporation

    Universal Pictures, a division of Universal City Studios

    Warner Bros. Inc.; the Board of the Alliance of Motion Picture and Television Producers:

    Universal City Studios, Inc.

    Warner Bros. Inc.

    Twentieth Century Fox Film Corp.

    Columbia Pictures Industries, Inc.

    Paramount Pictures Corp.

    Walt Disney Productions

    Aaron Spelling Productions

    Mary Tyler Moore Enterprises, Inc.

    Leonard Goldberg Co.

    Tandem/Embassy Communications Co.

Metro-Goldwyn-Mayer/United Artists; and the Coalition to Preserve the American Copyright:

Children's Television Workshop

Volunteer Lawyers for the Arts

National Association of Theater Owners

Screen Actors Guild

Association of Talent Agents

National Cable TV Association

International Alliance of Theatrical Stage Employees and Moving Picture Operators

Producers Guild of America, Inc.

CBS, Inc.

Authors

League Writers Guild of America

Training Media Distributors Association

Directors Guild of America

Actors Equity Association

AFTRA

National Association of Broadcasters.

69. U.S. House, H.R. 5705, 97th Cong., 1st Sess., March 3, 1982.

70. U.S. Senate, S. 31, S. 32, S. 33, 98th Cong., 1st Sess., January 26, 1983.

71. Lardner (Part l),p. 51.

72. U.S. House, Committee on the Judiciary, Subcommittee on Courts, Civil Liberties, and the Administration of Justice, *Home Recording of Copyrighted Works—Part 1* and *Part 2*, Hearings on H.R. 4783, H.R. 4794, H.R. 4808, H.R. 5250, H.R. 5488, and H.R. 5705,97th Cong., 1st. Sess and 2nd Sess., April 12, 13, 14, June 24, August 11, September 22 and 23, 1982, Washington, DC: U.S. Government Printing Office, 1983, Statement of David Ladd, Register of Copyrights and Assistant Librarian of Congress for Copyright Services, pp. 617-675, p. 633.

73. *Home Recording and Copyrights—Part 1,* Statement of Jack Valenti, President, MPAA, pp. 4-66. Valenti had served as MPAA president since 1966 after having served as a presidential assistant to Lyndon B. Johnson. Lardner reports that the motion picture companies found him so valuable that by 1981 they were paying him nearly $500,000 per year.

74. *Home Recording and Copyrights—Part 1,* Statement of Jack Valenti, President, MPAA, pp. 4-16, pp. 7-8.
75. *Home Recording and Copyrights—Part 1,* Prepared Statement of Jack Valenti, President, MPAA, pp. 17-66, p. 38.
76. *Home Recording and Copyrights—Part 1,* p. 38.
77. *Home Recording of Copyrighted Works—Part 1,* Statement of Clint Eastwood, pp. 115-116.
78. *Home Recording of Copyrighted Works—Part 1,* Statement of Gene Allen, Vice President, IATSE, p. 139.
79. *Home Recording and Copyrights—Part 1,* "An Assessment of the Impact to Consumers from a Royalty Fee on Videocassette Recorders and Blank Tapes," pp. 1145-1209.
80. Although the Betamax case did not apply to home taping from cable and pay-cable television, the comprehensive proroyalty bills did.
81. *Home Recording of Copyrighted Works—Part 1,* Statement of Stanley M. Gortikov, President, Recording Industry Association of America, pp. 311-381, p. 319.
82. The two-part published volumes of the 1982 House hearings (Home Recording and Copyrights — Part 1 *Copyrights—Part I* and *Part 2)* included the following studies: Media Statistics Incorporated, "1981 VCR Report," prepared tor the Coalition to Preserve the American Copyright (Summary), pp. 27-28, and "Analysis of Third (1981) Media Statistics Survey of Video Recorder Owners' Recording and Playback Behavior," pp. 1141-1144; Warner Communications Inc., "A Consumer Survey: Home Taping," 1980, pp. 382—433; William R. Hamilton and Staff, "A Survey of Households with Tape Playback Equipment," prepared for Copyright Royalty Tribunal, September 1979, pp. 434-452; CBS Record Market Research, "Blank Tape Buyers: Their Attitudes and Impact on Pre-Recorded Music," Fall 1980, pp. 453-470; The Roper Organisation, Inc., "A Study on Tape Recording Practices Among the General Public," conducted for the National Music Publishers Association and the Recording Industry of America, June 1979, pp. 471-480; RCA, Inc., "RCA Video Disc Player Owner Survey," April 1982, pp. 851-867; Market Facts, Inc., "Video Price Elasticity Study: Rental Versus Purchase," prepared for Twentieth Century Fox Video, September 1982, pp. 868-888; 3M Corporation, "Prerecorded Videocassette Market Study—1982," pp. 889-902; Yankelovich, Skelly, and White, Inc., "Why Americans Tape: A Survey of Home Audio Taping in the United States," September

1982, pp. 927-1032; Robert N. Nathan Associates, Inc., "An Assessment of the Impact to Consumers from a Royalty Fee on Videocassette Recorders and Blank Tapes," prepared for the MPAA, April 5, 1982, pp. 1145-1209. A significant portion of the printed hearings is thus not testimony but "scientific" surveys that back one claim or another.

83. U.S. Senate, Committee on the Judiciary, *Copyright Infringements (Audio and Video Recorders),* Hearings on S. 1758, November 30, 1981, and April 21, 1982, 97th Cong., 1st Sess. 2nd Sess., Washington, DC: U.S. Government Printing Office, 1982, Testimony of Alan Greenspan, pp. 917 *ff.*

84. U.S. Senate, *Copyright Infringements (Audio and Video Recorders);* Melville B. Nimmer, "Legal Status of Home Audio Recording of Copyrighted Works," prepared for the Recording Industry Association and National Music Publishers Association, 1982, pp. 878-910; Laurence H. Tribe, "Memorandum of Constitutional Law on Copyright Compensation Issues Raised by the Proposed Congressional Reversal of the Ninth Circuit's Betamax Ruling," December 5, 1981, pp. 78-154.

85. U.S. Senate, *Copyright Infringements (Audio and Video Recorders);* U.S. Senate, Committee on the Judiciary, Subcommittee on Patents, Copyrights, and Trademarks, *Audio and Video Rental,* April 29, 1983, 98th Cong., 1st Sess., Washington, DC: U.S. Government Printing Office, 1983; U.S. Senate, Committee on the Judiciary, Subcommittee on Patents, Copyrights, and Trademarks, *Video and Audio Home Taping,* Hearings on S. 31 and S. 175, October 25, 1983, 98th Cong., 1st Sess., Washington, DC: U.S. Government Printing Office, 1984.

86. Lardner (Part 2), p. 69.87. Lardner (Part 2), p. 70; Howie Kuntz, "Chariots for Hire," *Washington Post,* July 4, 1982, p. BI.

88. "ABA's Copyright Hedge," *TV Digest,* August 8, 1983, p. 16.

89. Electronic Industries Association, *Consumer Electronics Annual Review—1985,* Washington, DC: Electronic Industries Association, p. 25.

90. U.S. Senate, *Audio and Video Rental;* U.S. Senate, *Video and Audio Home Taping;* U.S. House, Committee on the Judiciary, Subcommittee on Courts, Civil Liberties, and the Administration of Justice, *Audio and Video First Sale Doctrine,* Hearings on H.R. 1027 and H.R. 1029, October 6 and 27 and December 13, 1983, February 23 anti April 12, 1984. 98th Cong., 1st Sess. and 2nd Sess., Washington, DC: U.S. Government Printing Office, 1985.

91. *Record Rental Amendment Act of 1984*, Pub.L. 98-450, 98 Stat. 1727 (October 4, 1984).
92. U.S. House, Committee on the Judiciary, *Record Rental Amendment of 1984*, House Report 98-987, August 31, 1984, 98th Cong., 2nd Sess., Washington, DC: U.S. Government Printing Office, 1984.
93. U.S. Senate, Committee on the Judiciary, *The Record Rental Amendment of 1983*, Senate Report 98-162, June 23, 1983, 98th Cong., 1st Sess., Washington, DC: U.S. Government Printing Office, 1983.
94. U.S. Senate, Senate Report 98-162, p. 3.
95. U.S. House, House Report 98-987, p. 2.
96. 464 U.S. 417 (1984).
97. The majority included Justices Stevens, Burger, Brennan, White, and O'Connor. Justice Blackmun wrote the dissent and was joined by Justices Marshall, Powell, and Rehnquist.
98. 464 U.S. 417, 432.
99. 464 U.S. 417, 432.
100. 464 U.S. 417, 452.
101. 464 U.S. 417, 451.
102. 464 U.S. 417,444.
103. 464 U.S. 417, 455-456.
104. 464 U.S. 417, 456.
105. 464 U.S. 417, 457.
106. 464 U.S. 417, 457.
107. 480 F. Supp. 469.
108. 464 U.S. 417, 491-492.
109. 464 U.S. 417,504.
110. 464 U.S. 417, 471.
111. See U.S. Senate, Committee on the Judiciary, *Home Video Recording*, Hearing on Providing Information on the Issue of Home Video Recording, September 23, 1986, 99th Cong., 2d Sess., Washington, DC: U.S. Government Printing Office, 1986.
112. Joann S. Lublin, "VCR Advances May Increase Zapping," *Wall Street Journal*, January 4, 1991, pp. BI, B4.
113. Richard Turner, "Disney Leads Shift from Rentals to Sales in

Videocassettes," *Wall Street Journal*, December 24, 1992, pp. 1, 30. Data cited from Paul Kagan Associates, Carmel, CA, p. 30.

114. Marc Berman, "Rentals Reap Bulk of 1991 Vid Harvest," *Variety*, January 6, 1992, pp. 22, 104.

115. U.S. Department of Commerce, *U.S. Industrial Outlook 1994*, Washington, DC: U.S. Government Printing Office, 1994, pp. 31-34.

116. "Blockbuster Doubts on Deal," *New York Times*, May 25, 1994, p. D3.

117. "Blockbuster Denies Boycott," New *York Times*, December 2, 1992, p. 5.

118. Bagdikian, p. 36.

119. Bernard Weinraub, "Film Ratings Under Attack from More than One Angle," *New York Times*, September 6, 1994, pp. C13, C14.

120. Geraldine Fabrikant, "Video Sales Gaining on Rentals," *New York Times*. October 17, 1989, pp. Dl, D25.

121. Peter M. Nichols, "Home Video: Studios Pursue New Marketing Strategies," *New York Times*, May 21, 1992, p. C22.

122. Nichols, May 21, 1992, p. C22.

123. Nichols, May 21, 1992, p. C22.

124. Peter M. Nichols, "Home Video: Hollywood Is Lowering Prices," *New York Times*, July 16, 1992, p. C24.

125. Nichols, July 16, 1992, p. C24.

126. Peter M. Nichols, "Home Video," *New York Times*, October 22, 1992, p. C26.

127. Peter M. Nichols, "Home Video: The Cost of Hits," *New York Times*, June 18, 1992, p. C18.

128. Lewis Beale, "Short Shrift at the Video Store," *Philadelphia Enquirer*, March 19, 1992, pp. D, D9.

129. Stan Luxenburg, *Books in Chains: Chain Bookstores and Marketplace Censorship*, New York: National Writers Union, 1991.

130. See especially Bagdikian, chapter 4, "From Mythology to Theology," and chapter 5, "Dear Mr. President..."

131. Jeffrey Ressner, "You Can't Always Get What You Want," *Rolling Stone*, 638, September 3, 1992, pp. 13-14.

8 INTELLECTUAL PROPERTY RIGHTS AND THE EUROPEAN COMMUNITY

Introduction

1. On 1 January 1973[1] the United Kingdom became a member of the European Economic Community (EEC), now retitled the European Community (EC). The stated aims of the EC include the harmonisation of national laws[2] and the creation of a unified market, consisting of all member states, within which there are no unjustifiable barriers to free trade[3]. Since the rules of the EC, as a matter of British[4] and Community[5] law, take precedence over conflicting national law, it is obvious that no description of the British law can be complete if it fails to take into account the impact of any relevant EC law and, in particular, the Treaty of Rome and the many European Court of Justice decisions and Commission rules which seek to explain and implement it.

A Brief Overview of EC Competition Law[6]

2. The Treaty of Rome is founded upon the assumption that competition within any given market for goods or services is the most effective way of keeping prices down, of ensuring that industrial output keeps pace with existing

consumer demand and of fostering the creation and exploitation of new markets. Market competition itself has a tendency towards that market's self-destruction, as one competing concern succeeds in winning the market from its rivals, and competition can neither be protected from itself nor enhanced by means of competition; for this reason it is accepted that legal rules are desirable in order to establish an artificial economic environment within which competition is preserved, and that these rules should be enforceable both by market competitors and by the intervention of the EEC Commission in Brussels.

3. The intended function of these rules is basically to interfere with competition no more than is necessary in order to keep competition alive. Thus Articles 30 to 36 of the Treaty of Rome seek to prohibit unjustifiable restrictions upon what can be imported into or exported from one member state to another, while Article 85 prohibits the operation of cartels and concerted undertakings which have, as their object or effect, the distortion or prevention of competition, and Article 86 prohibits the abuse of a position of dominance within the Community by any commercial undertaking. Since the exercise of national intellectual property rights is ideally suited to the preservation of market exclusivity, and to the elimination or selective preservation of competition, it is natural that the EC competition policy and the exploitation of intellectual property rights should come into conflict.

'Existence' v 'Exercise' of Rights

4. The key to the European Court of Justice's resolution of the conflict between pro- and anti-competitive laws lies in its distinction of the *existence* of intellectual property rights from the *exercise* of them. All national property rights - including those of an intellectual nature - are expressly preserved by Article 222 of the Treaty; this is so

even where a form of property, such as copyright in a sound recording, subsists in only some of the member states of the Community[7]. But there is a world of difference between recognising a property right (and not vitiating or expropriating it) and allowing its unfettered exercise. Article 222 does not therefore render the exercise of intellectual property rights invulnerable from the provisions of Articles 31 to 36, 83 and 86. In a similar manner, Article 36, which permits restrictions upon imports if they are justified as protection of industrial or commercial property, does not allow an 'arbitrary-discrimination' or 'disguised restriction' of otherwise legitimate trade between .member states.

EC Competition Law in Action

5. This book is not the place for a detailed account of EC competition law[8], or for an analysis of its complex interrelations with intellectual property rights[9]; the following is a brief and necessarily superficial survey of the main features of the subject.

(i) The abuse of a dominant position[10] within the Common Market, or in a substantial part of it, is prohibited to the extent that it affects trade between the various member states[11]. This prohibition applies without reference to the means by which the abuse is carried out, and has been held to apply to the exercise of intellectual property monopolies[12]. Article 86 identifies four particular activities which the Treaty of Rome regards *as* abusive, of which three (the imposition of unfair purchase or sale conditions[13], the limitation of production output[14] and the imposition of conditions relating to unconnected transactions[15]) are echoed in the British Patents Act 1977.

(ii) Agreements and concerted practices entered into

between, or conducted by two or more parties, are prohibited if they affect trade between member states and have as their object or effect the prevention, restriction or distortion of competition[16]. This means that many types of clause once favoured in patent licences, such as those which prohibited a licensee from challenging the validity of the licensed patent or which divided a geographical market between licensor and licensee, are no longer of utility within the context of European trade.

(iii) Quantitative restrictions on imports, and all measures which have that effect, are prohibited[17]. National intellectual property laws, and especially trade mark laws, are ideally suited to the restriction of imports from one member state to another, since the same person, holding the identical trade mark in each member state in respect of the same goods, could otherwise charge different prices for those goods in different countries and then prevent the export of his lawfully manufactured and marketed goods from a 'cheap' country to an 'expensive' one[18].

(iv) So far as concerns (i) and (ii), but not (iii), it is possible for one or more traders to obtain 'negative clearance' from the Commission in respect of their prima facie unlawful acts". 'Negative clearance' is simply certification by the Commission's Directorate-General IV (which administers the Treaty's competition policy) that, on the basis offsets known to it, usually being facts communicated to it by interested parties, there are no grounds for initiating proceedings against the practices of agreement in question. It is therefore an expression of opinion, and is

not immutable. There is no duty to apply for 'clearance' or to disclose one's possibly wrongful trading practices but, if one does so, one enjoys an immunity from the possibly huge fines which the Commission can impose upon reluctant competitors[20], until the Commission decides that exemption from Article 85 will not be allowed. The Commission is slow to give negative clearances, but may indicate, informally, in a 'comfort letter' that it does not intend to pursue an agreement or practice notified to it. No 'comfort letter' is irrevocable, which means that parties may embark upon a course of action which initially appears to be commercially neutral but which turns out to be objectionable.

(v) Some types of agreement - including patent licences[21], franchise agreements[22] and know-how licences[23] - are exempt from notification if they consist wholly of clauses which are approved by the Commission. It cannot, however, be inferred from this that a patent licence is objectionable simply because its terms do not qualify it for such an exemption.

(vi) As a guiding principle, the EC's competition rules will not permit the holder of any national intellectual property right to exercise that right in respect of goods or any other facilities once they have been made and commercially exploited by him or with his permission[24]. This is known as the principle of 'exhaustion of rights'[25]. Thus, a record company can exercise its copyright and neighbouring rights so as to prevent any unauthorised exploitation of those rights, but not to prevent any unauthorised transaction with regard to a chattel which has been legitimately made and sold in consequence of its own exploitation of those rights. Thus the British manufacturer of *Succo* chocolate bars can use his trade mark to stop the import of *Succo* bars made by a rival in Italy, in which *Succo* has not been registered and may be used by any manufacturer but he cannot use it in order to stop legitimate *Succo* bars being imported from Belgium, where they were made and sold by his subsidiary company, and so on.

Approximation and Assimilation of National Laws

6. The Commission of the European Economic Community has in mind two ideals towards which future legal developments should, it feels, be aimed. One is that each member state should employ, as far as is possible, the same substantive intellectual property rules; the other is that intellectual property monopolies should run the length and breadth of the Community, irrespective of the country of their origin. The remainder of this chapter will indicate the extent to which these aims have been, and remain to be, fulfilled.

Patents

7. The majority of the twelve member states of the EC (the Benelux countries, the United Kingdom, France, Germany and Italy) have broadly identical laws governing the criteria of patentability, and the patent term. That they do so is not, however, attributable to their membership of the BC; it is instead a by-product of their membership of the European Patent Convention. A Ccmmuniy Patent Convention[26], which would provide inter alia that one unitary patent would cover the entire territory of the Community[27], and that the EC be treated as one country for the purposes of the European Patent Convention[28] has been waiting many years for implementation and is expected

to be in force in 1992 or shortly thereafter. Note that the Community Patent Convention is intended to offer a second tier of patent protection, running in parallel with existing national systems. It is however a moot point whether national patent systems will be financially viable or economically justifiable once the unitary system comes into force[29].

Copyright

8. There is little likelihood of the member states of the EC enjoying broadly similar national laws, since the nature and extent of the variation of national laws, both between common law and civil law systems and within the different civil law systems, is so great that it is in many cases difficult to identify common conceptual ground between them. A preliminary comparative study of the state of national copyright laws[30], conducted when the Community had only nine member states, served mainly to highlight the extent of national variation. One cannot escape the observation that, just as the laws of science are the same throughout Europe, patent systems run largely in parallel with each other but that, just as the culture of each European country is uniquely personal to it, so too are the copyright laws which govern the protection and exploitation of cultural products. In 1988 a Green Paper was published on copyright and the new technologies[31]. This Green Paper has been criticised as seeking to solve European copyright problems by employing the British 'copyright' approach in preference to the continental "droit d'auteur' philosophy[32]- indeed, it does seem to advance practical solutions in preference to moral principles. It has been followed, in similar vein, by a proposed Directive on Software Protection[33] which, it has been suggested, would subordinate the interests of software writers to the development of the overall market for computer technologies[34].

Trade Marks

9. It is in the field of trade mark law that the greatest degree of progress has been made towards the goal of a law common to all member states. The Trade Marks Approximation Directive of 1988 has already laid down the principles which should be common to the Community's national or regional trade mark systems[35]. The draft Community Trade Mark Regulation[36] will, when it is implemented, provide for a single standard of registrability for a trade mark which will grant protection to its proprietor throughout the Community's extensive territory, in addition to the protection already provided under national laws. Initially there are bound to be problems, since it is likely that many marks currently in use in Europe are owned by different, and possibly quite unrelated, proprietors in a number of countries; this will entail the resolution of issues of concurrent user[37]. It is also inevitable that nuances of meaning in the different languages used within the Community will make questions of whether a mark is descriptive of the goods to which it is applied a matter of comparative semantics. There is also the problem of selecting for the Community Trade Marks Office a location which will offend the least number of unsuccessful bidders for it. Indeed of all the complex topics arising out of the text of the draft Regulation, the location of the Office seems to be that which is debated with the greatest degree of enthusiasm, perhaps because it is the easiest to comprehend.

REFERENCES

1. The date of coming into force of the European Communities Act 1972.
2. Treaty Establishing the European Economic Community (Treaty of Rome) Art 3, particularly 3(h).
3. *Ibid* Art 2.
4. European Communities Act 1972, s 2.

5. See eg *Algemenc Transport-en Expeditie Onderneming van Gend & Loos NV* v *Nederlands Administratie der Belastingen* 26/62 : [1963] ECR 1, ECJ; *Application des Gaz SA* v *Falks Veritas Ltd* [1974] 2 CMLR 75.
6. For a more detailed view see R Whish *Competition Law* (2nd edn 1989); see also V Korah's popular *An Introductory Guide to EC Competition Law and Practice* (4th edn 1990).
7. *EMl Eleclrola GmbH* v *Patricia lm-& Export GmbH* : 341/87 [1989] 2 CMLR 413.
8. See works cited at para **13.2**, n 1 above, and D Raybould *Comparative Law of Monopolies* (1988).
9. On which see D Guy and G Leigh *The EEC and Intellectual Property* (1981). See also V Korah *An Introductory Guide to EEC Competition Law and Practice* (4th edn 1990), pp. 156-170.
10. Treaty of Rome, Art 86.
11. The effect upon trade between member states is determined not just by geographical but, more importantly, by economic factors such as the proportion of market share affected : see eg *Felixstowe Dock and Rly Co* v *British Docks Roard* [1976] 2 CMLR 405.
12. See eg *Volvo* v *Veng* [1989] 4 CMLR 122
13. Treaty of Rome. Art 86(a); cf Patents Act 1977, s 48(3)(b)(i).
14. Treaty of Rome, Art 86(b); of Patents Act 1977, s 48(3)(a).
15. Treaty of Rome, Art 86(d); cf Patents Act 1977, s 44.
16. Treaty of Rome, Art 85.
17. Treaty of Rome, Art 30.
18. See *Deutsche Grammophon Gesellschaft GmbH* v *Metro-SB-Grossmarkte GmbH & Co KG* [1971] ECR 487; *Centrafarm B V* v *American Home Products Corpn* [1979] FSR 189.
19. Council Regulation 17/62, Art 2.
20. *Ibid.* Art 15(5).
21. Commission Regulation No 2349/84 of 23 July 1984, noted by D Guy 'Latest Draft of the Commission's Block Exemption for Patent Licences'[1984] EIPR 164.
22. Commission Regulation No 4087/88 of 30 November 1988.
23. Commission Regulation No 556/89 of 30 November 1988.
24. See eg *Deutsche Grammophon*, n 11.
25. For a discussion of 'exhaustion' within its wider EC context see

V Korah *An Introductory Guide to EEC Competition Law and Practice* (4th edn 1990), pp. 150-170, and Ch 8.

26. The Convention for the European Patent for the Common Market, Luxembourg, 15 December 1975 (Cmnd 6553, 1976).
27. *Ibid* Art I.
28. *Ibid* Art 2.
29. See J Phillips 'Time to Close the Patent Office Doors' [1990] 5 EIPR 151.
30. A Dietz *Copyright Law in the European Community* (1978).
31. Green Paper on *Copyright and the Challenge of Technology* (1988).
32. Margaret Moller *Urheberrecht oder Copyright?* (1988).
33. *Proposed Directive on Legal Protection of Computer Programs* (1988).
34. See W T Lake, J H Harwood_II and T P Olson 'Seeking Compatibility or Avoiding Development Costs? A Reply on Software Copyright in the EC' [1990] 12 EIPR 431.
35. 89/l04/EEC of 21 December 1988.
36. Amended Proposal for a Council Regulation on the Community Trade Mark, (1984) 27 *Official Journal of the European Communities* C230, p 1.
37. See eg *Re Persil Trade Mark* [1978] I CMLR 395.

9 RECOLONISING COMMUNICATIONS AND CULTURE: THE EXPANDING REALM OF INTERNATIONAL INTELLECTUAL PROPERTY LAW

This chapter moves the analysis of intellectual property law from the national to the international level while maintaining the focus on cable television and the videocassette recorder. As these new communications technologies increased their presence throughout the world, copyright owners faced similar problems re- garding the control of their property as those surfacing in the U.S. market. This chapter develops two case studies examining how new communications technologies generated challenges to U.S. intellectual property rights as well as how rights owners responded to them.

The first case considers the contest between U.S. filmed entertainment companies and Canadian cable operators over the issue of copyrights for cable. The central conflict in this case parallels between copy right owners and cable operators in the United States. The problem for U.S. copyright owners was how to persuade Canadian cable operators to accept copyright liability for the use of filmed entertainment programming carried in retransmitted broadcasts and to develop a regime that would govern the distribu tion of royalties generated by this use.

The second case focuses on Hollywood's battle against videocassette piracy in international markets. In this case, copyright owners of filmed entertainment had to respond to the challenge to their copyrights from unauthorized users of their property. The challenge here was to compel foreign governments to recognize the illegality of unauthorized duplication of prerecorded videocassettes and then to enforce the intellectual property rights of filmed entertainment copy- right owners.

Given the international character of these intellectual property disputes, the filmed entertainment industry found itself engaged in foreign policy making alongside the U.S. government. These cases thus lend themselves to an integration of the frameworks laid out in previous chapters used to analyze the political economy of the media, the capitalist state, and the law. For purposes of continuity, the political economy of international intellectual property can be organised into the same three basic categories used in previous chapters. The first category considers the institutions, networks, and organisations utilised by the capitalist class to advance its international foreign policy goals. Although theoretically and empirically undeveloped, this approach examines the solidification of a global capitalist class and the mechanisms utilised by it for defending and expanding the global capitalist economy. Accordingly, the following account of this approach constitutes a rough sketch of possible lines of inquiry.

Internationalisation of the Capitalist Class

Kees van der Pijl argued that the conscious deployment of an international capitalist class emerged with the rise of the global revolutionary threat represented by the Bolshevik Revolution and with the internationalisation of production in the twentieth century.[1] At the core of this global capitalist class are the world's largest industrial firms and banks. In a network analysis of joint directorates, M. Fennema found a dense system of interlocks between the directorates of the world's largest transnational banks and corporations (TNCs).[2] The research suggested that there is indeed an international power elite that operates through the channels of private industry and finance. This system of corporate interlocks is the transnational parallel to the interlocking directorates revealed by power-structure analysts investigating national power structures. Accordingly, van der Pijl identified the transnational corporation as the "prime vehicle of the internationalisation of capital."[3]

It is also possible to identify global policy-planning networks and organisations akin to those operating at the national level. For example, van der Pijl argued that the Trilateral Commission, launched by David Rockefeller and Zbigniew Brzensinski in the early 1970s, represented an unprecedented effort to organise transnational policy planning and to reestablish the international unity of the capitalist class in the face of popular social movements operating within nations around the world. Armand Mattelart traced the emergence of such reactionary global forces to the structural crisis that hit Western capitalist societies during the mid-1970s.[4] He cited a report to the Trilateral Commission that contemplated the "potentially desirable limits to economic growth" and also the "potentially desirable limits to the indefinite extension of political democracy."[5] This is precisely the period during which challenges to transnational capital from the nonaligned nations of the Third World reached their most threatening level.[6] This effort to forge an organised response by international capital to popular social movements once again has its parallel to domestic-level politics. Similarly, Edelman argued that the newly organised Business Roundtable and revitalised U.S. Chamber of Commerce appeared at this time to respond to the challenges represented by popular social movements in the United States because of their effectiveness in securing policies that affected corporate profit rates.[7]

The most important international economic policy-planning organisations during the 1980s were clearly the International Monetary Fund (IMF) and the World Bank. By utilising their influence over international financial lending practices, these organisations imposed a blueprint for economic and social policies to be followed by debtor countries around the world. The basic goal of international finance capital has been to make monetarism the economic policy of necessity at the level of the nation-state, which includes market liberalisation, export-oriented production, and massive privatisation of state-owned industries. At the same time, the austerity plans promoted by the World Bank and IMF have ravaged the social welfare state, with the effect of pulling the floor out from under the poorest segments of a nation's people. Consequently, the gaps between the rich and the poor have widened significantly as the gains of popular social movements of the 1960s and 1970s have been reversed. Furthermore, the internationalist sectors of domestic capital have become increasingly integrated into the global capitalist economy, leading them to identify more and more with the interests of international capitalists and less and less with those of their own national populations. Free trade agreements, the World Trade Organisation, the successor to the General Agreement on Tariffs and Trade (GATT), and an increasingly militarised United Nations acting as a global police force serve as the pillars of the "New World Order" in which capital reigns supreme.

The Transnationalisation of Communications and Culture

The transnationalisation of communications and culture

is not a new phenomenon; indeed it can be traced back to the earliest decades of the printing press.[8] However, never before have so few firms controlled so much of the world's informational and cultural output. The same pattern of mergers, acquisitions, and joint ventures among U.S. based communications companies has been occurring at the international level. There is a long and well-documented history of involvement by U.S. communications companies in foreign markets going back to the earliest days of radio broadcasting[9] and film.[10] With regard to the latter medium, Robert Sklar concluded from a review of a number of studies that 75 to 90 per cent of the films exhibited in most countries between World War I and World War II were from the United States.[11] Herbert Schiller described how the number of U.S. global ventures in the communications sector escalated after World War II under the auspices of the "free flow of information" doctrine.[12] Guback explained how the U.S. filmed entertainment industry reestablished its firm grip on European markets after World War II with active support of the U.S. government.[13]

More recent trends not only involve U.S. capital venturing abroad but increasingly the acquisition and financing of informational and cultural industries by European and Japanese capitalists. This pattern is apparent in the filmed entertainment sector. As noted, two of the Hollywood majors—Columbia and Universal—have ownership links to Japanese electronics firms. Another electronics firm, Dutch-based Philips, owner of Polygram and several other record labels, bought out two independent film companies, Propaganda Films *(Truth or Dare)* and Working Title Films *(My Beautiful Launderette)*, in 1991, then launched its own filmed entertainment distribution company, Gramercy Pictures, in 1992. Earlier, it had extended its interests in filmed entertainment by taking a 35 per cent stake in Pan Europeene of France and a 30 per cent stake in Andrew Lloyd Webber's Really Useful Company, a deal that not only gave Polygram access to the composer's theater, film, and television productions but also to his music copyrights.[14] In 1992, Universal announced a pact with Polygram Filmed Entertainment, a subsidiary of Philips, to distribute films produced by Polygram subsidiaries in Canada and the United States.

As of this writing, MGM/United Artists remained in the hands of French bank Credit Lyonnais. However, the bank will be required to divest itself of the film-entertainment company by 1997 under U.S. laws that limit ownership of U.S. companies by foreign banks. A bankruptcy petition filed by filmed entertainment producer Roger Corman against MGM-Pathe in 1991 revealed the vast network of financial connections involved in ownership and operation of a major filmed entertainment company. Along with Corman's Concorde-New Horizon's Corp., MGM's list of creditors included Kristan & Co., New York; Century Insurance Ltd., Brisbane, Australia; Levy-Gardner-Laven Productions, Beverly Hills; Theatrical and Television Motion Picture Special Payments Fund, Los Angeles; and Bill Lanese Advertising and Public Relations, San Francisco.[15] Although MGM/United Artists has sold off many of its most valuable films, those that it retains, particularly the United Artists library, have enabled the company to stave off liquidation despite the demands of creditors.

Another of the Hollywood majors controlled by an externally based transnational corporation is Twentieth Century Fox. Although Rupert Murdoch became a naturalised U.S. citizen to enable him to own television stations, control of the company remains in the hands of his Australian-based News Corp. Murdoch continues to expand his international holdings in a variety of media formats. In 1993, News Corp. gained control of 63.6 per cent of the Asian satellite television service Star TV through cash payments and the sale of 2.7 per cent of News Corp.'s stock to Star TV's founders, Hutchison Whampoa Ltd. and the family of billionaire Li Ka-shing of Hong Kong. The deal demonstrates how the fusion of media capital is not exclusively a process involving the "trilateral" nations. Murdoch's plan to exploit the Asian media market coincided with the announcement of a joint-venture deal between Dow Jones & Company and TCI to program a satellite business news channel for the region. At the same time, the Turner Broadcasting System, Time Warner, Capital Cities/ABC and TVB, the dominant television network in Hong Kong, announced plans for a satellite programming service. The participation of TVB, owner of the world's largest library of Chinese-language television programs, underscores the fact that ownership and control of intellectual property is vital to media capitalists around the world.[16]

Time Warner's financial globalisation came with its efforts to reduce the huge debt load accrued in the merger of Time and Warner. This forced the company to sell a 12.5 per cent, $1 billion stake in its feature film, pay-TV, and cable operations to Japan's Toshiba Corp. and Itochu Corp. This followed the establishment of an earlier partnership between Warner Bros, and a group of European filmed entertainment companies to finance the production and distribution of some twenty films. This deal brought Warner Bros, together with Regency International Pictures, a Dutch company; Canal Plus, a French pay-TV company; and Scriba & Deyhle, a German motion picture and television company.[17] Terry Semel, president of Warner Bros., described the deal "as a model for others" and as "a union that represents the natural extension of Time Warner's philosophy of globalization, based on the understanding that long-term competitive success can be achieved only through major alliances and a presence in all the world's most important markets."[18]

Shortly after the infusion of Japanese capital, Time Warner sought to forge a $1 billion partnership with a Canadian-European consortium. Although the alliance was not consummated, the reports of the deal provided revealing insight into the increasingly intimate relationships among the international capitalist elite. The contract talks involved Time Warner with Paul Desmarais Sr., chairman of the Montreal-based Power Corp. of Canada, and Albert Frere, chairman of Groupe Bruxelles Lambert S.A., a Brussels holding company. The deal would have linked Time Warner with Europe's largest commercial television broadcaster and a number of other European media companies.[19] A *Wall Street Journal* report on the negotiations disclosed that the Power Corp. board of directors included F. Ross Johnson of RJR Nabisco and that its "international supervisory council" included Paul A. Volker, former chair of the U.S. Federal Reserve, and Ahmed Zaki Yamani, Saudi Arabia's former oil minister.[20] The report provided striking evidence of the existence of a global power elite composed of corporate and government officials, very much like those found at the national level.

Although Time Warner's effort to find a European partner did not come to fruition, European filmed entertainment companies have invested heavily in Hollywood-based filmed entertainment companies to secure programming for new broadcast and cable operations. In 1991, Silvio Berlusconi's Finivest, a major Italian conglomerate with interests in communications, finance, and real estate, announced a coventure with Cecchi Gori Group, an Italian movie production and distribution company, to invest $110 million for production of six "mainstream" Hollywood films.[21] In addition to the deal with Warner Bros, mentioned above, Canal Plus entered into an agreement with Mel Brooks Productions to coproduce two films and bought a 5 per cent stake in Carolco Productions in 1990. Following market-based logic, Canal Plus aimed to reduce license fees for the use of U.S. filmed entertainment while becoming a profit participant. In 1990, the company paid some $130 million for the rights to 160 U.S. films and figured that not only could it reduce these costs by entering into coproduction deals but also earn revenues as co-owners of copyrights.[22]

Not to be left out in the cold, Bertelsman, the world's second largest media company, confirmed in 1993 that it was shopping around Hollywood hoping to invest some $200 million in motion picture production but found prices on media companies to be inflated.[23] Primarily a music recording and publishing operation, Bertelsman felt compelled to expand its filmed entertainment and television holdings in order to maintain its strategic position vis-a-vis other global media conglomerates.[24] To this end, the company joined a partnership with Canadian-based Alliance Communications Corporation and the CTV network to produce Harlequin romance films for CBS, television movies that would be used by CBS to counterprogram against National Football League games on Sunday afternoons.[25]

To round out this account of the financial globalisation of the Hollywood majors, the focus turns to Disney. Disney has been at the forefront of efforts to bring outside investors into the motion picture financing process. By doing so, it reduces the risk of losses on expensive box-office failures and through creative accounting practices still manages to make a profit, or at least break even, despite revenue sharing with outside investors. Touchwood Pacific Partners, established in 1990, provided Disney with $600 million over the course of a year, enough to finance some thirty movies. The limited partnership involved a consortium of banks including Fuji Bank Ltd., the Long-Term Credit Bank of Japan Ltd., Citibank, and Manufacturers Hanover and one of Japan's largest investment firms, Yamaichi Securities.

Japanese investment in Disney was part of a larger trend. According to one estimate, from the late 1980s up through 1991, Japanese venture capitalists flocked to Hollywood, investing a total of between $750 million and $1.25 billion, not including the purchases of Columbia and MCA.[26] Another estimate put total Japanese investment in Hollywood from the beginning of 1989 to the end of 1990, including the purchases of Columbia and CBS records by Sony and MCA by Matsushita, at $13 billion.[27] According to one investment attorney, Japanese venture capitalists had come to realise that "film libraries could be as good an investment as Impressionist art."[28] In 1992, Disney turned to tap the European capital markets with a seven-year, $400 million issue in the Eurobond market that gave investors direct play in the financing of thirteen films. However, for investors to earn the maximum 13.5 per cent return on the bond, the thirteen films must earn revenues of $800 million over the seven-year span; otherwise their return would be just 3 per cent.[29]

The internationalisation of filmed entertainment industry finance has tremendous significance in understanding the case studies undertaken in this chapter. Global ventures of this scope inevitably result in the unification of national capitalists in securing the recognition and protection of intellectual property rights. Accordingly, as U.S. intellectual property - based industries sought to secure their rights in foreign markets, they were able to forge alliances with foreign capitalists concerned with the same goal. It is not surprising, therefore, that intellectual property protection was high on the agenda during the Uruguay Round of the GATT discussions. Except for a handful of Third World countries concerned about having to pay high royalty fees on patents and copyrights to U.S., European, and Japanese TNCs, the global business community was largely in agreement on the need to bring intellectual property under the auspices of GATT.

The Logic of Capital and Intellectual Property Rights

The second general area of international political economy focuses attention on the expansionary logic of capital. This level of analysis is raised from examination of global power-elite networks and financial interlocks to a higher level of abstraction—the structural characteristics of global capitalism. Approaches from the "capital theoretical" position are concerned with explaining and documenting the increasing penetration of capital into previously unexploited domains of human activity and geographic territories. They also seek to confirm the inherent tendencies within capitalism toward concentration of capital and accumulation crises. Furthermore, these approaches explore the role of the nation-state in facilitating the internationalisation of capital as well as its effort to produce coun-termeasures to crises in the global capitalist system.

The structural analysis of international capitalism can be narrowed for the purposes of examining and explaining matters having to do with intellectual property rights. Given the expansionary logic of capital, it is "natural" that existing and emerging forms of human artistic and intellectual creativity increasingly are being integrated into the global market system. The case studies in this chapter concentrate on two new forms of delivering and embodying filmed entertainment—cable television and videocassettes—and the ways in which these media are being incorporated into existing market systems. These new media have offered not only new opportunities for exploiting human creative activity but also the chance to market intellectual property in new geographic regions.

In sum, cable television and the VCR provided the Hollywood-based filmed entertainment industry the means through which to expand its reach. The expansionary logic of capital thus precedes the need to extend the realm of intellectual property law to encompass new technologies and incorporate the new territories in which they will be deployed. The process demonstrates the functional role of intellectual property law in underpinning private property rights in artistic and intellectual creativity.

The transnationalisation of capital is therefore driven by the logic of capital that in turn produces the necessity for intellectual property rights. This logic reflects the more practical level at which the transnational corporations and financial institutions operate. Bagdikian identifies a global "troika" responsible for the increasing importance of intellectual property rights, mainly patents, trademarks, and copyrights.[30] As consumer-goods producers began to expand beyond their saturated markets in the United States, Europe, and Japan, the need for patent and trademark protection emerged in countries that previously had failed to recognise and/or enforce these rights. Among the transnational firms moving abroad were makers of processed foods, soft drinks, tobacco products, and pharmaceuticals, which in turn necessitated that transnational advertisers follow.[31] Naturally, transnational advertisers have a need for media outlets through which to display their ads. The global troika therefore produces inevitable pressure on governments to open up media outlets to advertisers; increased incentives for expansion by local media firms; and an invitation to media transnationals to enter the market. This is turn exacerbates the process of media commercialisation and privatisation at the national level and the process of media conglomeration at the international level.

With increasing numbers of media outlets, the value of "scarce" media programming rises, making copyright protection ever more vital. Pressure on national governments for greater copyright protection comes from both the locally based oligopolistic media industry and transnational media companies. Media transnationals operating within the United States have come to expect the U.S. government to help apply this pressure on foreign governments from outside. Since the recognition and protection of private property rights is an essential role of the capitalist state, governments around the world have adopted, or are ready to adopt, intellectual property laws and to see to their enforcement.

In the particular area of intellectual property law, the determining role of the economic system of a global legal infrastructure is clearly apparent, as capital logic theorists hold. Intellectual property regimes at both the national and international levels are thus derivative of the process of enclosure of the intellectual commons. The basic outcome of efforts by the filmed entertainment industry to obtain copyrights for cable in Canada and to eliminate videocassette piracy around the world was predictable. This is not to say that the specific forms of intellectual property laws were precisely determined nor that there were no struggles to resist their imposition. Indeed, such struggles are evident and lead us to the third area of radical political economy research—class struggle.

The Class Theoretical Position

The international level of analysis brings several layers of struggle and resistance into focus. However, intraclass and interstate struggles took center stage in conflicts over cable copyrights and videocassette piracy. The efforts by U.S. filmed entertainment companies to secure copyrights for the use of broadcast signals by Canadian cable operators mainly produced intraclass struggles. Within the United States, copyright owners clashed with U.S. broadcasters operating along the Canadian border over short- and long-term strategics for gaining Canadian compliance. U.S. border broadcasters, not U.S. copyright owners, were the first to pursue copyright liability for Canadian cable operators in retaliation to Canadian cultural policies. As the conflict evolved, differences emerged between broadcasters and copyright owners on matters of strategy, though not principle. Within Canada, intraclass struggles surfaced between cable operators and Canadian broadcasters, reflecting those between the same industry sectors in the United States a decade earlier. Canadian broadcasters saw cable operators' use of their broadcast signals as an "unfair" competitive advantage and supported compulsory license legislation. Conflicts between the U.S. and Canadian governments were not over the principle of intellectual property rights but rather over the means by which they should be conferred.

Hollywood's war on videocassette piracy, supported by U.S. government intervention, spearheaded a generally united capitalist front against infringements on intellectual property in foreign markets. Large sectors of the U.S. economy stood to benefit from the extension of intellectual property law and enforcement at the international level. Even labor unions joined the effort, supporting their employers in congressional hearings in documenting the harm caused by piracy of copyrighted works. Intraclass struggles within nations accused of piracy emerged as a result of the U.S. campaign to broaden global copyright protection. For a while, Third World nations argued that the international intellectual property system served as a pillar of the global economic structure that helped maintain their dependency on imports of media products and technology. Fernando Cardoso, a leading writer on the "dependency approach," identified an emergent form of economic dependence for semiperipheral and peripheral nations where surplus value is increasingly extracted in the form of licenses and royalties on patents and copyrights and of interest payments on national debt.[32] It had been the policy of some Third World governments to refuse to recognise the intellectual property rights of foreign nationals out of resistance to dependency. Others made the moral claim that new technology, cultural products, literature, and so forth are the products of all humanity and should be made available to all peoples and nations for free, especially "developing" countries.[33] However, resistance to the in-ternational intellectual property regime based on moral principles has largely faded.

The problem of international piracy, counterfeiting, and other unauthorised expropriation of U.S. intellectual property came to the forefront of U.S. trade policy concerns in the early 1980s. Worldwide infringement of U.S. intellectual property rights gained the attention of the members of the corporate and state elite once it became apparent that the future of U.S. global economic hegemony would be predicated upon the production, ownership, and marketing of intellectual property-based goods and services. Accordingly, state efforts to advance the copyright interests of the filmed entertainment industry were part of a much larger effort to institute the international legal infrastructure to support intellectual property-based industries.

The policy-planning apparatus bolstered this effort by providing documentation of the costs of piracy on U.S.

companies and justifications for action. The American Enterprise Institute, the National Planning Association, and the Conference Board generated reports on intellectual property and service trade in order to help build a consensus on priorities and action.[34] A report by the U.S. International Trade Commission (ITC) that was declassified in 1988 came up with estimated losses to U.S. intellectual property industries based on a survey of the sector's 431 largest companies. The ITC recognised that industry losses were probably inflated but nevertheless concluded that worldwide losses as a result of inadequate intellectual property protection cost these companies $23.8 billion in 1986; that lost licensing revenues of 104 of the surveyed companies totaled $3.1 billion in 1986 (two-thirds of these losses were reported by the filmed entertainment and music recording industries, some 14.3 per cent of their worldwide sales); and that losses due to intellectual property infringement for U.S. business as a whole totaled $43-$61 billion in 1986.[35] According to U.S. Register of Copyrights Ralph Oman, intellectual property accounted for 25 per cent of U.S. exports by 1991 and could have been higher were it not for infringements of U.S. rights.[36]

The U.S. government has pursued three strategies to eradicate piracy in foreign markets: bilateral trade leveraging against countries where piracy was rampant; free trade agreements (FTA's) with selected partners that incorporate intellectual property protection into their frameworks; and multilateral efforts including U.S. accession to the Berne Convention and incorporation of service and intellectual property sectors within GATT. Its greatest success has come with the bilateral antipiracy campaign targeted at the nations of the Third World. Prompted by lobbying on behalf of intellectual property-based industries, Congress mandated trade retaliation against nations who failed to protect U.S. intellectual property rights with passage of the Caribbean Basin Initiative (CBI) in 1983 and the Generalised System of Preferences Renewal Act (GSP) in 1984.[37] With this legislation, participation in CBI and GSP became contingent upon protection of U.S. intellectual property rights. Due to the great economic inequalities between the United States and Third World countries, such bilateral copyright trade agreements are in fact much more unilateral in character.

U.S. intellectual property owners characterise infringements of their rights as "trade barriers." The familiar cry of the filmed entertainment industry is that these barriers restrict the "free flow" of U.S. motion picture and television entertainment throughout the world. But, in fact, the new communications technologies have caused this programming to flow too freely. It is evident now that "free flow" of information and entertainment never meant "without charge." In practice, free flow has always been a rhetorical device for justifying U.S government and transnational corporate efforts to pry foreign markets open for U.S. capital.

U.S. government support of the U.S. filmed entertainment industry in its an-tipiracy war can be linked to the larger role the government plays in helping U.S. capital exploit foreign markets. For additional "intelligence" in this war on piracy, the U.S. Copyright Office called on U.S. embassies to systematically collect and provide information from foreign countries about such matters as levels of indigenous copyright, patent, and trademark activity and the infrastructures for the publication, distribution, and performance of protected works. The embassies also were to provide the names of the appropriate foreign government agencies concerned with intellectual property policies. The war on piracy also included the use of U.S. "foreign advisers" in copyright training programs for foreign government and private sector officials. The idea all along has been to help local officials develop the "expertise" to deal with copyright law problems. Foreign experts are also needed to enforce the new copyright legislation that is being passed in the Far East and Pacific Basin. In this regard, U.S. advisers are training foreign lawyers, police, and customs officials to handle the enforcement aspects of copyright protection.

The successful track record of bilateral trade leveraging based on CBI and GSP privileges prompted imitation legislation aimed at strengthening existing tools or providing U.S. trade negotiators with new ones. The prototype was the Inter national Intellectual Property Protection and Market Access Act of 1986 (S. 2435) introduced by Sen. Pete Wilson (R-Calif), who had recognised the political value of speaking for the interests of Hollywood. His support culminated in a piece of legislation introduced in the spring of 1986 that addressed a broad range of the U.S. copyright industry's international problems (Republican Wilson, in turn, was strongly supported in his 1988 reelection bid by "Democrat-heavy Hollywood" to serve his second term as California governor).[38]

Congress incorporated Wilson's plan in the Omnibus Trade Act of 1988, which included provisions to gain protection of U.S. intellectual property rights in foreign markets and access to foreign markets for U.S. intellectual property-based products and services.[39] Again, the leveraging principle in this legislation was based on access to the U.S. market. Foreign nations were required to provide adequate and effective enforcement of U.S. intellectual property rights and access to their markets as conditions for access to U.S. import markets.

This trade law also requires the U.S. Trade Representative (USTR) to designate "priority foreign countries" (PFCs) with "unfair trading practices" toward U.S. intellectual property industries—either because of inadequate intellectual property protection or market barriers to U.S. intellectual property-based industries. The list of PFCs is drawn from the USTR's annual report on foreign trade problems required under section 303 of the Trade and Tariff Act of 1984. The USTR is required to enter into negotiations with those PFCs listed, with up to two years to reach an agreement. If no agreement is reached, the president is required to take some form of retaliatory action, ranging from termination of trade agreements to suspension of any trade benefits enjoyed by the importing nation.

With the Omnibus Trade Act of 1988, Congress provided U.S. trade negotiators with the "carrots" and "sticks" to expand the antipiracy campaign. According to U.S. Register of Copyrights Ralph Oman, Congress acted with the sense that:

> international protection of intellectual property rights is vital to the international competitiveness of the United States . . . The absence of adequate and effective protection of United States intellectual property rights, and the denial of fair and equitable access, seriously impede the ability of United States citizens who rely on the protection of intellectual property rights to export and operate overseas.[40]

The international struggle between U.S. copyright interests and the rest of the world prompted intranational struggles within target nations. Those industries involved in infringing activities, such as video and audiocassette piracy, clashed with the more advanced export-oriented sectors in their countries. The latter recognised that their ability to operate in the global capitalist economy was contingent upon the recognition and protection of intellectual property within their own countries. Following the long-term logic of capital, foreign governments have acceded to demands from U.S. intellectual property-based industries and advanced sectors of the domestic bourgeoisie by enacting intellectual property laws and seeking to enforce them. Again, differences and conflicts between the U.S. and foreign governments emerged over tactics, not fundamental principles. As a result, the building of a basic infrastructure for a global intellectual property regime is largely complete. How this was accomplished is illustrated in the two case studies that follow. The chapter concludes with a brief outline of other major developments in the international intellectual property system over the last decade.

Copyrights for Cable Retransmission in Canada

Through the late 1980s, the U.S. filmed entertainment industry estimated that Canadian cable operators' refusal to pay royalties cost it $25-$100 million per year.[41] Seeking to curb these losses, the filmed entertainment and other media industries, along with aligned special-interest groups and various officials of the U.S. government (especially in legislative and executive organisations), pursued changes in Canadian copyright law to make cable retransmission an exclusive right of the copyright owner. The retransmission of U.S. television broadcasts by Canadian cable operators brought charges of piracy by U.S. copyright owners, that is, the illegal use of their property for profit. Furthermore, the industry claimed this act of piracy deprived copyright owners of the right to authorise "legitimate" uses of their works (for example, to Canadian television stations). The persistent efforts of industry and government officials eventually paid off with the implementation of the U.S.-Canada Free Trade Agreement in January 1989 and a new Canadian broadcasting bill (Bill C-136). With these actions, the Candadian cable operators became liable for the retransmission of broadcasts and were incorporated into a compulsory license system similar to the one functioning in the United States.

Before passage of the compulsory license, Canadian law defined simultaneous retransmission of television broadcasts by cable television systems as a private use rather than "public performance" and stated that such a service was merely an extension of the broadcast, all required rights transfers having been completed between program copyright owners and broadcasters. In this way Canadian law resembled U.S. cable copyright policy as it stood prior to the U.S. Copyright Act of 1976. In fact, up until January 1978, when the new U.S. copyright law came into effect, U.S. cable companies could also simultaneously retransmit broadcasts without royalty payments to copyright owners of the programs contained in the broadcast. However, once U.S. law changed and the disparity with Canadian law developed, the filmed entertainment industry could turn its sights to its largest "foreign" market in the Western Hemisphere. The conflict between the United States and Canada over copyright liability for cable retransmissions was part of a larger war on piracy being waged by the United States worldwide.

The Internationalisation of Copyright Conflicts

The reception of electronically transmitted, U.S. produced information and entertainment programming by Canadians dates back to the early days of radio. Much of Canada's population is concentrated along the border with the United States and is within easy reach of U.S. broadcasts. With the development of television, Canadians could receive U.S. programming with simple rooftop antennas. U.S. television was popular in Canada, and Canadians developed the attitude that they were entitled to the reception of U.S. broadcasts that crossed their border.

The Canadian cable television industry founded its expansion on the delivery of U.S. television broadcasts to its subscribers. Babe cited two main factors leading to the growth of Canadian cable service that made it an important urban as well as rural phenomenon:

> First, the rapid construction of high-rise buildings in centres close to the U.S. border interfered with the previously adequate reception of U.S. stations: cable television was a technological solution to this problem.
>
> Second, cable systems located too far from the U.S. border to trap [U.S.] signals off-air by traditional means began constructing distant "head ends" (antennae facilities) closer to the border in order to transport these signals to their communities by means of microwave relay stations.[42]

Canada's cable system grew quickly as the country became one of the most heavily cabled nations in the world. By early 1988, 68 per cent (5.6 million) of Canada's households subscribed to cable.[43]

Canada based its exemption of cable rediffusion from copyright liabilily on judicial interpretation of the Canadian Copyright Act (R.S.C. 1970, C.C.-30) and on the Canadian Broadcasting Act (R.S.C. 1970, c. B-11), which defined the radio frequency spectrum as public property. Under the terms of the latter law, broadcasters could not claim ownership of their operating frequency; therefore copyrights could not be claimed in broadcasts. *Canadian Admiral Ltd. v. Rediffusion Inc. et. al.* (1954)[44] provided the judicial justification for cable copyright exemption. The Canadian court decided that broadcasts were indeed a "performance" but not a "public performance" because private, home viewers did not constitute a "public." As noted in the Chapter 5, the U.S. Supreme Court's decisions in *Fortnightly Corp. v. United Artists Television, Inc.* (1968)[45] and *Teleprompter Corp. v. Columbia Broadcasting System, Inc.* (1974)[46] produced a similar exemption for cable retransmission of broadcasts, though by slightly different reasoning.

These early judicial decisions reflected the ambiguities that often surround the introduction of new communications technologies into the body of copyright law. However, by the time the cable copyright conflict between the United States and Canada surfaced, international intellectual property law had determined that cable retransmission was a commercial use for which copyright owners must be remunerated. Being a member of the Berne Convention, Canada could not maintain its copyright exemption for cable and still remain honorable within the international intellectual property system.

The Berne Convention for the Protection of Literary and Artistic Property (Paris 1971 text) granted authors the exclusive right to authorise "any communication to the public by wire or by rebroadcasting of the broadcast when the communication is made by an organisation other than the original one (Article 11 bis [2])." The International Labour Office (ILO), the Secretariat of UNESCO, and the International Bureau of the World Intellectual Property Organisation (WIPO) supported this principle in a document on the distribution of programs by cable. Principle 1 on cable rediffusion of broadcasts declared that *"the author or other owner of the copyright has the exclusive right of authorising any distribution by cable of the broadcast of his work protected by copyright"*[47] This exclusive right applied even if the cable distribution of a broadcast was simultaneous and free of charge.

The ILO document stressed that cable rediffusion was a distinct and separate use of copyrighted works because such a service is provided to a different public than the original broadcast—"different from (although possibly partially overlapping) the public that the broadcast can reach, or is intended to reach, or one that it can reach only with diminished quality or at higher cost."[48] The consensus of these international policymaking organisations was that there would be no need for cable rediffusion if the broadcast was in fact entirely efficient in reaching its intended public. Since cable can be viewed as a distinct and separate use of the copyrighted programming contained in a broadcast, authorisation of the program owners was required. This provided copyright owners of filmed entertainment the option of licensing the cable operator directly or authorising the broadcaster to license the cable operator on their behalf. While this approach is consistent with copyrights in principle, it is quite complicated in practice as the U.S. cable copyright case demonstrated. When the market is largely competitive, the sheer number of copyright owners and cable operators results in high transaction costs. For this reason, the U.S. Congress established a compulsory license system for cable retransmissions with the intent of reducing transaction costs between copyright owners and cable operators. Compulsory license systems make sense when the market is relatively competitive. U.S. copyright policymakers urged their Canadian counterparts to adopt a U.S. style system.

The Copyright Foreign Policy Apparatus

In 1983, Congress launched the first salvo against the infringing practices of Canadian cable operators by introducing legislation and holding hearings. In the Senate, the Judiciary Committee's Subcommittee on Patents, Copyrights, and Trademarks held hearings on the Canadian cable copyright question.[49] In the House, Patrick Leahy

(D-Vt.) introduced S. 736, the International Copyright Fairness Bill, in order to establish a "regime of reciprocity" between the United States and Canada in cable rediffusion copyright practices. The bill aimed directly at Canada and sought to deny its copyright owners royalty payments collected by the U.S. Copyright Royalty Tribunal from U.S. cable operators using Canadian programming. The practical result would have been to cut off that share of CRT royalties flowing to Canadian program producers—mainly to the Canadian Broadcasting Corporation. In the first three years of CRT allocations, Canada's copyright owners received $172,670 (1979), $198,550 (1980), and $236,179 (1981).[50]

The origins of the bill go back to what is known as "the border broadcasting dispute" between the United States and Canada that stems from another Canadian cultural policy, this one relating to transborder advertising. A 1976 amendment codified in section 19.1 of the Canadian Income Tax Act (referenced as Bill C-58) eliminated tax deductions for Canadian advertisers who purchased airtime on U.S. border broadcast stations to reach Canadians with their messages. Bill C-58 intended to encourage Canadian advertisers to support the Canadian broadcasting system by keeping advertising dollars in Canada. Thus, Canadian advertisers could continue to deduct advertising expenses from income taxes when incurred from advertising on Canadian television stations. The Canadian government hoped that by aiding national broadcasters they could, in turn, afford to finance or purchase more Canadian program production.

From its inception, U.S. border broadcasters and allied U.S. policymakers considered this Canadian tax policy a "service-trade barrier." They consistently sought "mirror legislation" in response to C-58 to deny U.S. advertisers

tax deductions for buying advertising on Canadian broadcast television stations. The border broadcasters' involvement in the C-58 dispute helped them establish their contacts in the lobbying process that were later mobilised in the cable rediffusion copyright conflict. Leahy's S. 736 was, in fact, mirror legislation, seeking to deny Canadian copyright owners cable royalties from U.S. operators since Canadian cable operators were exempt from paying royalties to U.S. copyright owners. It was ironic that border broadcasters initiated this bill, since they were minimally affected by uncompensated cable retransmission of their broadcasts, being producers of only a small fraction of the copyrighted programming that Canadian cable systems picked up for retransmission. The primary issue for border broadcasters, therefore, was not immediate revenues lost from uncompensated uses but rather the unfair competitive advantage Canadian cable operators held over them by not having to pay copyright royalties. For the same reason, the Canadian Association of Broadcasters (CAB) also insisted that Canadian cable systems pay for the programming they used. Thus, Canadian cable operators found themselves pitted against U.S. and Canadian copyright owners, U.S. and Canadian broadcasters, and the U.S. government. The Canadian government, anxious to protect the infant cable industry, moved slowly toward resolving the issue. Nevertheless, the logic of copyright provided the underlying structural pressure in favor of the copyright owners and broadcasters.

However, both the Motion Picture Association of America (MPAA), the main beneficiary of the legislation, and the Reagan administration came to oppose S. 736 because it violated the basic principle of "national treatment" upon which the international intellectual property system is based. National treatment is an essential aspect of international copyright protection, as the major international

copyright agreements—the Berne Convention and the Universal Copyright Convention (UCC)—are not self-enforcing. Copyright protection ultimately rests on national legislation and national enforcement. The international conventions provide minimum standards and guidelines for protection, but actual copyright practices are national in scope and effect. National treatment means that foreign copyright owners are to be given the same rights and protection as national copyright owners. The philosophy behind national treatment is that general respect for the rights of all copyright owners, national and foreign, will create a mutuality of interests between all such owners on a global level. Copyright owners who receive better protection in a foreign country will put pressure on their own governments to improve protection at home, for themselves and their foreign counterparts, in a process that is seen as continually raising the level of copyright protection around the world.

Leahy's S. 736 would have violated this principle since it proposed differential treatment of U.S. and Canadian copyright owners. It would have discriminated against Canadian program producers, whose works were used by U.S. cable companies, by denying them royalties. The situation in Canada was different. Since no liability for cable rediffusion existed under Canadian law, no remuneration was necessary for the retransmission of copyrighted works, whether owned by a Canadian or anyone else. Canadian cable copyright policy did not violate the principle of national treatment since it treated both domestic and foreign cable operators in the same manner. For the U.S. Register of Copyrights, and other foreign policy makers who testified at the S. 736 hearings, the United States would seriously undermine the global interests of capital as a whole by passing the bill and subverting the principle of national treatment established in the UCC. As the world's leading exporter of copyrighted works, the United States benefits most from the principle of national treatment and, therefore, has the most to lose should the principle increasingly be subverted.

The U.S. Congress considered a couple of other proposals to compel Canada to adopt a copyright for cable. One bill linked resolution of the dispute to Canadian videotex hardware imports to the United States, proposing to deny U.S. businesses tax deductions or tax credit for purchases of Canadian equipment. Another bill sought to prohibit foreign ownership of U.S. cable systems. The latter measure was essentially directed at a small number of Canadian media entrepreneurs as a way of forcing them, out of the need to preserve access to U.S. markets, to join and strengthen the power bloc within Canada that supported more favorable treatment of U.S. copyright industries. Canadian media capitalists as a whole began to recognise that intellectual property protection would be essential to them as they entered foreign markets, leading them to reassess national copyright practices. Recognising this, the U.S. Copyright Office argued against trade retaliation, predicting that Canadian policymakers would eventually change their cable rediffusion policy.

Senator Pete Wilson's aforementioned trade legislation, proposed in 1986, offered to provide mechanisms for addressing the wide array of intellectual property-related disputes existing between the United States and other countries. Wilson made special note of "unfair" Canadian practices when testifying on behalf of his bill at the 1986 Senate hearings on intellectual property rights. One remark worth citing reflected the condescending attitude held by many U.S. policymakers toward Canadian cultural concerns. Wilson stated:

> I find it more than ironic that while Canada invokes the absurd notion of "cultural sovereignty" to force divestiture of U.S. printing interests and to prevent other U.S. businesses from operating within its borders, it condones the theft of our television shows for the benefit of Canadian audiences. The bottom line seems to be that the Canadians don't mind an "invasion" of U.S. culture as long as it arrives free of charge.[51]

Jack Valenti, president of the MPAA, also made special mention of Canada's cultural policies at these hearings, concluding that "'cultural sovereignty' has become a smoke screen to hide the most insidious restrictions on trade and investment."[52] Valenti claimed further that "we have the right to control and participate financially in the distribution of our products—this is a well recognised right under international copyright standards. It should not be denied under the guise of preserving 'cultural identity.'"[53] He repeated that "Canadian firms essentially pirate the programming of [U.S.] companies" under the existing rediffusion law but that Canada refused to discuss the matter because it was considered a "cultural" issue, not a trade issue.

However, retaliatory action against Canada was problematic, for it departed from historical efforts to avoid linkages in the discussion of bilateral trade issues and the possible escalation of disputes. But it was the threat of such measures by the U.S. Congress, in response to a variety of trade conflicts between the two countries, that soon prompted the Canadian government and its core corporate sector to propose a free trade agreement. The increasing number of these retaliatory threats began to appear to Canadian capitalists as symptomatic of how the U.S. government would react in the face of deteriorating

U.S. economic hegemony. The fear of being shut out of the U.S. market, which accounted for 80 per cent of Canadian exports, prompted the Canadian capitalist class to find a mechanism to guarantee long-term access. The strong desire of Canadian capitalists for a free trade agreement gave the U.S. government the opportunity to settle a number of trade disputes, the cable copyright conflict being one of them.

The U.S. copyright policy-making apparatus kept the pressure on the Canadian government to hasten its movement toward adopting a cable copyright system. A flurry of activity on this issue reflects the instrumental role played by the U.S. government in this case. It also reveals the intimate involvement of the private sector in foreign policy making. Efforts in Congress supplemented activity carried out by executive agencies. For example, the Department of State and the U.S. Copyright Office engaged Canadian copyright officials in high-level discussions on this issue. U.S. broadcasters, motion picture producers, and authors were also in on these discussions. The MPAA held talks with Canada's minister of communications. The assistant secretary for communications and information of the U.S. Department of Commerce, who sits on the National Telecommunications and Information Administration, also made a trip to Montreal to talk with Canadian officials.

The rediffusion issue came to the forefront of U.S. government foreign trade priorities when Hollywood's biggest lobbyist in Washington, President Ronald Reagan, took the issue up personally with Canada's prime minister, Brian Mulroney. Reagan received a pledge from Mulroney at the March 1985 U.S.Canadian Quebec Summit that Canada would make its best efforts to accommodate U.S. interests on this issue and to "cooperate to protect intellectual property rights ... from abuses of copyright and patent law."[54] At this meeting, Mulroney and Reagan also announced their goal of a more secure bilateral trade relationship through a free trade agreement.

Reagan's personal effort signaled a heightened concern for intellectual property trade issues at the highest level of the U.S. government. Similar signals were sent through the president's stated Trade Action Plan (September 1985) that stressed "the importance of improving international protection for intellectual property rights";[55] another such statement in the 1986 State of the Union address; and, finally, the "Administration Statement on the Protection of U.S. Intellectual Property Rights Abroad," announced by Secretary of Commerce Malcomb Baldridge, U.S. Trade Representative (USTR) Clayton Yeutter, and Attorney General Edwin Meese on April 7, 1986.[56] The administration followed up the announcement by forwarding a bill to Congress called the International Property Rights Improvement Act of 1986 on May 5, 1986. The president's Trade Strike Force worked out the administration's program; it was an interagency task force created in September 1985, headed by the secretary of commerce and charged with the task of uncovering unfair trade practices and recommending actions to counter them.[57]

Other contributors to the administration's program on intellectual property rights included the president's Advisory Committee on Trade Negotiations, made up of representatives from business, labor, and the "public-interest sector" and members of academia and the USTR's Industry Functional Advisory Committee, whose members represented a diverse group of companies that depended upon intellectual property protection in foreign trade. These two committees were particularly responsible for the GATT reform policy. The intellectual property industries also represented themselves through various organisations, such as the International Anti-Counterfeit Coalition, the Intellectual Property Committee, the Intellectual Property Owners Association, and the International Intellectual Property Alliance (IIPA).[58] This kind of close industry-government cooperation is typical of copyright trade policy making. The government relies on industry for information on trade barriers and "unfair" trade practices so that the agenda for government action is essentially based upon private sector initiatives.

After nearly a decade of pressuring both the U.S. and Canadian governments to address the cable copyright question, U.S. filmed entertainment copyright owners found their demands answered with the U.S.-Canada FTA. Article 2006 of the FTA required the Canadian government to create a statutory copyright for cable retransmission and a mechanism to govern the collection and distribution of royalties.[59] Canada's new Copyright Board, created in response to the FTA, ruled in October 1990 that Canadian cable operators had to pay filmed entertainment copyright owners $100 million (Canadian) in royalty fees by the end of 1991. About 85 per cent of this payment went directly to U.S. copyright owners. Although the Canadian government insisted that "cultural policies" be excluded from its provisions, the compulsory license issue reflected its accession to U.S. demands. Following on the heels of the agreement, the U.S. television networks attacked Canadian government subsidies to the Canadian Broadcasting Corporation for promoting unfair competition—subsidies that the government later reduced, ostensibly as a cost-cutting measure.

The U.S.-Canada FTA was part of a larger global trend involving the solidification of trading blocs. The then pending unification of European states into a single trading system prompted similar endeavors worldwide. The incorporation of Mexico into the U.S.-Canada FTA, known as the North American Free Trade Agreement (NAFTA), is part of a larger plan for a free trade zone spanning, in George Bush's words, from "the port of Anchorage to Tierra del Fuego." Through FTAs, the U.S. government hopes to eliminate a number of service and intellectual property "trade barriers" found throughout the Americas, such as limits on equity investments by foreign firms, lack of patent protection for chemicals, pharmaceuticals, alloys, and agricultural products, and inadequate and ineffective copyright protection.

Anticipating NAFTA, the Mexican government took a number of steps toward alleviating intellectual property tensions with the United States. In the early 1990s, the Mexican Congress passed a new patent law covering all industrial processes and products and lengthened the period of protection from fourteen to twenty years. Inventions patented in other countries also now qualify for a Mexican patent. The new law covers trademarks for a renewable period of ten years. Reforms to the copyright law, which became effective in August 1991, enhanced copyright protection for computer programs against unauthorised reproduction for a period of fifty years and increased sanctions and penalties against infringements.

NAFTA, which took effect in January 1994, resolved the remaining intellectual property disputes between the United States and Mexico and raised international intellectual property protection to new levels. For example, its copyright provision grants protection to sound recordings for a term of at least fifty years and gives copyright owners the right to authorise rentals of sound recordings and computer programs and to collect royalties from their use. NAFTA treats computer programs as literary works and databases as compilations, giving copyright owners the same protection given to traditional literary works. Finally, NAFTA set down the terms for effective enforcement of intellectual property rights internally and at the border. Thus, U.S. copyright owners can file complaints with the trade commission administering the agreement should either Mexico or Canada fail to protect their rights. Upon a finding by the commission of violations of NAFTA, the U.S. government is entitled to retaliate.

NAFTA enjoyed massive support from big capitalists in all three countries. For Mexico, the agreement signaled the end of any effort to pursue nationalistic economic policies and the beginning of the total integration of the richest Mexican capitalists into the international capitalist economy. From the Mexican Revolution until the 1980s, Mexico's capitalist class largely took a nationalistic outlook on capital accumulation strategies and policies. NAFTA signaled the shift in orientation of Mexican capital outward and a new class identity that recognised U.S. capitalists as "natural class allies."[60] Among these allies were the core organisations of the U.S. corporate community. Policy-planning organisations promoting NAFTA included the U.S. Chamber of Commerce, the Business Roundtable, the Business Council, the National Association of Manufacturers, several influential think tanks, and even six of the ten largest environmental groups. Major corporate U.S. promoters of NAFTA included the big-three auto companies, Kimberly-Clark Corp., IBM, American Express, Goldman Sachs, and Eastman Kodak, representing, a merger of manufacturing, service, and finance capital. For these TNCs, FTAs are a necessary pillar upon which the emerging post-Fordist, flexible regime of accumulation is to be built. For intellectual property-based industries, they provide a means of extending the law of intellectual property to new territories ripe for market penetration.

Hollywood's International Antipiracy Campaign

The unauthorised reproduction of feature-length motion pictures and television programs on videocassette and their subsequent sale for commercial gain emerged as a problem for the U.S. filmed entertainment industry in the late 1970s after Sony introduced a home-consumer version of the VCR. By the end of 1983, global television" household penetration of VCRs reached 8 per cent, with some 40 million units sold worldwide.[61] Although the highest rates of VCR households were originally found in the advanced industrialised nations, the VCR was well on its way to becoming a global mass medium by the end of the 1990s. The U.S. filmed entertainment industry's concern about videocassette piracy emerged around 1983 as it realised that the medium was here to stay. When the industry began to enter foreign videocassette markets, it found that wherever VCR hardware was available there also existed a predominantly pirated market of prerecorded videocassettes.

The VCR permitted, for the first time, the unauthorised mass reproduction and sale of motion pictures and television programs. Before the VCR motion picture piracy mainly took the form of unauthorised copying, of 35- and 16-millimeter prints and unauthorised exhibition of these copies. The public nature of theatrical motion picture exhibition, or of a television broadcast, made it easier to monitor unauthorised performances and halt such acts of copyright infringement (i.e., the copyright owner was more likely to find out about an infringement when it was committed in so "public" a manner). The VCR has increased the availability of copies of motion pictures and television programs; has reduced the costs and complexity of mass producing them (one master videocassette or videodisc player can be connected to several VCRs); and has "privatised" the act of viewing a pirated copy. In many cases, the act of copying also takes place in the privacy of the home, though not all types of home copying are considered piracy (e.g., time-shifting of television broadcasts).

The MPAA estimated worldwide losses due to videocassette piracy ranged around $1 billion per year during the late 1980s. By 1994, the Motion Picture Export Association of America (MPEAA) estimated that its member companies, the major Hollywood filmed entertainment companies, lost $2 billion worldwide due to unauthorised copying of film prints and videocassettes and unauthorised use of cable and satellite signals.[62] Of course, it is impossible to verify these figures, which are based on projected losses of sales revenues and probably inflated.

Nevertheless, these claims have enhanced the urgency of the industry's calls for action against pirates, especially in light of the burgeoning U.S. trade deficit.

Accordingly, the U.S. filmed entertainment industry recruited the U.S. government to help it wage war on videocassette pirates. Winning the war meant making foreign home-video markets accessible and stable for the major U.S. distributors. It also meant bringing the home-video market into the existing international feature film and television program distribution channels dominated by these same companies. For the U.S. government, helping the filmed entertainment industry capture foreign home-video markets meant establishing a beachhead for the much larger war on intellectual property rights infringements. Contributing to the problem was the failure of many new nations to join the multilateral intellectual property conventions — the Berne Convention and the UGC. Those countries in the Third World that remain outside the international system have the effect of reducing the overall level of global protection available to owners of intellectual property, as do those countries that are formally part of the international system but fail to provide, to use the term of industry and foreign policy officials, "adequate and effective" protection of intellectual property rights.

For a long time, refusal to recognise or enforce intellectual property rights was a deliberate policy on the part of many Third World nations- those seeking to prevent foreign monopoly control of culture or the outflow of badly needed foreign exchange. For example the Brazilian Cinema Council, knows as CONCINE, issued a resolution requiring that 25 per cent of the titles stocked by video outlets consist of Brazilian films. Colombia imposed a 20 per cent royalty ceiling on home-video contracts between foreign and local distributors. It is also in in these states, obviously, where piracy of filmed entertainment and other forms of intellectual property has been the most rampant.

U.S. intellectual property owners have convinced the U.S. government that lack of intellectual property rights protection is serious enough to warrant trade sanctions against those countries failing to recognise or respect their property rights. Bilateral negotiation based on trade leveraging has become a central strategy in the effort to eradicate videocassette piracy, with some apparent success, particularly in Southeast Asia. The U.S. government has been particularly tough on Third World countries with respect to intellectual property issues, seeking to force non-member countries to join the copyright conventions and to force those who are members to live up to their treaty obligations. The ultimate goal has been to raise the effectiveness and comprehensiveness of the international intellectual property system in order to create or extend markets exploitable not only for U.S. home-video distributors but for other communications and mass media transnationals as well.

Forms of Videocassette Piracy

Piracy occurs when the copyright is infringed, that is, when copies are made or copyrighted material is exhibited or sold for private, commercial gain without authorisation of or compensation to the copyright owner. Videocassette piracy thus takes multiple forms, for example:

- Copying a film print, videodisc, or videocassette version of a motion picture or other audiovisual work and using this copy as a master tor mass duplication of videocassette copies;
- Taping a broadcast, cablecast, or satellite-distributed television program or motion picture and mass producing videocassette copies;
- Distributing unauthorised copies of videocassettes however they are made;
- Selling or renting mass produced, unauthorised copies of videocassettes;
- Importing authorised or pirated versions of videocassettes into territories where licensing agreements have not been arranged for by the importer (known as "parallel imports"); and
- Holding unauthorised public performances using videocassette programming in cafes, bars, hotels, video theaters, and buses.

All these forms of piracy continue to be found wherever there are VCRs, despite Hollywood's antipiracy war.

Piracy is most common in countries of the Third World and Eastern Europe. Pirates copy and distribute only the international box-office hits or top-rated television programs, thereby guaranteeing sales. Pirates do not pay royalties and often use cheaper raw materials for manufacturing and packaging videocassettes and may significantly underprice authorised copies. The U.S. filmed entertainment industry's copyrights are infringed most often because it holds the dominant share of global motion picture and television markets and produces the biggest hits. However, piracy is a problem for any nation that exports cultural programming since it undercuts legitimate markets. The U.S. motion picture companies are leading the war on pirates, and they have been able to enlist other national-culture industries, governments, and international organisations by emphasising that so-called legitimate home-video markets will benefit all who want to participate. Current developments in international home-video markets indicate that "legitimising" markets means turning them over to the transnational filmed entertainment suppliers and extending their domination of global mass media markets.

All of the forms of piracy listed above still can be found in Western Europe, though on a much smaller scale than when the technology first became available due to the combined efforts of U.S. and European copyright owners and governments to eradicate piracy. These home-video markets, therefore, have largely become "legitimised" and centralised. As early as 1985, the major U.S. motion picture distributors controlled between 65 and 70 per cent of videocassette distribution revenues in European markets while U.S. independent distributors accounted for another 15 per cent.[63] By the late 1980s, the U.S. majors had solidified their hold on the European video rental and sell-through markets. In the United Kingdom, 65 per cent of the rental market was held by the top four labels: Warner (21.6 per cent), CBS/Fox (18.5 per cent), CIC Video (handling home-video distribution for MGM/UA, Universal, and Paramount, 12.7 per cent), and RCA/Columbia (11.6 per cent) in 1987. Approximately 90 per cent of the rental market consisted of U.S.-produced or -distributed motion pictures. British producer-distributors placed only four films among the top fifty rentals in 1987, and independents producing "B" and "C" titles found themselves increasingly marginalised.[64] By 1989, Hollywood productions were more dominant than ever, providing all but two of the top twenty-five rentals in the U.K. market.[65] In 1992, CIC dominated the British video rental market with a 20 per cent share of the $910 million market; Warner and Disney shared roughly 50 per cent of the $594 million sell-through market.[66] By 1992, videocassette piracy was a marginal problem in the United Kingdom.

Reports on home-video markets in continental Europe look much like those on the industry structure in the United Kingdom. In 1989, all twenty of the top video rentals in Germany came from the United States—fourteen from the major distributors and six from U.S. independents.[67] By 1992, German-made and -distributed videos earned only 3 per cent of the industry's total take of $877 million in rentals and sales.[68] Following a global pattern, piracy in Europe is found in poorer regions and states. In Germany, most videocassette piracy is found in the poorer east, where bootleg videos are sold in open-air markets for about $17, a mere fraction of the average retail price of $137.[69]

The USTR's 1994 report on foreign trade barriers called video piracy in Italy "a serious problem."[70] U.S. motion picture distributors claimed that 40 per cent of the Italian video market consisted of pirated copies, costing them $224 million annually, a figure disputed by Italian copyright officials who counterclaimed that piracy made up only 15 per cent of the legitimate market.[71] Nevertheless, U.S. distributors have held a firm grip on the Italian rental and sell-through markets. By 1987, seven of the top ten prerecorded videocassettes sold by distributors to dealers came from the U.S. majors.[72] In 1989, nine of the top ten videos sold direct to Italian consumers came from Disney.[73] The company controlled 50 per cent of the sell-through market in 1991[74] but dropped to a 34 per cent share in 1993 even though it had the year's top five sell-through titles.[75] Blockbuster's entry into the market in July 1994 was hailed by Sergio Simonelli of CIC as a "great event, as well as a natural evolution of the market."[76]

Reports from France and Spain again confirmed that the products of the major U.S. distributors topped the rental markets and that as "A" titles take up increasingly more space on video shop shelves the "B" and "C" titles are squeezed out.[77] In Spain, four major U.S. video distributors—RCA/Columbia, CBS/Fox, CIC (Paramount and Universal), and Warner—took 70 per cent of distribution revenues in 1990.[78] The next year, U.S. distributors captured 78 per cent of the industry's revenues. [79] The USTR reported that video piracy was down sharply in 1993 due to public and private sector enforcement actions using Spain's new intellectual property regimes.[80]

Hollywood's ability to capture European home-video markets away from videocassette pirates is a success story for U.S. video distributors. In the early 1980s, 50-70 per cent of all videocassettes in circulation in various European countries were unauthorised copies.[81] The formula for success proved to be a combination of active pursuit of copyright protection by copyright owners, stricter laws and penalties against piracy, and more effective enforcement of these laws. European film and television production industries, recognising a potential stake in home-video markets, worked with the U.S. motion picture industry in urging their governments to strengthen copyright legislation and to increase enforcement efforts. In France, for example, l'Association de Lutte Centre le Piratage Audiovisuelle (ALPA) had among its founding members the French professional associations of theatrical and home-video distributors, the feature film exporters, the over-the-air pay-TV network (Canel Plus), the local National Cinema Center, and the MPEAA. ALPA's investigative efforts and strict penalties for copyright infringement resulted in the eradication of videocassette piracy in France. In Spain, the Anti-Piracy Federation, strongly backed by the MPEAA, was spending about $700,000 per year to fight piracy. The MPEAA and Italian copyright-based associations and industries formed a new organisation in January 1988, called the Federation Against Audiovisual Piracy, that investigates and supports prosecution of pirates and conducts antipiracy public education campaigns.

Intellectual property rights owners have traditionally found high levels of protection in the states of Western Europe. These nations are original members of many of the international intellectual property conventions. Their protection of property rights with regards to any new communications media is therefore to be expected. Great Britain, France, and Italy are also among the few countries in the world that export the products of their culture industries. The film and television industries in these countries are also seeking to exploit the global home-video market. Furthermore, the fusion of European and U.S. finance capital within the media sector puts European and U.S. filmed entertainment companies directly into alliance, giving West European media capitalists a clear stake in an effective international intellectual property regime as well as in "legitimate" home-video markets.

Having secured the West European home-video market, U.S. industry and government officials turned eastward and today envision huge growth potential in East European countries. The two main problems they have encountered are the lack of copyright laws and ineffective enforcement of those on the books. This is one of the three regions, along with East Asia and the Middle East, where piracy is most formidable. The USTR made Hungary, Poland, and Russia its primary targets for intellectual property reform as their conversion to market systems began. Hungary responded to USTR pressure and signed a bilateral trade pact with the United States in mid-1993 that expanded protection and enforcement of Intellectual property rights. Poland followed one year later by enacting a copyright law that subjects copyright violators to hefty lines and lengthy prison terms. The actions were of particular delight to Disney officials, who expected their earnings from product licensing to rise from $15 million in 1993 to $50 million in 1996, making Poland the company's largest East European market.[82]

Clearly, the biggest potential market for U.S. filmed entertainment companies lies in Russia. The Soviet government took initial steps toward appeasing U.S. industry and government officials in 1988, granting U.S. film distributors copyright and trademark protection. Disney responded by registering trademarks on several of its characters, including Mickey Mouse and Donald Duck, as a prerequisite to film distribution.[83] However, enforcement of U.S. intellectual property rights was not forthcoming, and with piracy levels running 100 per cent, the U.S. filmed entertainment industry took matters into its own hands, following tactics tested after World War II in Western Europe. In the summer of 1991, the MPAA announced a ban on U.S. film distribution in the Soviet Union and proclaimed that its members would no longer provide prints for the Moscow Film Festival, a fixture on the international feature film circuit for some thirty years.[84] In

1992, the U.S. government bolstered the industry's effort by granting Russia most-favored-nation trading status, partly on the condition that it introduce new copyright legislation by the end of the year.

Russia's long-term trade policy goal of joining the Berne Convention converged with the interests of U.S. intellectual property owners and was one reason why the Russian Parliament enacted new copyright legislation. This came on the heels of mounting pressure from domestic copyright holders and licensees seeking to solidify their market positions. For example, Melodiya, the state-owned recording company, had seen its export opportunities significantly diminished when more than 100,000 of its Russian classical recordings were reproduced without authorisation and shipped as exports.[85] Microsoft Corp. invited Russian software pirates to become authorised dealers through various enticements and then organised a software manufacturers association, made up of fifteen Western companies and forty Russian producers, to lobby the Russian Parliament to protect copyrights out of national economic interests. The Supreme Soviet approved such a law in July 1993, permitting the country's accession to the Paris Convention for the Protection of Industrial Property and the UCC. The enrollment of domestic intellectual property owners in the antipiracy campaign is a procedure being followed around Eastern Europe, with homegrown organisations sprouting in Hungary, Romania, Poland, Bulgaria, and the Czech Republic. This combination of strategies is being utilised to fight piracy in the two other regions where it is most rampant, the Middle East and Asia.

Piracy in the Middle East

U.S. copyright owners learned that piracy in the Middle East was largely attributable to the lack of copyright relations between the United States and Middle Eastern nations, Many of these countries only recently gained political independence and have yet to join the international intellectual property conventions. For some time, many postcolonial governments, including those in the Middle East, retained the inadequate and outdated copyright systems inherited from their former colonisers. For copyright owners, the acuteness of the situation was exaggerated by the rapid introduction of new communications technologies. The oil boom of the early 1970s provided the nations of the Persian Gulf with considerable income, some of which was used to buy communications hardware. Kuwait and Saudi Arabia have ranked among the highest VCR-penetrated nations in the world in terms of the VCR-to-TV household ratio. Much of the proliferation of television-based technology in Saudi Arabia and other conservative Arab countries is due to a lack of motion picture theaters, a consequence of government restrictions. As a result, domestic film industries have not developed due to the lack of theatrical outlets. Of all the Arab states, only Egypt has any kind of significant domestic film production industry.

The lack of domestic mass media industries and the lack of copyright eligibility for foreign works in the Middle East produced a market situation that the U.S. Register of Copyrights described as "an international bazaar of 'stolen' intellectual properties."[86] Like the rest of the world, Western films and television programs make up the bulk of the pirated VCR programming available in the Middle East. Other pirated videocassettes contain Arab-produced television and film, mostly from Egypt.[87] The International Intellectual Property Alliance included Saudi Arabia on its April 1989 list of twelve "problem" countries with regard to trade losses due to piracy and market access barriers.[88] The IIPA estimated that motion picture piracy in Saudi

Arabia cost U.S. distributors $75 million in 1989. U.S. filmed entertainment industry sources claimed revenues lost to videocassette piracy in Egypt alone totaled $125 million in 1988.[89]

U.S. filmed entertainment companies were eager to move into Middle Eastern home-video markets, but first they had to confront the piracy problem. The nations of the Middle East are both major importers of pirated videocassettes (from the Far East) and a major world site for illegal manufacture of pirated videocassettes. Some of the world's most advanced duplicating equipment is found there. The illegal copies are then exported throughout Africa and Europe. Middle Eastern governments, therefore, have cause to ignore imports of unauthorised copyrighted works because they reduce the outflow of foreign exchange and to ignore unauthorised copyright operations within their borders due to the export revenues they earn. Thus, although U.S. and European filmed entertainment companies have targeted the Middle East as a regional antipiracy battlefield, progress has been slow.

In the mid-1980s, the U.S. government began pressuring the countries of the Gulf Cooperation Council (GCC: Saudi Arabia, Kuwait, the United Arab Emirates [UAE], Bahrain, Qatar, and Oman) to adopt copyright laws. For example, the U.S. embassy in Riyadh arranged and participated in several meetings with U.S. film industry representatives and Saudi officials. As a result of U.S. pressure, Saudi Arabia enacted a patent and copyright law in 1989; the UAE enacted copyright, trademark, and patent laws in 1992; Bahrain's emir issued his country's first copyright law in 1993; and Kuwait and Oman began drafting laws in 1993. Part of this success was due to the convergence of U.S. and GCC geopolitical interests. Much of the action of the intellectual property front followed on the heels of expanded U.S. military presence in the region for the Gulf War. And though the laws are on the books, U.S. copyright owners continue to complain about lack of enforcement. As a result of these complaints, Saudi Arabia was put on the USTR's "priority watch list" in 1993 under the "Special 301" provision of the 1988 trade act.

Outside of the GCC, the U.S. has targeted two other key Middle Eastern nations: Egypt and Turkey. Egypt also made the USTR's 1993 watch list due to inadequate copyright protection. The Egyptian Peoples' Assembly began considering copyright reform legislation in 1988 and passed amendments to its 1954 copyright law in June 1992, but by 1994 it had still not fully implemented the new provisions. U.S. home-video distributors claimed to be losing an estimated $37 million per year by 1994.[90] The pirated copies are made from broadcast or cable television programs, or illegal copies are made from videos bought or rented in Europe or the United States. Occasionally, Egyptian video clubs rent titles that are still having their theatrical runs; copies are also made in the United States from studio prints or captured by 8-millimeter video cameras at U.S. theaters.[91] In response to U.S. copyright industries, the USTR has used the Generalised System of Preferences (GSP) review to bring up discussions about copyright matters with Turkey, threatening to withhold trade privileges unless U.S. copyrights are respected.

The filmed entertainment industry has also resorted to market strategies to capture Middle Eastern home-video markets for "legitimate" distributors. These efforts include offering a video product with a superior visual image to that of pirated products, supplying a dubbed audio track on the prerecorded videocassette or Arabic subtitling, and releasing prerecorded videocassettes closer to the date of initial release in the United States. The same combination of government pressure and market-based strategies are being used throughout Asia to combat piracy.

Video Piracy in Asia

When U.S. filmed entertainment copyright owners turned to the Asian market they found a piracy situation similar to that in the Middle East. The root causes in most countries were also the same: lack of intellectual property laws, lax enforcement of those laws on the books, minimal participation in international or bilateral intellectual property agreements, and a rapid proliferation of recording technologies—both consumer and industrial. Furthermore, most of the indigenous film and television production industries in this region of the world are weak and underdeveloped, making it ripe for imported products. Videocassette pirates often have had the tacit approval of governments who recognised the valuable foreign exchange generated by them. Some resistance has been carried out to protect these domestic interests. For example, demonstrators in the Philippines met the antipiracy campaign with rallies and protests, asserting that government efforts to curb piracy would only promote foreign interests.[92]

Public demand for video software fuels video piracy, of course. The notion of intellectual property is foreign to many Far Eastern societies. Traditionally, Asian authors and artists have viewed the copying of their works as an honor. Thus, tradition makes it difficult to convince Asian video consumers that buying or rentingpirated programming is a criminal activity. Demand for prerecorded videocassettes is even higher in those states where broadcasting is state-controlled, where there are screen quotas, or where theater exhibition of films requires the approval of state censors. These factors have made Asia fertile ground for pirating, for both domestic video consumption and export. Pirated products produced in Asia have become available as far away as Africa, Western Europe, and Latin America.

The filmed entertainment industry began paying serious attention to the problem of videocassette piracy in the Far East and Pacific Basin beginning in 1984. The countries that generated the most immediate concern were Singapore, Taiwan, and South Korea because of their emerging status as newly industrialising countries (NICs). Losses to U.S. copyright industries in 1984 due to piracy in each of these countries were estimated at $358 million, $186 million, and $146 million, respectively.[93] Soon after, Indonesia, Malaysia, Thailand, and the Philippines were added to the list of top ten pirate countries (along with India, Brazil, and Mexico). The IIPA estimated that the U.S. copyright industries' losses in these ten countries totaled $1.3 billion in 1984.[94]

Looking to past experiences with piracy in Asia, U.S. copyright industries took the Hong Kong antipiracy campaign, initiated in 1973 by the International Federation of Phonographic Industries (IFPI) to combat record and tape piracy, as their model for addressing the problem in these other Southeast Asian and Pacific Basin countries. In this case, the MPAA Film Security Office and a local headquarters of the IFPI provided the catalyst for generating local action on the piracy front. The copyright industries worked with local government and enforcement authorities (police, customs, and tax agents) and managed to secure increased criminal penalties for copyright infringement, crackdowns on duplicating labs, and enhanced export laws that led to a significant reduction in piracy. Frank G. Wells testified to a joint congressional committee that Disney had its own investigative force in Hong Kong whose work had led to the filing of some sixty infringement lawsuits per year.[95] At the same time, the filmed entertainment industry began to undercut pirates by establishing "legitimate" relations with select local video dealers and cutting prices on prerecorded videocassettes to reduce the differential between pirate copies and legitimate copies.

However, private market and legal efforts proved insufficient for dealing with piracy on the grand scale that it existed in the region, so the copyright industries as a whole once again turned to the U.S. government for help. In petitioning Congress for assistance, Nesuhi Ertegun, president of the IFPI and chair of the Atlantic Recording Group (a subsidiary of Warner Communications), argued that piracy could not be beaten in Asia unless copyright industries had the U.S. government's "active support."[96]

By 1986, the U.S. private sector and government operation vis-a-vis Asian governments reached full force. The USTR, in particular, used the GSP review during the summer of 1986 to apply pressure to a number of foreign governments to act on copyright issues. At the same time, it had to fight in Congress to retain the very tools with which it was conducting its antipiracy campaign. Sen. Bob Dole (R-Kans.) introduced a bill to "graduate" (remove) the NICs—Taiwan, Hong Kong, and Korea—from the list of eligible GSP beneficiaries because of the large trade deficits that had developed between these three countries and the United States ($13.1 billion, $6.2 billion, and $4.8 billion, respectively).[97] In House hearings on the bill, the Reagan administration strongly opposed the graduation, citing its success with using the GSP to move Taiwan, Korea, and Singapore, in particular, toward action on copyright legislation.[98] Stanley Gortikov, president of the Recording Industry Association of America and representing the IIPA, also testified that the organisation itself had "fully utilised the tools provided by the GSP Renewal Act" and had done so successfully.[99] The IIPA's estimated losses of its members due to piracy declined dramatically in Singapore, Indonesia, Taiwan, and Malaysia between 1984 to 1988, as shown in Table 7.1.

The intellectual property industries and the Reagan administration successfully thwarted efforts to graduate the NICs from the list of GSP beneficiaries. The long-term interests of the information-entertainment copyright sector won out over the short-term trade-deficit reduction measure proposed by Dole. What was more important, from the perspective of capital as a whole, was achieving enhanced intellectual property rights protection in these countries that are playing an increasingly important role in the world capitalist system. Accordingly, many Asian nations have adopted intellectual property systems for the first time, others have upgraded the protections they provide, and enforcement of intellectual property laws has become a government priority.

Among the nearly vanquished are India and China, the U.S. entertainment industry's two largest potential markets on the Asian continent. The IIPA added both countries to its report on "problem countries" in 1989, citing estimated annual losses to member companies at $418 million in China and at $123 million in India.[100] In India, the U.S. filmed entertainment industry not only encountered piracy but also came up against a strong domestic film industry heavily protected by government policies. For example, Indian import laws restricted U.S. companies from distributing films, excluded them from the home-video market, and subjected motion picture and video imports to quotas.[101] Initial studies indicated that VCRs were used mostly to watch pirated feature films—mostly Indian productions—in video theaters and cafes, at video parties, and on buses.[102]

TABLE 9.1

Estimated Losses from Intellectual Property Piracy in Four Southeast Asian Countries (in $millions)

	1984	*1988*
Singapore	358	10
Indonesia	206	45
Taiwan	186	90
Malaysia	73	32

SOURCE: International Intellectual Property Alliance, 1989, p. vi.

In 1991, the USTR put India on the "priority foreign country" list under the "Special 301" provision of the 1988 trade act and initiated a section 301 investigation due to rampant infringements of U.S. intellectual property rights and a wide range of service trade "barriers." The action prompted the Indian government to pursue drastic policy changes in the areas of copyrights and film and video importation regulations. Amendments to the copyright law provided for rental rights for videocassettes; protection for works transmitted by satellite, cable, or another means of simultaneous retransmission; and less judicial discretion in determining levels of penalties for infringements. The Indian government also took steps to increase enforcement efforts. Changes in government regulation of film imports and distribution were even more dramatic. Foreign motion picture companies are now allowed to import and distribute their products in India. Import quotas on motion pictures or videos and restrictions on the number of prints that may be exported have been lifted. Films no longer must go through a government film review board for approval, and the restriction on dubbing foreign films into local languages was abolished. In response to the new legislation, CIC Video began the push into India, releasing such titles as *Samson and Delilah, Stalag 17, Scent of a Woman,* and *Beverly Hills Cop* for sale to video libraries.[103]

India's revised intellectual property laws prompted the announcement of a number of new market entries, joint ventures, and alliances involving several U.S., European, and Japanese TNCs, most dependent on such laws in one way or another. The Indian government listed the new market entrants in a full-page ad taken out in the *New York Times* in May 1994.[104] Among them were Kellogg's, McDonald's, Polaroid, AT&T, General Electric, IBM, and Coca-Cola. Gillette, Pepsi, Merck, Nestle, Proctor & Gamble, Colgate-Palmolive, Unilever, Philips, Glaxo, and Honda all took advantage of new foreign investment regulations, permitting them to take a majority 51 per cent stake in their Indian joint ventures. The U.S. trade policy apparatus utilised similar tactics and made similar gains in China.

The Chinese government published the country's first copyright law in May 1991. U.S. trade officials had been pressuring China on intellectual property legislation since normalisation of relations in 1979 and escalated these efforts in the late 1980s.[105] Despite China's commitment to a new copyright law, the USTR identified China as a major site of piracy, designated the country a "priority," and initiated a section 301 investigation of its intellectual property practices in April 1991. When China failed to respond to U.S. complaints, the USTR took procedures for the first time to enact trade sanctions against a country in retaliation for intellectual property violations. A full-scale trade war was avoided when the United States and China signed a "Memorandum of Understanding" in which the latter committed itself to enhancing protection of U.S. intellectual property rights. China promised to bring its copyright laws up to global standards to facilitate accession to the Berne Convention and the Geneva Phonograms Convention and to toughen the protection of patents.

Shortly after the signing of the memorandum, Disney

announced that it would reenter the Chinese market, which it had abandoned in 1989, in the consumer products, publishing, and television programming sectors.[106] Subsequently, China has made several changes to its intellectual property laws and joined the major copyright conventions. However, lack of enforcement of the new laws brought China under the scrutiny of U.S. trade officials once again. The USTR charged that piracy of videos, tape cassettes, compact discs, laser discs, computer games, computer software and manuals, and books and magazines was costing U.S. businesses $800 million in lost sales.[107] In July 1994, the USTR again initiated an investigation into China's copyright practices and gave the government six months to enhance copyright protection. Just five days after the USTR action, the Chinese legislature approved prison terms and stiffer fines for copyright violators, responding to a principle U.S. demand. However, lack of enforcement of new laws prompted the United States to continue to put pressure on China, and retaliatory trade measures loomed once again early in 1995. It is clear that the Chinese government is steadily moving toward the institution of an intellectual property system that conforms to global standards. The government must demonstrate its resolve to adhere to new global trading rules if China is to eventually gain entry into the World Trade Organisation.[108]

The cases of India and China demonstrate how Asian countries are caving in to U.S. trade leveraging. However, it is not trade leveraging alone that is driving the expanding realm of intellectual property. The economic interests of U.S. capitalists have tended to converge with those of foreign governments and the internationalist sectors of foreign capital. It is generally agreed that integration into the world intellectual property system is more beneficial in the long run than short-term gains from the export of pirated products. The NICs, such as South Korea, Taiwan, and Singapore, want to establish the appropriate national legal structure that will support an economy based on the export of high technology and its intellectual property-based products. India and China are seeking greater integration into the global economy and therefore have been compelled to open their domestic markets and adopt legal infrastructures conducive to a favorable business climate. These nations have concluded that in order to draw transnational investment and to be able to participate in emerging global markets, they must play by the rules of the game. Furthemore with the collapse of the international bipolar geopolitical system, every country in the world is now involved in the global competition to provide a "favorable investment climate."

Multilateralism: U.S. Accession to Berne and GATT Reform

U.S. trade officials could not insist that foreign governments accede to the Berne Convention until March 1989, when the United States itself first became a member. The United States could not join until it made changes in its copyright registration procedures and trade policy on book publishing. Formal copyright registration procedures, such as the requirement that two copies of the work be deposited with the U.S. Library of Congress, stood in violation of the Berne Convention. The 1976 Act largely resolved this problem with simplified copyright registration procedures. The remaining sticking point for U.S. accession was the "manufacturing clause" (17 U.S.C. section 601), a piece of protectionist policy that for almost 100 years required first publication in either the United States or Canada for a copyright owner to qualify for copyright protection under U.S. law. Although the United States was not a member of Berne, U.S. copyright owners had received the higher level of protection offered by the Berne Convention by simultaneously publishing in those nations that belonged to both UCC and Berne, for example, Canada. Most U.S. copyright owners recognised the greater protection they would have if the United States joined Berne, though it took quite a while for them to overcome the vested interests of another communications sector, the printing industry (usually not copyright owners), which was the main beneficiary of the manufacturing clause and its biggest supporter.

Congress allowed this century-old protectionist measure to expire July 1, 1986, since it represented a major barrier to U.S. accession to Berne. It was also found to be in violation of GATT. The book printing industry represented a declining hegemonic faction of capital based in manufacturing that could at one time effectively promote its interests through the state (i.e., protectionist copyright law) but was challenged by a larger, emergent sector of capital represented by copyright industries (including book publishers). As the larger fraction of copyright industries established its economic hegemony within capital as a whole, it increasingly was able to restructure the state apparatus to advance its own interests (e.g., eliminating the manufacturing clause and gaining U.S. accession to Berne).

Hearings on U.S. adherence to Berne were held in the Senate in May 1985 and April 1986.[109] Throughout these hearings, the intellectual property industry representatives from the MPAA, the American Association of Publishers, the Computer and Business Equipment Manufacturers Association (CBEMA), the Information Industry of America (whose representative, Morton David Goldberg, also served on the State Department's Ad Hoc Working Group on U.S. Adherence to the Berne Convention), the U.S. Council for International Business, and CBS, Inc., called for retirement of the manufacturing clause and for U.S. accession to Berne. The acting commissioner for the U.S. Patent and Trademark Office, testifying on behalf of the Cabinet Council of Commerce and Trade, supported accession to Berne because the World Intellectual Property Organisation, Berne's governance forum, was "not as politicised as UNESCO, and the influence of the developing nations in WIPO is not so disproportionate as in UNESCO."[110] At this time, the United States found itself outside the policymaking structure of the UCC due to its withdrawal from UNESCO, the governing body of the UCC. Accession to the Berne Convention would give the United States a role in developing international copyright policymaking.

Some copyright owners nevertheless opposed U.S. accession to the Berne Convention due to its moral rights clause (Article 6 bis)—the general right to claim authorship of a work and the specific right to object to actions (distortion, mutilation, or other modification) that would prejudice the author's honor and reputation. The filmed entertainment industry had long opposed U.S. accession to Berne because of the moral rights clause. Industry owners and executives felt it would interfere with the normal practice whereby the filmed entertainment production company buys screenplays from writers and retains the right to make any changes it wants. Screenwriters and film directors also linked the moral rights clause to legal efforts to halt the "colorisation" of black-and-white feature films.[111] However, industry concerns about the moral rights clause were easily outweighed by the need to protect filmed entertainment copyrights in the face of new communications technologies. The filmed entertainment industry had not suffered from lack of U.S. membership in Berne when its product was distributed primarily on 35-millimeter and 16-millimeter film since it was able to maintain strict control and contract governance for usage. Norman Alterman, vice president for the MPAA, testified that the new technologies of satellites, cable television, and VCRs now made U.S. adherence to Berne essential.[112]

President Reagan transmitted the Berne Convention to the Senate for advice and consent in June 1986.[113] Additional activity in 1987 produced a split between book publishers over the moral rights provision. The Coalition to Preserve the American Copyright Tradition (PACT), led by Time, Inc., and McGraw-Hill and represented by former Register of Copyrights David Ladd, opposed U.S. accession to Berne because it would surely lead to increased moral rights litigation and end up costing publishers enormously, especially if damages to reputation mirrored those awarded in libel cases.[114] Other book publishers, allied with most representatives of the copyright industries, formed the National Committee for the Berne Convention in response to PACT and clearly reflected the interests of the hegemonic faction of capital in this matter. Pro-Berne forces highlighted the symbolic value of U.S. accession to the treaty in bolstering U.S. efforts to fight piracy and promote higher standards of protection and enforcement worldwide. Accordingly, Congress approved legislation that made the necessary changes in U.S. copyright law to permit U.S. accession to Berne.

The treaty itself was approved by the Senate on October 20,1988, with only five members present. To circumvent the need for a two-thirds majority vote ordinarily required to approve a treaty, Senator Robert Byrd (D-W.Va.) used a special device called a "division," where members stand to indicate approval or dissent, to gain this treaty's passage.[115] With the live senators standing,[116] the U.S. Senate; voted to become a full member of the Berne Convention beginning in March 1989. In the implementation act however, Congress asserted that the moral rights provision should not be enforced by U.S. courts, a resolution that once again privileged economic rights over those of actual creators of intellectual and artistic works.[117]

GATT Revision

The major pillar of U.S. multilateral strategy to expand the global range of intellectual property involved revision of GATT. Ninety-two nations launched the Uruguay Round of discussions in September 1986, concentrating on strengthening and extending the rules governing the international trading system. Originally, GATT rules applied only to manufactured goods—sectors in which the United States had been dominant for most of the twentieth century. With the decline of U.S. competitiveness in manufacturing sectors, the importance of service and intellectual property trade increased. U.S. foreign policy makers thus took the lead in bringing services and intellectual property under the auspices of GATT.[118] They sought to establish minimum standards of protection and develop a dispute-settlement mechanism, which was lacking in both the Berne Convention and UCC.

Corporate officialdom of the largest TNCs also pushed for the incorporation of services and intellectual property in GATT. One notable event occurred when the U.S.-based Intellectual Property Committee joined with the Japan Federation of Economic Organisations and the Union of Industrial and Employers' Confederation of Europe in producing a report that urged their governments to negotiate a comprehensive multilateral agreement in GATT that would stop theft and illegal copying of intellectual property.[119] It was an historic occasion, being the first time that the world business community had jointly expressed the need for such action in GATT. The participation of the corporate and governmental elite throughout the Uruguay Round of negotiations underscored the importance of the revisions to big capital. For example, at the interim meetings in Montreal in 1988, the U.S. Trade Representative, Clayton K. Yeutter, who had served as head of the Chicago Stock Exchange before becoming the top U.S. trade official, took a delegation of 150 people to the meetings including two cabinet secretaries (Commerce and Agriculture), chairpersons of the House and Senate agriculture committees, other legislators, and so-called private sector advisers.[120]

At the Montreal meetings, the outlines of international struggles emerged among and between the rich countries of the North and the poor countries of the South. Agricultural subsidies surfaced as the primary area of contention, with France, Germany, and Japan, among other nations, claiming the right to protect their agricultural industries and thereby minimise dependence on food imports. European farmers rallied in Brussels during the December 1990 talks to defend their livelihood. Agriculture-exporting nations, such as Australia, Argentina, and Brazil, among others, demanded abolition of agriculture subsidies.

India and Brazil criticised the effort to bring intellectual property rights into GATT and to erect high standards of protection, fearing that such economic barriers would inhibit the spread of advanced technology needed in the fights against hunger and disease.[121] The Third World delegations added that bringing intellectual property into GATT was inappropriate and would increase tension in the global trading system. They expressed their confidence in WIPO and UNESCO in handling intellectual property matters. Of course, these were fora in which North-South politics had become quite intense, with the Third World nations able to exercise some clout as a majority. GATT is structured to minimise politics and to emphasise the principles of economics and law. Such principles are never neutral, nor do they provide a level playing field. Biases built into the form and content of GATT favor the dominant economic powers.

Cultural struggles also emerged during the Uruguay Round. The European Community (EC), led by France, refused to allow filmed entertainment subsidies and quotas into the agreement. The U.S. filmed entertainment industry sought to use GATT as a means of securing a greater share of tax revenues raised on the sal of video and audio equipment and tapes. Many European nations collected royalty fees on home-taping products and redistributed them to domestic filmed entertainment companies to foster domestic production. In France, for example, taxes on theater tickets and audio and video cassettes amounted to $350 million in 1992.[122] Most of this revenue was plowed back into French filmed entertainment, a practice the U.S. industry finds "unfair" since much of the tax is generated by its products. The EC also refused to negotiate on the issue of film and television quotas, asserting the right to seek to protect a distinctly European market for television programming.

The struggles over agricultural subsidies and intellectual property rights were resolved through compromise. The economically disadvantaged nations of the South agreed to a new intellectual property regime in exchange for deep cuts in agricultural subsidies. Intellectual property issues were settled under the Agreement on Trade-Related Aspects of Intellectual Property Rights, Including Trade in Counterfeit Goods (the "TRIPS Agreement"). Its copyright provisions require members of the new World Trade Organisation to comply with the Berne Convention, including granting protection to databases and to computer programs as literary works under Berne. They also grant computer program and sound recording copyright owners the right to authorise or prohibit rental of their property. Sound recordings are granted protection for fifty years, and duration of copyright protection in general must be compatible with Berne. The enforcement component of the provisions requires Imposition of criminal penalties as a deterrent to copyright piracy.[123] The enforcement provisions are unique to GATT. Their purpose is to compensate for the lack of such provisions in the Berne Convention and the UCC. That the "moral rights" provision in the Berne Convention was excluded from the revised GATT demonstrates its primary function—to protect the rights of intellectual property owners.

Intellectual property industry advisers to the U.S. government found the baseline provision of the TRIPS Agreement satisfactory but criticised the five- to ten-year grace period granted to "developing countries" during transitions toward the new intellectual property rules, arguing that this sanctioned continued piracy for the immediate future.[124] They recommended that the USTR sustain its efforts to eradicate intellectual property infringements through bilateral trade strategies. The grace period turned out to be a victory for the advanced industrialised countries. The TRIPS Agreement ultimately prohibits less industrialised nations from applying intellectual property laws so as to foster technological and economic development, a political-economic strategy, as Chakravarthi Raghavan points out, that has been utilised by countries for centuries, including the United States.[125] This is a complete reversal of the commitments made by the advanced industrialised countries two decades earlier to help promote development in the Third World by reforming the international intellectual property system.

The EC gave ground on farm subsidies but refused to budge on filmed entertainment levies and quotas, much to the chagrin of the United States. However, the importance of the broader GATT revisions outweighed the specific sectoral interests of the U.S. filmed entertainment industry. Clearly, the long-term interests of capital as a whole won out over short-term industry gains. Although some government officials in the EC, such as Jack Lang, former culture minister of France, hailed this resistance to the United States as "a victory of art and artists over the commercialisation of culture," the U.S. Industry Sector Advisory Committee on Services, made up of top officials from the largest service sector companies, recommended that the United States use its trade leveraging tools to open foreign filmed entertainment markets and push for "liberalisation" of the "audiovisual" sector in the next round of GATT negotiations beginning in 2000.[126]

Despite the compromises, the reduced tariffs and more open global trading system promised by GATT are most beneficial to the United States. Indeed, the global economic hegemon historically has been the strongest advocate for free trade—Great Britain in the nineteenth century and the United States in the twentieth century. The previous case studies have shown how establishing the rules for "fair trade" permit the most economically powerful entities to solidify and extend their market shares. For example, the new GATT regime will do nothing to change the balance of trade in theatrical feature films between the United States and the EC, a situation in which the United States takes roughly 80 per cent of the EC box-office revenues while the EC earns a mere 2 per cent of the U.S. domestic box-office. This disparity is not based on government trade regulations by on oligopolistic market power.

Conclusion

The evidence presented in this chapter demonstrates the role of the U.S.power elite, made up of officials from industry and government, in promoting the long term interests of U.S. capital as a whole. At the same time, the evidence also suggests that a parallel international power-elite network, involving international finance capital, transnational corporate owners, executives, and representative and high-level government officials, has become an effective force in the global economic system. It is clear that there are concrete .struggles that take place due to conflicts between national and international capital. However, the deeper determining logic of capital has tipped the balance in favor of the latter. The expanding range of intellectual property is driven by this deeper expansionary logic of capital. The developments described in this chapter concern the most recent evolutionary stages in the international intellectual property system

The institution of intellectual property emerged with the dawn of capitalism and intellectual property owners established organisations ot govern global trade in intellectual and artistic works in the nineteenth century. However, the scale and intellectual property trade by the late twentieth century required drastic reform of the international intellectual property system. The reformed needed to support the emerging flexible regime of accumulation that was increasingly organised on an international level. Industries dependent upon rights, patents, and trademarks required a legal infrastructure that transcended national borders to allow them to take advantage of favorable capital and lab markets. They could also be assured of protection of their investments as they entered foreign markets.

Raghavan predicted that for the industrialised countries the new international intellectual property system would largely serve to protect the monopoly rentier incomes of their TNCs. At the same time, however, it could also deny

Third World countries access to knowledge, block their capacity for innovation and technical change, and prevent any serious increase in their competitive capacity.[127] The evidence in this chapter suggests that new rules governing intellectual property will greatly facilitate the process of global commodification of human intellectual and artistic creativity. Cultural activities, in particular, will continue to be incorporated into the global market system, produced and sold primarily for their exchange value. This commodification will lead to an even greater concentration of copyright ownership in the hands of the global cultural industries. The profit orientation of these industries leads them to produce and distribute homogenous cultural products. Their market power, in turn, fosters the erosion of national, regional, ethnic, and group autonomy, undermines democratic participation in cultural expression, and increases inequalities between people and nations. Struggle.

NOTES

1. Kees van der Pijl, "The International Level," in T. Bottomore and R. J. Brym (eds.), *The Capitalist Class: An International Study*, New York: New York University Press, 1989, pp. 237—266, p. 237.
2. M. Fennema, *International Networks of Banks and Industry*, The Hague: Nijhoff, 1982.
3. Van der Pijl, p. 259.
4. Armand Mattelart, "Introduction: For a *Class* and *Group* Analysis of Popular Communication Practices," in A. Mattelart and S. Siegelaub (eds.), *Communication and Class Struggle*, Volume 2: *Liberation, Socialism*, New York: International General, 1983, pp. 17-67.
5. M. Crozier, S. Huntington, and J. Watanuki, *The Crisis of Democracy: Report on the Governability of Democracies to the Trilateral Commission*, New York: New York University Press, 1975. Cited in Mattelart, p. 60.

6. Herbert Schiller, *Culture, Inc.: The Corporate Takeover of Public Expression*, New York: Oxford University Press, 1989, pp. 141-143; and *Mass Communications and American Empire* (2nd ed.), Boulder: Westview Press, 1992, pp. 23-24.

7. Thomas B. Edsall, *The New Politics of Inequality*, New York: W. W. Norton, 1985, pp. 107-125.

8. Elizabeth Eisenstein, *The Printing Press as an Agent of Change*, Cambridge: Cambridg University Press 1979.

9. James Schwoch, *The American Radio Industry and Its Latin American Activities, 1900-1939*, Urbana: University of Illinois Press, 1990.

10. Thomas Guback, "Hollywood's International Market," in T. Balio (ed.), *The American Film Industry*, Madison: University of Wisconsin Press, 1985, pp. 463-486.

11. Robert Sklar, *Film: An International History of the Medium*, New York: H. N. Abrams, 1993, pp. 94-95.

12. Herbert Schiller, *Communication and Cultural Domination*, White Plains, NY: M. E. Sharpe, 1976, pp. 24-33; Schiller, 1992, pp. 123-151.

13. Thomas Guback, *The International Film Industry, Western Europe, and America Since 1945*, Bloomington: Indiana University Press, 1969.

14. Meg Cox, "Polygram Plans Outlay on Movies of $200 Million," *Wall Street Journal*, September 25, 1991, p. B6.

15. Kathleen A. Hughes, "Creditors File for Liquidation of MGM-Pathe," *WalkStreet Journal*, April 1, 1991, p. B5.

16. Marcus W. Brauchli and S. Karene Witcher, "News Corp. Purchases Majority Stake-in Star TV of Asia for $525 Million," *Wall Street Journal*, July 27, 1993, p. B5; Philip Shenon, "Star TV Extends Murdoch's Reach," *New York Times*, August 23, 1993, pp. Dl, D6.

17. Richard W. Stevenson, "Warner to Make 20 Films with European Companies," *New York Times*, January 15, 1991, p. D7.

18. Stevenson, p. D-7.

19. Johnnie L., Roberts " Time Warner Attempt to Find Partner in Europe Remains Far from Fruition," *Wall Street Journal*, July 30, 1992, p.A3.

20. Roberts . p. A3.

21. 'Berlusconi of Italy to Invest $110 Millions in Six Hollywood Films," *Wall Street Journal* , March 7, 1991, p. C16.

22. Alan Riding, "French TV Seeks to Slice of the Hollywood Pie," *New York Time* March, 19 1991, pp. C11, C14.
23. Cacilie Rohwedder and Audrey Choi, "Bertelsman Goes Shopping for a Film Studio," *Wall Street Journal*, August 10, 1993, pp. B1, B6.
24. Don Jeffrey, "Challenge Await Zelnick at BMG; Hiring New Head for RCA Label a Priority," *Billiboard*, September 24, 1994, p. 6.
25. Bull Carter, "CBS Gives Romance a Chance," *New York Times*, September 26, 1994 pp. D1, D6.
26. Yumiko Ono, "Hollywood Is Losing Some Glitter for Tinsel-Weary Japan Investors," *Wall Street Journal*, July 10, 1991, p. A6.
27. Alan Citron, "Japan's Thirst for Hollywood Unquenched," *Los Angeles Times* December 10, 1990, pp. A1, A20.
28. Citron, p. A20.
29. Shoba Purushothaman, 'Walt Disney Sets a Eurobond Issue Tied to Film Results," *Wall Street Journal*, October 12, 1992, p. C17.
30. Ben Bagdikian, *The Media Monopoly* (4th ed.,) Boston, 1992, p. 246.
31. For a history and case study fo this process, see Kwangmi Ko Kim, "The Globalisation of te Korean Advertising Industry: History of Early Penetration of TNAAs and Their Impacts on Korean Society," Ph.D. Dissertation University Park: The Pennsylvania State University, 1994.
32. Fernando Henrique Cardoso, "Dependency and Development in Latin America," in H. Alavi and T.Shanin (eds.) *Introduction to the Sociology of Developing Countries*, London: MacMillan, 1982, pp. 112-127, p. 121.
33. World Intellectual Property Organisation, *WIPO Worldwide Forum on the Piracy of Broadness and the Printed Word*, Geneva: World Intellectual Property Organisation, 1983, "Statement" of Tom Tavares-Finson, Representative from Jamaica, pp. 78-81; Fidel Castro, "Communism Will Be Abundance Without Egoism: On Intellectual Property," in M. Kenner and J. Petras (eds.) *Fidel Castro Speaks*, New York:: Grove Press, 1969, pp. 237-246.
34. See, for example, these studies from the American Enterprise Institute on the funture U.S. global economic role: Sven W. Arendt and Lawrence Bouton. *The United States in World Trade*, 1987; Robert P. Benko, *Protecting Intellectual Property Rights*,

1987; and Jonathan D. Aronson and Peter E Cowhey, *Trade in Services: A Case for Open Markets*, 1984, all works Washington, DC: American Enterprise Institute for Public Policy Research. See also Ronald E, Berenheim, *Safeguarding Intellectual Property*, New York: The Conference Board, 1989; and Helena Stalson, *Intellectual Property Rights and U. S. Competitiveness in Trade*, Washington, DC: National Planning Association, 1987.

35. U.S. International Trade Commission, *Foreign Protection of Intellectual Property Rights and the Effect on U.S. Industry and Trade*, Washington, DC: US. International Trade Commission, 1988.

36. Ralph Oman, "Report from the Copyright Office to the ABA Annual Meeting," *PTC Newletter*, 10:1, 1991, pp. 22-35, p. 22.

37. Caribbean Basin Economic Recovery Act of 1983, Pub. L. 98-67, 97 Stat. 369 (August 1983.); Trade and Tariff Act of 1984, Title V: Generalised System of Preferences Renewal Act, Pub., 98-573 Stat. 2948 (October 30, 1984).

38. Frank Clifford, "Race for Senate Shifting Out of Low Gear," *Los Angeles Times*, June 1988, p. 3.

39. Trade and Competitiveness Act of 1988, Pub. L. 100-418, 102 Stat: 1107 (August 23, 1988).

40. U. S. House, Committee on the Judiciary, Subcommittee on Courts, Intellectusal Property, and the Adminstration of Justice, *Intellectual Property, Domestic Productivity, and Trade*, Hearings, July 25, 1989, 101st Cong., Ist Sess., Washington, DC: U.S. Government Printing Office, 1989, Statement of Ralph Oman, Register of Copyrights, pp. 62-82, p. 66.

41. U.S. Trade Representiative, *National Trade Estimates 1986*, Washington, DC: U.S. Government Printing Office, 1986, p. 53.

42. Robert E. Babe and Conrad Winn, *Broadcasting Policy and Copyright Law*, Ottawa: Department of Communications, Government of Canada, 1981, pp. 123-124.

43. "Canadian TV Facts and Figures," *Variety*, April 27, 1988, p. 242.

44. *Canadian Admiral Corporation v. Rediffusion, Inc.*, Ex C.R. 362 (1954).

45. *Fortnightly Corp. v. United Artists Elevision, Inc.*, 392 U.S. 390 (1968).

46. *Telecrompter Corp. v. CBS, Inc.*, 415 U.S. 394 (1974).

47. International Labour Office (ILO), Secretariat of Unesco, and the International Bureau of the WIPO, *Annotated Principles of*

Protection of Authors, Performers, Producers of Phonograms, and Boradcasting Organisations in Connection with the Distribution of Programs by Cable, in International Satelite and Cable television, Los Angeles, CA: U.C.L.A,. Communications Law Program 1985, reprinted at pp. 341 *ff.*, p. 351 (italics in original text).

48. ILO et al., p. 344.
49. U.S. Senate, Committee on the Judiciary, Subcommittee on Patents, Copyrights, and Trademarks, *International Copyright/ Communication Policies,* Hearings, November 16, 1983, 98th Cong., Ist Sess., Washington, DC: U.S. Government Printing Office, 1983.
50. U.S. Senate, *International Copyright*, p. 127.
51. U.S. Senate, Committee on Finance, Subcommittee on International Trade, *Intellectual Property Rights,* Hearings of S. 1860 and S. 1869, May 14, 1986, 99th Cong,, 2nd Sess., Washington, DC: US Government Printing Office, 1986, Statement of Sen. Pete Wilson, pp. 26 *ff.*, p. 28.
52. U.S. Senate, *Intellectual Property Rights,* statement of Jack Valenti, President, MPAA, pp. 133-142, p. 141.
53. U.S. Senate, *Intellectual Property Rights*, p. 138.
54. U.S. Trade Representative, *Trade Estimates 1985,* Washington, DC: U.S. Government Printing Office, 1985, p. 48.
55. U.S. Senate, *Intellectual Property Rights,* Statement of Harvey E. Bale Jr., Assistant U.S. Trade Representative for Trade Policy, pp. 86-96, p. 87.
56. U.S. Senate, *Intellectual Property Rights,* Adminstration Statement on the Protection of U.S. Intellectual Property Rights Abroad, April 7, 1986, pp. 96-100.
57. U.S. Senate, *Intellectual Property Rights*: Prepared Statement of James Moore, Deputy Assistant Secretary for International Economy Policy, International Trade Administration, Department of Commerce pp. 101-123, p. 109.
58. Copyright owners formed the International Intellectual Property Alliance in 1984 lobby for the inclusion of intellectual property provisions in the GSP. Its members included:

    the Recording Industry Association of America

    the Motion Picture Association of America

    the Amercian Film Marketing Association (the trade association of independent motion picture and television producers).

the National Music Publishers Association

the American Association of Publishers

the Computer Software and Services Industry Association and

the Computer Software and Services Industry Association.

59. U.S. Canada Free Trade Agreement, Ottawa: Dpartment of External Affairs, 1987.
60. Matt Witt, "Don't Trade on Me," *Dollars& Sense*. April 1991, pp. 18-21, p. 20.
61. *Video Data Book* (4th ed.), Washington, DC: Television Digest, 1986, p. 78.
62. Rex Weiner, "Video Pirates Find Rough Seas Abroad," *Variety*, May 9, 1994, p. 86.
63. Video Marketing Newsletter, May 5, 1986, p. 2 (citing data from RCA Corp.0.
64. UK Homevideo Posted Record Numbers in 87: Outlook Even Brighter for the Current Year," *Variety*, May 4, 1988, p. 245.
65. Don Groves, "Discribs Cheer as U.K. Audiences Soak Up Hollywood Products *Variety*, January 24, 1990, p. 94.
66. Geoff Watson, "Sell-Through Salvation," *Variety*, November 16, 1992, pp. 57, 62.
67. "German Video on Rocks: Yanks Prevent Disaster," *Variety*, February 21, 1990, 266.
68. Rebecca Lieb, "German Vidbiz Sales Up, Rentals Down," *Variety*, November 1992, pp. 57, 60.
69. Lieb, p. 60.
70. U.S. Trade Representative, *Foreign Trade Barriers, 1994*, Washington, DC: U.S. Government Printing Office, 1994, p. 88.
71. Jennifer Clark, "Maturing Italy Grows, but the Room is Over, " *Varitey*, November In 1992, p. 60.
72. Mark Thomas, " Italian Homevideo Trade Valued at $200,000,000, Priacy Down *Variety*, May 4, 1988, pp. 505, 515.
73. Hank Werba, "Roger, the Rabbit Who Changed the Face of Italian Hoevideo Variety, February 21, 1990, p. 294.
74. Clark p. 60.
75. Anna Matranga, "Italy's Unrest Impacts Homevid Market," *Variety*, August 29, 1994 p. 38.

76. Matranga, p. 38.

77. Peter Besas, "Spanish VCR Penetration 21 per cent, `Community Video' Haunt Market," *Variety*, May 4, 1988, p. 506; Bruce Alderman, "Sell-Through Is Where Action in French HV," *Variety*, May 4, 1988, p. 506.

78. "Spain's TV Explosion Could Mean a Gloomy Year for Homevid Biz," *Variety* February 21, 1990, p. 167.

79. Linda Moore, "Growing Pains in Spain", *Variety*; November 16, 1992, p. 62.

80. U.S. Trade Representative, *Foreign Trade Barriers* 1994; p. 241.

81. U.S. Copyright Office, *To Secure Intellectual Property Rights in World Commen* Report to the U.S. House, Committee on the Judiciary, Subcommittee on Patern Copyrights, and Tradewmarks, and to the U.S. House, Committee on Foreign Affairs Sub Committee on Western Hemisphere Affairs, September 21, 1984, p. 99.

82. Matthew Brzenzinski, "New Polish Law Takes Alm at Copyright Piracy," *New York Times*, June 14, 1994, p. D6.

83. Andrea Adelson, "Entertainment Industry Adds Anti-Piracy Triscks," *New York Times*, November, 11, 1988, p. D8.

84. Will Tusher, "MPAA Bans the Sale of U.S. Pictures to USSR," *Variety*, June 10, 1991, p. D8.

85. Celestine Bohlen, "In Russia's Free Market, Cultural Piracy Thrives," *New York Times*, July 2, 1993, p. A4.

86. U.S. Copyright Office, p. 84.

87. Douglas Boyd. "VCRs in Developing Countries; The Arab Case." *Media Development*, 32:1, 1988, pp. 5-7.

88. International Intellectual Property Alliance, Trade Loisses Due to Piracy and Other Market Access Restrictions Affecting the U.S. Copyright Industries, Washington, DC; International Intellectual Property Alliance, 1989.

89. U.S. Trade Representative, *Foregin Trade Barriers 1989*, Washington, DC: U.S. Government Printing Office, 1989, p.-55.

90. U.S. Trade Representative, *Foreign Trade Barriers* 1994, Washington, DC: U.S. Government Printing Office, 1994, p. 68.

91. William E. Schmidt, "Cairo's Rule on Tape and Video: Copy It and Sell It," *New York Times*, August 18, 1991, pp. 1. 12.

92. Marietta Giron, "Filipino Video Piracy Virtually 100 per cent," *Variety*, October 22, 1986, p. 443.

93. International Intellectual Property Alliance, p. vi.
94. International Intellectual Property Allinance p. ii.
95. U.S. Congress, Joint Economic Committee, Subcommittee on Trade, Productivity, and Economic Growth, *International Piracy Involving Intellectual Property,* Hearing, March 31, 1986, 99th Cong., 2nd Sess., Washington, DC:US. Government Printing Office: 1987, Prepared Statement of Frank G. Wells, President, Walt Disney Co., pp. 83-93, p. 89.
96. U. S. Congress, *International Piracy,* Testimony of Nesuhi Ertegun, President, International Federation of Phonogram and Videogram Producers, pp. 74-76.
97. U.S. Senate, Committee on Finance, Subcommittee on International Trade; *Generalised System of Preferences,* Hearing on S. 1867 and Title VI of S. 1860, June 17, 1986, 99th Cong., 2nd Sess., Washington, DC.U.S. Government Printing Office, 1986, pp. 6-7.
98. U.S. House, Committee on Energy and Commerce, Subcommittee on Oversight and Investigations, Unfair Foreign Trade Practices, Hearings on Intellectual Property Rights, February 18, 1987, 100th Cong., 1st Sess., Washington, DC: U.S. Government Printing Office, 1987, Statement of Michael B. Smith, Deputy U.S. Trade Representatives, pp. 8-13, p. 8.
99. U.S. Senate *Genealised System of Preferences,* Statement of Stanley Gortikov, President, Recording Industry of America, pp. 81-96.
100. International Intellectual Property Alliance, p. ix.
101. U.S. Trade Representatives, *Foreign Trade Barriers 1992,* Washington; DC: U.S. Government Printing Office, 1992, pp. 119-120.
102. Binod C. Agarwal, "Video—A New Diversion for India's Rich," *Media Development,* 32:1, 1985; pp. 14-17; and "India," in M. Alvarado, *Video World-Wide: An International Study,* London: John Libby, 1988, pp. 83-101.
103. Don Groves "Video Vendors View a Feast in the East," *Variety,* June 27, 1994, p. 1.
104. "India: Foreign and U.S. Investment is Soaring [Advertisement]," *New York Times,* May 19, 1994, pp. D10-D12.
105. See U.S. Trade Representative, 1991 *Trade Policy Agenda and 1990 Annual Report,* Washington, DC: U.S. Government Printing Office, 1991, p. 57; and 1992 *Trade Policy Agenda and 1991 Annual Report,* Washington, DC: U.S. Government Printing Office, 1992 pp. 42-44.

106. Michael Duckworth, "Disney Plans to Re-Enter China Market as Beijing Promiser Copyright Reforms," *Wall Street Journal*, March 24, 1992, p. C19.
107. U.S. Trade Representative. *Foreign Trade Barriers 1994*, p. 51.
108. The Clinton administration delayed the USTR's investigatin for three months in order to delink it from broader discussions on China's most-favored-nation (MFN) status and its human rights practices. The adminstration renewed China's MFN status after intense lobbying on the part of big business and despite broad opposition from human rights groups, who claimed that profits were being promoted ahead of human rights. What is telling about U.S. foreign policy vis-a-vis China is that property rights violations, prompted real steps toward trade retaliation, wheres human rights violations do not merit the same when U.S. economic interests are at stake.
109. U.S. Senate, Commitee on the Judiciary, Subcommittee on Patents, Copyrights, and Trademarks, *U.S. Adherance to the Berne Convention*, Hearings, May 16, 1985, and April 15, 1986, 99th Cong., 1sr and 2nd Sess., Washington, DC: U.S. Government Printing Office, 1987.
110. U.S. Senate, *U.S. Adherence to the Berne Convention*, Testimony of Donald J. Quigg, Acting Commissioner for Patents and Trademarks. p. 116.
111. Herbert Mitgang, " Old Copyright Treaty: New Shield for U.S. Artists, "*New York Times*, March 10, 1989, p. B7.
112. U.S. Senate, *U.S. Adherence to the Berne Convention*, Letter from Norman Alternman Re: Implementing Legislation to Permit Berne Aherence, Vice President, MPAA, p. 230.
113. U.S. Senate, *Message from the President of the United States Transmitting the Berne Convention for the Protection of Literary and Artistic Works....*, Treaty Doc. 99-27, 99th Cong., 2nd Sess., Washington, DC: U.S. Government Printing Office, June 1986.
114. Howard Fields, "New Coalition of 47 Joints battle over Berne," *Publishers Weekly*, September 25, 1987, p. 10; " Berne Hearings: Witnesses Argue Question of Joining or Not," *Publishers Weekly*, October 9, 1987, p. 29 and " 10 Publishers Say Ahdrence Would Not Affect Moral Rights Issue," *Publishers Weekly*, October 16, 1987, p. 13.
115. "Resolution of Ratification fo the Berne Convention," *Congressional Record*, 134:150, October 20, 1988, p. S16939.

116. Robert byrd (D-W.Va.), Paul Simon (D-III.), Robert Dole (R-Kans.), Jesse Helms (R-N.C.) and David Prior (D-Ark.).
117. See S. 1301, A bill to Amend Title 17, U.S.C, to implement the Berne Convention for the Protection of Literary and Artistic Works, as revised July 24, 1971, and for other purposes, 100th Cong., 2nd Sess.
118. Sydney Golt, *The GATT Negotiations, 1986-1990; Origins, Issues, Prospects,* London: British-North American Commitee, 1988.
119. Kenneth Winikoff, "New Protections Urged for GATT," *Hollywood Reporter*, June 17, 1988, p. 7.
120. Cycle H. Farnsworth, "Farm Aid is Top Issue at Trade Talks," *New York Times*, December 5, 1988, p. D1.
121. Clyde H. Parnsworth, "Brazil and India Fight Copyright Rules," *New York Times*, December 7, 1988, p. D2.
122. Keith Bradsher, "Relying on the Irresisitible Force of GATT's Appeal," *New York Times*, December 13, 1993, p. D2.
123. U.S. Advisory Committee on Trade Policy and Negotiations, *The Uruguay Round of Multilateral Trade Negotiations*, Washington, DEC: U.S. Trade Representative, 1994, p. 69.
124. U.S. Industry Functional Advisory Committee on Intellectual Property Trade Policy Matters (ISAC/IFAC), Industry Sector and Functional Advisory Committees. *The Uruguay Round of Multilateral Trade Negotiations*, Washington, DC: U.S. Trade Representative, 1994.
125. Chakravarthi Raghavan, *Recolonisation: The GATT, the Uruguay Round, and the Third World*, London; Zed, 1990.
126. ISAC/IFAC, *The Uruguay Round*, Washington, DC: U.S. Trade Representative, 1994, p. 26.
127. Raghavan, p. 114.

INDEX

D

E

□□□